AI Innovations for Customer Experience Optimization in the Service Sector

Mourad Aarabe
Sidi Mohamed Ben Abdellah University, Morocco

Nouhaila Ben Khizzou
Sidi Mohamed Ben Abdellah University, Morocco

Lhoussaine Alla
Sidi Mohamed Ben Abdellah University, Morocco

Ahmed Benjelloun
Sidi Mohamed Ben Abdellah University, Morocco

IGI Global
Scientific Publishing
Publishing Tomorrow's Research Today

Published in the United States of America by
IGI Global Scientific Publishing
701 East Chocolate Avenue
Hershey, PA, 17033, USA
Tel: 717-533-8845
Fax: 717-533-7115
Website: https://www.igi-global.com E-mail: cust@igi-global.com

Library of Congress Cataloging-in-Publication Data

Names: Aarabe, Mourad, 1993- editor. | Ben Khizzou, Nouhaila, 1999- editor. | Alla, Lhoussaine, 1969- editor. | Benjelloun, Ahmed, 1991- editor.
Title: AI innovations for customer experience optimization in the service sector / edited by: Mourad Aarabe, Nouhaila Ben Khizzou, Lhoussaine Alla, Ahmed Benjelloun.
Other titles: Artificial intelligence innovations for customer experience optimization in the service sector
Description: Hershey, PA : IGI Global Scientific Publishing, [2025] | Includes bibliographical references and index. | Summary: "From chatbots and virtual assistants to predictive personalization and sentiment analysis, artificial intelligence (AI) allows companies to gain deeper insights into their customers' needs and preferences, enabling them to deliver more tailored and effective customer experiences"-- Provided by publisher.
Identifiers: LCCN 2024409182 (print) | LCCN 2024409183 (ebook) | ISBN 9798337309187 (hardcover) | ISBN 9798337309194 (paperback) | ISBN 9798337309200 (ebook)
Subjects: LCSH: Customer services--Technological innovations. | Artificial intelligence--Marketing applications.
Classification: LCC HF5415.5 .A39 2025 (print) | LCC HF5415.5 (ebook) | DDC 658.8/12028563--dc23/eng/20250326
LC record available at https://lccn.loc.gov/2024409182
LC ebook record available at https://lccn.loc.gov/2024409183
British Cataloguing in Publication Data
A Cataloguing in Publication record for this book is available from the British Library.

Table of Contents

Detailed Table of Contents

Zouhair Allal, School of Engineering Sciences (EMSI), SMARTiLab Laboratory, Rabat, Morocco
Hajar Kobi, School of Engineering Sciences (EMSI), SMARTiLab Laboratory, Rabat, Morocco
Lamyae Khattabi, Sidi Mohamed Ben Abdellah University, Morocco
Laila Zamzami, NPG Laboratory, Cadi Ayyad University, Marrakesh, Morocco
Elmahdi Lemrami, Economics and Public Policy Laboratory (LSPP), Ibn Tofail University, Kenitra, Morocco

The integrated use of artificial intelligence (AI) is rapidly transforming the service industry and fundamentally reshaping the customer experience (CX) through automation, personalization, and predictive analytics. With global AI adoption projected to exceed $500 billion by 2025, service organizations are increasingly adopting AI-based solutions to enhance customer engagement and operational efficiency. Yet, the dynamic interplay between AI and CX remains under-researched, particularly with regard to ethical implications, trust drivers, and consumer preferences. To address this knowledge gap, this study employs a systematic literature review to develop an integrative heuristic model for understanding the impact of AI on CX. The results reveal that while AI improves service efficiency and personalization, its effectiveness depends on consumer trust, ethics, and industry-specific characteristics. The study provides a conceptual framework for assessing the role of AI in CX, highlighting both the opportunities and challenges associated with AI deployment in the service sector.

Artificial intelligence (AI) is considered as key driver of innovation in many sectors, including hospitality. The gaps in the literature highlight the need for a thorough and integrated study of the impact of AI in hospitality, particularly in relation to the customer experience. This research fills this gap by shedding light on how AI can transform value creation practices through interactions between hotels and their guests by providing an analysis of the main current applications of AI applied in the hotel sector. A systematic literature review was carried out to explore the role of AI in the hospitality sector, highlighting its impact on customer experience and value creation. The PRISMA method was adopted and data were collected from Scopus. A final list of 54 Book chapters of IGI GLOBAL and journal articles were included to broaden perspectives. Thematic analysis was used in this systematic review to effectively structure the results and properly address the research objectives.

Background: Patient data and artificial intelligence are widely explored concepts for improving healthcare services. However, little is known about the application of lean thinking to quantify these two elements. Objective: The aim of this study is to develop a theoretical framework combining patient data and artificial intelligence, aimed at optimizing the care pathway by identifying the theories to be mobilized to address this issue. Methods: A systematic review of the literature was carried out. Inclusion criteria were that the article should focus on optimizing the patient's care pathway. Twenty articles were included. Results: The proposed framework can be used to create an overview of the potential of driving patient-related data with AI for optimizing the patient care pathway. Further research is needed to investigate the use of patient-related quantifications of this data. Conclusions: This research paper analyzes the application of artificial intelligence in data science to optimize patient care pathways.

Ikram Ed-Daakouri, LAREMEF Laboratory, Sidi Mohamed Ben Abdellah University, Fez, Morocco
Lhoussaine Alla, LAREMEF Laboratory, Sidi Mohamed Ben Abdellah University, Fez, Morocco

Generative AI is transforming customer retention strategies in emerging markets by enabling hyper-personalization, predictive analytics, and automation to enhance customer engagement. This chapter explores the role of AI-driven solutions in optimizing retention strategies across diverse socio-economic and cultural contexts in Southeast Asia, Africa, and Latin America, based on a systematic review of 30 academic sources and comparative case studies in e-commerce, mobile telecommunications, and fintech. The findings highlight the effectiveness of AI in delivering personalized experiences, optimizing dynamic pricing models, and leveraging predictive analytics to identify and prevent customer churn. This chapter presents a conceptual framework that provides actionable guidelines for businesses to harness generative AI effectively while maintaining ethical standards and scalability. The chapter concludes with managerial insights, limitations, and future research directions, highlighting the potential of AI in shaping customer experiences and long-term loyalty in emerging markets.

Metasebia Adula, Bule Hora University, Ethiopia
Shashi Kant, Bule Hora University, Ethiopia

This study investigates the effect of customer journey mapping on Omni channel optimization, mediated by real-time personalization of contact points in Eastern Africa. Study used a sample size of 390 respondents. To ensure the robustness of the data, the Kaiser-Meyer-Olkin (KMO) measure was utilized, confirming the adequacy of the sample for factor analysis. Exploratory Factor Analysis (EFA) was performed to uncover latent variables and refine the measurement model, followed by Confirmatory Factor Analysis (CFA) to validate the proposed constructs and their relationships. Structural Equation Modeling (SEM) was implemented using AMOS software to explore the direct and mediated effects of customer journey mapping on Omni channel optimization through real-time personalization. Results indicate that effective customer journey mapping significantly enhances Omni

customer satisfaction. Eco hotels should direct their efforts towards implementing AI technologies and showcasing their unique offerings while consistently monitoring these technological developments for success. Theoretical implications deepen understanding of technology's role in hospitality while practical suggestions provide actionable strategies for managers.

Muhammad Younus, Universitas Muhammadiyah Yogyakarta, Pakistan
Halimah Abdul Manaf, Universiti Utara Malaysia, Malaysia
Eliza Meiyani, Universitas Muhammadiyah Yogyakarta, Indonesia
Achmad Nurmandi, Universitas Muhammadiyah Yogyakarta, Indonesia
Dyah Mutiarin, Universitas Muhammadiyah Yogyakarta, Indonesia
Imron Sohsan, Khon Kaen University, Thailand
Hajira Gul, College of Nursing, University of Lahore, Pakistan
Ibrahim Shah, College of Nursing, University of Lahore, Pakistan
Nurlina Subair, Universitas Muhammadiyah Makassar, Indonesia
Fatmawati A. Mappasere, Universitas Muhammadiyah Makassar, Indonesia

Artificial Intelligence is revolutionizing the service sector with intelligent solutions that optimize customer experience and reimagine service delivery. The article captures the ability of AI technologies such as machine learning, natural language processing etc., in developing faultless, tailored, and seamless customer experiences. Pilgrim applications like AI-based chatbots, recommender systems, and customer behavior analysis are claimed to refer to its potential towards business success and customer satisfaction. It is used to demarcate problems in embracing AI like moral issues, privacy, and integration problems, also mentioned in the research study, depicting an integrated concept regarding its extent and magnitude. From retailing, hospitality, and healthcare industries case studies, the paper presents lessons of practical applications based on real practices regarding how to employ AI innovation in constructing customer engagement and creating competitive advantage.

Preface

The rapid and widespread adoption of artificial intelligence (AI) across all sectors—particularly within the service industries—has emerged as a defining trend of our era. With each passing day, new AI applications are being introduced, continuously expanding the boundaries of what is possible in enhancing and personalizing the customer experience. Fueled by the digital revolution and the exponential growth of customer data, AI is now an essential tool across a broad range of service fields, including tourism and leisure, professional services, healthcare, banking and insurance, commerce, transportation and logistics, education and training, technology, telecommunications, and beyond.

In the wake of the COVID-19 pandemic, digital transformation efforts have intensified, further accelerating the adoption of AI technologies. This shift has redefined the customer relationship paradigm, ushering in an era of hyper-personalization and seamless customer interactions. Today's consumers expect more than basic service—they demand experiences that are personalized, fluid, responsive, and anticipatory. The fact is that, developers having got their hands on new AI (such as Claude) are increasingly opening up new doors, through the creation of tools that are readily accessible, such as chatbots, virtual assistants, offers customized to a user's preferences or the analysis of the emotions of customers.

Although AI is progressing rapidly and its application within the service sector is becoming more widespread, there remain significant areas for further investigation. From a theoretical standpoint, it is essential to deepen our understanding of how AI influences customer experiences and behaviors. Methodologically, traditional research approaches may be inadequate for capturing the complexities inherent in human-AI interactions and for accurately assessing customer satisfaction in these environments. Additionally, existing studies frequently face limitations in scope or depth, which hampers cross-industry comparisons and comprehensive insights.

The project "AI Innovations for Customer Experience Optimization in the Service Sector" aims to address these shortcomings by providing new theoretical insights, original research methods and concrete results. The goal is to increase knowledge about how AI is revolutionizing customer experience management in the service sector. The work will be conducted in a serious and practical manner, making it useful for researchers, practitioners, and policy makers alike.

The project addresses the following key questions: What is the real impact of artificial intelligence innovations on consumer satisfaction and the commercial performance of service companies? How are these companies addressing the challenges of adopting these innovations?

What are the ethical considerations that need to be respected for the responsible use of artificial intelligence in service provision?

The chapters in this publication take a multidisciplinary approach to these questions. Each section explains how AI can change the way companies manage the customer experience, and how they are inventing new ways to deal with the new possibilities offered by the technology.

Chapter 1 lays the groundwork by presenting a comprehensive systematic literature review that examines the interplay between AI and customer experience across service industries. It introduces an integrative heuristic model that captures how AI-driven automation, personalization, and analytics influence CX. The chapter emphasizes the importance of consumer trust, ethical considerations, and sector-specific dynamics in shaping AI's effectiveness.

Chapter 2 focuses on the hospitality sector, offering a systematic analysis of how AI innovations enhance guest engagement and value co-creation. By adopting the PRISMA method and conducting a thematic review of 54 publications, the chapter uncovers the evolving applications of AI in hotel services and provides structured insights into its impact on customer satisfaction.

Chapter 3 transitions to healthcare, where it proposes a theoretical framework integrating patient data with AI to optimize the care pathway. Drawing on a systematic literature review, the chapter explores how lean thinking and AI can improve patient-centric services and identifies opportunities for data-driven healthcare transformation.

Chapter 4 discusses how artificial intelligencc (AI) can help companies better retain customers in developing countries, such as those in Southeast Asia, Africa, and Latin America. Using concrete examples and studies, he explains how AI can personalize offers, adjust prices in real time, and prevent customers from leaving. He also emphasizes the importance of respecting ethics and adapting to change.

Chapter 5 looks at how understanding each customer's journey and offering real-time services can improve the customer experience in several stores and online shops in East Africa. Using advanced mathematical analysis, it shows that personalizing each stage of the customer relationship creates a more enjoyable experience and enables different channels (phone, web, physical store) to work better together.

Chapter 6 looks at how customer relationship management and new AI technologies can be combined to make the service sector more sustainable. Using numbers-based research methods, it shows that when companies align the way they manage their customers with new technologies, they strengthen customer loyalty and improve performance. It also provides valuable advice for managers on how to make better decisions.

Chapter 7 delves into the use of sentiment analysis in online retail. Through comparative analysis of machine learning algorithms—Naive Bayes, SVM, and Neural Networks—the chapter demonstrates the ability of AI to extract valuable sentiment data from customer reviews, thereby enabling more precise personalization and satisfaction tracking.

Chapter 8 evaluates how AI-driven service automation, personalization, and proactive network management affect customer satisfaction in the Moroccan telecommunications industry. Based on survey data analyzed with SEM, the study confirms the critical role of AI in improving service quality and enhancing customer loyalty.

Chapter 9 highlights the strategic integration of AI in eco-conscious hotels. It investigates how AI contributes to guest satisfaction and competitive advantage, revealing that the indirect effects of AI through strategic alignment yield substantial CX improvements. The chapter offers both theoretical contributions and practical recommendations for sustainable service providers.

Chapter 10 provides a holistic view of AI's integration across retail, hospitality, and healthcare, using real-world case studies to illustrate best practices and implementation challenges. It discusses the technological, ethical, and managerial implications of deploying AI for CX innovation, positioning AI as both a strategic asset and a complex organizational undertaking.

By bringing together diverse perspectives and sectors, this book offers a comprehensive and forward-thinking examination of AI's evolving role in shaping the future of service delivery.

Mourad Aarabe
Sidi Mohamed Ben Abdellah University, Morocco

Nouhaila Ben Khizzou
Sidi Mohamed Ben Abdellah University, Morocco

Lhoussaine Alla
Sidi Mohamed Ben Abdellah University, Morocco

Ahmed Benjelloun
Sidi Mohamed Ben Abdellah University, Morocco

Chapter 1
Systematic Analysis of the Role of Artificial Intelligence in Customer Experience in the Service Sector:
Towards the Development of a Conceptual Model

Zouhair Allal
https://orcid.org/0009-0002-8537-0301
School of Engineering Sciences (EMSI), SMARTiLab Laboratory, Rabat, Morocco

Hajar Kobi
School of Engineering Sciences (EMSI), SMARTiLab Laboratory, Rabat, Morocco

Lamyae Khattabi
Sidi Mohamed Ben Abdellah University, Morocco

Laila Zamzami
NPG Laboratory, Cadi Ayyad University, Marrakesh, Morocco

Elmahdi Lemrami
Economics and Public Policy Laboratory (LSPP), Ibn Tofail University, Kenitra, Morocco

DOI: 10.4018/979-8-3373-0918-7.ch001

ABSTRACT

The integrated use of artificial intelligence (AI) is rapidly transforming the service industry and fundamentally reshaping the customer experience (CX) through automation, personalization, and predictive analytics. With global AI adoption projected to exceed $500 billion by 2025, service organizations are increasingly adopting AI-based solutions to enhance customer engagement and operational efficiency. Yet, the dynamic interplay between AI and CX remains under-researched, particularly with regard to ethical implications, trust drivers, and consumer preferences. To address this knowledge gap, this study employs a systematic literature review to develop an integrative heuristic model for understanding the impact of AI on CX. The results reveal that while AI improves service efficiency and personalization, its effectiveness depends on consumer trust, ethics, and industry-specific characteristics. The study provides a conceptual framework for assessing the role of AI in CX, highlighting both the opportunities and challenges associated with AI deployment in the service sector.

INTRODUCTION

The development of artificial intelligence has launched an extensive transformation of consumer behavior and transformed the relationships between businesses and their client base. According to Lemon & Verhoef (2016) service companies must achieve exceptional CX because it acts as a decisive factor for standing apart from competitors in a quickly evolving consumer expectations market. The service sector depends heavily on personal interaction for delivering good service yet artificial intelligence brings along both positive opportunities and difficult technical obstacles. AI delivers automation of mundane duties simultaneously with individualized suggestion features and service availability expansion through virtual assistant implementations (Wirtz et al., 2018). The development of advanced technologies leads to concerns about both ethical matters and individual data security as well as customer acceptance of these systems (Parasuraman et al., 2005).

The relevance of this subject gains additionnal importance because of the acknowledgment and the acceptance of companies that customer experience is their biggest differentiating factor in competitive markets. A study conducted by McKinsey and Company (2022), revealed that 80% of consumers are more likely to choose businesses that deliver customized service experiences while AI functions as the key driver of this shift. What's more, Gartner (2023) forecasts that by 2025, over 50% of customer interactions in service-oriented businesses will be tackled by AI-driven systems, thus pointing to the speed-up of this trend.

As AI is gaining ground in customer experience management, its integration is not only confined to automating tasks. A thought-out strategically focused approach, that takes into full account consumer expectation, industry-specific characteristics, and the ethical concerns, is required. Consumers' perception of these technologies play a key role in shaping their satisfaction and loyalty. Research has shown that consumers in particular contexts, such as those entailing emotional sensitivity or complexity, do still prefer to interact with humans over AI (Huang & Rust, 2018). Despite ongoing studies into the potential of AI for automation and personalization, there remains a marked gap in the literature. While prior research had investigated AI's role in automation and personalization, they have not yet developed a comprehensive model that encompass the full scope of AI's effect on customer interactions. Furthermore, the extent to which AI adoption differs across sectors and shift consumer perceptions over time are still understudied areas.

Building on this, the current focuses on bridging this gap by putting foward an integrative heuristic model that invisgates systematically the role of AI in customer experience optimization. The guiding question is: *What integrative heuristic model can be used to understand and optimize AI's role in enhancing customer experience?*

The study has three goals: (1) identify key factors and barriers to AI implementation in CX, (2) examine AI's theoretical and empirical contributions in service industries, and (3) develop a framework to evaluate AI's effectiveness in improving CX. By combining insights from various fields, this chapter aims to provide practical guidance for academics and professionals navigating the AI-CX relationship.

I. CONCEPTUAL FRAMEWORK

1. EMERGING DIGITAL TECHNOLOGIES

1.1 A focus

The digital transformation of businesses arises primarily from modern digital technological innovations. Big Data, blockchain and IoT, as well as artificial intelligence, are making up these innovations (Bharadwaj et al., 2013). These technologies offer benefits that go further than process improvement features Industrial automation enables companies to deliver more tailored products and personalized services to customers. Their ability to transform both the economy and society substantially comes through these technologies, while at the same time benefiting from their vast areas of use. The uncertain future of these technologies has not lessened their importance as strategic business advantages, according to Boon and Moors (2008) and Martin (1995).

Different theoretical approaches underpin these technologies. There are studies that center on the substantial impact that transforms entire industrial sectors and markets (Danneels, 2004). Innovation via the technology surge model starts with advanced technologies before seeking specific market applications. Technology development is initially unrelated to current market demands (Di Stefano et al., 2012). Verganti (2011) refers to this phenomenon as "technological epiphanies", which demonstrate the discovery of new values with examples of use for current technologies. While these approaches aim to enhance technological capabilities (Adner & Kapoor, 2016), they do not always provide a clear distinction between emerging technologies and well-established, mature technologies (Haleem et al., 2019 ; Rotolo, Hicks & Martin, 2015, cited in Artusi et al., 2024). Such an observation underscores the need for further research into development methodologies that facilitate the adoption and growth of emerging technologies (Danneels, 2004).

According to Rotolo et al. (2015, cited in Artusi et al., 2024), there are five fundamental characteristics of emerging technologies. First, they are marked by radical newness, introducing unprecedented innovations. Their development and adoption experience rapid growth, characterized by significant expansion. Secondly, they are internally coherent, meaning that their evolution follows a structured trajectory. Their prospective applications are highly relevant because they have the potential to fundamentally change economic processes and society as a whole. By their very nature, they are unpredictable, which makes forecasting these technologies more difficult. Emerging digital technologies, by reason of their defining characteristics, act as the main drivers of innovation while driving industrial development. Successful integration of digital technologies calls for unique approaches to address a number of identified challenges.

1.2. Artificial intelligence

The research field of artificial intelligence aims to convert human thought processes into machine-operated systems. The roots of the concept go back to 1956, to the time when Minsky and McCarthy ran a workshop at Dartmouth. The study cited in Kühl et al. (2022) presents McCarthy et al. (1956, cited in Kühl et al., 2022). Ever since, AI has included Being among the key disciplines are computer science (He et al., 2016) and others. neuroscience (Ullman, 2019), robotics (Brady, 1984), linguistics (Clark et al., 2010) and philosophy (Witten et al., 2011). Despite the fact that each discipline defines AI differently, modern society is heavily reliant on AI. from one scientific discipline to another. Information Systems understands artificial intelligence as the aptitude of machines to perform cognitive tasks related to human intellectual operations. Human-like intellectual behaviors, such as perception and reasoning, associate learning with interactions with the environment, problem-solving tasks and decision-making capabilities. Similar to the definition used by Kühl et al (2022) in their research, Rai et al (2019) confirm this definition. The stated definition corresponds to this particular framework. With its service AI approach, the system acts simultaneously as a provider of innovation while effecting a profound organizational transformation of professional roles and models. the other a factor in the in-depth transformation of organizational models and professions (Huang & Rust, 2018).

AI is thus regarded not only as an instrument for optimizing performance, but as a strategic lever enabling companies to stand out from the crowd, particularly in services with high levels of customer interaction.

Yet the terminology encompassing AI remains open to debate. According to Russell and Norvig (2020), two fundamental dimensions characterize the study of AI: on the one hand, the depth of imitation (thought processes versus concrete actions) and, on the other, the intended goal (replicating human intelligence or optimizing rational decision-making). It is imperative to delineate between weak AI (or narrow AI), based on the execution of precise tasks without consciousness, and strong AI (or general AI), which seeks to reproduce the full range of human cognitive abilities (Russell & Norvig, 2020).

Indeed, the AI AI's field encompasses a several technological subfields. Machine learning is a process by which machines are capable of acquiring knowledge from data without the necessity of explicit programming. This technology is fundamental to the operation of modern personalized recommendation systems, such as those employed by prominent companies such as Netflix and Amazon (Pizzi, Scarpi & Pantano, 2021).

Deep learning, an advanced branch of machine learning, leverages neural networks to parse large datasets and identify complex patterns, providing the basis for speech and facial recognition systems (Huang & Rust, 2018). Natural language processing (NLP) empowers machines to understand and respond to human language, as Siri as well as Alexa do (Du & Xie, 2021). Computer vision, for its part, enables systems to interpret images and videos, facilitating applications in security, road surveillance, medicine and autonomous vehicles (Davenport et al., 2020).

AI is also analyzed in light of intelligence levels. Huang and Rust (2018) have pinpointed four levels of AI progression: intuitive, mechanical, analytical and empathic intelligence. Mechanical intelligence consists of automating simple, repetitive tasks, such as self-service kiosks or kitchen robots (Bowen & Morosan, 2018). Analytical intelligence deals with data to solve problems, as seen in chatbots and reservation management systems. As evidenced the effectiveness of personalized recommendation applications and robotic hotel assistants (Gursoy et al., 2019), artificial intelligence (AI) systems equipped with intuitive intelligence are able to effectively traverse and react to new or changing circumstances. In the meantime, the advancement of AI has made it possible to build systems that can identify and figure out human emotions. According to Wirtz et al. (2018), this ability is especially obvious in sophisticated humanoid devices that are emotionally aware. This classification of AI intelligences supplies an organized method for comprehending the development of AI and its possible use in contemporary service sectors.

2. CUSTOMER EXPERIENCE

2.1. Definitions

Customer experience is a complex part of customer relationship management, yet it serves as the primary factor that distinguishe companies from each other, especially in service industries. According to Meyer and Schwager (2007), customer experience (CX) represents the set of impressions that customers develop throughout their business interactions, based on all their encounters with both company-owned products/services and marketing-initiated and branded experiences.

According to Lemon and Verhoef (2016), CX is characterized as a complete journey that transcends the traditional boundaries of the purchase. Those three parts, which include pre-purchase exploration and transaction as well as post-purchase engagement, create a complete CX journey. There are two types of encounters that shape this strategy - the digital and the physical, such as mobile app usage and social media connection in addition to chatbot interaction. Customers experience physical encounters when they visit retail stores or speak with customer service representatives.

Since 1988, research by Parasuraman, Zeithaml, and Berry, combined with Lemon and Verhoef in 2016, has shown that customer experience is a complex phenomenon that controls consumers' evaluation processes and interaction tendencies (Alla et al., 2025) and drives sustained customer loyalty.

2.2. The Multidimensional Nature of Customer Experience

Customer experience is not just a singular construct, but a multidimensional phenomenon, that comprises cognitive, emotional, sensory, and behavioral components (Gentile, Spiller & Noci, 2007):

- **Cognitive Dimension:** This refers to the rational assessment of a product or service, especially in regard to perceived quality and alignment with customer expectations (Oliver et al., 1997).
- **Emotional Dimension:** This reflects the affective responses evoked by an experience, ranging from positive emotions (such as satisfaction and delight) to negative ones (such as frustration or disappointment) (Brakus, Schmitt & Zarantonello, 2009).
- **Sensory Dimension:** This encompasses sensory stimuli (visual, auditory, tactile, and olfactory) that shape the customer's perception, playing a particularly significant role in both physical and digital environments (Krishna, 2012).
- **Behavioral Dimension:** This concerns customer actions resulting from their experience, including purchase intentions, brand loyalty, and engagement (Verhoef et al., 2009).

Customer experience is fundamentally intertwined with the customer journey, a construct referring to the sequential stages a consumer navigates before, during, and after interacting with a business. As Lemon and Verhoef (2016) highlight, this journey has increasingly become multichannel, integrating physical, digital, and social interaction points. The proliferation of digital platforms, the growing influence of the social media, and the emergence of omnichannel strategies have considerably broadened the scope of the customer experience. Today, interactions extend far beyond the traditional point of sale, encompassing websites, mobile Apps, and social media platforms, all of which contribute to shaping the overall experience.

Assessing customer experience presents a methodological challenge, insofar as it is intrinsically subjective and multidimensional. Various techniques have been developed to evaluate its quality, among which customer satisfaction surveys, loyalty measurements, Net Promoter Score (NPS) and customer feedback analysis are the most widely used. Homburg et al. (2006) emphasize that studying customer experience (CX) demands complete attention to the originality of each relationship together with the particularities of contacts and personal customer expectations.

The assessment of CX through emotion has gained significance because emotion drives customer loyalty and engagement according to Schmitt (1999). Businesses implement tools that monitor voice tones and track physical responses and social media sentiments to instantly modify their interaction methods.

CX factors are influenced by service quality perception which serves as a central driver according to SERVQUAL model developed by Parasuraman et al. (1985). The model puts forward reliability as well as assurance along with tangibles and responsiveness and empathy because they remain vital to customer satisfaction.

How well customers expect their experiences to match the service industry standards alongside their personal background and history determines satisfaction results. Customer perceptions depend heavily on the gap between what they expect from the service and what they actually receive according to Oliver et al. (1997). Service industries benefit from employee interactions through customer retention because customers value both employee expertise and their ability to empathize (Groening et al., 2018).

II. METHODOLOGICAL PROTOCOL

A systematic literature review (SLR) was the methodology used to address the research question of this chapter. A research protocol was followed according to the principles outlined in the Preferred Reporting Items for Systematic Reviews (PRISMA) statement, as set forth by Page et al. (2021).

A comprehensive SLR is entirely dependent on a well-designed protocol. The core components of a SLR include defining a clear research question (in the introduction) and establishing study eligibility requirements along with selected search protocols (e.g., databases to be searched and selected keywords, as well as quality assessment procedures and methods of analysis) (Aarabe et al., 2024, 2025; Zaugg et al., 2014). In order to successfully conduct an SLR, a research team composed of experts in the field must be assembled and the methodological protocol must be designed (Zaugg et al., 2014).

To conduct our analysis, we undertook a meticulous search of the most prominent international databases. To collect and select articles for the analysis database, we adopted an approach that incorporates the frameworks advanced by Tranfield et al. (2003) and Zaugg et al. (2014). The protocol that was followed is outlined in (***Table 1***):

- Defining the research question and establishing eligibility criteria ;
- Selecting relevant databases and determining the temporal scope of the review ;
- Developing a precise search strategy to ensure comprehensive literature coverage ;
- Identifying and selecting journals and studies ;
- Classifying and organizing the collected documents for in-depth analysis.

Table 1. Methodological Protocol of the Systematic Review

Steps	Description		
Eligibility criteria	**Elements**	**Inclusion Criteria**	**Exclusion Criteria**
	Type of Document	Journal article, official report, conference paper, empirical and theoretical article, bulletin, working paper, and book chapter.	Thesis, dissertation.
	Type of Journal/ Review	Recognized national and international journals.	Unrecognized or predatory journals and publications.
	Research Subject	All research conducted on AI and its relationship with customer experience in the service sector.	Studies focusing solely on AI or customer experience, or examining the interaction between these two variables in sectors other than the service industry.
	Unit of Analysis	Service sector companies and their customers.	Companies operating in sectors other than the service industry.
	Type of Research	Research studies with a well-defined theoretical and methodological framework, along with detailed empirical findings.	Low-quality empirical research (unclear or irrelevant theoretical and methodological framework, inadequate empirical analysis methods, or insufficiently detailed empirical results).
Databases	Scopus, Web of Science, ScienceDirect, Jstor, Springer, Taylor & Francis, Wiley Online Library, Emerald Insight, Google Scholar, HAL Open Archive, ResearchGate, PsycINFO, PsycNet, Cairn, Érudit, and ProQuest.		
Time Horizon	**Open Search Strategy** (due to the emerging nature of studies on AI and CX).		
Search Strategy	**The research strategy should be based on a list of keywords and synonyms.** These terms must be included in the search according to a precise logic and linked using Boolean operators (AND, OR, NOT). The list of keywords includes: *Artificial Intelligence (AI); Customer Experience; Digital Innovation; Customer Service; Customer Relationship; Emerging Technologies.*		
Journal Selection	**The selected keywords are combined with the terms:** *"optimization," "effect," "role," and "service sector."*		

Source: authors

Moreover, we had to define the conceptual boundaries of the "service sector" to specify the activities that are part of it. This sector is described as all economic activities that do not fall under agriculture or industry and whose production primarily involves the provision of intangible services to individuals or businesses. It incorporates a wide spectrum of activities, which may be classified into three main categories. First, market services, which include commerce, financial services, transportation, communication, hospitality, and catering, as well as business services such as consulting, auditing, advertising, and information technology. Second, non-market services, mainly provided by public administrations, educational institutions, healthcare services, and non-profit organizations. Finally, personal services cover activities such as education, medical care, social assistance, and domestic and leisure-related services. This sector is characterized by its intangible nature, high labor intensity, and direct interaction between service providers and beneficiaries.

Selecting relevant databases and determining the temporal scope of the

The selection of a database is of particular importance, as it determines the scope of the study. To ensure the inclusion of relevant articles, a meticulous selection process was employed. Initially, the Scopus and Web of Science databases were utilized. The latter two databases are particularly pertinent to interdisciplinary research, encompassing domains such as management, epidemiology, economics, and applied sciences. Subsequently, we conducted a comprehensive search through numerous databases, including ScienceDirect, Jstor, Springer, Taylor & Francis, Wiley Online Library, Emerald Insight, Google Scholar, HAL Open Archive, Researchgate, PsycINFO, Psycnet, Cairn, Erudit, and ProQuest, to obtain a comprehensive list of articles pertinent to our research subject.

Given the narrow temporal scope of the work dealing with AI and customer experience in the service sector, an open search strategy was employed (due to the emerging nature of AI and customer experience studies).

Study Selection Process

The initial search yielded 1,552 studies (*N = 1552*). The first step involved removing duplicate entries to refine the dataset. Next, a screening process was conducted based on titles and abstracts, allowing us to discard studies that did not align with our research focus.

In the final stage, we assessed the full-text relevance of the remaining studies, ensuring they met the predefined selection criteria. Following this rigorous filtering, a definitive set of 30 studies was retained (Figure 1). Each selected study underwent a detailed examination during the review phase to support the development of a comprehensive and SLR.

Figure 1. The PRISMA diagram of our systematic analysis

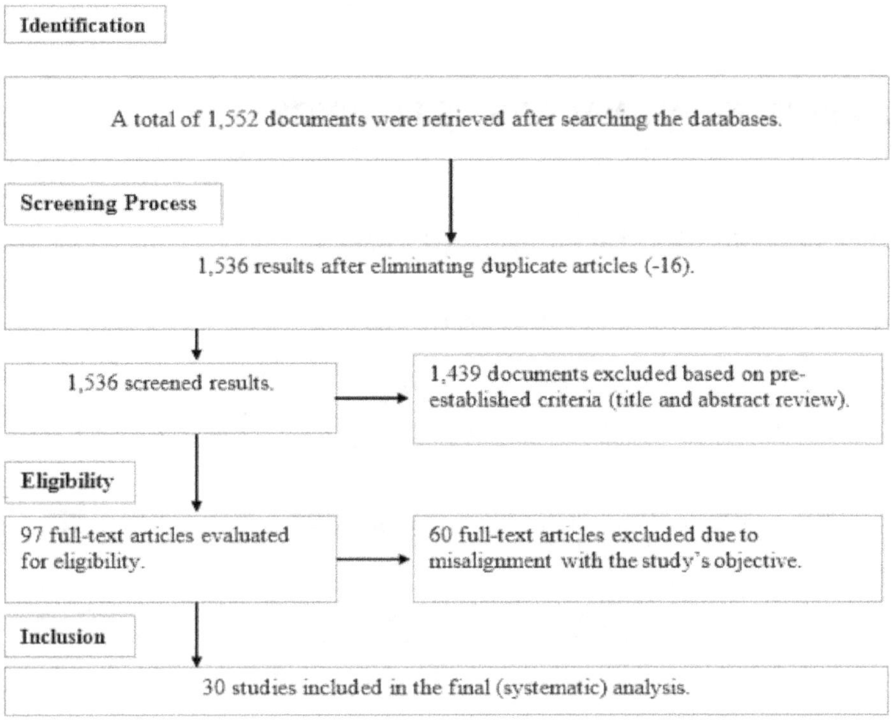

Source: authors

Organization of Documents

The final dataset comprises N_f=30 documents (journal articles, conference papers, and book chapters). To systematically structure our research, we developed an Excel file to categorize the documents based on key aspects such as title, authors, study context, document type, research design, theoretical frameworks applied, methodology employed, study variables, unit of analysis, sample size, main findings, limitations, and future research directions. The subsequent sections highlight what we have learned from our analysis of the selected literature.

III. ANALYSIS OF RESULTS

1. DESCRIPTIVE ANALYSIS OF FINDINGS

1.1. Classification by Document Type

Figure 2. Classification of Documents by type

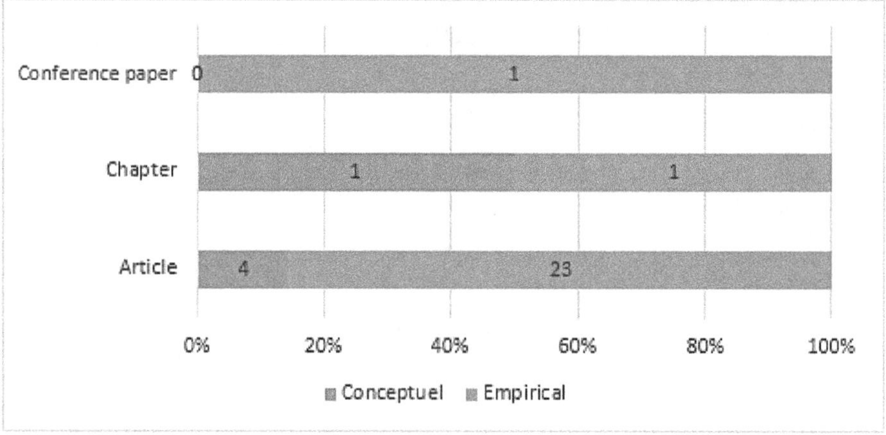

Source: Our analysis

On a global scale, research exploring the interplay between AI and customer experience in the service industry is largely empirical, with most studies published as journal articles. However, discussions on this topic remain relatively scarce in academic conferences. Our dataset includes only two conference papers: one presented at the ICRITO Conference (2020) and another published as a book chapter in the *International Conference on Economics and Social Sciences*, Cham: Springer Nature Switzerland (2023). This limited presence in conference proceedings suggests a lack of interdisciplinary dialogue on this emerging subject.

1.2. Quality of Journals and Citation Impact

Most of the reviewed articles are published in Scopus-indexed journals, with 17 appearing in Q1-ranked journals. Among these, *Computers in Human Behavior* has the highest H-index (251), and the selected article from this journal (Ameen et al.,

2020) has accumulated 708 citations. Additionally, four articles were published in Q2-ranked journals, with *Cogent Business & Management* (H-index = 44) being the most prominent in this category. Two recent articles from this journal (Hung & Le, 2024 ; Lopes et al., 2024) have yet to receive citations. The dataset also includes one article from *WSEAS Transactions on Business and Economics* (Q4; H-index = 22), which has been cited 56 times (Al-Araj et al., 2022). Notably, the most frequently cited article in our dataset is by Martin et al. (2019), with 1,020 citations. This study examines the growing role of humanoid service robots and their effect on customer experiences, particularly in shaping compensatory consumer behaviors. Through seven experimental studies, the authors explore whether humanoid robots evoke responses such as status-driven consumption, social affiliation, and increased food intake. Their findings suggest that these behaviors stem from consumer perceptions that humanoid service robots are unsettling and may pose a threat to human identity.

1.3. The historical evolution of documents and their context of development

Figure 3. The historical evolution of documents

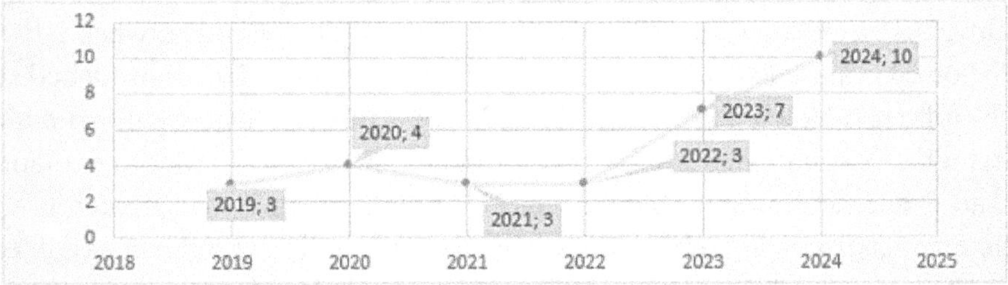

Source: Our analysis

Figure 4. The continental distribution of documents

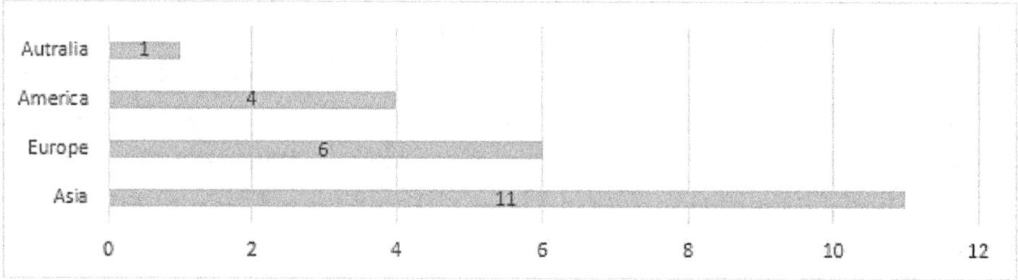

Source: Our analysis

The findings of this analysis clearly demonstrate that the study of the interaction between AI and customer experience has gained considerable momentum since the COVID-19 crisis (Fig. 3). Specifically, concerns surrounding social distancing, combined with evolving competitive pressures and the need to meet customer expectations across geographical distances, have been major catalysts for the integration of AI into business strategies.This research area remains emerging because it only received three empirical investigations through the year 2019 (Abu Daqar & Smoudy, 2019 ; Martin et al., 2019; Qiu et al., 2019). The period between 2019 and 2022 showed minimal changes in publication numbers until 2023 introduced seven notices followed by ten publications in 2024. This research has examined multiple aspects which explain AI's effects on customer experience in order to explain this intricate phenomenon better. For instance, researchers have investigated how the characteristics of service robots shape customer reception experiences (Qiu et al., 2019); the impact of AI adoption in call centers on call duration, demand for human assistance, and customer complaints (Wang et al., 2020); the impact of chatbots on online customer experience and satisfaction in e-commerce, as well as the moderating effect of user personality (Chen et al., 2021); and the chatbot's anthropomorphic role in online food retailing, along with its effects on consumer satisfaction and behavior (Klein & Martinez, 2023).

The service industry within Asia attracts most academic research interested in AI Apps since 11 publications originate from this region according to the geographical distribution of studies (Fig. 4). China along with Malaysia and countries from the Middle East particularly Oman serve as major contributors to this research field. Academic research activity related to AI apps in the service sector shows a higher level in Asia compared to Europe since Asia contributes 11 studies while Europe generates 6 studies and the Americas produce only 4 studies. Most research happens through international teamwork since 17 studies unite authors who come from different nations and continents. Research related to AI in customer experience shows both global scope and interdisciplinary nature according to current data.

1.4. Theoretical and Methodological Framework

Researchers lack a shared understanding of how to explore the relationship between artificial intelligence and customer experience within service settings. The reviewed studies present different combinations of models alongside theories. Research applications of the Technology Acceptance Model (TAM) constitute the majority since it appears in five studies (Aw et al., 2022; Chen et al., 2021; Lopes et al., 2024; Sadhu et al., 2024; Wang et al., 2020). The subject's technological base explains why these assessment models have become popular because they exist solely to examine digital adoption and integration.

Beyond TAM researchers used models focusing on frontline service technologies and service encounters and also applied the uncanny valley theory and machine learning theories and the Unified Theory of Acceptance and Use of Technology (UTAUT). A combination of theoretical perspectives is mostly used in research through the integration of consumer-oriented frameworks. Researchers have utilized self-completion theory along with emotional consumption theory together with behavioral theories of customer satisfaction and trust and customer experience theory and humor theories. A multi-disciplinary research strategy presents a complete examination of consumer emotional and behavioral reactions to AI-based exchanges.

Researchers have developed multiple study methods which portray the subject's intricate nature in their systematic investigation. Research limitations stem from the fact that all reviewed studies use cross-sectional designs to study this topic. This approach prevents the potential establishment of causal relationships. Research studies have used mixed-method analysis to increase the strength of their results when facing this methodological limitation. Many studies make use of quantitative methods which primarily employ SEM modeling and experimental scenario-based methods (both natural and controlled) to forecast causal effects between brand experience factors and consumer reactions.

Various researchers use qualitative approaches to deliver more complex customer experience understanding by conducting in-depth interviews and interactive focus groups and performing comprehensive case studies. Mixed-methods research serves as part of triangulation methods to enhance result validity through providing exhaustive insights into the study phenomenon. Researchers use this methodology to overcome the weaknesses that occur when researchers employ a single method independently.

Research based on analyzing literature has been performed through systematic reviews and bibliometric studies and meta-analyses to examine current publications, combine existing knowledge and determine research gaps in this field of study. Research teams work together to achieve innovation for both theoretical understanding and empirical knowledge regarding the impacts of AI on customer experiences.

2. FINDINGS FROM THE CRITICAL ANALYSIS

The critical analysis of the main results is based on a logic of identification of central themes as well as a correspondence analysis to identify the links between the concepts.

Table 2. Summary of key results from a systeùatic analysis

Authors	Main theoretical anchoring	Methodological Approach	Key findings
Qiu et al. (2019)	Theories on the infusion of frontline service technologies and service encounters: Uncanny Valley Theory	Three Approaches: **Qualitative Study (In-Depth Interviews); Scenario-Based Experiment; Quantitative Study.**	Study 1 reveals a dual attitudinal response among hotel guests: an attraction to technological innovation and the anthropomorphism of robots, alongside certain reservations. Additionally, service robots can enhance service quality and increase employee satisfaction, ultimately contributing to improved customer satisfaction. Study 2 finds that participants spent more time interacting with robots exhibiting higher levels of anthropomorphism or perceived intelligence compared to those with lower levels. Study 3 demonstrates that the attributes of service robots facilitate the hospitality experience through the mediating role of customer-employee relationship building.
Martin et al. (2019)	Escape theory; self-completion theory; emotional eating theory	Seven Experimental Studies; Meta-Analysis.	Consumers exhibit compensatory behaviors when interacting with humanoid service robots (HSRs) instead of human employees. For instance, they are more likely to purchase prestige goods, seek social affiliation, and consume larger quantities of food. This research identifies boundary conditions affecting these compensatory responses. Specifically, the effects are: (1) attenuated when consumers perceive high levels of social affiliation, (2) reduced when the food is perceived as healthier, and (3) diminished when the robot appears machine-like rather than anthropomorphized. Participants were more likely to choose a premium product over a generic alternative when assisted by a humanoid service robot rather than a human employee.

continued on following page

Table 2. Continued

Authors	Main theoretical anchoring	Methodological Approach	Key findings
Daqar and Smoudy (2019)	Blake Morgan's model on AI's benefits in CX. Machine learning theories; Behavioral theories related to customer satisfaction and trust.	Mixed Approach.	AI accounted for 26.4% of the variance in overall customer experience (CX). Personalized services demonstrated a significant positive impact on customer satisfaction. Chatbots and virtual assistants reduced waiting times and enhanced post-purchase experiences
Samala et al. (2020)		Qualitative Approach.	AI and robotics are advancing service personalization, process automation, and operational efficiency in the tourism sector. Emerging technologies, including chatbots, virtual reality, and facial recognition, are transforming customer interactions and enhancing the user experience. Despite their potential, these technologies do not fully replace the importance of human contact in tourism.
Sikandar et al. (2020)	Machine learning model	Systematic Literature Review.	AI enhances the customer experience through personalization, automation, and tailored recommendations. AI positively impacts every stage of the customer journey, including need recognition, research, evaluation, purchase, and post-sale interactions. However, challenges remain, such as ethical concerns, implementation complexity, and dependency on technology.

continued on following page

Table 2. Continued

Authors	Main theoretical anchoring	Methodological Approach	Key findings
Wang et al. (2020)	Technology Acceptance (TAM)	Empirical Approach Based on a Natural Experiment.	The introduction of AI significantly increases call duration compared to traditional interactive voice response (IVR) systems. AI implementation significantly reduces customer complaints. AI extends call duration while decreasing complaints, particularly for simple tasks. Older customers benefit more from AI, experiencing a greater reduction in complaints and shorter call durations. Women experience a greater reduction in complaints with AI implementation.
Ameen et al. (2020)	Service quality model; Trust and commitment theory	Quantitative Approach (Structural Equation Modeling).	Service quality enhanced by AI directly improves the customer experience and fosters trust. Perceived sacrifice moderates the relationship between certain factors (such as personalization) and customer experience. Relationship commitment has a direct positive effect on customer experience.
Neuhofer et al. (2021)		Qualitative Approach Based on Scenarios with Six Interactive Focus Groups.	The adoption of AI will profoundly impact the nature of experiences and value creation at events. Initially, people may be skeptical, but as trust develops, acceptance will increase. Integrating event technologies with personal devices can help mitigate initial skepticism.
Khan and Iqbal (2021)	Technological evolution in customer service	Qualitative Study (Review of Secondary Data and Semi-Structured Interviews with Key Stakeholders).	AI enhances efficiency, personalization, and CX but struggles to replicate human empathy. Challenges to adoption include customer perceptions and operational complexities.
Chen et al. (2021)	Technology Acceptance Model (TAM); Information Systems Success Model (IS Success Model).	Quantitative Approach.	Responsiveness positively influences intrinsic values but does not affect extrinsic values. Perceived values significantly enhance customer satisfaction. Personality moderates only the relationship between usability and extrinsic values.

continued on following page

Table 2. Continued

Authors	Main theoretical anchoring	Methodological Approach	Key findings
Aw et al. (2022)	Unified Theory of Acceptance and Use of Technology (UTAUT); Parasocial Interaction Theory; Technology Acceptance Model (TAM)	Quantitative Study (Partial Least Squares Structural Equation Modeling (PLS-SEM)).	Human-like attributes (e.g., perceived intelligence) have a significant impact on customer experience (CX). Parasocial interactions and smart-shopping perceptions promote positive shopping behaviors. AI-enabled CX and social influence shape continued usage intentions.
Al-Araj et al. (2022)	SERVQUAL model; Commitment-trust theory	Quantitative Approach	AI has a significant impact on all five dimensions of service quality, with a positive correlation ranging from 0.594 to 0.753. AI exhibits a moderate yet positive impact on customer satisfaction ($r = 0.538$). Findings indicate that while customers perceive AI-based services favorably, overall satisfaction remains suboptimal.
Bhattacharya and Sinha (2022)	Natural language processing (NLP); Machine learning.	Mixed Approach	Chatbots are widely adopted for customer support and personalized recommendations. A positive correlation ($r = 0.247$) exists between chatbot usage for support and recommendations, indicating a beneficial impact on customer experience.

continued on following page

Table 2. Continued

Authors	Main theoretical anchoring	Methodological Approach	Key findings
Punga et al. (2023)	The trend-setter approach and the wait-and-see approach	Qualitative Approach	Several respondents emphasized the need for caution, as AI lacks the ability to demonstrate empathy. This is particularly crucial for companies operating in niche markets, where human interaction is prevalent and communication involves high levels of emotional engagement. Various factors influence the implementation of AI in customer interactions, both positively and negatively. Among the key success factors, the most frequently mentioned are consumer-relevant content (ensuring both the message and the marketing channel align with customer expectations—"the right content in the right place"), return on investment (ROI), gradual integration within an omnichannel strategy, and well-defined key performance indicators (KPIs). Conversely, the primary obstacles include high costs, rushed implementation, and a lack of necessary expertise.

continued on following page

Table 2. Continued

Authors	Main theoretical anchoring	Methodological Approach	Key findings
Holz, Becker, Blut, and Paluch (2023)	Customer Experience Theory	Qualitative Approach Comprising Three Sub-Studies	Study 1: Identification of experiential pain points in the customer experience across three key themes: information, performance, and reception. Customer experience dimensions: Interpersonal or organizational. Most frequent emotional responses to high-intensity pain points: Anger and fear. Study 2: The most frequently cited emotions associated with customer pain points include disgust, anger, and sadness. Study 3: Implementation of smart service solutions to address traveler pain points: • Smart service solutions for information-related pain points: Real-time flight information, smart luggage, and airport navigation systems. • Smart service solutions for performance-related pain points: Smart kiosks and service robots, automated security systems, and smart queue management systems. • Smart service solutions for hospitality-related pain points: Personalized recommendation systems and smart cleaning scheduling.
Klein and Martinez (2023)	Anthropomorphism theory, Agent theory,	Quantitative Experimental Scenario-Based Approach	Anthropomorphic chatbots are positively correlated with customer satisfaction, with this relationship being mediated by enjoyment, attitude, and trust.
Nazir et al. (2023)	Stimulus-Organism-Response (SOR) theory.	Quantitative Approach (Using SmartPLS)	AI has a positive impact on social media engagement and conversion rates. Engagement enhances customer satisfaction, which in turn increases repurchase intentions. Consumer habits significantly moderate the relationship between satisfaction and repurchase intentions.

continued on following page

Table 2. Continued

Authors	Main theoretical anchoring	Methodological Approach	Key findings
Youssofi et al. (2023)	Reinartz et al.'s framework for digital transformation	Qualitative Approach with Thematic Content Analysis	Maintaining a balance between automation and human interaction is essential. Psychological mechanisms, such as empathy, play a key role in shaping the guest experience. Ethical and confidentiality concerns are critical considerations in digital implementations.
Shin et al. (2023)	Theory of anthropomorphism; Theories of humor	Experimental Approach Through Three Experiments	The strategic use of affiliative humor in chatbots enhances the customer experience by increasing engagement, satisfaction, and the perceived human-like qualities of chatbots, ultimately providing businesses with a competitive advantage.
Pappas et al. (2023)	"seven C" approch	Literature Review and Conceptual Analysis	AI and human capabilities are complementary. AI excels in repetitive and analytical tasks ("raising the floor"), while humans contribute relational and emotional value ("raising the ceiling").
Mariani and Borghi (2024)	The three-factor theory of customer satisfaction	Quantitative Approach Based on Penalty-Reward Contrast Analysis	AI, particularly service robots, plays a significant role beyond merely enhancing productivity. In service contexts, customer interactions with mechanical AI positively influence overall satisfaction with AI-enabled service operations. The positive performance of AI-enabled delivery services enhances consumers' online ratings of their overall experience, subsequently increasing their overall perceived satisfaction.

continued on following page

Table 2. Continued

Authors	Main theoretical anchoring	Methodological Approach	Key findings
Peruchini et al. (2024)	Behavioral theories applied to technology adoption.	Bibliometric and Thematic Analysis	Research frequently explores conversational agents, including chatbots and voicebots, alongside machine learning prediction models and recommendation systems, as tools for enhancing customer experience. The most commonly studied industries include tourism, banking, and e-commerce. Improving customer experience via AI, is done through personalization, predictive analytics, and operational efficiency. AI adoption for customer experience stands at the highest level among banking institutions and e-commerce entities even though other industries demonstrate more moderate integration.
Yunanda et al. (2024)	Technology adoption models and trust frameworks.	Quantitative Study	AI strengthens trust by enabling service customization and ensuring security. The trust levels and also the adoption of AI-driven solutions depend heavily on cultural differences in the workplace. The substantial cybersecurity challenges act as primary obstacles for user trust in AI-developed solutions.
Roy et al. (2024)	Customer Equity Framework; Relationship Marketing Theory	Hybrid Approach Combining Two Analytical Methods: PLS-SEM (Partial Least Squares Structural Equation Modeling) and Artificial Neural Networks (ANN)	Trust functions as a fundamental linking element between customer equity aspects and the general quality of customer interactions that occur within social robot environments. Alpha Systems demonstrates the requirement to build trust in service providers who operate social robots because it promotes prolonged trust in robotic systems while improving customer satisfaction.

continued on following page

Table 2. Continued

Authors	Main theoretical anchoring	Methodological Approach	Key findings
Sadhu et al. (2024)	Service-Dominant Logic (SDL); SERVQUAL model; Nielsen's (1993) usability heuristics; Technology Acceptance Model (TAM)	Mixed Approach: Qualitative (Case Study) and Quantitative	Users generally express satisfaction with chatbots due to their ease of use; however, limitations persist in addressing complex queries. Customer service agents have benefited from reduced workload, enabling them to focus on more complex tasks. Chatbots exhibit limitations in handling emotionally nuanced and intricate queries, highlighting the need for further improvements.
Sigala et al. (2024)	-	Qualitative Approach Based on Expert Perspectives	Contributors recognize ChatGPT's potential to significantly transform service offerings, enhance customer experiences, optimize service costs, and generate societal benefits through improved digital services.
Tula et al. (2024)	Customer Engagement Theory; Ethical Approaches to AI	Systematic Analysis	AI enhances the customer experience by enabling personalized interactions and increasing efficiency in business operations..
Tran (2024)		Conceptual Analysis	AI facilitates greater personalization, strengthens customer engagement, and supports data-driven decision-making. Key challenges include data privacy concerns, algorithmic bias, and the absence of human empathy.
Lopes et al. (2024)	Technology Acceptance Model (TAM); Flow Theory	Quantitative Approach (Using PLS-SEM)	AI usability improves customers' perceived control, concentration, and cognitive appreciation. Findings indicate that concentration does not directly impact purchase intention but exerts a significant effect when mediated by a sense of awe
Nguyen and Le (2024)	Information Systems Success Model (ISS); Post-Adoption Intentions Model	Quantitative Approach (Using Structural Equation Modeling)	Chatbot attributes—personalization, interactivity, and comprehension—positively influence the customer experience. Customer satisfaction strongly correlates with the intention to continue using chatbots.

Source: *Our analysis*

2.1. Key Themes

In a bid to identify the main themes analyzed in the studies selected for this SLR, we carried out a content analysis using IRaMuTeQ software (Fig. 5).

Figure 5. Word Cloud of the Most Frequent Terms in AI-Customer Experience Research

Source: Output IRaMuTeQ

The word cloud reveals the centrality of concepts such as AI, consumer, experience and service. These constructs are examined in conjunction with other variables to further our understanding of how AI and consumer experience interact in the service sector. Our analysis enabled us to identify several related topics addressed in the selected studies. Analysis has shown that AI-based technologies have significant effects on service sector customer experience while introducing important aspects about consumer AI sentiment and operational best practices for AI and service quality issues and technical boundaries the system faces.

2.1.1. Consumer attitudes towards AI

The study of Qiu et al. (2019) (in the hospitality sector) points to a duality in customer attitudes towards the integration of robots into hospitality services. Customers are drawn by robots' technological nature and robotic appearance which they view as exciting new additions to their service encounters. Both positive and negative sentiments emerge from their perspective as they show a mixture of feelings about including robots in their operations. Mende et al. (2019) proved through seven experimental studies that humanoid robots generate psychological discomfort in consumers which appears as an unpleasant emotional state. People develop doubts when they first encounter AI systems because systems that operate improperly can cause user frustration. AI acceptance grows stronger with higher degrees of trust because trust stands as the main factor influencing human-AI interaction (Neuhofer et al., 2021). The degree of trust as well as the rate of AI adoption demonstrates sensitivity to cultural variations (Yunanda et al., 2024).

2.1.2. Conditions for AI effectiveness

AI systems succeed better when users can identify human qualities in them because people tend to connect with products that display human characteristics (Klein & Martinez, 2023; Mende et al., 2019). System quality attributes together with ease of use (Chen et al., 2021) contribute to creating an uninterrupted seamless user experience. When AI demonstrates its ability to adapt to personal preferences it drives better user loyalty together with engagement (Ameen et al., 2020). The degree to which consumers believe AI processes information determines their system trust directly (Aw et al., 2022). Human interaction stays vital for key customer interactions because machines still find it difficult to demonstrate empathy (Pugna et al., 2023; Youssofi et al., 2023). Smart solutions including smart baggage and airport navigation and automated security services and intelligent cleaning planning should be designed to combine well with existing human services for achieving best results in user value and AI-human expertise synergy (Klein & Martinez, 2023).

2.1.3. Relational aspects and service quality

The use of artificial intelligence enables organizations through process automation which reduces both human mistakes and promotes standardized service delivery according to Salama et al (2020). Performance upgrades together with standardization practices enable delivery of dependable and consistent customer service. Beyond production benefits service quality depends on essential human factors which shape interaction dynamics as well as determine users' acceptance towards the technology (Mende et al., 2019). The relationship between customers and employees (Qiu et al., 2019) stays essential in its social dimension because AI lacks the capabilities to replace human empathy and emotion management (Khan & Iqbal, 2020 ; Punga et al., 2023) in specific situations. The combination of AI support and customized and pseudo-social interactions brings about improved customer happiness according to Aw et al. (2022). Critical service quality improvement demands both automated optimization of processes and respect for human relational elements to achieve maximum service quality with social and empathetic customer engagement (Youssofi et al., 2023).

2.1.4. Limits and challenges of AI

Among the main obstacle for AI developers are ethical issues which researchers such as Sikandar et al. (2020), Tula et al. (2024) and Youssofi et al. (2023) have discussed. Proper accountability and trust in AI systems become major questions due to these factors. A major roadblock to AI implementation arises because artificial intelligence systems lack the ability to empathize with humans specifically in situations where personal care and health service operations require extensive human contact and deep emotional patient-provider relationships (Punga et al., 2023). AI development faces two main obstacles: the requirement for specialized technical personnel and strong IT infrastructure and smooth integration to current organizational systems (Sikandar et al., 2020). Increasing dependence on AI in technology leads to two unfavorable outcomes which include erosion of human abilities and system failure vulnerabilities (Sikandar et al., 2020).

2.2. Model development: relationships between concepts

The research used Correspondence Factor Analysis (CFA) through the Similarity Analysis Using ADS in the IRaMuTeQ software enabled identification of relationships together with their level of strength between variables and key concepts. The Correspondence Factor Analysis implemented ADS method in IRaMuTeQ software demonstrates both variable relationships and main concept connections. The fig. 6 illustrates the obtained results.

Figure 6. Results of the Similarity Analysis (ADS)

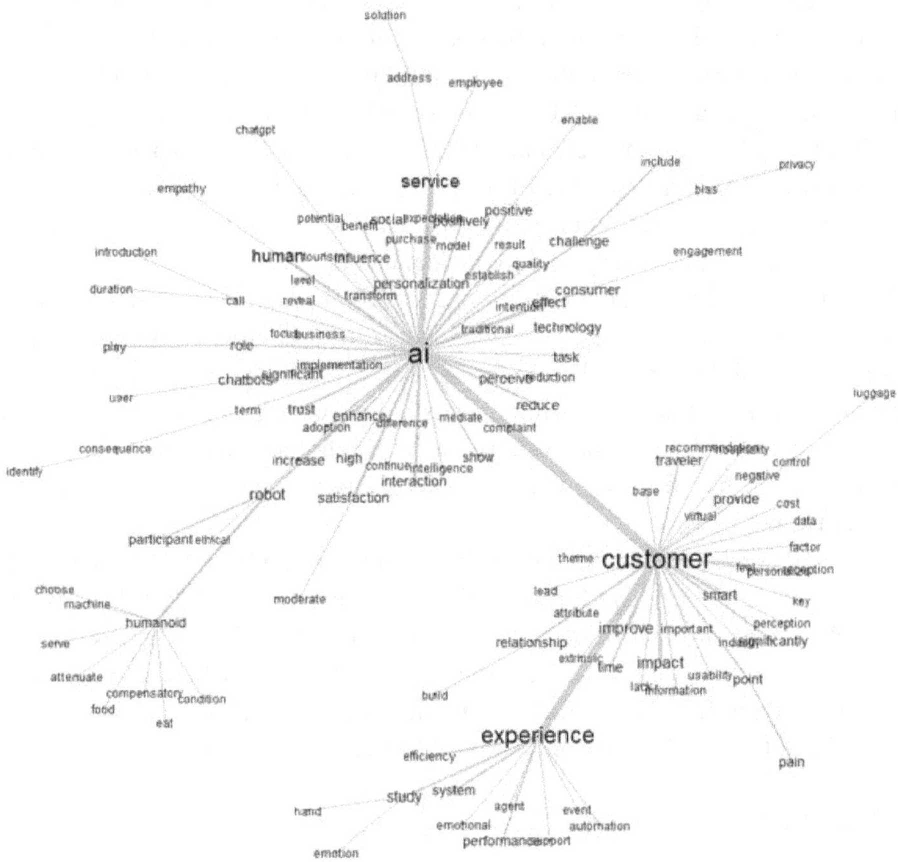

Source: Output IRaMuTeQ

2.2.1. The direct-effect relationship: AI → Customer experience in the services sector

Across the services sector, AI facilitates the personalization of offers, enhancing the customer experience through recommendations based primarily on users' past behaviors. This finding was emphasized in the study by Abu Daqar and Smoudy (2019), which demonstrated that personalized services have a significant effect on customer satisfaction. Likewise, AI-powered chatbots and virtual assistants helped reduce waiting times and improve post-purchase experiences. Empirical findings from these researchers indicate that AI accounted for 26.4% of the variance in overall customer experience in the banking sector.

Consistent findings were previously reported by Samala et al. (2020), who noted that emerging technologies such as chatbots, virtual reality and facial recognition are transforming customer interactions and improving user experience in the tourism industry (Aarabe et al., 2025 ; Khizzou et al., 2024). Through systematic analysis, Sikandar et al. (2020) discovered that AI enhances the customer experience through personalization, automation and relevant recommendations. According to their findings, every stage of the customer journey - needs recognition, research, evaluation, purchase and after-sales - is positively influenced by AI.

The call center sector displays the impact of AI on customer experiences according to Wang et al. (2020). Their research determined that older adults together with women receive higher advantages from AI-controlled systems. AI-driven service quality optimization improves customer satisfaction and increases trust levels across the e-commerce platform (Ameen et al., 2020). Neuhofer et al. (2021) revealed that AI implementation will make major changes to event experiences and their value creation methods.

The impact of AI on customer experience finds strong backing in the scientific literature documented by multiple studies including those written by Aw et al. (2022), Bhattacharya & Sinha (2022), Khan & Iqbal (2020), Klein & Martinez (2023), Mariani & Borghi (2024), Pugna et al. (2023), and Sigala et al. (2024). The obtained data from our research validating the initial hypothesis which states:

P1: AI positively influences customer experience in the service sector

2.2.2. Indirect relationships

Mediation relationships

AI's influence on the customer experience is not always direct. Sikandar et al. (2019) have emphasized that this influence operates through personalization, automation and relevant recommendations. In the same vein, AI enhances the customer experience via personalization, predictive analytics and efficiency (Peruchini et al., 2024 ; Tula et al., 2024). Tran (2024) has recently added that AI enables increased personalization, improved customer engagement and more informed decision-making. In addition, the quality of AI-driven services directly improves the customer experience and builds trust (Ameen et al., 2020). Furthermore, AI system quality is closely linked to user acceptance of the technology (Neuhofer et al., 2021).

In addition, Mende et al. (2019) found that service robot attributes facilitate the customer reception experience through the mediating role of customer-employee relationship building. Similarly, Roy et al. (2024) emphasized that trust plays a central role in the relationship between customer value factors (value, brand, relationship) and customer experience quality in environments where social robots are deployed.

In light of the aforementioned, we suggest the following:

P2: AI's influence on customer experience is mediated by service personalization.
P3: AI's influence on the customer experience is mediated by service automation.
P4: AI's influence on the customer experience is mediated by relevant recommendations.
P5: AI's influence on the customer experience is mediated by service quality.
P6: AI's influence on the customer experience is mediated by the establishment of a customer-employee relationship.
P7: AI's influence on the customer experience is mediated by trust.

Moderation relationships

Studies have suggested that human-like attributes (e.g. perceived intelligence) have a significant impact on customer experience (Aw et al., 2022). However, beyond this relationship, scenario-based experiments revealed that participants tended to spend more time with robots with higher levels of anthropomorphism or perceived intelligence. More specifically, it has been shown that consumers interact more with named humanoid robots than with mechanized humanoid robots (Mende et al., 2019). Therefore, we hypothesize that:

- **P8: Attributes such as the level of anthropomorphism moderate the influence of AI on customer experience.**

In addition, gender and age are other factors that have been shown to moderate the influence of AI on customer experience. Indeed, Wang et al. (2020) demonstrated that older customers and women benefit more from AI, with a greater reduction in complaints and shorter call durations. Based on this result, we propose that:

- **P9: Age moderates the influence of AI on customer experience.**
- P10: Gender moderates the influence of AI on customer experience.

Moderate mediating relationships

It has been suggested that personalization plays a mediating role in the relationship between AI and customer experience (Peruchini et al., 2024 ; Sikandar et al., 2019 ; Tula et al., 2024). However, scientific data has shown that the influence of certain factors, such as personalization, on this experience is moderated by the "perceived sacrifice" variable (Ameen et al., 2020). This concept refers to the voluntary abandonment by a consumer during a purchasing process. We therefore propose that:

- P11: Perceived sacrifice moderates the relationship between personalization and customer experience.

2.2.3. Control variable

Given that this paper focuses on customer experience in the service sector, it seems prudent to consider control variables related to the specific industries in this sector. This is justified by the fact that the sectors most studied are banking, e-commerce and tourism. The first two are at the forefront of AI adoption for customer experience, while the other sectors are lagging behind (Peruchini et al., 2024). In addition, it proved relevant to control for the effect of company size and type, as regardless of sector, company type or size, participants in some studies consider that AI already plays an important role in customer interactions (Holz et al., 2023).

We schamitize the proposed relationships in the following model (Fig. 7).

Figure 7. Our developed conceptual model

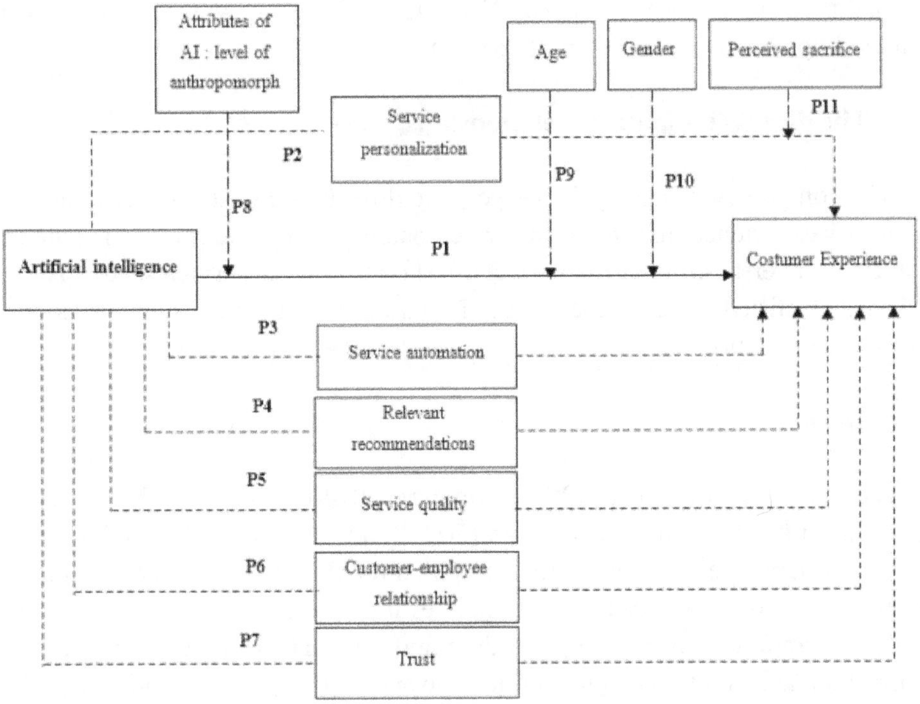

Source: authors

DISCUSSION

The SLR conducted as part of this study provides substantial support for the overarching hypothesis concerning the significant impact of AI on CX within the service sector. The results demonstrate that AI, through personalization, automation, and the provision of relevant recommendations, significantly improves customer satisfaction, trust, and experience.

- **The discussion of direct relationships:**

The extant literature has demonstrated that the use of AI has been shown to enhance CX in the service sector through personalization, automation, and the provision of relevant recommendations (e.g., TAM model; Abu Daqar & Smoudy, 2019; Sikandar et al., 2020; Wang et al., 2020). Research has established that customers view AI devices as productive tools which tailor services and decrease waiting period and boost interaction efficiency. The technological acceptance of the AI system relies on quality features as established by Neuhofer et al. (2021) which demonstrates the critical importance of user-friendly design.

- **The discussion indirect relationships:**

The comprehensive analysis has generated fresh knowledge describing the AI-customer experience alignment in service businesses by using intermediate effect patterns. Understanding of the impact of AI on CX in the service sector. The analysis has identified three distinct types of relationships: mediation, moderation, and moderate mediation.

- ***Mediation***

A research by Ameen et al. (2020), Mende et al. (2019) and Peruchini et al. (2024) together with Roy et al. (2024), Tran (2024) and Tula et al. (2024) demonstrates how AI systems perform operations on CX through mediation mechanisms based on personalization, service automation, relevant recommendations, service quality, customer-employee relationship building and trust. The research concept of auto-completion and emotional consumption showed how AI impacts consumer identity needs and emotional consumption dimensions to meet expectations. trust (according to Roy et al., 2024) plays an intermediary function which highlights the essentiality of maintaining long-lasting positive customer relationships (behavioral theories).

- ***Moderation***

The relationship between AI technology and CX requires consideration based on individual consumer attributes and AI platform features because these aspects act as moderators in this connection. Anthropomorphism serves as a moderator according to Mende et al. (2019) to emphasize the social element of customer experience which should inform human-machine interactions when emotional obligations are crucial. This explanation establishes heterogeneity in consumer expectations and preferences through the age and gender findings of Wang et al. (2020). AI's influence on customer experience requires a method based on segmentation and personalization when delivering services to customers.

- ***Moderate mediation***

The mediation through perceived sacrifice (Ameen et al., 2020) identify key factors which explain how AI influences service sector customer experience. While personalization has been shown to be generally beneficial for customer experience (see Peruchini et al., 2024 ; Sikandar et al., 2019 ; Tula et al., 2024), it can be counterproductive if the customer perceives the sacrifice to be excessive and does not yield the anticipated benefits. This variable underscores the significance of a balanced exchange of value in the customer-IA relationship.

- **The discussion of the control variables**

The choice to control the effect of the variables: sector of activity (Peruchini et al., 2024), size and type of company (Holz et al., 2023) is justified by the explanatory role of contextual factors in the AI- CX relationship in the service sector. Indeed, the banking, e-commerce and tourism sectors are the most studied in the reviewed works. This affects the nature of the models developed and the results obtained, which can be considered specific and limited in scope. On the other hand, the control of the variable "sector of activity", in addition to that of the size and type of company, makes it possible to isolate the effect of AI systems on customer experience, independently of sectoral or organizational specificities.

Beyond the causal relationships identified, this study makes an original contribution to the current state of research by offering a systematic and structured perspective on the link between AI and customer experience. While much of the existing literature focuses on isolated use cases or specific technologies, this chapter provides a comprehensive theoretical synthesis, grounded in a rigorous methodology and a cross-cutting analytical framework. In doing so, it addresses a critical gap by bringing together and articulating technical, psychological, relational, and contextual dimensions. This strategic positioning creates a reference point for investigations regarding AI effects on customer engagement that helps both scholars and practitioners and decision-makers. The chapter enhances the whole book's scholarly value by using customer experience to promote digital transformation in service industries.

CONCLUSION

The structured evaluation demonstrates how AI influences service sectors to undergo customer experience evolution. Service automation together with the real-time data analysis and customized offerings through AI generates digital age business advantages. When succeeding in AI deployment organizations need to create equilibrium between robotic systems and human contact to prevent AI from damaging consumer relationships.

The research presents a valuable addition to existing knowledge through an integrative heuristic format that explains AI influence across multiple customer management areas. This research focuses on three main aspects of personalization together with predictive analytics alongside automation but it addresses related issues of consumer trust concerns and ethical matters and service characteristics. Interdisciplinary research findings culminate in this study to develop an organized structure for evaluating AI-based support for optimized customer experiences.

Nevertheless, it is crucial to underscore the existing lacunae concerning the study's design., its primary underpinning is built on available literature which supersedes the pace AI customer experience strategies are evolving at. Additionally, the differing levels of AI application within industry and cultural settings suggest the need further research to test the framework empirically. Later studies could employ a more longitudinal approach to gauge the timeline impacts of AI on consumer trust, brand loyalty, and behavior on deep structural levels.

Looking ahead, it is predicted that the evolution of AI in enhancing customer experience will greatly depend on the development of adaptive learning technologies, the deepening of human-machine collaboration, and the integration of ethical guidelines. It remains important to note that with the increase of AI-based tools within a business, there should still be a balance between communication and automation. AI’s success in customer relationship management domains will greatly depend not just on technological advances but also on the ability of the system to build genuine, trusted relationships with clients.

REFERENCES

Aarabe, M., Bouizgar, M., Khizzou, N. B., Alla, L., & Benjelloun, A. (2025). The Transformative Impact of Artificial Intelligence on Tourism Experience: Analysis of Trends and Perspectives. *AI Technologies for Personalized and Sustainable Tourism*, 277-310.

Aarabe, M., Bouizgar, M., Khizzou, N. B., Alla, L., & Benjelloun, A. (2025). Technology-Driven and Personality in the Travel Experience Within a Destination: Literature Review and Proposal for Analysis Model. *Adapting to Evolving Consumer Experiences in Hospitality and Tourism*, 267-300.

Aarabe, M., Khizzou, N. B., Alla, L., & Benjelloun, A. (2024). Smart Tourism Experience and Responsible Travelers' Behavior: A Systematic Literature Review. Promoting responsible tourism with digital platforms, 128-147.

Al-Araj, R. E. E. M., Haddad, H. O. S. S. A. M., Shehadeh, M. A. H. A., Hasan, E., & Nawaiseh, M. Y. (2022). The effect of artificial intelligence on service quality and customer satisfaction in Jordanian banking sector. *WSEAS Transactions on Business and Economics*, *19*(12), 1929–1947. DOI: 10.37394/23207.2022.19.173

Alla, L., Bouhtati, N., Aarabe, M., & Khizzou, N. B. (2025). Social Media Analytics for Effective Customer Brand Engagement Assessment: A Theoretical Exploration. In Leveraging AI for Effective Digital Relationship Marketing (pp. 385-418). IGI Global.

Ameen, N., Tarhini, A., Reppel, A., & Anand, A. (2020). Customer experiences in the age of artificial intelligence. *Computers in Human Behavior*, *114*, 106548. DOI: 10.1016/j.chb.2020.106548 PMID: 32905175

Artusi, F., Magistretti, S., Bellini, E., & Dell'Era, C. (2024). Technology-aided customer experience innovation: Implementation modes in retail. *Creativity and Innovation Management*, *0*(1), 1–13. DOI: 10.1111/caim.12646

Aw, E. C. X., Tan, G. W. H., Cham, T. H., Raman, R., & Ooi, K. B. (2022). Alexa, what's on my shopping list? Transforming customer experience with digital voice assistants. *Technological Forecasting and Social Change*, *180*, 121711. DOI: 10.1016/j.techfore.2022.121711

Bharadwaj, A., El Sawy, O. A., Pavlou, P. A., & Venkatraman, N. (2013). Digital business strategy: Toward a next generation of insights. *Management Information Systems Quarterly*, *37*(2), 471–482. DOI: 10.25300/MISQ/2013/37:2.3

Bhattacharya, C., & Sinha, M. (2022). The role of artificial intelligence in banking for leveraging customer experience. *Australasian Accounting. Business and Finance Journal, 16*(5), 89–105.

Bouizgar, M., Aarabe, M., Khizzou, N. B., Alla, L., & Benjelloun, A. (2025). Smart Territorial Marketing and Promotion of Customer Engagement Towards the Territorial Brand: A Systematic Review of Literature. Sustainable and Intelligent Territorial Marketing and Entrepreneurship, 129-158.

Bouizgar, M., Aarabe, M., Khizzou, N. B., Alla, L., & Benjelloun, A. (2025). AI and Digital Technologies for Transforming Territorial Branding Management: A Systematic Review. *Corporate Management in the Digital Age*, 35-68.

Bowen, J. T., & Morosan, C. (2018). Beware hospitality industry: The robots are coming. *Cornell Hospitality Quarterly, 59*(3), 236–245.

Brady, M. (1984). Robotics and artificial intelligence. In M. Brady, L. A. Gerhardt, & H. F. Davidson (Eds.), *Artificial intelligence* (Vol. 26, Issue 1). Springer. https://link.springer.com/book/10.1007/978-3-642-82153-0

Brakus, J. J., Schmitt, B. H., & Zarantonello, L. (2009). Brand experience: What is it? How is it measured? Does it affect loyalty? *Journal of Marketing, 73*(3), 52–68. DOI: 10.1509/jmkg.73.3.052

Chen, J. S., Tran-Thien-Y, L., & Florence, D. (2021). Usability and responsiveness of artificial intelligence chatbot on online customer experience in e-retailing. *International Journal of Retail & Distribution Management, 49*(11), 1512–1531. DOI: 10.1108/IJRDM-08-2020-0312

Clark, A., Fox, C., & Lappin, S. (2010). *The handbook of computational linguistics and natural language processing*. Wiley-Blackwell., DOI: 10.1002/9781444324044

Danneels, E. (2004). Disruptive technology reconsidered: A critique and research agenda. *Journal of Product Innovation Management, 21*(4), 246–258. DOI: 10.1111/j.0737-6782.2004.00076.x

Daqar, M. A. A., & Smoudy, A. K. (2019). The role of artificial intelligence on enhancing customer experience. *International Review of Management and Marketing, 9*(4), 22–31. DOI: 10.32479/irmm.8166

Davenport, T. H., Guha, A., Grewal, D., & Bressgott, T. (2020). How artificial intelligence will change the future of marketing. *Journal of the Academy of Marketing Science, 48*(1), 24–42. DOI: 10.1007/s11747-019-00696-0

Di Stefano, G., Gambardella, A., & Verona, G. (2012). Technology push and demand-pull perspectives in innovation studies: Current findings and future research directions. *Research Policy, 41*(8), 1283–1295. DOI: 10.1016/j.respol.2012.03.021

Du, S., & Xie, C. (2021). Paradoxes of artificial intelligence in consumer markets: Ethical challenges and opportunities. *Journal of Business Research, 129*, 961–974. DOI: 10.1016/j.jbusres.2020.08.024

Gartner. (2023). Future of AI in Service Industry. *Gartner Research.*

Gentile, C., Spiller, N., & Noci, G. (2007). How to sustain the customer experience: An overview of experience components that co-create value with the customer. *European Management Journal, 25*(5), 395–410. DOI: 10.1016/j.emj.2007.08.005

Groening, C., Sarkis, J., & Zhu, Q. (2018). Green marketing consumer-level theory review: A compendium of applied theories and further research directions. *Journal of Cleaner Production, 172*, 1848–1866. DOI: 10.1016/j.jclepro.2017.12.002

Gursoy, D., Chi, O. H., Lu, L., & Nunkoo, R. (2019). Consumers acceptance of artificially intelligent (AI) device use in service encounters: The role of perceived control, innovation, and machine learning orientation. *International Journal of Information Management, 49*, 157–169. DOI: 10.1016/j.ijinfomgt.2019.03.008

He, K., Zhang, X., Ren, S., & Sun, J. (2016). Deep residual learning for image recognition. *2016 IEEE Conference on Computer Vision and Pattern Recognition (CVPR).* DOI: 10.1109/CVPR.2016.90

Holz, H. F., Becker, M., Blut, M., & Paluch, S. (2023). Eliminating customer experience pain points in complex customer journeys through smart service solutions. *Psychology and Marketing, 41*(3), 592–609. DOI: 10.1002/mar.21938

Homburg, C., Koschate, N., & Hoyer, W. D. (2006). The role of cognition and affect in the formation of customer satisfaction: A dynamic perspective. *Journal of Marketing, 70*(3), 21–31. DOI: 10.1509/jmkg.70.3.021

Huang, M. H., & Rust, R. T. (2018). Artificial intelligence in service. *Journal of Service Research, 21*(2), 155–172. DOI: 10.1177/1094670517752459

Khan, S., & Iqbal, M. (2020, June). AI-Powered Customer Service: Does it optimize customer experience? In *2020 8th International Conference on Reliability, Infocom Technologies and Optimization (Trends and Future Directions)(ICRITO)* (pp. 590-594). IEEE.

Khizzou, N. B., Aarabe, M., & Alla, L. (2024). The impact of digitalisation on the customer experience in medical tourism: A systematic review. *Impact of AI and tech-driven solutions in hospitality and tourism*, 408-428.

Khizzou, N. B., Aarabe, M., Bouizgar, M., Alla, L., & Benjelloun, A. (2025). The Digital Transformation of Medical Tourism: A Systematic and Bibliometric Review of the Literature. *Revolutionizing Healthcare Experience With Digital Medical Tourism*, 355-382.

Klein, K., & Martinez, L. F. (2023). The impact of anthropomorphism on customer satisfaction in chatbot commerce: An experimental study in the food sector. *Electronic Commerce Research*, *23*(4), 2789–2825. DOI: 10.1007/s10660-022-09562-8

Krishna, A. (2012). An integrative review of sensory marketing: Engaging the senses to affect perception, judgment and behavior. *Journal of Consumer Psychology*, *22*(3), 332–351. DOI: 10.1016/j.jcps.2011.08.003

Kühl, N., Schemmer, M., Goutier, M., & Satzger, G. (2022). Artificial intelligence and machine learning. *Electronic Markets*, *32*(4), 2235–2244. DOI: 10.1007/s12525-022-00598-0

Lemon, K. N., & Verhoef, P. C. (2016). Understanding customer experience throughout the customer journey. *Journal of Marketing*, *80*(6), 69–96. DOI: 10.1509/jm.15.0420

Lopes, J. M., Gomes, S., Nogueira, E., & Trancoso, T. (2024). AI's invisible touch: How effortless browsing shapes customer perception, experience and engagement in online retail. *Cogent Business & Management*, *12*(1), 2440628. DOI: 10.1080/23311975.2024.2440628

MacCormack, A., & Verganti, R. (2003). Managing the sources of uncertainty: Matching process and context in software development. *Journal of Product Innovation Management*, *20*(3), 217–232. DOI: 10.1111/1540-5885.2003004

Mariani, M. M., & Borghi, M. (2024). Artificial intelligence in service industries: Customers' assessment of service production and resilient service operations. *International Journal of Production Research*, *62*(15), 5400–5416. DOI: 10.1080/00207543.2022.2160027

McCarthy, J., Minsky, M. L., Rochester, N., & Shannon, C. E. (1956). A proposal for the Dartmouth summer research project on artificial intelligence. *Dartmouth Conference*. DOI: 10.1609/aimag.v27i4.1904

McKinsey & Company. (2022). *The state of AI in customer experience*. McKinsey Insights.

Mende, M., Scott, M. L., Van Doorn, J., Grewal, D., & Shanks, I. (2019). Service robots rising: How humanoid robots influence service experiences and elicit compensatory consumer responses. *JMR, Journal of Marketing Research*, *56*(4), 535–556. DOI: 10.1177/0022243718822827

Meyer, C., & Schwager, A. (2007). Understanding customer experience. *Harvard Business Review*, *85*(2), 116. PMID: 17345685

Nazir, S., Khadim, S., Asadullah, M. A., & Syed, N. (2023). Exploring the influence of artificial intelligence technology on consumer repurchase intention: The mediation and moderation approach. *Technology in Society*, *72*, 102190. DOI: 10.1016/j.techsoc.2022.102190

Neuhofer, B., Magnus, B., & Celuch, K. (2021). The impact of artificial intelligence on event experiences: A scenario technique approach. *Electronic Markets*, *31*(3), 601–617. DOI: 10.1007/s12525-020-00433-4 PMID: 38624486

Nguyen, T. H., & Le, X. C. (2024). Artificial intelligence-based chatbots–a motivation underlying sustainable development in banking: Standpoint of customer experience and behavioral outcomes. *Cogent Business & Management*, *12*(1), 2443570. DOI: 10.1080/23311975.2024.2443570

Nouhaila, B. K., Aarabe, M., & Alla, L. (2024). The impact of digitalisation on the customer experience in medical tourism: A systematic review. *Impact of AI and tech-driven solutions in hospitality and tourism*, 408-428.

Oliver, R. L., Rust, R. T., & Varki, S. (1997). Customer delight: Foundations, findings, and managerial insight. *Journal of Retailing*, *73*(3), 311–336. DOI: 10.1016/S0022-4359(97)90021-X

Page, M. J., McKenzie, J. E., Bossuyt, P. M., Boutron, I., Hoffmann, T. C., Mulrow, C. D., ... & Moher, D. (2021). The PRISMA 2020 statement: an updated guideline for reporting systematic reviews. *bmj, 372*.

Pappas, A., Fumagalli, E., Rouziou, M., & Bolander, W. (2023). More than Machines: The Role of the Future Retail Salesperson in Enhancing the Customer Experience. *Journal of Retailing*, *99*(4), 518–531. DOI: 10.1016/j.jretai.2023.10.004

Parasuraman, A., Zeithaml, V. A., & Berry, L. L. (1985). A conceptual model of service quality and its implications for future research. *Journal of Marketing*, *49*(4), 41–50. DOI: 10.1177/002224298504900403

Parasuraman, A., Zeithaml, V. A., & Berry, L. L. (1988). Servqual: A multiple-item scale for measuring consumer perc. *Journal of Retailing*, *64*(1), 12.

Parasuraman, A., Zeithaml, V. A., & Berry, L. L. (2005). A conceptual model of service quality and its implications for future research. *Journal of Marketing*, *49*(4), 41–50. DOI: 10.1177/002224298504900403

Parasuraman, R., Sheridan, T. B., & Wickens, C. D. (2000). A model for types and levels of human interaction with automation. *IEEE Transactions on Systems, Man, and Cybernetics. Part A, Systems and Humans*, *30*(3), 286–297. DOI: 10.1109/3468.844354 PMID: 11760769

Peruchini, M., da Silva, G. M., & Teixeira, J. M. (2024). Between artificial intelligence and customer experience: A literature review on the intersection. *Discover Artificial Intelligence*, *4*(1), 4. DOI: 10.1007/s44163-024-00105-8

Pizzi, G., Scarpi, D., & Pantano, E. (2021). Artificial intelligence and the new forms of interaction: Who has the control when interacting with a chatbot? *Journal of Business Research*, *129*, 878–890. DOI: 10.1016/j.jbusres.2020.11.006

Pugna, I. B., Popescu, I. C., & Henson, M. (2023, June). AI and New Forms of Market Interaction to Enhance Customer Experience—A Management Perspective. In *International Conference on Economics and Social Sciences* (pp. 35-47). Cham: Springer Nature Switzerland.

Qiu, H., Li, M., Shu, B., & Bai, B. (2019). Enhancing hospitality experience with service robots: The mediating role of rapport building. *Journal of Hospitality Marketing & Management*, *29*(3), 247–268. DOI: 10.1080/19368623.2019.1645073

Rai, A., Constantinides, P., & Sarker, S. (2019). Next generation digital platforms: Toward human-AI hybrids. *Management Information Systems Quarterly*, *43*(1), iii–ix.

Rotolo, D., Hicks, D., & Martin, B. R. (2015). What is an emerging technology? *Research Policy*, *44*(10), 1827–1843. DOI: 10.1016/j.respol.2015.06.006

Roy, S. K., Singh, G., Sadeque, S., & Gruner, R. L. (2024). Customer experience quality with social robots: Does trust matter? *Technological Forecasting and Social Change*, *198*, 123032. DOI: 10.1016/j.techfore.2023.123032

Russell, S. J., & Norvig, P. (2020). *Artificial intelligence: A modern approach* (3rd ed.). Pearson.

Sadhu, A. K. R., Parfenov, M., Saripov, D., Muravev, M., & Sadhu, A. K. R. (2024). Enhancing customer service automation and user satisfaction: An exploration of ai-powered chatbot implementation within customer relationship management systems. *Journal of Computational Intelligence and Robotics*, *4*(1), 103–123.

Samala, N., Katkam, B. S., Bellamkonda, R. S., & Rodriguez, R. V. (2020). Impact of AI and robotics in the tourism sector: a critical insight. *Journal of tourism futures, 8*(1), 73-87.

Shin, H., Bunosso, I., & Levine, L. R. (2023). The influence of chatbot humour on consumer evaluations of services. *International Journal of Consumer Studies, 47*(2), 545–562. DOI: 10.1111/ijcs.12849

Sigala, M., Ooi, K. B., Tan, G. W. H., Aw, E. C. X., Cham, T. H., Dwivedi, Y. K., Kunz, W. H., Letheren, K., Mishra, A., Russell-Bennett, R., & Wirtz, J. (2024). ChatGPT and service: Opportunities, challenges, and research directions. *Journal of Service Theory and Practice, 34*(5), 726–737. DOI: 10.1108/JSTP-11-2023-0292

Sikandar, M. A., Munari, P. K., & Arli, M. (2020). A Systematic Literature Review of the Impact of Artificial Intelligence on Customer Experience. *Machine Learning for Business Analytics*, 117-127.

Tran, M. T. (2024). Unlocking the AI-Powered Customer Experience: Personalized Service, Enhanced Engagement, and Data-Driven Strategies for E-Commerce Applications. In *Enhancing and Predicting Digital Consumer Behavior with AI* (pp. 375-382). IGI Global.

Tranfield, D., Denyer, D., & Smart, P. (2003). Towards a methodology for developing evidence-informed management knowledge by means of systematic review. *British Journal of Management, 14*(3), 207–222. DOI: 10.1111/1467-8551.00375

Tula, S. T., Kess-Momoh, A. J., Omotoye, G. B., Bello, B. G., & Daraojimba, A. I. (2024). Ai-enabled customer experience enhancement in business. *Computer Science & IT Research Journal, 5*(2), 365–389. DOI: 10.51594/csitrj.v5i2.789

Ullman, S. (2019). Using neuroscience to develop artificial intelligence. *Science, 363*(6428), 692–693. DOI: 10.1126/science.aau6595 PMID: 30765552

Verganti, R. (2011). Radical design and technology epiphanies: A new focus for research on design management. *Journal of Product Innovation Management, 28*(3), 384–388. DOI: 10.1111/j.1540-5885.2011.00807.x

Verhoef, P. C., Lemon, K. N., Parasuraman, A., Roggeveen, A., Tsiros, M., & Schlesinger, L. A. (2009). Customer experience creation: Determinants, dynamics and management strategies. *Journal of Retailing, 85*(1), 31–41. DOI: 10.1016/j.jretai.2008.11.001

Wang, L., Huang, N., Hong, Y., Liu, L., Guo, X., & Chen, G. (2020). Effects of voice-based ai in customer service: evidence from a natural experiment.

Wirtz, J., Patterson, P. G., Kunz, W. H., Gruber, T., Lu, V. N., Paluch, S., & Martins, A. (2018). Brave new world: Service robots in the frontline. *Journal of Service Management, 29*(5), 907–931. DOI: 10.1108/JOSM-04-2018-0119

Witten, I. H., Frank, E., & Hall, M. A. (2011). *Data mining: Practical machine learning tools and techniques* (3rd ed.). Morgan Kaufmann.

Youssofi, A., Jeannot, F., Jongmans, E., & Dampérat, M. (2023). Designing the digitalized guest experience: A comprehensive framework and research agenda. *Psychology and Marketing, 41*(3), 512–531. DOI: 10.1002/mar.21929

Yunanda, R. A., Rusmanto, T., Tareq, M. A., & Putri, N. K. S. (2024). Can ai-driven features alone foster customers'trust in indonesian and malaysian banks? *Journal of Theoretical and Applied Information Technology, 102*(24).

Zaugg, V., Savoldelli, V., Sabatier, B., & Durieux, P. (2014). Améliorer les pratiques et l'organisation des soins: Méthodologie des revues systématiques. *Santé Publique (Vandoeuvre-Les-Nancy, France), 26*(5), 655–667. DOI: 10.3917/spub.145.0655 PMID: 25490225

Chapter 2
The Contribution of AI Applications to Customer Value Creation in Hospitality

Ridouan Nejjari
https://orcid.org/0000-0002-5127-0364
Sidi Mohamed Ben Abdellah University, Morocco

Youssef El Fakir
https://orcid.org/0009-0002-5556-8130
Sidi Mohamed Ben Abdellah University, Morocco

ABSTRACT

Artificial intelligence (AI) is considered as key driver of innovation in many sectors, including hospitality. The gaps in the literature highlight the need for a thorough and integrated study of the impact of AI in hospitality, particularly in relation to the customer experience. This research fills this gap by shedding light on how AI can transform value creation practices through interactions between hotels and their guests by providing an analysis of the main current applications of AI applied in the hotel sector. A systematic literature review was carried out to explore the role of AI in the hospitality sector, highlighting its impact on customer experience and value creation. The PRISMA method was adopted and data were collected from Scopus. A final list of 54 Book chapters of IGI GLOBAL and journal articles were included to broaden perspectives. Thematic analysis was used in this systematic review to effectively structure the results and properly address the research objectives.

DOI: 10.4018/979-8-3373-0918-7.ch002

1. INTRODUCTION

1.1. Theoretical foundation and the relevance of the subject

Artificial intelligence (AI) is now considered as key driver of innovation in many sectors such healthcare (Khizzou et al., 2024a, 2024b, 2024b, 2025) and also in hospitality. By 2027, the global market of IA in hotel sector is expected to overcome 1.2 Billion dollars (Brand et al., 2023). Hotel businesses need to adopt new technologies to gain prominence and rise above other competitors, allowing better understanding customer preferences, predicting their needs, automating certain tasks and offering a tailored experience. In this sector, digital transformation is no longer an option, but a necessity to maintain sustainable competitiveness (Alla et al., 2025; Khizzou et al., 2024a; Saputra et al., 2024). AI can improve customer satisfaction (Sankar & David, 2023), strengthen loyalty and support hotel performance (Prentice et al., 2020). Nonetheless, certain ethical and technological challenges, such as technological cost, the management of personal data, and the customer privacy still need to be overcome to fully maximise the benefits of this technology.

Most studies of literature review are carried out in both hospitality and tourism settings (Aarabe et al., 2024b; Aarabe, Bouizgar, et al., 2025b, 2025a; Aarabe, Khizzou, et al., 2025; Nouhaila et al., 2024) and in marketing (Aarabe et al., 2024a), the gaps in the literature highlight the need for a thorough and integrated study of the impact of AI in hospitality, particularly in relation to the customer experience. This research will not only fill this gap, but also offer a more nuanced analysis of AI applications in the hospitality sector.

1.2. Research problem

In the hotel sector, the integration of AI is significantly transforming the customer experience, enabling personalised services, process automation and improved operational efficiency. Nonetheless, even though AI has great benefits in improving customer satisfaction and loyalty (Sankar & David, 2023), a number of challenges relating to the use of these technologies remain, including the management of personal data, confidentiality and ethical issues (Bhaskar & Sharma, 2022).

This research aims firstly to explore the specific applications of AI in the hotel industry, secondly assess the impact of these technologies on the customer experience and value creation, operational efficiency and historical heritage, and thirdly to identify the challenges faced by hotel businesses.

1.3. Research objective

The contribution of this study is twofold. First, it represents an academic breakthrough by documenting the current digital transformations occurring in the hotel industry and their impacts, an area that still remains underexplored in the scientific literature. Second, it offers managerial perspectives to hotel managers, providing them with insights to properly and effectively integrate AI into their operations in order to maintain their competitiveness. The conclusions of this research will therefore inform the technological choices made by hotels and suggest concrete solutions for making maximum of benefits of AI, while overcoming or at least minimising the ethical and technological risks associated with its adoption (Bhaskar & Sharma, 2022).

2. METHODOLOGY

This systematic literature review was carried out to explore the role of AI in the hospitality sector, highlighting its impact on customer experience and value creation. The PRISMA method (Preferred Reporting Items for Systematic Reviews and Meta-Analyses) was adopted (Swartz, 2021).

Data were collected from Scopus. Book chapters of IGI GLOBAL and journal articles were included to broaden perspectives. The words used are: Artificial Intelligence AND Hospitality, applications IA AND experience client, applications IA AND customer value, digital transformation AND hospitality. Only papers in English between 2010 and 2024 are kept while focusing on the application of AI in hospitality.

An initial total of 145 of both book chapters of IGI GLOBAL and article papers were identified through database Scopus. 72 articles were retained for thorough evaluation after analysis of titles and abstracts. Ultimately, 54 papers were selected, representing a variety of methodologies, geographical contexts, theoretical approaches, and distinct themes.

We opted for a manual thematic analysis, as the corpus studied is limited to synthesised research articles, and not to huge voluminous qualitative data that would require software such as Nvivo.

3. RESULTS AND DISCUSSION

The rise of intelligent technologies of AI has profoundly changed the hotel industry, introducing various solutions that reshape how customer value is created. From this perspective, AI offers hotels specific applications such as robots, chatbots and personalisation systems, leading to more efficient offerings that perfectly meet the customers' needs. The first theme explores what technologies are enabling a radical transformation of customer-business interactions. Another focus of this review of customer experience at the second theme, as AI plays a crucial role in improving the customer experience, by providing advanced personalisation, expectation management and anticipation of needs that enrich customer satisfaction (Sankar & David, 2023). However, the benefits of AI are not limited to the customer experience; its ability to improve operational efficiency in the hospitality sector is a third strand of this review, with implications for resource management, cost reduction and process optimisation. Finally, the integration of AI in cultural and heritage contexts is a final field of study, where technologies can enhance the authenticity of the guest experience while preserving historical, cultural and local specificities.

3.1. Theme 1: Specific Applications of Artificial intelligence in hospitality

The articles under investigation have revealed that advances in AI are deeply transforming the hotel sector through specific applications such as robots, chatbots and personalised services (Astuti et al., 2024; Doborjeh et al., 2022). These tools are reshaping the relationship between customers and hotels (Alla et al., s. d.; Belanche et al., 2019; Bhaskar & Sharma, 2022), providing innovative solutions to enhance the customer experience, operational efficiency, and historical and cultural heritage. The findings point out the positive benefits of these intelligent tools, the concerns they raise and recommendations for managers to optimise these positive impacts.

The integration of AI in the hotel industry has profoundly changed the interactions between hotels and their guests (Doborjeh et al., 2022), introducing innovative solutions that make services faster, more efficient and personalized. According to (Chan et al., 2022; Samala et al., 2020), robots, chatbots and service personalization are three emerging specific applications of AI in hospitality. The table below describes the benefits for each of the three applications:

Table 1. Current emerging applications of IA in hospitality:

Applications	Benefit	Description
Robots	service automation	They are adopted in hospitality sector to accomplish various tasks such as delivering luggage, greeting guests at reception, or providing room service (Doborjeh et al., 2022). In addition, (Nam et al., 2021; Tung & Au, 2018) point out that Robots increase the availability of services. Therefore, hotels can better meet demand, reduce operational costs (Ivanov et al., 2017) and improve service efficiency through automating these functions. Nonetheless, this automation can sometimes come into conflict with the human dimension of the service. In this sense, (Ivanov et al., 2017; Jabeen et al., 2022) indicate that customers can perceive these robots as impersonal, which limits the ability of these technologies to establish an emotional connection with customers. The human touch remains a crucial factor in quality hospitality (Jabeen et al., 2022), and robots can hardly replace the warm, personal hospitality that customers expect.
Chatbots	Digital interactions	For managing reservations, complaints and also frequently asked questions, chabots are successful to provide seamless interactions and then fast available service. According to the (Dwivedi et al., 2024; Neuhofer et al., 2021; Nguyen et al., 2022), these systems allow hotels to respond to customer inquiries immediately and faster, in many languages at most times, enabling hotels being accessible internationally (Hasan et al., 2021). They also reduce costs related to employees by automating most repetitive tasks of exchange (Ivanov et al., 2017). Nonetheless, the quality of machine learning algorithms and databases is a crucial factor for their effectiveness. In fact, poorly trained chabots can produce inaccurate and irrelevant responses, which can lead to customer frustration and poor customer experience.
Systems recommendation	Customization	Service customization is another area where AI tools give benefits, in particular through platforms like those explored in (Gavalas et al., 2014). These systems use customer data, such as past preferences or online behaviors, to provide personalized recommendations, activity suggestions, room choices or promotions. Customization improves the customer experience by increasing the relevance of the services provided and offering services more tailored to individual needs. This customization generates a feeling of appreciation and satisfaction, which can lead to increased customer loyalty.

Source: author own creation

Reviewing papers that are part of this first theme indicate that the AI reshapes practices in the hospitality industry and offer high prospects. These prospects cover areas such as enriching the guest experience, enhancing operational efficiency and preserving historical and cultural heritage. Nonetheless, these new benefits come with major challenges that should be taken into consideration. Therefore, the positive impacts of AI will be explored while providing recommendations to fully leverage its potential by maintaining a balance between technology and customer satisfaction.

It is effectively shown that the use of AI in the hotel industry generates a series of notable advantages and positive impacts (Cain et al., 2019; Chan et al., 2022). First, technology helps improve the operational efficiency of hotels by reducing waiting times and enabling instant response to customer requests. This reduction of time service contributes to a significant enhancement of customer value and the experience lived with customized services (Nejjari & Slaoui, 2024). Second, AI also enhances the role of hotels to preserve and promote the historical and cultural heritage. This role enables them to properly meet the needs of guests from diverse countries and cultures. This impact become more significant and important as AI enables multilingual interactions which facilities international expansion of hotels, thereby strengthening competiveness on a global scale (Saputra et al., 2024). The table below shows the papers that focused on applications used in hospitality while also highlighting the essence of the paper.

Table 2. Theme 1: Specific applications of Artificial intelligence in hospitality

Article	Essence
(Astuti et al., 2024)	Exploration of current state of technologies adoption for customer service in hospitality in Indonesia
(Belanche et al., 2019)	proposition a framework to better understand robo-advisor adoption among customers
(Bhaskar & Sharma, 2022)	Exploration of AI systems and applications implemented and available in hospitality
(Chan et al., 2022)	Presentation of major enabling technologies for AI in hospitality
(Deepthi & Bansal, 2023)	Investigation of existing applications of IA technologies and proposition of the main obstacles limiting their usefulness
(Doborjeh et al., 2022)	exploration of applications within the hospitality sector ranging from data modelling for demand forecasting, tourism destination and behaviour pattern to enhanced customer service and experience
(Doğan & Niyet, 2024)	Advantages of adopting AI technologies to offer tailored recommendations and support data-driven decision-making
(Dwivedi et al., 2024)	Analyse of the existing practices to establish a research agenda for the implementation of generative artificial intelligence (AI) (such as ChatGPT) and similar tools and raising challenges
(Gretzel, 2011)	Identification of research gaps in literature to address them for more use and effectiveness of intelligent systems
(Ivanov et al., 2017)	Exploration of the current state and the potential adoption of service automation and robots by actors involved in hospitality sector and addressing challenges when adapting these service robots
(Jabeen et al., 2022)	Development of a framework identifying the key factors in automation and AI implementation in the hospitality industry.
(Jain et al., 2024)	Systematic literature review through the PRISMA technique to present an extensive and in-depth analysis of existing research on adopting AI and robotics in hospitality industry.
(Kaur & Chauhan, 2024)	Examination of AI's role in the hospitality field (effective and harmful roles) and highlighting the emerging trends

continued on following page

Table 2. Continued

Article	Essence
(Knani et al., 2022)	proposition a bibliometric approach through systematic review aiming to examine the current state of art of AI research in hospitality
(Law et al., 2024)	analyse the state-of-the-art knowledge of AI research in hospitality.
(Li et al., 2021)	Investigating the effect of quality dimensions of chabots on use confirmation and use continuance of customers
(Manthiou et al., 2021)	Literature review to harmonize the meaning and the foundations of AI and service robots based on three themes (deployment, acceptance and ethics)
(Murphy et al., 2017)	Review literature on robotics emphasizing the importance of autonomy and human robot interaction and explaining three robot categories (industrial, professional service and personal service)
(Nam et al., 2021)	Investigation of trends and the underlying factors related to the adoption of AI and robotics in the hotel industry
(Gavalas et al., 2014)	Exploration of mobile recommender systems in tourism and hospitality, highlighting their ability to personalize recommendations according to user preferences and context
(Saputra et al., 2024)	Proposition of a typology of AI robots based on anthropomorphism in the hotel industry, classifying robots into four types: chatbots, mechanoids, humanoids and android.
(Cain et al., 2019)	Review of hospitality literature on the state of art of robotics in the sector by examining studies focusing on robots' impacts.
(Huang et al., 2022)	Qualitative study aiming at summarizing results and rating current emerging applications of AI in hospitality based on the diffusion theory of Rogers.
(Go et al., 2020)	Identification of key determinants of customer perception that impact accepting IA technology in hospitality using technology acceptance model (TAM).

Source: author own creation

The benefits, when using these tools by hotels, come with their challenges. Indeed, (Deepthi & Bansal, 2023) indicate that one of the main obstacles is the absence of human warmth in interactions with robots or chatbots. For many customers, this technological coldness can harm their experience, particularly in settings where human contact is at the heart of satisfaction (at reception or personalized service). Additionally, automated systems ensured by robots or chatbots can be prone to technical failures, such as bugs or inaccuracies. These imperfections harm the perceived quality of service and consequently reduce customer confidence by generating frustration in the technology used.

It is highly recommended to conceive and implement a hybrid strategy which reconciles AI and human interaction in order to optimize the benefits (Astuti et al., 2024). This aims to maintain automated service efficiency while ensuring emotional satisfaction for customers. in this sense, repetitive and logistic tasks could be assigned to robots while humans keep their role in maintaining their high level of emotional engagement. Likewise, it is also crucial to invest in continuous improvement of algorithms (Nguyen et al., 2022) to ensure that all used AI tools are permanently updated and trained to provide customers with suitable and relevant responses.

3.2. Theme 2: Artificial intelligence and improving the customer experience

The finding of the articles studied reveal that AI plays a fundamental role in transforming the customer experience in the hotel industry (Belanche, Casaló, & Flavián, 2021; Belanche, Casaló, Schepers, et al., 2021), by introducing more personalisation, immersive experiences (Das et al., 2024) and proactive management of needs (Doğan & Niyet, 2024). These technologies are contributing to add value to services, meeting the expectations of increasingly connected and demanding customers (Al-Emadi et al., 2021). The findings emphasize the contribution that AI has the ability to enhance the customer experience, while suggesting that related challenges should be met, indicating the need for exploration of prospects for enabling sustainable innovative dynamic.

in hospitality, AI is a crucial tool enabling customer experience improvement, (Chung et al., 2022). This is possible by providing adapted expectations. First, the paper of (Ghesh et al., 2024) reveals how AI plays a crucial role in adapting services to customers preferences, zhci enables memorable experiences (Doğan & Niyet, 2024). In addition, (Al-Emadi et al., 2021) focus on the importance of customization when predicting behavior of consumers.

Second, technologies such as augmented reality, investigated in (Das et al., 2024; Gretzel, 2021), enable customers to have immersed and enriched virtual environments (Gupta et al., 2022; Huang et al., 2022). These tools make visits more interactive and educational, increasing consequently guest satisfaction (Chen & Prentice, 2024).

Third, (Avula & Sithole, 2024; Bedu et al., 2024) highlight how AI anticipates customer needs, when hotels deliver solutions before a problem even occurs. This anticipation is highly relevant in some particular contexts such as in complex stays or corporate events management. This reveals the ability of AI to ensure a high level of proactive managements of customers' needs. The table below shows the papers highlighting the role of AI in improving the customer experience.

Table 3. Theme 2: Artificial intelligence and improving the customer experience

Article	Essence
(Al-Emadi et al., 2021)	How to predict consumer behaviour (passengers that purchase premium promotions) using the PAX model
(Avula & Sithole, 2024)	an overview of AI technologies and their possible uses for enhancing experiences in the hotel and tourist industries
(Bedu et al., 2024)	Examination of the impact of IA systems on the customer experience
(Belanche, Casaló, & Flavián, 2021)	Examination the impact of service Robots on the service enhancement
(Belanche, Casaló, Schepers, et al., 2021)	Examination of the impact of robots' perceived physical human-likeness, perceived competence, and perceived warmth on the customers' service value expectations and their loyalty intentions
(Chen & Prentice, 2024)	focus on the relationship between AI and customer experience to gain a competitive advantage
(Chung et al., 2022)	Proposition of framework of AI tools and technologies for achieving better business outcomes as well as improving customer experience management
(Ghesh et al., 2024)	Exploration of existing academic research on the AI-enabled customer experience (AICX), identification of gaps in literature and opportunities for future research in this domain.
(Gündüz, 2023)	Investigation of how AI impacts customer experience and enables to deliver competitive advantage to hospitality companies
(Gupta et al., 2022)	examination and exploration of AI enabled robots in hotels to enhance guest experience in a smart city
(Gursoy & Cai, 2024)	Examination of AI research trends in hospitality and impacts on customer service experience creation and delivery, service failure and recovery, human resources and organizational behavior.
(Hasan et al., 2021)	Broadening the understanding of anthropomorphic AI in physical and digital environments by presenting different characteristics and real life uses cases and examples and their relationships with improving customer experience
(Nejjari & Slaoui, 2024)	Investigating the impact of value creation on the performance of hotels. The customer value is seen as a process while performance focused on internal and external lens.
(Nejjari & Slaoui, 2025)	Comparing customer value from three perspectives that of managers, frontline employees and guests among three, four and five-star hotels.
(Nguyen et al., 2022)	extending the current body of knowledge in relation to the role of AI in the development of service experience and the relationship between customers and an organization through dimensions affecting customer-brand identification
(Prentice et al., 2020)	Examination of the impact of AI applications and employee service quality on customer satisfaction and loyalty
(Sankar & David, 2023)	Quantitative study showing that AI has a significant positive impact on service quality underlining its key role in improving customer satisfaction.
(Singh & Dhankhar, 2024)	quantitative research identifying the customer experience from the use of AI in Indian hotels

continued on following page

Table 3. Continued

Article	Essence
(Tung & Au, 2018)	Exploration of consumer opinions on robotics based on five dimensions of experience evaluation in human-robot interactions: embodiment, emotion, human-oriented perception, sense of security and co-experience
(Samala et al., 2020)	Systematic review of current emerging applications in hospitality and their roles in enhancing service and customer experience.

Source: author own creation

Although AI improves highly customer experience in hotels, it raises considerable issues (Bhaskar & Sharma, 2022), such as fear of dehumanization and concerns around data confidentiality (Manthiou et al., 2021). In fact, over-reliance on AI can lead to feelings of dehumanization, because some customers prefer personal interactions (Singh & Dhankhar, 2024), suggesting the need that hospitality businesses should strike a balance. Moreover, data privacy concerns remain a major obstacle (Bhaskar & Sharma, 2022). In this sense, in order to build consumer trust, hotels should invest to make their intelligent systems more transparent and ethical (Gursoy & Cai, 2024). Thereby, hotels are held to adopt a management model combining both automation and human presence, which could be considered as the most promising avenue. Moreover, (Murphy et al., 2017) indicate that hotels can not only overcome these obstacles, but also open the way for ethical and sustainable innovation for the future. As a result, AI will enable hotels to respond quickly and efficiently to customer needs, while delivering value that fit customers' expectations (Chung et al., 2022).

In sum, AI plays a crucial role in improving customer value in the hotel industry (Chen & Prentice, 2024) through increased customisation and proactive needs management. Nonetheless, challenges such as data confidentiality, ethics and technological accessibility need to be overcome (Bhaskar & Sharma, 2022). Therefore, hotels are invited to adopt an AI strategic adoption integrating these concerns to optimise value creation and thereby their overall performance.

3.3. Theme 3: Artificial intelligence and operational efficiency

The findings of the articles studied reveal that AI redefines operational efficiency in the hotel industry. In fact, hotels can reach this benefit by adopting innovative solutions such as decision optimisation through predictive analysis, process automation, and cost reduction (Al-Emadi et al., 2021; Belanche, Casaló, & Flavián, 2021).

Therefore, AI has become a strategic lever to improve the operational efficiency of hotels, by optimizing internal processes and reducing costs. More specifically, first, studies focused on process automation such as (Bhaskar & Sharma, 2022) and highlight the ability of AI to automate tasks such as inventory management, predictive maintenance or even human resources management and planning (Process automation). This automation enables employees, especially frontline employees, to focus on tasks with higher added value.

Second, AI systems, through predictive analysis, analyze data in real time to predict trends (Das et al., 2024). These predictions, such as peak bookings or seasonal preferences, are crucial to enable better resource management and efficient planning (Al-Emadi et al., 2021).

Third benefit is about staff cost reduction (Belanche, Casaló, & Flavián, 2021; Ivanov et al., 2017), because robots and chatbots gradually replace some important tasks and functions ensured by humans, in particular at reception.

The table below shows the papers highlighting the role of AI in enhancing operational efficiency.

Table 4. Theme 3: Artificial intelligence and operational efficiency

Article	Essence
(Alt, 2021)	Current developments implications of digital tools in maximizing efficiency
(Avula & Sithole, 2024)	an overview of AI technologies and their possible uses in for further efficiency in the hotel and tourist industries
(Belanche, Casaló, & Flavián, 2021)	Examination the impact of service Robots on the cost reduction
(Belanche et al., 2020)	Proposition of research agenda to guide scholars and help practitioners implement service robots successfully to finally increase productivity and reduce costs
(Das et al., 2024)	Emphasizing the importance of AI in learning and adapting behaviour standards of customers through predictive analytics

Source: author own creation

The integration of AI in the hotel industry opens up new perspectives in terms of efficiency and competitiveness (Saputra et al., 2024). Although it involves significant initial costs, its advantages, such as financial savings and a notable improvement in the operational efficiency, make it an essential strategic lever. Nonetheless, these innovations must be accompanied by proactive management of challenges, in particular to guarantee their harmonious and lasting adoption.

Moreover, the introduction of AI in the hotel industry has revolutionised operational efficiency by automating repetitive tasks, improving accuracy through predictive analysis (Das et al., 2024) and reducing costs (Belanche, Casaló, & Flavián, 2021). Nonetheless, these advances are not without their challenges, not least the need to train employees to use the new technologies and maintain reliable, high-performance systems. To fully capitalise on the potential of AI, hotels need to adopt a balanced strategy, combining technological innovation and human development. This combination will not only overcome current limitations, but will also guarantee a sustainable improvement in operational performance in the sector of hospitality that is constantly evolving.

In short, the AI tools bring significant benefits in terms of operational efficiency, while at the same time raising challenges, such as adapting teams and managing technologies. A gradual approach, supported by investment in training and maintenance, is essential to overcome these obstacles and exploit the full potential of AI.

3.4. Theme 4: Artificial intelligence and cultural and heritage context

The findings of the articles reviewed highlight the transformative role of AI in enhancing cultural and historical heritage, by offering immersive, interactive and widely accessible experiences. Digital applications and enriched representations allow not only to preserve and promote heritage (Bouizgar et al., 2025a), but also to create unique emotional connections between travellers and visitors. Nonetheless, these innovations raise significant challenges, particularly in terms of the authenticity of content and equity of access to technologies, suggesting the need for a balance between modernity and respect for cultural values.

In fact, AI plays a key role in promoting and preserving cultural heritage (Jing et al., 2021), while enriching the visitor experience. Some works focusing on digital applications for heritage like the work of (Jing et al., 2021) explore the use of AI to create virtual tours, educational applications and multilingual translation tools.

Moreover, AI enables to model virtual environments where visitors can interact with historical reenactments or personalized virtual guides (Huang et al., 2022).

The table below shows the papers highlighting the role of AI in cultural and historical heritage.

Table 5. Theme 4: Artificial intelligence and cultural and heritage context

Article	Essence
(Gretzel, 2021)	Suggestion of a conceptualization of smart tourism development and identification of values to build smart tourism mindset.
(Gretzel et al., 2015)	proposition of definition for smart tourism, its current trends and its technological and business foundations
(Hunter, 2021)	Investigation of the link between online representations and their physical counterparts in the context of smart tourism research
(Jing et al., 2021)	Proposition of a set of intangible digital application models in the light of the cultural ecology theory and verification its application in the sustainable development of cultural tourism.

continued on following page

Table 5. Continued

Article	Essence
(Xiang, 2021)	This article highlights the growing importance of the concept of 'smart tourism' in tourism development, national policies and destination management, while underlining the need for empirical and theoretical approaches to meet modern technological and socio-cultural challenges
(Yim et al., 2021)	This study uses deep learning algorithms to analyse the subjective dimensions (authenticity, creativity, emotion) of travel photos generated by consumers, showing their impact on user engagement on online tourism review sites.

Source: author own creation

Nonetheless, some challenges should be indicated as the fact that technology AI can reduce the authenticity of the cultural experience. Likewise, limited infrastructure in some heritage regions slows the adoption of these tools.

As a result, a combination of technological and human interventions could preserve authenticity while benefiting from IA advantages.

It is therefore crucial to note that the cultural and heritage context directly concerns hotels in a number of ways, including integrating AI into the management of local cultural heritage, creating immersive experiences for visitors and enhancing the value of the region's cultural resources. Hotels can thus have significant roles in the following specific aspects described in the table below:

Table 6. Roles of hotels in the cultural and heritage context

Aspects	Description
Promoting local heritage	When providing tours in historical sites, hotels can promote cultural heritage of a city while using AI tools. This enables more understanding by customers about historical sites.
Immersive experiences	Mobile applications and chatbots enables tourists to receive information in real time about features of hotels, which is part of the heritage of the city. This enriches the experiences of guests.
Accessibility and personalisation	Hotels can use AI to customize offerings by recommending tours and events based on what tourists react.
Targeted marketing and differentiation	By highlighting cultural heritage and using AI to promote these elements in their marketing strategy, hotels can differentiate themselves in a competitive market. Hotels are thus enabled by AI tools to create a niche when integrating cultural heritage in their offering.
Supporting sustainability and environment preservation:	Ai is also used as a tool to manage sustainability of historical elements within hotels.

Source: author own creation

In conclusion, the integration of cultural heritage into hotels, via digital technologies, offers an innovative way to enrich the guest experience while contributing to the enhancement and preservation of local cultural resources. It can also deliver hotels a competitive edge by responding to a growing demand for authentic and enriching tourism experiences. Likewise, the analysis of travel photos is essential for destinations as well as hotels, as it provides a better understanding of customer preferences and emotions (Yim et al., 2021).

4. PRACTICAL IMPLICATIONS

The findings of this chapter is useful to managers of hotels as it provides insights to optimize value creation. Through various emerging applications, from the personalization of services to the optimization of operational processes, AI helps to enrich the customer experience while improving the efficiency of hotels and historical heritage. Nonetheless, its adoption raises significant challenges, particularly on the ethical, organizational and technological levels. Through this synthesis, we want to point out the key contributions of AI, their identified limits, challenges and perspectives, while evidencing its strategic role in hospitality, which is rapidly changing sector.

4.1. The impact of AI in the hotel sector: towards better customer value creation

Through this literature review, it is clearly shown that AI is redefining traditional practices in the hospitality industry, providing unique opportunities to optimize customer value creation (Ghesh et al., 2024). From personalizing services (Doğan & Niyet, 2024) to predicting traveler needs (Al-Emadi et al., 2021), AI actually seems a strategic lever to improve the customer experience and strengthen the competitive advantage of hotel companies (Gündüz, 2023).

In the same way, by exploring innovative applications of generative AI, intelligent systems and the concept of smart tourism, it is aimed at highlighting the multiple facets of impacts of AI. This analysis allow to better understand how these technological tools, grounded in foundations of smart tourism (Gretzel, 2021; Hunter, 2021), are able to define a new dynamic of customer value in the current hotel industry.

4.1.1. AI Applications for enhancing customer value creation in hospitality

The hospitality industry has witnessed significant transformation in recent years, due in large part to the emergence of digital technologies (Gupta et al., 2022; Kaur & Chauhan, 2024). Among these technologies, AI is considered as one of the most influential forces that is reshaping the sector. In hospitality, the applications of AI cover a wide range, from automation to customization, improving both operational efficiency and customer experience. In an increasingly competitive environment, hoteliers are increasingly using AI-powered solutions to meet the growing demand for personalized services.

Finally, by saving time and reducing human errors (Ivanov et al., 2017), automated services lead to an enriched and enjoyable customer experience.

In sum, the automated services in hotels contribute to customer satisfaction and loyalty (Prentice et al., 2020). Nonetheless, several issues are of great interest (Dwivedi et al., 2024). The major challenge lies in the absence of human warmth during interactions with these devices (Singh & Dhankhar, 2024). This can provoke a feeling of dehumanization among some particular customers (Manthiou et al., 2021, Gursoy & Cai, 2024)), who prefer human interactions. Moreover, automated services can be prone to technical failures and imperfections, which can lead to dissatisfaction of customers. Consequently, in order to optimize the implementation and adoption of AI with quality of human interactions, it is recommended to adopt a combined approach (Kaur & Chauhan, 2024). In this sense, robots can be used for repetitive logistics tasks, while human employees can focus on personalized, emotionally engaging interactions.

4.1.2. Leveraging Generative AI for Customer Value Creation in Hospitality

As a branch of AI, generative AI has shown immense potential for creating personalized and dynamic customer experiences in hospitality (Gupta et al., 2022). Unlike traditional AI systems that rely on pre-existing data and algorithms, generative AI is capable, based on the information provided by their customers, of creating new content, such as emails, special offers, loyalty programs, dynamic pricing models and unique customer experiences. The content creation is one of the most promising applications of generative AI in the hospitality industry that hotels can leverage to offer more flexible and tailored services (Doğan & Niyet, 2024). This way, hotels create stronger emotional connections with customers, thereby increasing customers' perception of value, which leads ultimately to customer loyalty (Nejjari & Slaoui, 2024).

4.1.3. Intelligent systems: role and implications in creating customer value in hospitality

Smart tourism relies on the integration of AI, Internet of Things (IoT) and big data analytics (Bouizgar et al., 2025b; Gretzel, 2011; Gretzel et al., 2015). These technologies work together to create a more personalized and efficient travel experience. Smart tourism therefore refers to the integration of all these digital technologies to enhance the travel experience. Hotels are increasingly adopting this mindset as the implementation of AI and other smart technologies has become fundamental to create higher customer value.

Another concept is used to mean smart tourism is intelligent systems, which integrate AI and machine learning. In hospitality, machine learning algorithms draw on past booking (reservations) and some other factors such as local event and weather, to optimize room rates by predicting demand.

Overall, the concept of smart tourism points out the importance of the integration between digital services in real-time information and customized stay experience (Hunter, 2021; Xiang, 2021). Having the ability to analyze data from various and different sources, hotels can therefore deliver real time recommendations and provide customers with higher customized experience. Finally, it is important to note that most research in smart tourism tend to be conceptual or case study-based (Xiang, 2021).

4.2. Digital revolution with strategic and sustainable issues

The findings of the reviewed articles highlight the main strategic and sustainable issues related to the integration of AI in hospitality.

4.2.1. AI and resource management: a lever for sustainability

AI goes beyond simply improving the guest experience by also enabling more efficient resource management. Automating repetitive tasks (Ivanov et al., 2017), such as check-in or inventory management, not only reduces operational costs but also allows employees to focus on higher value-added tasks (Gursoy & Cai, 2024; Ivanov et al., 2017). In addition, AI can optimize energy consumption by automatically adjusting heating, air conditioning and lighting systems based on room occupancy, thus contributing to more sustainable management of the property.

In a context where sustainability is a major issue for consumers and companies, this ability of AI to optimize the use of resources while reducing operational costs represents a double benefit (Deepthi & Bansal, 2023; Ivanov et al., 2017). Hotels can thus meet the growing expectations of customers in terms of environmental responsibility while reducing their ecological footprint and aligning their practices with sustainability objectives.

Overall, beyond customer value creation, integrating AI into hospitality also helps to optimize resource allocation, reduces waste and improves energy management in hotels, contributing to sustainability goals. Therefore, AI is shown to be a powerful lever for innovation and optimized resource management, contributing to sustainable performance. Consequently, hotels can focus on providing high added value services, a key factor in customer loyalty and satisfaction (Nejjari & Slaoui, 2024).

4.2.2. The ethical and technological challenges of AI

Customers increasingly expect hotels to treat their data with the utmost confidentiality, while offering them a personalized experience. So, one of the main obstacles is the management of personal data of customers. This issue related to transparency of data use, privacy, and secure information management are at the heart of the debates on the adoption of AI in this sector (Gursoy & Cai, 2024).

In addition, the integration of AI requires a high initial investment (Nguyen et al., 2022), which can be a barrier for small structures. Moreover, resistance to change from employees is another barrier to widespread adoption.

To overcome these challenges, hotels must find a balance between the legal and ethical requirements of data management and the benefits of AI. Likewise, the implementation of these technologies can require significant investments in terms of infrastructure and staff training (Kaur & Chauhan, 2024), which represents a challenge for many companies, especially smaller hotels. Finally, hotel companies must invest in employee training and integrate modular and scalable AI tools.

4.2.3. AI as a driver of innovation in the hotel industry

In a constantly evolving sector, the adoption of AI is not only a question of competitiveness (Saputra et al., 2024), but represents a strategic lever to transform the way hotels gain competitive advantage and create value for their customers. The study of AI in the hotel sector is part of a framework where technological innovation and customer satisfaction have become the main drivers of success (Li et al., 2021).

5. CONCLUSION

The objective of this book chapter was to provide an analysis of the main emerging applications of AI in the hotel industry. This firstly involves identifying and studying the AI technologies currently used in hotels, such as robots, chatbots, personalized recommendation systems, and predictive analytics, and secondly understanding their contribution to improving the customer experience. This book chapter also aims to provide an analysis of the challenges and opportunities when integrating these technologies in the hotel industry, while suggesting recommendations to fully optimize their adoption and implementation.

The selected papers under review contribute highly to broadening the understanding of the impact of AI in hospitality, particularly on creating value for customers and operational efficiency. They highlight several specific applications of AI such as robots, chatbots and personalization systems, and explain how these technologies can transform the customer experience and improve the operational efficiency of hotels. Hence, hotels can build stronger relationships with their clients, improve operational performance, and ensure long-term success.

In fact, the integration of robots in hotels allows automation of various repetitive and logistical tasks, such as welcoming guests, baggage delivery and room service. As highlighted by several studies, including the work of (Tung & Au, 2018), robots enable to reduce operational costs while responding to labor shortages in certain contexts. These devices increase the availability of services, which is particularly useful during peak periods. Hotels improve therefore the efficiency of their services and become more responsive.

The use robots like those (Nam et al., 2021; Tung & Au, 2018) whose task concerns front desk and room service, is a real-world example of how AI is being applied to automate repetitive tasks and improve service efficiency. This kind of robots are able to interact with customers and complete essential tasks, such as reception related tasks and baggage delivery (Ivanov et al., 2017), contributing to create a fruitful experience. Nonetheless, a major challenge of this automation lies in customer perception. Some guests still prefer human interaction which can be perceived as more warm and empathetic. Robots, while effective, struggle to create an emotional connection with customers, which limits their impact in some situations where hospitality is the key.

Moreover, chatbots also play a central role in managing reservations, complaints, and customer frequently asked questions, providing permanent support. Therefore, they automate conversations with guests, providing instant answers to their questions and reservations. A great example is multilingual chatbots deployed to handle customer inquiries, as in the article of (Li et al., 2021). These tools enable quick and efficient interaction with guests of different nationalities, making hotels more accessible and increasing their competitiveness in the international market. These systems are increasingly sophisticated, able to understand and respond to requests in a variety of contexts, from managing reservations to providing personalized recommendations for leisure activities.

These based-machine learning tools therefore allow responding instantly to guest inquiries, often in multiple languages, making hotels more accessible to an international market. According to (Nam et al., 2021), chatbots also help reduce operational costs by automating interactions that would otherwise require staff intervention. However, their effectiveness depends heavily on the quality of the learning algorithms and the databases on which they are trained. In this sense, poorly trained chatbots can generate inaccurate responses, causing customer frustration and thereby dissatisfaction. Thus, careful attention to systems training is crucial to maintaining a positive customer experience.

In addition, the personalization of services using AI-based recommendation systems represents another major area of innovation in the hotel industry (Doğan & Niyet, 2024), like those mentioned in (Gavalas et al., 2014; Hasan et al., 2021). Through intelligent systems to analyze guest behaviors and preferences, hotels can offer tailored services, such as personalized activity or room recommendations. The recommendation algorithms can therefore offer specific services or products based on the guest's past preferences, contributing to a unique and tailor-made experience. The data collected through these tools feeds predictive models that anticipate guest needs, optimize room management and improve resource allocation, contributing to smoother and more profitable hotel management. In this sense, studies like those conducted in (Gavalas et al., 2014; Sankar & David, 2023) demonstrate that this approach increases customer satisfaction by making their experiences more relevant and tailored to their specific needs. This type of personalization is also a key factor in customer loyalty, as it creates a feeling of valuation and recognition. Therefore, the use of AI in this area allows hotels to better anticipate customer expectations, which strengthens their competitiveness (Saputra et al., 2024) and positioning in the market (Nam et al., 2021).

Another area on the impact of IA is the cultural and heritage context, which represents an exceptional opportunity for hotels to modernise and democratise access to heritage (Laoute et al., 2025). Indeed, IA facilitates interactive and accessible experiences and helps therefore to preserve and promote cultural riches to a diverse target. However, there are challenges related to these advances, particularly in terms of the authenticity of content and inequalities in technological access. To fully optimise its impact, it is essential to adopt a balanced approach that combines technological innovation with respect for cultural values. In this way, AI can become a real lever for cultural enhancement, enriching human interaction while protecting the common cultural heritage. Therefore, this heritage delivers hotels a great opportunity to create a competitive edge to be differentiated from other competitors.

The findings highlight that AI plays a pivotal role in reshaping the hospitality industry. From improving customer value through chatbots and predictive analytics to optimizing operations efficiency and historical heritage, AI helps hotels deliver more personalized and efficient guest experiences. The use of these technologies is thus not just a trend but a necessity for hotel businesses looking to keep and maintain their competitiveness in an increasingly digital changing world. Moreover, the potential to create customer value in the hospitality industry is expected to grow with the continuous evolution and use of AI, providing new areas and opportunities to innovate and improve service offerings. The following figure (Figure 1) illustrates how IA applications in hospitality influence customer experience, operational efficiency and cultural heritage.

In sum, the analysis of the studied articles reveals that AI tools are numerous and powerful and consequently plays a strategic role in improving customer value, operational efficiency in the hotel industry, and the historical heritage. Nonetheless, these technological advances come with major challenges, particularly in terms of ethics, data privacy and sustainability. Consequently, hotels must balance innovation and social responsibility to fully maximize the benefits of AI by adopting a combined approach that aligns innovation, sustainability and customer value. This particular perspective provides a solid foundation to guide research and guide the strategies of hospitality industry players in a constantly evolving technological environment. Likewise, hospitality academics should, through their role of teaching, integrate in this novel era of technologies and reposition themselves, students and the whole industry (Murphy et al., 2017).

Although existing literature is growing and has widely explored the contributions of AI and digital transformation in hospitality (Kaur & Chauhan, 2024; Knani et al., 2022; Law et al., 2024), several areas remain under-researched, suggesting the need for future research. These gaps provide opportunities to deepen the understanding of less studied aspects, such as the impact of AI on cultural or emotional dimensions of customer experience (Tung & Au, 2018).

These key missing areas can be stated and described by the following table:

Table 7. Key missing areas and Future research

Key missing areas	State of literature	Future research
Emotional impact of interactions with robots and chatbots	Much of current research focuses on the technical and functional aspects of AI, but few studies focus on the emotional impact of interactions with robots and chatbots.	Another avenue of research could be on how AI can be used to create more empathetic and emotionally engaging interactions, and thereby better emotional experience.
AI Adoption in SME Hotels	While large hotel chains are investing heavily in AI technologies, SMEs (Nguyen et al., 2022), particularly in less developed regions, remain largely behind. The literature on AI adoption by small and medium enterprises (SMEs) in hospitality is limited.	Future studies could focus on the challenges these companies face in integrating AI, as well as solutions that fit their limited resources. So, they should explore specific strategies to help SMEs overcome barriers to AI adoption, such as high implementation costs and lack of technical skills (Deepthi & Bansal, 2023). Studies also could focus on the specific benefits these companies could gain from adopting simple, less expensive technologies.
Ethics and social implications	The social and ethical impact of the adoption of AI in the hotel industry also remains understudied, which makes ethics in the application of AI in hospitality represents a significant gap. For example, concerns around customer privacy, data security, and the impact of robots on employment in the hospitality industry merit further investigation (Jain et al., 2024).	It would be relevant to explore these ethical dimensions to better understand how hotels can deploy AI while respecting social and legal standards. Thereby, particular attention should be paid in future research to the balance between the effectiveness of technologies and social expectations, particularly in terms of humanizing customer service.
Effect of AI on long-term satisfaction and loyalty	Although studies have shown that AI improves immediate customer satisfaction, longitudinal research on the impact of AI on the long term customer loyalty is lacking.	It would be useful that future studies examine whether the use of technologies such as robots and chatbots generates lasting relationships with customers or whether they risk remaining superficial.

Source: author own creation

Even though the existing literature makes important contributions to understanding the application of AI in hospitality, there are still several areas where future research is needed to deepen understanding of the impact of AI on customer experience, particularly in more local contexts, and to explore the ethical and social aspects of its adoption. So, researchers can contribute to significant advances in exploring areas that are still little studied, such as the interaction between AI and cultural specificities, or the emotional impacts on the customer experience. Exploring these areas will fill theoretical gaps, guide professional practices, and prepare the sector to meet the technological and ethical challenges of tomorrow, while strengthening its capacity to create lasting value for customers.

REFERENCES:

Aarabe, M., Bouizgar, M., Khizzou, N. B., Alla, L., & Benjelloun, A. (2025a). Technology-Driven and Personality in the Travel Experience Within a Destination : Literature Review and Proposal for Analysis Model. *Adapting to Evolving Consumer Experiences in Hospitality and Tourism*, 267-300.

Aarabe, M., Bouizgar, M., Khizzou, N. B., Alla, L., & Benjelloun, A. (2025b). The Transformative Impact of Artificial Intelligence on Tourism Experience : Analysis of Trends and Perspectives. *AI Technologies for Personalized and Sustainable Tourism*, 277-310.

Aarabe, M., Khizzou, N. B., Alla, L., & Benjelloun, A. (2024a). Marketing applications of emerging technologies : A systematic literature review. In *AI and data engineering solutions for effective marketing* (pp. 23–47). IGI Global. DOI: 10.4018/979-8-3693-3172-9.ch002

Aarabe, M., Khizzou, N. B., Alla, L., & Benjelloun, A. (2024b). Smart Tourism Experience and Responsible Travelers' Behavior : A Systematic Literature Review. *Promoting responsible tourism with digital platforms*, 128-147.

Aarabe, M., Khizzou, N. B., Alla, L., & Benjelloun, A. (2025). Marketing Applications of Emerging Technologies and Business Performance of Tourism SMEs : A Systematic Literature Review. *Models, Strategies, and Tools for Competitive SMEs*, 217-242.

Al-Emadi, N., Thirumuruganathan, S., Robillos, D. R., & Jansen, B. J. (2021). Will you buy it now? : Predicting passengers that purchase premium promotions using the PAX model. *Journal of Smart Tourism*.

Alla, L., Bouhtati, N., Aarabe, M., & Khizzou, N. B. (2025). Social Media Analytics for Effective Customer Brand Engagement Assessment : A Theoretical Exploration. In *Leveraging AI for Effective Digital Relationship Marketing* (p. 385-418). IGI Global.

Alla, L., Bouhtati, N., Aarabe, M., & Khizzou, N. B. (2025). Social Media Analytics for Effective Customer Brand Engagement Assessment: A Theoretical Exploration. In Leveraging AI for Effective Digital Relationship Marketing (pp. 385-418). IGI Global.

Alt, R. (2021). Digital transformation in the restaurant industry : Current developments and implications. *Journal of smart tourism, 1*(1), 69-74.

Astuti, E., Harsono, I., Uhai, S., Muthmainah, H. N., & Vandika, A. Y. (2024). Application of artificial intelligence technology in customer service in the hospitality industry in Indonesia : A literature review on improving efficiency and user experience. *Sciences Du Nord Nature Science and Technology*, *1*(01), 28–36. DOI: 10.71238/snst.v1i1.15

Avula, M., & Sithole, T. (2024). Artificial Intelligence's Potential to Improve Operational Efficiency and Customer Experience in the Hospitality and Tourism Sectors. In *Impact of AI and Tech-Driven Solutions in Hospitality and Tourism* (pp. 351–382). IGI Global. DOI: 10.4018/979-8-3693-6755-1.ch018

Bedu, E. J., Foroudi, P., & Palazzo, M. (2024). Artificial intelligence (AI) systems, customer experience and preference in the tourism industry in Ghana : Focus on Accra Metropolis. In *Contemporary Marketing and Consumer Behaviour in Sustainable Tourism* (pp. 208–222). Routledge. DOI: 10.4324/9781003388593-15

Belanche, D., Casaló, L. V., & Flavián, C. (2019). Artificial Intelligence in FinTech : Understanding robo-advisors adoption among customers. *Industrial Management & Data Systems*, *119*(7), 1411–1430. DOI: 10.1108/IMDS-08-2018-0368

Belanche, D., Casaló, L. V., & Flavián, C. (2021). Frontline robots in tourism and hospitality : Service enhancement or cost reduction? *Electronic Markets*, *31*(3), 477–492. DOI: 10.1007/s12525-020-00432-5

Belanche, D., Casaló, L. V., Flavián, C., & Schepers, J. (2020). Service robot implementation : A theoretical framework and research agenda. *Service Industries Journal*, *40*(3-4), 203–225. DOI: 10.1080/02642069.2019.1672666

Belanche, D., Casaló, L. V., Schepers, J., & Flavián, C. (2021). Examining the effects of robots' physical appearance, warmth, and competence in frontline services : The Humanness-Value-Loyalty model. *Psychology and Marketing*, *38*(12), 2357–2376. DOI: 10.1002/mar.21532

Bhaskar, P., & Sharma, K. D. (2022). A critical insight into the role of artificial intelligence (AI) in tourism and hospitality industries. *Pacific Business Review International, 15*(3).

Bouizgar, M., Aarabe, M., Khizzou, N. B., Alla, L., & Benjelloun, A. (2025a). AI and Digital Technologies for Transforming Territorial Branding Management : A Systematic Review. *Corporate Management in the Digital Age*, 35-68.

Bouizgar, M., Aarabe, M., Khizzou, N. B., Alla, L., & Benjelloun, A. (2025b). Smart Territorial Marketing and Promotion of Customer Engagement Towards the Territorial Brand : A Systematic Review of Literature. *Sustainable and Intelligent Territorial Marketing and Entrepreneurship*, 129-158.

Brand, J., Israeli, A., & Ngwe, D. (2023). Using GPT for market research. *Harvard business school marketing unit working paper, 23-062*.

Cain, L. N., Thomas, J. H., & Alonso, M.Jr. (2019). From sci-fi to sci-fact : The state of robotics and AI in the hospitality industry. *Journal of Hospitality and Tourism Technology*, *10*(4), 624–650. DOI: 10.1108/JHTT-07-2018-0066

Chan, L., Hogaboam, L., & Cao, R. (2022). Artificial intelligence in tourism and hospitality. In *Applied artificial intelligence in business : Concepts and cases* (pp. 213–229). Springer. DOI: 10.1007/978-3-031-05740-3_14

Chen, Y., & Prentice, C. (2024). Integrating Artificial Intelligence and Customer Experience. *Australasian Marketing Journal*, •••, 14413582241252904. DOI: 10.1177/14413582241252904

Chung, K., Quach, S., & Thaichon, P. (2022). A framework of artificial intelligence (AI) applications in marketing. In *Artificial Intelligence for Marketing Management* (pp. 41–51). Routledge. DOI: 10.4324/9781003280392-4

Das, I. R., Talukder, M. B., & Kumar, S. (2024). Implication of Artificial Intelligence in Hospitality Marketing. In *Utilizing Smart Technology and AI in Hybrid Tourism and Hospitality* (pp. 291–310). IGI Global. DOI: 10.4018/979-8-3693-1978-9.ch014

Deepthi, B., & Bansal, V. (2023). Applications of Artificial Intelligence (AI) in the Tourism Industry : A Futuristic Perspective. In *Impact of Industry 4.0 on Sustainable Tourism : Perspectives, Challenges and Future* (p. 31-43). Emerald Publishing Limited.

Doborjeh, Z., Hemmington, N., Doborjeh, M., & Kasabov, N. (2022). Artificial intelligence : A systematic review of methods and applications in hospitality and tourism. *International Journal of Contemporary Hospitality Management*, *34*(3), 1154–1176. DOI: 10.1108/IJCHM-06-2021-0767

Doğan, S., & Niyet, İ. Z. (2024). Artificial Intelligence (AI) in Tourism. In *Future Tourism Trends Volume 2 : Technology Advancement, Trends and Innovations for the Future in Tourism* (p. 3-21). Emerald Publishing Limited.

Dwivedi, Y. K., Pandey, N., Currie, W., & Micu, A. (2024). Leveraging ChatGPT and other generative artificial intelligence (AI)-based applications in the hospitality and tourism industry : Practices, challenges and research agenda. *International Journal of Contemporary Hospitality Management, 36*(1), 1–12. DOI: 10.1108/IJCHM-05-2023-0686

Gavalas, D., Konstantopoulos, C., Mastakas, K., & Pantziou, G. (2014). Mobile recommender systems in tourism. *Journal of Network and Computer Applications, 39*, 319–333. DOI: 10.1016/j.jnca.2013.04.006

Ghesh, N., Alexander, M., & Davis, A. (2024). The artificial intelligence-enabled customer experience in tourism : A systematic literature review. *Tourism Review, 79*(5), 1017–1037. DOI: 10.1108/TR-04-2023-0255

Go, H., Kang, M., & Suh, S. C. (2020). Machine learning of robots in tourism and hospitality : Interactive technology acceptance model (iTAM)–cutting edge. *Tourism Review, 75*(4), 625–636. DOI: 10.1108/TR-02-2019-0062

Gretzel, U. (2011). Intelligent systems in tourism : A social science perspective. *Annals of Tourism Research, 38*(3), 757–779. DOI: 10.1016/j.annals.2011.04.014

Gretzel, U. (2021). Conceptualizing the smart tourism mindset : Fostering utopian thinking in smart tourism development. *Journal of Smart Tourism, 1*(1), 3–8. DOI: 10.52255/smarttourism.2021.1.1.2

Gretzel, U., Sigala, M., Xiang, Z., & Koo, C. (2015). Smart tourism : Foundations and developments. *Electronic Markets, 25*(3), 179–188. DOI: 10.1007/s12525-015-0196-8

Gündüz, C. (2023). Customised Holiday Experiences through Artificial Intelligence : Case Studies from the Aviation and Hospitality Sectors. *Journal of Aviation, 7*(3), 337–345. DOI: 10.30518/jav.1351472

Gupta, S., Modgil, S., Lee, C.-K., Cho, M., & Park, Y. (2022). Artificial intelligence enabled robots for stay experience in the hospitality industry in a smart city. *Industrial Management & Data Systems, 122*(10), 2331–2350. DOI: 10.1108/IMDS-10-2021-0621

Gursoy, D., & Cai, R. (2024). Artificial intelligence : An overview of research trends and future directions. *International Journal of Contemporary Hospitality Management.*

Hasan, R., Thaichon, P., & Weaven, S. (2021). Are we already living with Skynet? Anthropomorphic artificial intelligence to enhance customer experience. In *Developing digital marketing* (pp. 103–134). Emerald Publishing Limited. DOI: 10.1108/978-1-80071-348-220211007

Huang, A., Chao, Y., de la Mora Velasco, E., Bilgihan, A., & Wei, W. (2022). When artificial intelligence meets the hospitality and tourism industry : An assessment framework to inform theory and management. *Journal of Hospitality and Tourism Insights*, *5*(5), 1080–1100. DOI: 10.1108/JHTI-01-2021-0021

Hunter, W. C. (2021). Cultural representations and experience in tourism : Two forms of mimesis. *Journal of Smart Tourism*, *1*(1), 65–67. DOI: 10.52255/smarttourism.2021.1.1.8

Ivanov, S. H., Webster, C., & Berezina, K. (2017). Adoption of robots and service automation by tourism and hospitality companies. *Revista Turismo & Desenvolvimento (Aveiro)*, *27*(28), 1501–1517.

Jabeen, F., Al Zaidi, S., & Al Dhaheri, M. H. (2022). Automation and artificial intelligence in hospitality and tourism. *Tourism Review*, *77*(4), 1043–1061. DOI: 10.1108/TR-09-2019-0360

Jain, A., Singh, K., & Jain, P. (2024). Understanding the Impact of Artificial Intelligence and Robotics in the Tourism and Hospitality Industry Through Customer Experience : A Systematic Literature Review. *Impact of AI and Tech-Driven Solutions in Hospitality and Tourism*, 329-350.

Jing, X., Tan, F., & Zhang, M. (2021). Digital application of intangible cultural heritage from the perspective of cultural ecology. *Journal of Smart Tourism*, *1*(1), 41–52. DOI: 10.52255/smarttourism.2021.1.1.6

Kaur, G., & Chauhan, P. (2024). Artificial Intelligence and Invigoration of the Hospitality Industry : An Analysis. In *Artificial Intelligence for Smart Technology in the Hospitality and Tourism Industry* (p. 49-62). Apple Academic Press.

Khizzou, N. B., Aarabe, M., & Alla, L. (2024a). *Current trends in scientific research on managerial innovations in healthcare supply chain : A bibliometric analysis*. 1-9.

Khizzou, N. B., Aarabe, M., & Alla, L. (2024b). Practices of Qualitative Studies in Medical Sciences : The Focus Groups Method Applied to Patients. In *Data Collection and Analysis in Scientific Qualitative Research* (pp. 229–252). IGI Global. DOI: 10.4018/979-8-3693-8689-7.ch009

Khizzou, N. B., Aarabe, M., Bouizgar, M., Alla, L., & Benjelloun, A. (2025). The Digital Transformation of Medical Tourism : A Systematic and Bibliometric Review of the Literature. *Revolutionizing Healthcare Experience With Digital Medical Tourism*, 355-382.

Knani, M., Echchakoui, S., & Ladhari, R. (2022). Artificial intelligence in tourism and hospitality : Bibliometric analysis and research agenda. *International Journal of Hospitality Management*, *107*, 103317. DOI: 10.1016/j.ijhm.2022.103317

Laoute, C., Aarabe, M., Khizzou, N. B., Alla, L., Alj, B., & Benjelloun, A. (2025). Digital Marketing and Territorial Attractiveness of Innovative Entrepreneurship : Exploratory Qualitative Study. In *Sustainable and Intelligent Territorial Marketing and Entrepreneurship* (p. 33-68). IGI Global.

Law, R., Lin, K. J., Ye, H., & Fong, D. K. C. (2024). Artificial intelligence research in hospitality : A state-of-the-art review and future directions. *International Journal of Contemporary Hospitality Management*, *36*(6), 2049–2068. DOI: 10.1108/IJCHM-02-2023-0189

Li, L., Lee, K. Y., Emokpae, E., & Yang, S.-B. (2021). What makes you continuously use chatbot services? Evidence from chinese online travel agencies. *Electronic Markets*, *31*(3), 1–25. DOI: 10.1007/s12525-020-00454-z PMID: 35603227

Manthiou, A., Klaus, P., Kuppelwieser, V. G., & Reeves, W. (2021). Man vs machine : Examining the three themes of service robotics in tourism and hospitality. *Electronic Markets*, *31*(3), 511–527. DOI: 10.1007/s12525-020-00434-3

Murphy, J., Hofacker, C., & Gretzel, U. (2017). Dawning of the age of robots in hospitality and tourism : Challenges for teaching and research. *European Journal of Tourism Research*, *15*, 104–111. DOI: 10.54055/ejtr.v15i.265

Nam, K., Dutt, C. S., Chathoth, P., Daghfous, A., & Khan, M. S. (2021). The adoption of artificial intelligence and robotics in the hotel industry : Prospects and challenges. *Electronic Markets*, *31*(3), 553–574. DOI: 10.1007/s12525-020-00442-3

Nejjari, R., & Slaoui, S. (2024). Customer value creation and Moroccan hotels' performance : A multi-party and multi-phase vision. *Journal of Hospitality and Tourism Insights*, *7*(5), 2504–2524. DOI: 10.1108/JHTI-04-2023-0224

Nejjari, R., & Slaoui, S. (2025). Towards a comparison of three customer value perspectives in the hotel industry : Insights from Moroccan context. *Journal of Hospitality and Tourism Insights*, *8*(4), 1602–1620. DOI: 10.1108/JHTI-03-2024-0236

Neuhofer, B., Magnus, B., & Celuch, K. (2021). The impact of artificial intelligence on event experiences : A scenario technique approach. *Electronic Markets, 31*(3), 601–617. DOI: 10.1007/s12525-020-00433-4 PMID: 38624486

Nguyen, T., Quach, S., & Thaichon, P. (2022). The effect of AI quality on customer experience and brand relationship. *Journal of Consumer Behaviour, 21*(3), 481–493. DOI: 10.1002/cb.1974

Nouhaila, B. K., Aarabe, M., & Alla, L. (2024). The impact of digitalisation on the customer experience in medical tourism : A systematic review. *Impact of AI and tech-driven solutions in hospitality and tourism*, 408-428.

Prentice, C., Dominique Lopes, S., & Wang, X. (2020). The impact of artificial intelligence and employee service quality on customer satisfaction and loyalty. *Journal of Hospitality Marketing & Management, 29*(7), 739–756. DOI: 10.1080/19368623.2020.1722304

Samala, N., Katkam, B. S., Bellamkonda, R. S., & Rodriguez, R. V. (2020). Impact of AI and robotics in the tourism sector : A critical insight. *Journal of tourism futures, 8*(1), 73-87.

Sankar, J. G., & David, A. (2023). Measuring the Service Quality of Artificial Intelligence in the Tourism and Hospitality Industry. In *Handbook of Research on Innovation, Differentiation, and New Technologies in Tourism, Hotels, and Food Service* (p. 133-155). IGI Global. DOI: 10.4018/978-1-6684-6985-9.ch007

Saputra, F. E., Buhalis, D., Augustyn, M. M., & Marangos, S. (2024). Anthropomorphism-based artificial intelligence (AI) robots typology in hospitality and tourism. *Journal of Hospitality and Tourism Technology, 15*(5), 790–807. DOI: 10.1108/JHTT-03-2024-0171

Singh, L., & Dhankhar, D. (2024). Artificial Intelligence for Innovative Customer Services in the Hospitality Industry of India. In *Leveraging AI and Emotional Intelligence in Contemporary Business Organizations* (pp. 219–239). IGI Global.

Swartz, M. K. (2021). PRISMA 2020 : An update. *Journal of Pediatric Health Care, 35*(4), 351. DOI: 10.1016/j.pedhc.2021.04.011 PMID: 34243844

Tung, V. W. S., & Au, N. (2018). Exploring customer experiences with robotics in hospitality. *International Journal of Contemporary Hospitality Management, 30*(7), 2680–2697. DOI: 10.1108/IJCHM-06-2017-0322

Xiang, Z. (2021). Journal of Smart Tourism. *Journal of Smart Tourism, 1*(1), 1–2. DOI: 10.52255/smarttourism.2021.1.1.1

Yim, D., Malefyt, T., & Khuntia, J. (2021). Is a picture worth a thousand views? Measuring the effects of travel photos on user engagement using deep learning algorithms. *Electronic Markets*, *31*(3), 1–19. DOI: 10.1007/s12525-021-00472-5

Chapter 3
Driving Patient Data With AI for Patient Care Path Optimization:
A Theoretical Framework

Nouhaila Ben Khizzou
https://orcid.org/0009-0002-3355-5224
National School of Commerce and Management, Sidi Mohamed Ben Abdellah University, Fez, Morocco

Mourad Aarabe
https://orcid.org/0009-0003-9772-6683
National School of Business and Management, Fez, Morocco

Meryem Bouizgar
https://orcid.org/0009-0009-0943-2057
National School of Business and Management, Morocco

Lhoussaine Alla
https://orcid.org/0000-0002-7238-1792
Sidi Mohamed Ben Abdellah University, Fez, Morocco

Ahmed Benjelloun
https://orcid.org/0009-0004-9673-2747
Sidi Mohamed Ben Abdellah University, Fez, Morocco

ABSTRACT

Background: Patient data and artificial intelligence are widely explored concepts for improving healthcare services. However, little is known about the application of lean thinking to quantify these two elements. Objective: The aim of this study is to

DOI: 10.4018/979-8-3373-0918-7.ch003

develop a theoretical framework combining patient data and artificial intelligence, aimed at optimizing the care pathway by identifying the theories to be mobilized to address this issue. Methods: A systematic review of the literature was carried out. Inclusion criteria were that the article should focus on optimizing the patient's care pathway. Twenty articles were included. Results: The proposed framework can be used to create an overview of the potential of driving patient-related data with AI for optimizing the patient care pathway. Further research is needed to investigate the use of patient-related quantifications of this data. Conclusions: This research paper analyzes the application of artificial intelligence in data science to optimize patient care pathways.

1. BACKGROUND

The fact that more and more people need healthcare, combined with a lack of staff to help them, creates a big problem that could become even more difficult in the years to come. (Wallin et al., 2019). But there are ways of overcoming these difficulties by using simpler methods that are better suited to patients' needs. The idea of "improving the care pathway" means trying to organise and use resources more intelligently and efficiently. This can help build trust between health professionals and patients. (Scholz et al., 2021). Healthcare is changing rapidly, with an increasing emphasis on creating personalised care pathways tailored to the needs of each individual. Studies show that care coordinators play an important role in identifying patients with complex needs, helping them to understand their options and assessing their medical and social care needs.(Vijverberg et al., 2022). This just goes to show how important it is for all healthcare professionals to work together, putting the individual at the center of their concerns, and for there to be well-organized managers to ensure the smooth running of support and care coordination services. Furthermore, the work of Vanasse et al. highlights a crucial aspect of healthcare: every patient is unique, and it is essential that care is personalized to meet their specific needs.(Vanasse, s. d.). By taking into account different individual and environmental factors, we can not only better understand care pathways, but also significantly improve patient outcomes. This paves the way for a real breakthrough in the organization of healthcare services, making our system more efficient and more humane. In addition, the concept of care trajectories can offer an enriching perspective on patients' healthcare pathways. Indeed, this approach, which links different clinical episodes by common themes, provides a global vision of the care provided (Alla et al., s. d.). (Laveault-Allard, 2022). In addition, the integration of artificial intelligence into digital medicine is transforming our approach to healthcare. By personalizing treatments through in-depth analysis of patient data, we have the opportunity to make significant advances in individual well-being. (Budde et al., 2021). It's exciting to think of the new treatment strategies that may emerge from this exploration of patient trajectories. AI technologies really do seem to be a key to improving clinical decision-making and delivering better-tailored care (De Man et al., 2016). It is essential to encourage interdisciplinary partnerships that will unite expertise and enable innovative solutions to emerge(Aarabe et al., 2025b). The integration of technologies such as artificial intelligence opens up a multitude of possibilities for improving not only the delivery of care, but also the overall patient experience. (Peltzer, 2009). By focusing on an ethical, patient-centered approach, we can truly transform the healthcare landscape and ensure that every individual benefits from a personalized, efficient care pathway. (Savina & Boidin, 1996) .

1.1. Gaps De Recherche

Analyzing patient trajectories enables researchers to better understand patterns of care utilization, which are key to improving patient outcomes and reducing overall healthcare costs. However, the lack of a comprehensive definition or operational framework for care trajectories is a major challenge in this field (Laveault-Allard, 2022). Current literature often draws on concepts such as continuity of care, care pathways or episodes of care, but fails to provide a unified structure. This fragmentation highlights the need for further research to develop a coherent model that encompasses the various aspects of the patient journey. In addition, the integration of artificial intelligence (AI) solutions offers the opportunity to harness the value of patient trajectories in digital medicine (Saleem et al., 2022). Personalized approaches are essential to effectively analyze longitudinal patient data and derive insights conducive to patient data-driven strategies and the use of AI technologies to enable researchers to explore patient trajectories more thoroughly and optimally, identifying new patterns that can aid clinical decision-making.

This chapter aims to review the current literature on patient pathways. Following this review, clarifying key concepts and assessing implications for future research and practice. We address three research questions within this framework.

(RQ1) How might the evolving literature on patient pathways prompt reflection on how healthcare has been conceptualized over the years.and what themes are emerging?

(RQ2) What are the specific features of patient care pathways, and what distinguishes them from other methods of care?

(RQ3) What impact might this have on practice and future research?

1.2 Literature background

1.2.1. Patient care pathway

The fact that 17 different terms have been identified underlines the growing importance of this concept in the medical field. The inclusion of "critical pathway" in specialized dictionaries shows the extent to which this concept has gained recognition since its inception in 1996. (Anderson, 2002). It's encouraging to see that the healthcare sector continues to evolve and seek ways to optimize care through increasingly elaborate and coordinated treatment protocols. The definition provided by De Bleser et al. underlines just how essential it is to approach care with a global, coordinated vision. By integrating this method, we can really improve the efficiency of resources while preserving patients' well-being. (De Bleser et al., 2006). The idea of using lean thinking to optimize every step of the way is brilliant. Not only does it promote a seamless system, it also ensures that every patient receives the care they need, in line with their unique pathway. (Diallo et al., 2024).

1.2.2. Care pathways

the concept of care trajectories, often used interchangeably with care pathways, encompasses a series of clinical episodes linked by a common theme with varying temporal constraints (Patwala et al., 2024). This method models the sequence and nature of episodes, interventions, and financial and health outcomes over time. Effective patient care pathways involve the structured use of healthcare services over a specific period of time, with the aim of improving the overall well-being and outcomes of individuals within the healthcare system. These trajectories offer valuable insights into how patients navigate through different stages of care, ensuring that their needs are met in a timely and efficient manner. As mentioned in(Quigley et al., 2021)

1.2.3. Dimensions of the patient care pathway

the multidimensional model enriches our understanding of care pathways for patients, particularly those suffering from chronic illnesses (Pinaire et al., 2017). This model focuses on important ideas like long-term illness, ongoing care, care plans, and the different stages and changes in a patient's health journey. It looks at the details like who the patient is, why they need care, where they go for treatment, what kind of care they receive, and when these events happen. For example, a person with a chronic illness may see their family doctor, specialists, or other healthcare providers. They might visit clinics, emergency rooms, or hospitals. Throughout their health journey, the person will go through regular check-ups, tests, and treatments in outpatient or hospital settings, at different times.(Vanasse, s. d.). Potential predictors of outcomes can be found in the care pathway (figure1).

Figure 1. Illustration of the dimensions of the patient care pathway

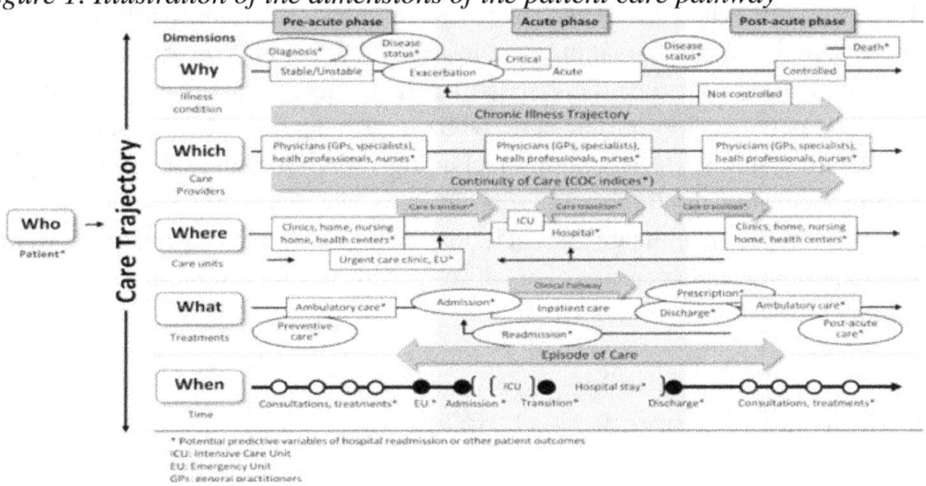

Source: (Vanasse, s. d.)

1.2.4. Patient care pathway characteristics

After looking at various studies about how things are sorted into three main groups, we found that a clear explanation of a clinical pathway should include the following parts. (De Bleser et al., 2006).

There are three main categories: a name, certain characteristics and certain aspects concerning the course's objectives and results. This will undoubtedly make it easier to interpret and understand the various terms.

Figure 2. Characteristics of the patient care pathway

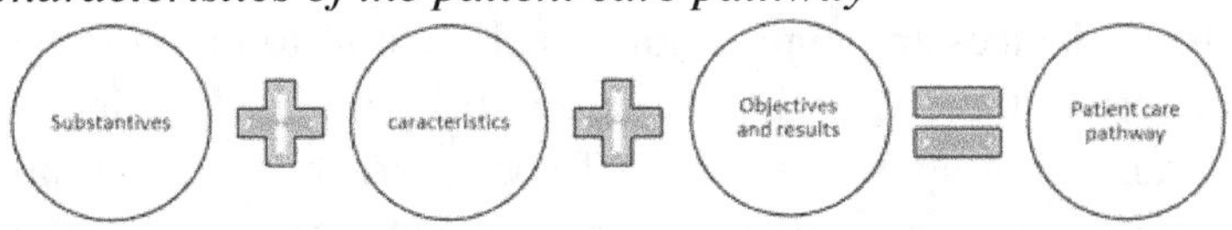

Source: (Authors,2025)

Main items or things, such as plans, documents, or rules.(El-Razek, 2019) ;

Features such as having a team with different skills or working with patients who share similar conditions. (Kercsmar & Myers, 2002).
Goals and outcomes (such as health improvements, financial gains, and other results)

However, a clinical pathway isn't just a paper with instructions to follow. It's also a way of organizing and managing care to make sure patients receive better, more consistent treatment. On the other hand, optimizing this care pathway is essential to delivering timely and appropriate care, while improving the operational efficiency of healthcare systems. By leveraging technology solutions such as AI and digital transformation, and adopting a value-driven approach focused on patient outcomes and quality of life, healthcare organizations can effectively improve the overall patient experience and optimize care pathways via AI. What we're going to see in this chapter (objective).

1.2.5. The use of technology to make patient care more efficient and easier to follow.

The use of artificial intelligence (AI) tools in digital medicine offers a great opportunity to better monitor and understand the evolution of patients. Tailoring treatments to each individual is very important to effectively analyze their data over time. This uncovers valuable information that helps to propose more appropriate care for each patient. (Allam et al., 2021). Advances in healthcare through digital technologies, particularly artificial intelligence, are making it possible to deliver care faster and more efficiently. AI can analyze vast amounts of patient information to identify trends or emerging issues, helping physicians make better treatment decisions. What's more, this digital evolution is making life easier for patients by making it easier to book appointments, access their medical records online, and communicate with their healthcare professionals.(Hechinger et al., 2022). The use of new technologies, such as computerized medical records and telemedicine, allows different healthcare professionals to share information more effectively. This facilitates teamwork and ensures that patients receive more coordinated care.(Barelds et al., 2010). Digital devices and applications, such as tools to monitor their health or consult their doctor remotely, enable patients to be more involved in planning their treatment and care.(Stoumpos et al., 2023). To better organize patient care pathways, it's important for decision makers to analyze existing healthcare rules and policies to see what can be improved. By proposing changes to these rules, we can facilitate communication between different healthcare professionals and encourage them to work as a team. The result will be more cohesive, better coordinated care that is always focused on the needs of the patient.(Patwala et al., 2024).

Figure 3. development of prognostic pathways.

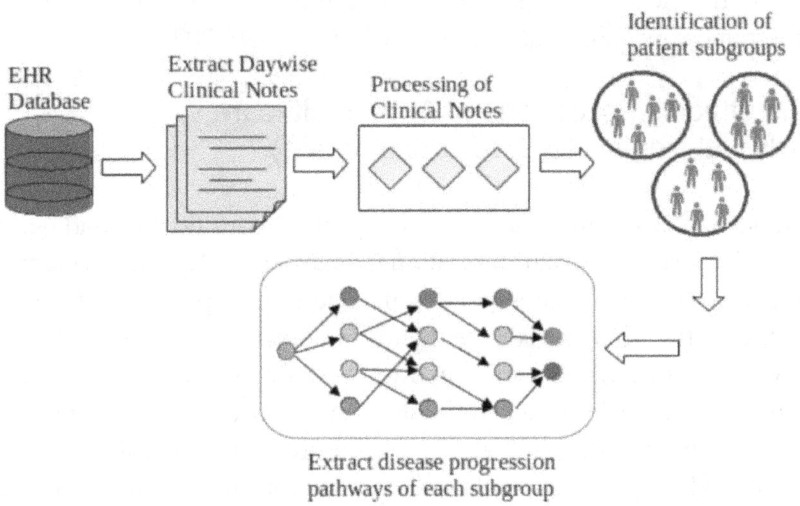

Source: (Arias et al., 2020)

1.2.6. The difficulties encountered by hospitals in keeping patient records.

By integrating electronic health records into their operations, providers have been able to move towards remote consultations and follow-ups, ensuring timely and appropriate care for patients. The use of EHR systems has facilitated continuity of care, enabling a smooth transition between various healthcare services while keeping critical patient data readily accessible. The benefits of using electronic health records go beyond the simple exchange of information. Electronic health record systems help healthcare providers access complete patient information, so they can make better decisions and choose the most suitable and effective treatments. (Hechinger et al., 2022). What's more, electronic health records help reduce the administrative burden, increase productivity and minimize errors in clinical documentation (Montravers, P. 2000). In essence, integrating electronic health records into the patient care pathway is vital to optimizing healthcare delivery. However, a number of obstacles stand in the way of the smooth progression of electronic health records through the healthcare system. These include a lack of knowledge among healthcare professionals and patients about the disease, the absence of standardized treatment protocols, and insufficient stakeholder commitment to the treatment process.(Miller & Brown, 2018). What's more, hospitals can struggle to cope with complex and innovative treatments without the necessary expertise and structures, resulting in sub-optimal satisfaction of patients' needs. To achieve effective treatment, it is imperative that doctors and patients are well informed and trained, and that the appropriate frameworks are established(Manktelow et al., 2022).

1.2.7. The ethical implications of AI in healthcare, particularly with regard to data confidentiality

Using tools like electronic health records (EHRs) helps doctors and healthcare workers share important patient information more easily and quickly. Telemedicine allows patients to have medical appointments and check-ups remotely, which can save time, reduce the need to visit the doctor in person, and make it easier to see specialists when needed. In addition, empowering patients through shared decision-making processes, as exemplified by glaucoma management programs, enables individuals to choose treatments that match their preferences.(Sealey et al., 2015). Patient forums and support groups play an essential role in facilitating communication between patients and healthcare professionals, fostering mutual understanding and cooperation. In addition, the operational framework for primary healthcare emphasizes It's important to include patients, their families, and the local community in efforts to make healthcare better. By involving these groups in planning, providing, and reviewing healthcare services, we can ensure the care meets everyone's needs, healthcare systems can effectively connect communities with services while enhancing overall service quality.(Gearhart et al., 2020). It is essential to address policy and regulatory matters to support efficient care pathways. Evaluating current healthcare policies that influence the optimization of patient care and recommending necessary adjustments can help eliminate barriers to delivering optimal care. By aligning policies with the goal of improving patient outcomes, healthcare systems can create an environment that promotes effective care coordination.(Gearhart et al., 2020). In summary, empowering patients to engage actively in decision-making processes necessitates a transition to personalized care models that consider individual preferences and values. By promoting open communication, encouraging patient involvement, and incorporating patient feedback into care plans, we can develop more efficient, patient-centered care pathways. (Cuevas et al., 2016).

1.3. Research objectives

The aim of this study is to create a theoretical framework for analyzing patient data with AI. We answered the following questions:

1. What is known in the current literature about steering patient data with AI in patient care pathways?
2. How does the use of AI in data steering optimize a patient care pathway?

1.4. Plan to be followed

The document is arranged in the following way:

- Section 1: presents the research methodology and literature selection process.
- Section 2: gives an overview of the results obtained from the literature to answer the research gaps related to the topic.
- Section 3: discusses what the results mean.
- Section 4: shares the main takeaways.

summary of the literature:

To summarize, the notion of optimal patient care pathways plays a significant role in modern healthcare by delivering high-quality patient care. In essence, optimizing patient care pathways requires a holistic approach that takes into account individual characteristics, environmental influences and the fluid coordination of services across various healthcare settings. So, to optimize patient care pathways, it's important to consider different perspectives, including communication barriers and facilitators from a patient-centric perspective, data-driven care pathway mapping and holistic chronic disease management models. Addressing these challenges, adopting multidisciplinary approaches and integrating socio-economic considerations are essential to improving patient outcomes and overall quality of care.

2. METHODS

2.1. Eligibility criteria

Table 1. Research Design.

Background to the study	**Focused on optimizing the patient's care pathway.**
Types of study	All types of studies were considered, but only peer-reviewed articles were retained.
Report language	Published in English.
Years of publication	All years of publication have been taken into account for this review.
Included items	The articles studied the optimization of a patient care pathway using patient data mobilization and the application of AI, The authors explicitly mentioned the use of AI Patient Data Mobilization.

Source: (Authors,2025)

2.2. Information sources

We created plans to find information using online databases called Scopus, Pubmed, and Web of Science. (Khizzou et al., 2024). These three databases were selected for their excellent coverage of healthcare research and innovation. (Allen et al., 2009). The search was carried out in February 2025. We carefully checked the list of sources in the articles we included to make sure we didn't miss any important studies. (Bouizgar et al., 2025b).

2.3. Search strategy

Below is the plan used to find articles on PubMed. We've also made similar plans for other databases. The plan has two parts: one for finding articles that study (1) Mobilizing Patient Data with AI and (2) Optimizing the Patient Care Pathway. It consists of the following terms:

(*"care pathways") AND ("conceptual framework"*) AND *("care trajectory" OR "care pathway") AND ("optimization"OR "management") AND ("AI" OR "Data Driven").*

2.4. Selection process

All the search results were added to the ZOTERO reference manager. Any repeated items were removed before choosing the final ones. Titles and abstracts were reviewed to select articles deemed eligible for inclusion. Full-text articles were then checked for eligibility. The selection process was carried out using the Rayyan web application, an online tool dedicated to the selection of articles (Ouzzani, M., Hammady, H., Fedorowicz, Z., & Elmagardmid, A. (2016).

2.5. Data collection process

We used Microsoft Excel 2017 to gather and organize your information. Also, taking the time to review the data for any mistakes or errors helps ensure that the results are accurate and trustworthy.

2.6. Data elements

Information was gathered about the main details of each article, such as the year it was published, the type of study, how many people participated, and who the patients were. We also looked at how they defined medical terms and the steps involved in patient care.

2.7. Analysis and presentation of results

The flowchart explained how articles were chosen. The information gathered was summarized with numbers and simple details.

Figure 4. Document search strategy

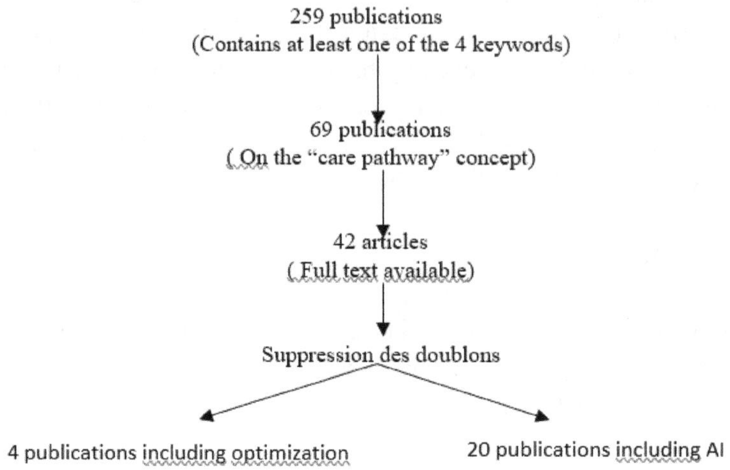

Source: (Authors,2025)

2.8. Development Proposed framework

The proposed framework focuses on the piloting of patient data with AI for the optimization of the patient care pathway, and subsequently retains a theoretical perspective.

3. RESULTS

3.1. Analysis of patient care pathway results

3.1.1. History of patient care

Figure 5. Patient Care History

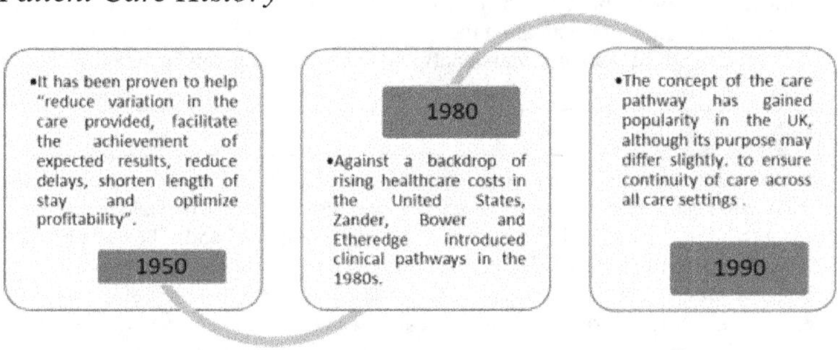

Source: (Authors,2025)

Because costs are now a concern in healthcare, making procedures better and ensuring good quality are very important topics that need a lot of focus. (Nouhaila et al., 2024), and it's encouraging to see those innovative solutions, such as the critical path method, have begun to take hold. The emergence of clinical pathways in the 1980s truly marked the beginning of a significant transformation in the way we think about care.(Rais & Viana, 2011). Since then, the concept of the pathway has been adopted worldwide and has continued to evolve under various names, things like treatment plans, health care plans, coordinated care plans, care routes, and care cards.(De Bleser et al., 2006). Table 1, which reflects the conceptual evolution over time. Patient care pathways represent an expanded version of clinical pathways: they involve a greater number of stakeholders at every stage of their lifecycle, from development to implementation and use, while placing the patient at the center of concerns. This approach, less widespread in the past, is now increasingly encouraged by the scientific community. (Ersek et al., 2017).

Table 2. patient care pathway results

A clinical pathway
This concept enables evidence to be integrated into local structures. It specifies the steps to follow for treatment or care (Aspland et al., 2021). It also helps ensure that the treatment for a particular health issue, procedure, or medical situation is consistent and similar for everyone in a specific group of people.(Kinsman et al., 2010).
The patient's journey
This idea involves goals related to how well the treatment works, the patient's health and well-being, and their personal needs. It also covers the different steps of care for each patient who has complicated health issues within a similar group of people.$.(Richter & Schlieter, 2019). This tool is essential for informing the patient, documenting, monitoring and evaluating the quality of the care process. It thus serves as an evidence-based guide for patients, as well as for all professionals and informal caregivers involved in the care pathway. (Richter et al., 2021).
Patient care pathways
Paths are only designed for a particular visit or treatment and usually include only people from the same organization, which can limit how many others are involved. (Hipp et al., 2016). You need to physically reach the equipment to access it, so sharing information has to be done by hand. The team members also have to manually include scientific knowledge into the process. These procedures are inflexible and can't automatically change to fit different patient needs.(Ersek et al., 2017). Human recording errors are a frequent occurrence. There are many paper forms, such as medication and test orders, as well as laboratory reports, which contain information relevant to a patient's pathway. Once a plan has been made, it can be hard to quickly include new steps that weren't thought of beforehand. Also, the way results are understood and explained depends a lot on how knowledgeable and experienced the person in charge is.(Cheah, 1998).
Digitizing the Patient Care Pathway
Information can be shared and exchanged easily and quickly between different people or groups using digital tools. Patients can now be more involved in their own care because most people have smartphones and access to the Internet. Using electronic records to keep and share information helps prevent unnecessary repetition and mistakes. Artificial intelligence (AI) can automatically provide an updated version of a given patient's prospective course, based on advanced analysis of variability and data relating to the patient population.(Awad et al., 2021). Team members who are responsible can automatically receive alerts about important information from these sources. Also, helpful details like the time, date, and person's name can be added automatically. The system can figure out the order in which events happened, making it easier to put together information from different sources in a clear way. By using standard methods to connect different systems, information about various steps or processes can be combined smoothly into the pathway management system. AI can also help healthcare professionals identify potential reasons for observed discrepancies(Stoumpos et al., 2023). The elderly, often being more vulnerable, benefit particularly from the use of digitized care pathways. However, it should be noted that digitization can present communication barriers, challenges that should resolve themselves over time. In addition, interactive elements such as quizzes, virtual reality and touchscreen functions can be integrated into digital formats, promoting greater patient adherence. This approach allows us to compare new patient information with data from similar groups of people. Using artificial intelligence and machine learning, we can then predict possible future developments. This helps healthcare providers suggest personalized treatment options for each patient. (Awad et al., 2021).

Source: (Authors,2025)

3.1.2. Topics covered in patient pathway documentation

It's clear that, no matter the topic, more and more people are becoming interested in understanding how patients move through different stages of care in both research and everyday practice. This is reflected in the rising number of articles and studies published each year, as shown in the chart.

Figure 6. Number of publications per year (n = 24)

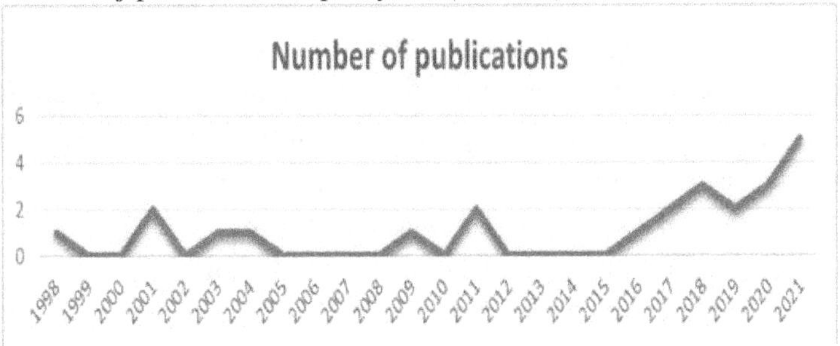

Source: (Authors,2025)

3.2. Analysis of the results obtained in managing patient data to implement digital pathways

3.2.1. The challenges of implementing digital pathways

Achieving this goal promises to be a complex undertaking. Successful implementation of digital care pathways depends to a large extent on patients' willingness to share their personal data.(Manktelow et al., 2022). Unlike traditional electronic medical records, these digital care pathways allow patients to actively benefit from sharing their health data during treatment. In exchange for this contribution, patients gain access to educational resources and receive immediate feedback on their health status whenever possible throughout their care journey.(Allen et al., 2009). Furthermore, patients have the opportunity to communicate effectively with a dedicated clinic team, enabling them to receive tailored assistance or reach out when necessary. With the support of their healthcare provider, they can access an online dashboard to review their health information, receive personalized reports, and obtain health predictions. This approach fosters greater patient engagement in their healthcare management.(Nasir & Dang, 2017). There are growing worries about how well artificial intelligence (AI) systems can explain their decisions and actions. This is especially important when using AI to plan patient care or when using chatbots and other AI tools in healthcare programs. People involved in setting up these digital health tools should understand this need for clear explanations, which is a key topic that many experts are studying and discussing. (Saleem et al., 2022). Another common problem, which many people have noted, is that different healthcare computer systems and digital tools often don't work well together. This can make it more difficult to put new digital ways of caring for patients into practice.

3.2.2. Data piloted to implement digital pathways

Integration of outcome data, biomarkers, treatment guidelines, co-morbidities and other medical information provides a deeper understanding of patient trajectories. (Ratti et al., 2023). Recent studies highlight the importance of tracking patients' health trajectories in disease management and the associated economic aspects. Since the introduction of Diagnosis-Related Grouping (DRG) systems in the USA in 1983, tracking patient pathways through national hospital financing systems and comprehensive databases has provided essential information on the evolution of care over time.

Table 3. AI-driven data science in patient care pathways

Data pilot	Scope or definition
Results	Clinical results
Biomarkers	Clinical markers are signs or measurements, like a particular chemical in the body or other features, that help identify or understand a disease or patient.
Guidelines	Official instructions or recommendations from healthcare or official organizations
Comorbidities/complications	The pathology-based perspective
Specifications	A prescription-based perspective on the journey
Clinical classification	Sorting?
Physical information	Includes multi-site care processes.
Other medical data	Simple categories for medical and surgical treatments

Source: (Authors,2025)

Integrating numerical and categorical data from vital signs, laboratory results and drug prescriptions (Rotter et al., 2008). Nevertheless, analysis of the clinical notes associated with these records can offer deeper insights into patients' medical conditions, symptoms, treatments, pathological histories and prescriptions. This contributes to a better understanding of their state of health and the optimization of treatment decisions.

3.2.3. Methods or techniques for managing patient-related medical data to optimize the care trajectory.

Table 4. methods for handling patient health information to improve the way care is provided.

techniques	*Definition*	*utility*
Lean management in healthcare(Ben Khizzou et al., 2024)	The Toyota model is a way for organizations to focus on their patients while getting rid of waste. It uses helpful tools and techniques to cut out activities that don't really add value. The goal is to boost the organization's performance.	reduce hospitalization time, costs and waiting times, while guaranteeing quality of care and patient safety.
Time Driven activity-based costing (Khizzou et al., 2024a)	TDABC is a model for evaluating logistics-related costs.	Assign costs directly to each activity or care pathway.
activity-based costing	is a method of evaluating the cost	a method for assessing the costs of an outpatient clinic
Deep Learning Overview (Aarabe et al., 2024a)	Deep Learning (DL) aims to make the hard work of choosing the right features simpler and less complicated.	attempt to learn optimal representations from the data itself
Machine Learning Models (Aarabe et al., 2024b)	Machine learning arose from the idea that computers can teach themselves to recognize patterns, without needing to be programmed for specific tasks.	seek health information to help them plan and manage future scenarios
simulation as part of a kaizen approach	a continuous improvement approach based on Lean management principles to tackle the problem.	It has been designed to study patient movements, as it applies mainly to emergency situations, such as emergency departments or walk-in clinics.
PSPLIB bodies(Aarabe et al., 2025a)	It involves organizing a set of tasks that need to be carried out in a certain order and that require a precise quantity of resources. The aim is to optimize one or more criteria, such as reducing the total time needed to complete the project.	Examination planning with resource allocation.
TraMineR (Bouizgar et al., 2025a)	TraMineR is an R tool for working with sequences of states or events. It helps to describe, visualize and analyze them.	Patient sequence analysis tools

Source: (Authors,2025)

3.2.4. Study on how to improve patient pathways.

This study aims to better understand and improve the care of women with early breast cancer. In particular, it looks at the timing of care and how it is organized depending on where patients live. Because each care pathway may be different, the study will take into account regional differences in treatment, medical practices and costs. The project, called "OPTISOINS01", brings together several hospitals with large numbers of patients to analyze in detail how care is organized for these women.(Kumlin et al., 2022).

The aim of this study is to examine the patient journey through different health-care systems in order to better understand the difficulties and challenges faced by patients, their families and healthcare professionals. It focuses in particular on older people with complex care needs. To do this, researchers are using a method that involves studying a few specific cases in depth, allowing them to gather all the important information to better understand the challenges and barriers to managing care throughout these patients' journeys. (Fernandes et al., 2020). In addition, the Schizophrenia Care Pathway Study uses a method that allows us to observe how patients progress through their treatment. This involves tracking the sequence and duration of various steps, such as psychiatrist visits, psychological support activities, and antipsychotic medication use, over a fixed period of time.(Fernandes et al., 2020). These studies offer valuable insights into optimizing patient care.

3.3. Summary of results:

It's important to make the patient's healthcare journey simpler and clearer. This will ensure that everyone gets the help they need, at the right time and in the right place. In hospitals, we often see patients waiting for long periods of time, which shows that their journey through the care system needs to be better organized. By understanding the different stages patients go through, we can provide care that is tailored to their needs and circumstances. It's also very important that everyone involved in care - physicians, administrators, educators, and even patients themselves - work together to create simple, effective care pathways. When everyone works together and patients have a say in their care, services will be better and the patient experience will be more positive.

4. DISCUSSION

Making patient care easier and faster can help people get diagnosed and treated faster. It can also reduce stress and promote better recovery. (Araghi et al., 2018). Providing patients with more consistent and reliable care helps them feel more independent and less disoriented about their treatment. In addition, a clearer organization of care helps prevent errors in diagnosis and treatment, resulting in healthier outcomes for patients.(Williams & Radnor, 2018).

But we must also be wary of certain problems that can arise when we try to be more efficient. For example, too much emphasis on speed and efficiency can make care seem cold or mechanical. This can lead to doctors and nurses paying less attention to the feelings and needs of individual patients.(Peng et al., 2024). This trend could make care worse and limit patients' options. What's more, as these new methods make it more expensive to prevent and correct errors, some patients with serious health problems or physical disabilities may find it harder to get the help they need.(Barelds et al., 2009). Another problem is that patients may be discouraged from participating in decisions about their health when treatments are very tightly planned.(Khizzou et al., 2025),

Patients can sometimes feel less connected or involved in their care. It's difficult to strike the right balance between empowering seniors to make decisions about their health and ensuring that they receive the best possible care, especially for those with complicated health problems.(Wynne, 2004). However, it's good to know that the use of organized care plans has saved money and improved the health of older people with complex needs. If more health care professionals adopted these plans, everyone would benefit: costs would be reduced and patients would have more control over their care. These simplified plans offer many benefits, including faster diagnosis and treatment, more consistent care, fewer errors, and potential cost savings. But they also present challenges that must be carefully considered. (Clarke et al., 2000). These concerns relate primarily to patients who feel they are being treated as a number, care that is becoming more expensive, healthcare professionals who are less satisfied with their jobs, and the reduction of different roles within medical teams. It's important to find the right balance between getting things done quickly and providing personalized care. Thanks to new digital tools and artificial intelligence (AI), healthcare is changing: these technologies help analyze large amounts of patient information to identify trends. This makes it possible to offer treatments that are better suited to each individual.(Gearhart et al., 2020). These tools help patients by making it easier to schedule appointments, view their medical information, and communicate with their doctors and nurses. By leveraging new digital technologies and focusing on what's really important to patients and their health, healthcare professionals can make the experience more enjoyable and responsive to their needs. (Rosa et al., 2023). The use of new technologies, such as online medical records and telemedicine, makes it easier for healthcare professionals to share information. This enables better communication and more efficient care coordination. Digital tools such as connected health monitoring devices and remote consultations also enable patients to play a greater role in making decisions about their care.(Colodette et al., 2018).

To effectively optimize patient care routes, it is imperative that decision-makers examine existing healthcare policies that have an impact on optimization efforts. (Hechinger et al., 2022). Suggesting changes to policies that make healthcare more straightforward will help improve communication between providers and encourage teamwork across different professions to better focus on the needs of patients.

5. CONCLUSION

In essence, optimizing patient care trajectories requires a holistic approach that takes into account individual characteristics, environmental influences and the fluid coordination of services across diverse healthcare settings. By deepening our understanding of these trajectories and implementing evidence-based practices, we can improve patient outcomes, elevate the quality of care and drive positive transformations in healthcare practices. Further exploration is needed to investigate innovative strategies for effectively implementing optimal care trajectories in diverse healthcare settings, but also act on patient data, AI, patient pathway dimensions and optimization techniques (Figure 5).

Figure 7. Key elements for an optimal patient care pathway

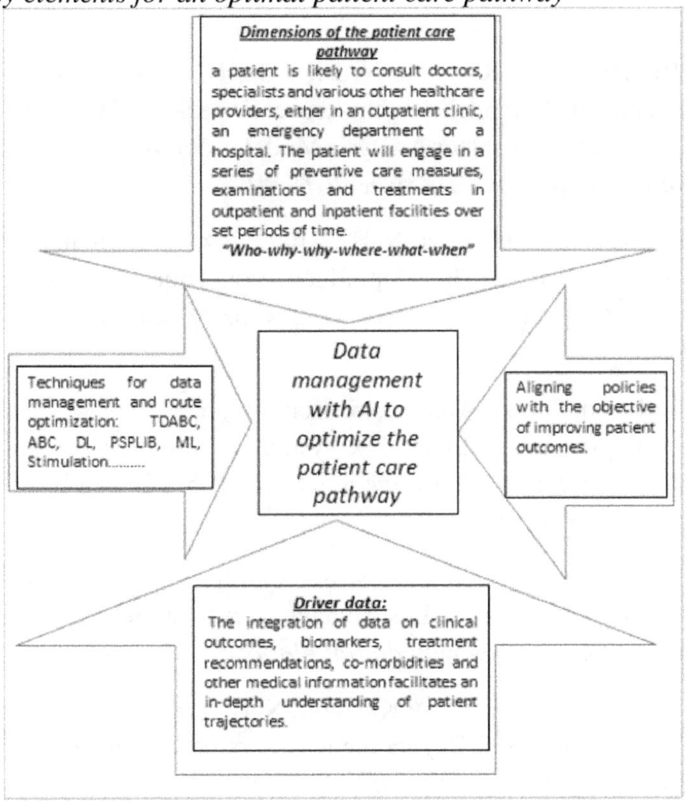

Source: (Authors,2025)

6. REFERENCES

Aarabe, M., Bouizgar, M., Khizzou, N. B., Alla, L., & Benjelloun, A. (2025a). Technology-Driven and Personality in the Travel Experience Within a Destination : Literature Review and Proposal for Analysis Model. *Adapting to Evolving Consumer Experiences in Hospitality and Tourism*, 267-300.

Aarabe, M., Bouizgar, M., Khizzou, N. B., Alla, L., & Benjelloun, A. (2025b). The Transformative Impact of Artificial Intelligence on Tourism Experience : Analysis of Trends and Perspectives. *AI Technologies for Personalized and Sustainable Tourism*, 277-310.

Aarabe, M., Khizzou, N. B., Alla, L., & Benjelloun, A. (2024a). Marketing applications of emerging technologies : A systematic literature review. In *AI and data engineering solutions for effective marketing* (pp. 23–47). IGI Global. DOI: 10.4018/979-8-3693-3172-9.ch002

Aarabe, M., Khizzou, N. B., Alla, L., & Benjelloun, A. (2024b). Smart Tourism Experience and Responsible Travelers' Behavior : A Systematic Literature Review. *Promoting responsible tourism with digital platforms*, 128-147.

Alla, L., Bouhtati, N., Aarabe, M., & Khizzou, N. B. (s. d.). Social Media Analytics for Effective Customer Brand Engagement Assessment. *Advances in Marketing, Customer Relationship Management, and E-Services.*

Allam, A., Feuerriegel, S., Rebhan, M., & Krauthammer, M. (2021). Analyzing Patient Trajectories With Artificial Intelligence. *Journal of Medical Internet Research, 23*(12), e29812. DOI: 10.2196/29812 PMID: 34870606

Allen, D., Gillen, E., & Rixson, L. (2009). Systematic review of the effectiveness of integrated care pathways : What works, for whom, in which circumstances? *International Journal of Evidence-Based Healthcare, 7*(2), 61–74. DOI: 10.1111/j.1744-1609.2009.00127.x PMID: 21631848

Analyse de l'impact économique de l'expérience patient : Une revue systématique—PMC. (s. d.). Consulté 15 mars 2025, à l'adresse https://pmc.ncbi.nlm.nih.gov/articles/PMC11087015/

Anderson, K. (2002). *Mosby<<'>>s Medical, Nursing & Allied Health Dictionary ; editor /.*

Araghi, S. N., Fontaili, F., Lamine, E., Salatge, N., Lesbegueries, J., Pouyade, S. R., Tancerel, L., & Benaben, F. (2018). A Conceptual Framework to Support Discovering of Patients' Pathways as Operational Process Charts. *2018 IEEE/ACS 15th International Conference on Computer Systems and Applications (AICCSA)*, 1-6. DOI: 10.1109/AICCSA.2018.8612822

Arias, M., Rojas, E., Aguirre, S., Cornejo, F., Munoz-Gama, J., Sepulveda, M., & Capurro, D. (2020). Mapping the Patient's Journey in Healthcare through Process Mining. *International Journal of Environmental Research and Public Health, 17*(18), 6586. Advance online publication. DOI: 10.3390/ijerph17186586 PMID: 32927669

Aspland, E., Gartner, D., & Harper, P. (2021). Clinical pathway modelling : A literature review. *Health Systems (Basingstoke, England), 10*(1), 1–23. DOI: 10.1080/20476965.2019.1652547 PMID: 33758656

Awad, A., Trenfield, S. J., Pollard, T. D., Ong, J. J., Elbadawi, M., McCoubrey, L. E., Goyanes, A., Gaisford, S., & Basit, A. W. (2021). Connected healthcare : Improving patient care using digital health technologies. *Advanced Drug Delivery Reviews, 178*, 113958. https://www.sciencedirect.com/science/article/pii/S0169409X21003513. DOI: 10.1016/j.addr.2021.113958 PMID: 34478781

Barelds, A., Van De Goor, I., Bos, M., Van Heck, G., & Schols, J. (2009). Care and service trajectories for people with intellectual disabilities : Defining its course and quality determinants from the client's perspective. In *Journal of Policy and Practice in Intellectual Disabilities* (Vol. 6, Numéro 3, p. 163-172). DOI: 10.1111/j.1741-1130.2009.00224.x

Barelds, A., van de Goor, I., van Heck, G., & Schols, J. (2010). Quality of care and service trajectories for people with intellectual disabilities : Defining the aspects of quality from the client's perspective. In *Scandinavian Journal of Caring Sciences* (Vol. 24, Numéro 1, p. 164-174). DOI: 10.1111/j.1471-6712.2009.00701.x

Ben Khizzou, N., Alla, L., & Aarabe, M. (2024). Contribution of the Evaluation of Infection Control Committees to the Development of a Computerized Infection Risk Management Tool. *International Conference on Digital Technologies and Applications*, 443-453. DOI: 10.1007/978-3-031-68653-5_42

Bouizgar, M., Aarabe, M., Khizzou, N. B., Alla, L., & Benjelloun, A. (2025a). AI and Digital Technologies for Transforming Territorial Branding Management : A Systematic Review. *Corporate Management in the Digital Age*, 35-68.

Bouizgar, M., Aarabe, M., Khizzou, N. B., Alla, L., & Benjelloun, A. (2025b). Smart Territorial Marketing and Promotion of Customer Engagement Towards the Territorial Brand : A Systematic Review of Literature. *Sustainable and Intelligent Territorial Marketing and Entrepreneurship*, 129-158.

Budde, H., Williams, G. A., Winkelmann, J., Pfirter, L., & Maier, C. B. (2021). The role of patient navigators in ambulatory care : Overview of systematic reviews. *BMC Health Services Research, 21*(1), 1166. DOI: 10.1186/s12913-021-07140-6 PMID: 34706733

Cheah, T. S. (1998). Clinical pathways–the new paradigm in healthcare? *The Medical Journal of Malaysia, 53*(1), 87–96. https://europepmc.org/article/med/10968144 PMID: 10968144

Clarke, T., Mackinnon, E., England, K., Burr, G., Fowler, S., & Fairservice, L. (2000). A review of intensive care nurse staffing practices overseas : What lessons for Australia? In *Intensive and Critical Care Nursing* (Vol. 16, Numéro 4, p. 228-242). DOI: 10.1054/iccn.2000.1524

Colodette, R. M., Moreira, T. R., Gomes, A. P., & Siqueira-Batista, R. (2018). The oral health team in the family health strategy : Trajectories and challenges. In *Open Public Health Journal* (Vol. 11, Numéro 1, p. 438-450). Bentham Science Publishers B.V. DOI: 10.2174/1874944501811010438

Cuevas, A. G., O'Brien, K., & Saha, S. (2016). African American experiences in healthcare : « I always feel like I'm getting skipped over ». *Health Psychology: Official Journal of the Division of Health Psychology, American Psychological Association, 35*(9), 987–995. DOI: 10.1037/hea0000368 PMID: 27175576

De Bleser, L., Depreitere, R., De Waele, K., Vanhaecht, K., Vlayen, J., & Sermeus, W. (2006). Defining pathways. *Journal of Nursing Management, 14*(7), 553–563. DOI: 10.1111/j.1365-2934.2006.00702.x PMID: 17004966

De Man, J., Roy, W. M., Sarkar, N., Waweru, E., Leys, M., Van Olmen, J., & Criel, B. (2016). Patient-centered care and people-centered health systems in sub-Saharan Africa : Why so little of something so badly needed? *International Journal of Person Centered Medicine, 6*(3), 162–173. https://www.academia.edu/download/61640113/JeroenDeManRoyWilliamMayegaNandiniSarkarEvelynWaweruMartLeysJosefienVanOlmen-2016-Patient-CenteredCareandPeopl20191230-20568-yv2rg.pdf. DOI: 10.5750/ijpcm.v6i3.591

Diallo, E. M., Traore, F. B., Camara, B. S., Langlet, A., Delamou, A., Diallo, O. O., Gerbaud, L., & Camara, A. (2024). Analysis of care-seeking pathways and factors influencing early and appropriate care-seeking for malaria patients in the Republic of Guinea : A cross-sectional study. *Malaria Journal*, *23*(1), 273. DOI: 10.1186/s12936-024-05102-x PMID: 39256721

El-Razek, A. (2019). Effect of Implementing Clinical Pathway to Improve Child-Birth and Neonatal Outcomes. *American Journal of Nursing Research*, *6*(6), 6. Advance online publication. DOI: 10.12691/ajnr-6-6-13

Ersek, J. L., Nadler, E., Freeman-Daily, J., Mazharuddin, S., & Kim, E. S. (2017a). Clinical pathways and the patient perspective in the pursuit of value-based oncology care. *American Society of Clinical Oncology Educational Book*, *37*(37), 597–606. https://www.academia.edu/download/53658904/2017_ASCO_Educational_Book.pdf#page=615. DOI: 10.1200/EDBK_174794 PMID: 28561657

Ersek, J. L., Nadler, E., Freeman-Daily, J., Mazharuddin, S., & Kim, E. S. (2017b). Clinical pathways and the patient perspective in the pursuit of value-based oncology care. *American Society of Clinical Oncology Educational Book*, *37*(37), 597–606. https://www.academia.edu/download/53658904/2017_ASCO_Educational_Book.pdf#page=615. DOI: 10.1200/EDBK_174794 PMID: 28561657

Fernandes, Ó. B., Netshiombo, M., Gulácsi, L., Klazinga, N. S., Péntek, M., & Baji, P. (2020). *Patient experiences in a public primary health care clinic : A South African case study*. DOI: 10.1556/204.2020.00014

Gearhart, A., Gaffar, S., & Chang, A. C. (2020). A primer on artificial intelligence for the paediatric cardiologist. In *Cardiology in the Young* (Vol. 30, Numéro 7, p. 934-945). Cambridge University Press. DOI: 10.1017/S1047951120001493

Hechinger, M., Hentschel, D., Aumer, C., & Rester, C. (2022). A Conceptual Model of Experiences With Digital Technologies in Aging in Place : Qualitative Systematic Review and Meta-synthesis. In *JMIR Aging* (Vol. 5, Numéro 3). JMIR Publications Inc. DOI: 10.2196/34872

Hipp, R., Abel, E., & Weber, R. J. (2016). A Primer on Clinical Pathways. *Hospital Pharmacy*, *51*(5), 416–421. DOI: 10.1310/hpj5105-416 PMID: 27303097

Kercsmar, C., & Myers, T. (2002). Clinical pathways in treatment of asthma. *Current Opinion in Allergy and Clinical Immunology*, *2*(3), 183–187. DOI: 10.1097/00130832-200206000-00005 PMID: 12045412

Khizzou, N. B., Aarabe, M., & Alla, L. (2024a). Current trends in scientific research on managerial innovations in healthcare supply chain : A bibliometric analysis. *2024 IEEE 15th International Colloquium on Logistics and Supply Chain Management (LOGISTIQUA)*, 1-9.

Khizzou, N. B., Aarabe, M., & Alla, L. (2024b). Practices of Qualitative Studies in Medical Sciences : The Focus Groups Method Applied to Patients. In *Data Collection and Analysis in Scientific Qualitative Research* (pp. 229–252). IGI Global. DOI: 10.4018/979-8-3693-8689-7.ch009

Khizzou, N. B., Aarabe, M., Bouizgar, M., Alla, L., & Benjelloun, A. (2025). The Digital Transformation of Medical Tourism : A Systematic and Bibliometric Review of the Literature. *Revolutionizing Healthcare Experience With Digital Medical Tourism*, 355-382.

Kinsman, L., Rotter, T., James, E., Snow, P., & Willis, J. (2010). What is a clinical pathway? Development of a definition to inform the debate. *BMC Medicine*, *8*(1), 31. DOI: 10.1186/1741-7015-8-31 PMID: 20507550

Kumlin, M., Berg, G. V., Kvigne, K., & Hellesø, R. (2022). Dilemmas and deliberations in managing the care trajectory of elderly patients with complex health needs : A single-case study. *BMC Health Services Research*, *22*(1), 1030. DOI: 10.1186/s12913-022-08422-3 PMID: 35962337

Laveault-Allard, P. (2022). *Les effets de la défavorisation matérielle et sociale sur les coûts et les trajectoires de soins et services en périnatalité.*

Manktelow, M., Iftikhar, A., Bucholc, M., McCann, M., & O'Kane, M. (2022). Clinical and operational insights from data-driven care pathway mapping : A systematic review. *BMC Medical Informatics and Decision Making*, *22*(1), 43. DOI: 10.1186/s12911-022-01756-2 PMID: 35177058

Miller, D. D., & Brown, E. W. (2018). Artificial Intelligence in Medical Practice : The Question to the Answer? In *American Journal of Medicine* (Vol. 131, Numéro 2, p. 129-133). Elsevier Inc. DOI: 10.1016/j.amjmed.2017.10.035

Nasir, J. A., & Dang, C. (2017). An integrated model for home health care and patients cluster based care. *2017 International Conference on Robotics and Automation Sciences (ICRAS)*, 204-208. DOI: 10.1109/ICRAS.2017.8071945

Nouhaila, B. K., Aarabe, M., & Alla, L. (2024). The impact of digitalisation on the customer experience in medical tourism : A systematic review. *Impact of AI and tech-driven solutions in hospitality and tourism*, 408-428. https://www.igi-global.com/chapter/the-impact-of-digitalisation-on-the-customer-experience-in-medical-tourism/354144

Patwala, A., Barker, D., Da Costa, A., Bayard, G., Brunner-La Rocca, H.-P., Fontes-Carvalho, R., De la Fuente, L., Goralski, M., Mahon, N. G., Roque, D., Santos, M., Yousef, Z., Ben Hamouda, H., Teal, M., Christory, F., Ahmed, F. Z., & Mebazaa, A. (2024). Optimizing heart failure pathways to enhance patient care : The Program to Optimize Heart Failure Patient Pathways (PRO-HF). *ESC Heart Failure*, *11*(5), 2578–2590. DOI: 10.1002/ehf2.14911 PMID: 38924644

Peltzer, K. (2009). Patient experiences and health system responsiveness in South Africa. *BMC Health Services Research*, *9*(1), 117. DOI: 10.1186/1472-6963-9-117 PMID: 19602290

Peng, Z., Augusto, V., Perrier, L., & Xie, X. (2024). Optimal Process Mining of Traces With Events and Transition Attributes With Application to Care Pathways of Cancer Patients. *IEEE Transactions on Automation Science and Engineering*, *21*(3), 4364–4381. DOI: 10.1109/TASE.2023.3295947

Pinaire, J., Azé, J., Bringay, S., & Landais, P. (2017). Patient healthcare trajectory. An essential monitoring tool : A systematic review. *Health Information Science and Systems*, *5*(1), 1. DOI: 10.1007/s13755-017-0020-2 PMID: 28413630

Quigley, D. D., Reynolds, K., Dellva, S., & Price, R. A. (2021). Examining the Business Case for Patient Experience : A Systematic Review. *Journal of healthcare management / American College of Healthcare Executives, 66*(3), 200-224. DOI: 10.1097/JHM-D-20-00207

Rais, A., & Viana, A. (2011). Operations Research in Healthcare : A survey. *International Transactions in Operational Research*, *18*(1), 1–31. DOI: 10.1111/j.1475-3995.2010.00767.x

Ratti, M., Milicia, O., Rescinito, R., Coeckelberghs, E., Seys, D., Vanhaecht, K., & Panella, M. (2023). The determinants of expert opinion in the development of care pathways : Insights from an exploratory cluster analysis. *BMC Health Services Research*, *23*(1), 211. DOI: 10.1186/s12913-023-09139-7 PMID: 36869326

Rayyan : Plateforme de gestion des revues systématiques alimentée par l'IA. (s. d.). Consulté 18 février 2025, à l'adresse https://www.rayyan.ai/

Richter, P., Hickmann, E., & Schlieter, H. (2021). Validating the Concept of Patient Pathways : A European Survey on Their Characteristics, Definition and State of Practice. *PACIS*, 32. https://www.researchgate.net/profile/Hannes_Schlieter/publication/354209554_Validating_the_Concept_of_Patient_Pathways_A_European_Survey_on_Their_Characteristics_Definition_and_State_of_Practice/links/6197875e3068c54fa5007579/Validating-the-Concept-of-Patient-Pathways-A-European-Survey-on-Their-Characteristics-Definition-and-State-of-Practice.pdf

Richter, P., & Schlieter, H. (2019). *Understanding patient pathways in the context of integrated health care services-implications from a scoping review*. https://aisel.aisnet.org/wi2019/track08/papers/6/

Rosa, W. E., Izumi, S., Sullivan, D. R., Lakin, J., Rosenberg, A. R., Creutzfeldt, C. J., Lafond, D., Tjia, J., Cotter, V., Wallace, C., Sloan, D. E., Cruz-Oliver, D. M., DeSanto-Madeya, S., Bernacki, R., Leblanc, T. W., & Epstein, A. S. (2023). Advance Care Planning in Serious Illness : A Narrative Review. In *Journal of Pain and Symptom Management* (Vol. 65, Numéro 1, p. e63-e78). Elsevier Inc. DOI: 10.1016/j.jpainsymman.2022.08.012

Rotter, T., Kugler, J., Koch, R., Gothe, H., Twork, S., Van Oostrum, J. M., & Steyerberg, E. W. (2008). A systematic review and meta-analysis of the effects of clinical pathways on length of stay, hospital costs and patient outcomes. *BMC Health Services Research*, *8*(1), 265. DOI: 10.1186/1472-6963-8-265 PMID: 19094244

Saleem, F., Al-Ghamdi, A. S. A.-M., Alassafi, M. O., & AlGhamdi, S. A. (2022). Machine Learning, Deep Learning, and Mathematical Models to Analyze Forecasting and Epidemiology of COVID-19 : A Systematic Literature Review. *International Journal of Environmental Research and Public Health*, *19*(9), 5099. DOI: 10.3390/ijerph19095099 PMID: 35564493

Savina, M.-D., & Boidin, B. (1996). Privatisation des services sociaux et redéfinition du rôle de l'État : Les prestations éducatives et sanitaires au Bénin. *Revue Tiers Monde*, •••, 853–874. https://www.jstor.org/stable/23592377

Scholz, M., Haase, R., Schriefer, D., Voigt, I., & Ziemssen, T. (2021). Electronic health interventions in the case of multiple sclerosis : From theory to practice. *Brain Sciences*, *11*(2), 180. https://www.mdpi.com/2076-3425/11/2/180. DOI: 10.3390/brainsci11020180 PMID: 33540640

Sealey, M., Breen, L. J., O'Connor, M., & Aoun, S. M. (2015). A scoping review of bereavement risk assessment measures : Implications for palliative care. In *Palliative Medicine* (Vol. 29, Numéro 7, p. 577-589). SAGE Publications Ltd. DOI: 10.1177/0269216315576262

Stoumpos, A. I., Kitsios, F., & Talias, M. A. (2023a). Digital transformation in healthcare : Technology acceptance and its applications. *International Journal of Environmental Research and Public Health*, *20*(4), 3407. https://www.mdpi.com/1660-4601/20/4/3407. DOI: 10.3390/ijerph20043407 PMID: 36834105

Stoumpos, A. I., Kitsios, F., & Talias, M. A. (2023b). Digital transformation in healthcare : Technology acceptance and its applications. *International Journal of Environmental Research and Public Health*, *20*(4), 3407. https://www.mdpi.com/1660-4601/20/4/3407. DOI: 10.3390/ijerph20043407 PMID: 36834105

Vanasse, A. (s. d.). *Cohorte sur les trajectoires de soins des personnes ayant une condition propice aux soins ambulatoires.*

Vijverberg, J. R., Daniels, K., Steinmann, G., Garvelink, M. M., van der Voort, M. B. R., Biesma, D., Bos, W. J. W., van Merode, F., & van der Nat, P. (2022). Mapping the extent, range and nature of research activity on value-based healthcare in the 15 years following its introduction (2006–2021) : A scoping review. [abstract]. *BMJ Open*, *12*(8), e064983. https://bmjopen.bmj.com/content/12/8/e064983. DOI: 10.1136/bmjopen-2022-064983 PMID: 35973705

Wallin, M. T., Culpepper, W. J., Nichols, E., Bhutta, Z. A., Gebrehiwot, T. T., Hay, S. I., Khalil, I. A., Krohn, K. J., Liang, X., Naghavi, M., Mokdad, A. H., Nixon, M. R., Reiner, R. C., Sartorius, B., Smith, M., Topor-Madry, R., Werdecker, A., Vos, T., Feigin, V. L., & Murray, C. J. L. (2019). Global, regional, and national burden of multiple sclerosis 1990–2016 : A systematic analysis for the Global Burden of Disease Study 2016. *Lancet Neurology*, *18*(3), 269–285. https://www.thelancet.com/journals/laneur/article/PIIS1474-4422(18)30443-5/fulltext. DOI: 10.1016/S1474-4422(18)30443-5 PMID: 30679040

Williams, S. J., & Radnor, Z. (2018). Using bandwidths to visualize and improve patient pathways. *Public Money & Management*, *38*(1), 21–28. DOI: 10.1080/09540962.2018.1389495

Wynne, R. (2004). Variable definitions : Implications for the prediction of pulmonary complications after adult cardiac surgery. In *European Journal of Cardiovascular Nursing* (Vol. 3, Numéro 1, p. 43-52). DOI: 10.1016/j.ejcnurse.2003.11.001

Chapter 4
Generative AI Solutions for Unlocking Customer Loyalty and Retention Strategies in Emerging Markets

Ikram Ed-Daakouri
https://orcid.org/0009-0001-8207-5502
LAREMEF Laboratory, Sidi Mohamed Ben Abdellah University, Fez, Morocco

Lhoussaine Alla
https://orcid.org/0000-0002-7238-1792
LAREMEF Laboratory, Sidi Mohamed Ben Abdellah University, Fez, Morocco

ABSTRACT

Generative AI is transforming customer retention strategies in emerging markets by enabling hyper-personalization, predictive analytics, and automation to enhance customer engagement. This chapter explores the role of AI-driven solutions in optimizing retention strategies across diverse socio-economic and cultural contexts in Southeast Asia, Africa, and Latin America, based on a systematic review of 30 academic sources and comparative case studies in e-commerce, mobile telecommunications, and fintech. The findings highlight the effectiveness of AI in delivering personalized experiences, optimizing dynamic pricing models, and leveraging predictive analytics to identify and prevent customer churn. This chapter presents a conceptual framework that provides actionable guidelines for businesses to harness generative AI effectively while maintaining ethical standards and scalability. The chapter concludes with managerial insights, limitations, and future research

DOI: 10.4018/979-8-3373-0918-7.ch004

directions, highlighting the potential of AI in shaping customer experiences and long-term loyalty in emerging markets.

INTRODUCTION

Customer loyalty in the pre-AI era relied principally on rewards schemes, behavioral segmentation, and rule-driven interactions (Lemon & Verhoef, 2016). All these are now shifting towards hyper-personalization, adaptation, and conversation as generative AI has stepped in, redefining customer relationships in real-time (Davenport et al., 2023).

Customer loyalty and retention are fast-growing business priorities for companies as they contend with an intense global economy that is increasingly competitive and interconnected. Traditional ways of connecting with customers are giving way to advanced, data-driven customer-engagement methods focusing on personalization, flexibility, as well as scalability. At the forefront of this revolution is Generative Artificial Intelligence (AI), technology enabling businesses to sift through vast amounts of data, predict consumer behavior, and create highly personalized customer experiences. By leveraging generative with AI, businesses can form in-depth relationships with consumers, gaining long-term loyalty as well as improved retention.

The Southeast Asian, Sub-Saharan African, and Latin American emerging markets are of particular opportunities for the growth of generative AI. Such markets are dominated by young highly dynamic consumer attitudes, high penetration of mobiles, and increasingly digitalized infrastructure. A case in point is that smartphone penetration in such markets is predicted to exceed 70% by 2025, driving significant expansions in digital services such as fintech, e-commerce, and telecommunications via cellular networks. (GSMA, 2022). These opportunities are supplemented by special problems, such as inadequate infrastructure, economic uncertainty, as well as multicultural communities. The companies doing business in these markets are faced with navigating these challenges alongside satisfying customers in a highly localized, culturally customized manner. Generative AI has tremendous potential to help meet these challenges through tools that can enable companies to tailor their customer retention strategies to complex and heterogeneous environments. AI-driven chatbots, for instance, can provide personalized assistance in local languages, as predictive analytics can flag customer risk of churn and deliver actionable information for renewal campaigns (Tadepally et al., 2022). Even with such potential, applied generative AI in emerging economies has been under-explored in academic scholarship as well as business practice. The majority of available studies are concentrated on developed economies, where AI maturity as well as data infrastructure is far superior (Celik & Manson, 2021). This creates a very important gap in knowing how generative AI may be adapted to specific requirements of emerging economies, especially in resource-scarce as well as culturally heterogeneous environments.

Digital transformation has dramatically impacted customer interaction, as artificial intelligence has become a primary force behind it. Two dimensions of the technology are worth special consideration: its opportunities and challenges. At one level, generative AI facilitates sophisticated personalization strategies, improving customer experience through dynamic suggestions, natural language interactions, and fine-grained prediction analysis (Rust & Huang, 2021). At another level, it creates complex challenges, especially in terms of ethics, private information, and the trustworthiness of generated answers (Brynjolfsson & McAfee, 2022). Balancing the two dimensions is necessary to ensure effective as well as responsible implementation of these technologies in customer loyalty management.

This chapter aims to bridge this gap by examining how generative AI can be utilized to drive customers' loyalty and retention in emerging markets. This chapter aims to bridge the gap by examining how generative AI can be utilized to drive customers' loyalty and retention in emerging markets. The central question guiding this analysis is:

How can generative AI help emerging market businesses retain customers by adapting to local economic as well as cultural settings?

As an answer to this question, the chapter explores the relationship between generative AI and customer interactions, providing actionable insights as well as applied frameworks for practitioners and researchers. There are three objectives of this chapter. Firstly, it aims to promote a theoretical and conceptual understanding of how generative AI can transform customer retention strategies in emerging markets. Secondly, it employs a systematic literature review to synthesize what is already known about the topic area, distilling key trends, challenges, and opportunities. Thirdly, it considers actual applications in the form of case studies, showcasing real-world findings on how firms in emerging regions, such as Southeast Asia, Sub-Saharan Africa, and Latin America, are advancing retention with AI technologies.

The chapter introduces the theoretical and conceptual foundation of generative AI and its customer retention value. It then discusses the methodology, which involves a systematic review of literature accompanied by a comparative analysis of case studies in emerging markets. It then discusses key findings as well as strategic suggestions for firms that are adopting generative AI solutions. In doing so, it provides insight into the impact on customer retention in emerging markets.

1. THEORY AND CONCEPTUAL FRAMEWORK

Generative Artificial Intelligence is an innovative technological leap that provides companies effective means for customizing customer experiences, anticipating needs, as well as encouraging loyalty-building. In the new markets, where the socio-economic as well as cultural aspects are so differentiated, generative AI possesses a vast capability for combating challenges in customer retention. This framework provides a systematic examination of how generative AI is utilized in customer retention policy, integrating theoretical insights, practical applications, as well as analytical aspects.

1.1. Definition and Capabilities of Generative AI

Generative AI is one of the forms of artificial intelligence that utilizes models such as Generative Adversarial Networks (GANs), Variational Autoencoders (VAEs), and transformers for the creation of new content. Unlike rule-based programming in initial AI, generative AI learns patterns in the data in order to create realistic as well as novel outputs. Table 1 gives the descriptive overview of significant generative AI models as well as their customer-retention applications.

Table 1. Main Generative AI models and their uses in customer retention

Model	Description	Applications	References
GANs	Learn data distributions to create realistic content	Personalized advertising, fraud detection	Gupta et al., 2024
Transformers	Process text as a sequence	Chatbots, recommendation systems	Madanchian, 2024
VAEs	Encode the data into latent variables for reconstruction	Anomaly detection, data augmentation	Tadepally et al., 2022

Source: Authors

Generative AI encourages customer interaction via personalized content generation, behavioral forecasting, as well as adjust to multiple cultures. It enables companies to build tailored emails, discounts, and product recommendations based on personal tastes, optimizing Marketing campaigns. AI-driven analytics also identify customer behavioral patterns, enabling businesses to predict churn and take preventive action. AI may also customize suitable for individual linguistic, cultural, and geographic contexts, so interactions are significant for diverse consumers, building improved relationships with customers across global markets.

1.2. Emerging Markets: Opportunities and Challenges

1.2.1. Distinct Features

Southeast Asian, Sub-Saharan African, and Latin American emerging markets are rapidly changing due to technological advancements as well as shifting consumer trends. High mobile penetration, for instance, is a key feature, with smartphone penetration estimated at above 70% in most of their regions by 2025 (GSMA, 2022), allowing for higher digital services coverage. These economies are also rapidly digitalizing, especially in online commerce, fintech, and telecommunications, opening new opportunities both for consumers and businesses. Finally, the regions are highly diverse in cultures, with multilingual populations having different consumption habits, necessitating companies to adapt their offerings to meet the local needs and wants.

1.2.2. Challenges in Customer Retention

Customer retention challenges come with several factors. The first is scarcity of data, whose limited availability makes it difficult to train deep AI models. The second is economic uncertainty, whose unfolding affects consumer sensitivity to prices. The third is the major challenge posed by the scattered legal frameworks that regulate AI deployment as well as the protection of data.

Figure 1. Digitalization and AI readiness in emerging markets

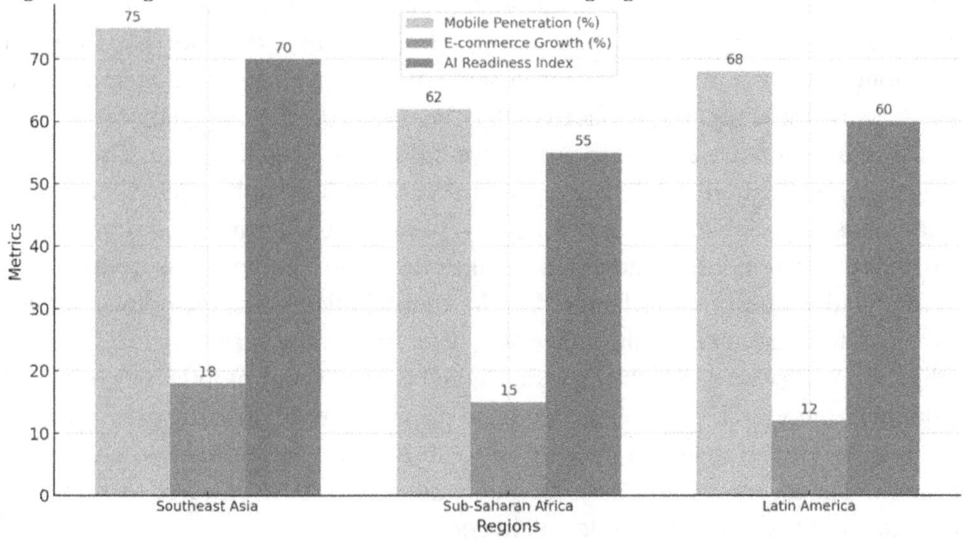

Source: GSMA. (2022), Shevchyk, Y. (2024), Madanchian, M. (2024)

The relative mobile penetration, growth of e-commerce, as well as AI readiness indicators, across Southeast Asia, Sub-Saharan Africa, and Latin America reveal distinguishing factors in digitalization and technology adoption among emerging markets. The indicators serve as a basis on which the potential of generative AI to improve customer retention strategies in these regions can be understood.

Mobile penetration is a leading driver of digital adoption and a prerequisite for the deployment of AI-powered solutions. The GSMA Mobile Economy Report (2022) states that Southeast Asia has the highest mobile penetration at 75%, followed by 68% in Latin America and 62% in Sub-Saharan Africa. This is because of massive investments in telecommunication infrastructure and the extensive availability of low-cost smartphones in Southeast Asia, especially in Indonesia, Vietnam, and the Philippines. Through the provision of access to digital services, high mobile penetration supports the integration of generative AI into customer loyalty strategies, such as mobile-based chatbots and recommenders.

E-commerce growth is another key indicator, capturing the velocity of digital economic growth. Led by Southeast Asia at 18%, as reported by Shevchyk (2024) in the generative AI e-commerce study, this region has rapidly embraced digital shopping channels. This is compared to 15% growth in Sub-Saharan Africa and 12% growth in Latin America. Although slower, both regions indicate promising developments driven by rising internet penetration and digital payment solutions. These can be built on by generative AI to deliver personalized experiences, improving retention and loyalty in the e-commerce market.

AI readiness quantifies the level of preparedness of a region to embrace and deploy AI technologies. According to Madanchian (2024), Southeast Asia has the highest AI readiness score of 70, indicating strong infrastructure and a pool of AI-trained practitioners. Latin America has a lower score of 60, as well as Sub-Saharan Africa at 55, because these regions are faced with issues like a shortage of AI professionals, inconsistent regulatory environments, as well as a lack of quality data. These gaps imply that though Southeast Asia is poised better to employ sophisticated generative AI solutions, Sub-Saharan Africa and Latin America need customized strategies to help their respective infrastructural as well as regulation-related constraints.

The relative observations featured in the figure indicate that the uptake of generative AI for customer retention needs to take into account regional differences in digital preparedness. Southeast Asia's high penetration of mobile networks and e-commerce acceleration place the region at the forefront of utilizing generative AI in personalization of customer interactions. Sub-Saharan Africa and Latin America, on the other hand, are opportunities for innovations that are AI-powered to overcome infrastructural and regulation-related challenges.

1.3. Theoretical Foundations

1.3.1. Behavioral Economics

Generative AI takes cues from behavioral economics to forecast customers' preferences and develop strategies for their retention. Predictive algorithms, for example, determine the most probable drivers of customer churn, allowing for preventive interaction (Madanchian, 2024).

1.3.2. Consumer Engagement Theories

Theories of consumer participation identify the implications of trust, relevancy, and personalized experiences for fostering loyalty among customers (Gupta et al., 2024). Generative AI helps to reinforce such principles by automating personalized interactions, including local-language-based chatbots, as well as improving customers' experiences by making contextual suggestions based on individual tastes.

1.3.3. Scalability Frameworks

Scalable solutions are needed in emerging markets because they are characterized by limited resources (Tadepally et al., 2022). The use of generative AI helps companies overcome problems by employing cost-efficient retention measures as well as automating tasks for them, thus minimizing overhead costs in operations and enhancing efficiency. Table 2 presents an overview of the key theoretical contributions that support the role of generative AI in customer retention.

Table 2. Theoretical contributions to Generative AI for customer retention

Theory	Relevance to Generative AI	Practical implications	References
Behavioral economics	Determines what triggers churn based on predictive models	Proactive strategies for retaining	Madanchian, 2024
Theory of consumer engagement	Emphasizes personalization and trust as drivers	Culturally customized communication	Gupta et al., 2024
Scalability frameworks	Provides for adaptability in varied and limited-resource environments	Scalable AI campaign	Tadepally et al., 2022

Source: Authors

Table 2 offers a framework overview of the theoretical foundations that support the generative AI role in customer retention. It also illustrates how various theories are used to understand and optimize AI-powered retention campaigns. Behavioral economics is used to discover the triggers behind churn through prediction models, allowing companies to initiate preventive retention strategies (Madanchian, 2024). Consumer engagement theory focuses on trust and personalization as the most important factors in retaining customers, with real-world applications in culturally conditioned communication to improve customer relationships (Gupta et al., 2024). Lastly, scalability frameworks address the need for adaptable solutions in resource-constrained contexts, demonstrating how AI-driven campaigns can be replicated across different market contexts (Tadepally et al., 2022). In most cases, the table outlines the multi-disciplinary nature of customer retention generative AI, showing how theoretical principles are translated into practice in order to create actionable business measures.

1.4. Applications of Generative AI in Emerging Markets

Generative AI has emerged as an innovative technology in numerous sectors in the emergent markets, enabling businesses to transcend resource constraints, cultural variations, and in the face of limited data, companies are able to enhance customer loyalty and retention through customized and responsive tactics.

1.4.1. Case Study: AI-Driven Retention in Fintech

Generative AI has significantly contributed to the fintech industry in Sub-Saharan Africa, particularly in mobile banking. Local datasets are used for customizing generative AI chatbots Offer personalized finance advice in local tongues such as Swahili, Yoruba, as well as Zulu localizes the services, establishing confidence and convenience for users who would otherwise be hampered by linguistic problems or illiteracy.

A case in point is the use of AI-driven chatbots in banking mobile applications, which has assisted in increasing customer retention by 20%. The chatbots offer a number of services including budget guidance, loan eligibility checks, as well as payment reminder services, enhancing user experience as a whole (Tadepally et al., 2022). It shows how generative AI can be used to close financial inclusion gaps as well as establish long-term customer relationships.

1.4.2. Case Study: E-Commerce in Southeast Asia

Southeast Asian e-commerce sites have used generative AI to transform the online shopping experience. Platforms base personalized product recommendations as well as tailored promotion offers on real-time analysis of customers' behavior. For example, leading e-commerce players such as Lazada and Shopee have utilized

AI models with natural language processing (NLP) to decipher customer questions and inclinations.

A top online shopping platform in the area experienced a 15% rise in repeat-shopping after adopting AI-based personalization (Shevchyk, 2024). The findings demonstrate how generative AI not only promotes customer satisfaction but also boosts revenues. Furthermore, the platforms use AI for dynamic pricing, allowing the businesses to be competitive in a price-conscious market.

1.4.3. Comparative Analysis of Generative AI Adoption

Adoption of generative AI is quite diverse across emerging economies based on differences in infrastructure, adaptability, and economic priorities. Table 3 offers a summary of applications of generative AI in different sectors in emerging economies.

Table 3. Generative AI applications in emerging markets

Region	Primary Application	Key Outcomes	References
Sub-Saharan Africa	Financial chatbots	Greater accessibility and trust	Tadepally et al., 2022
Southeast Asia	Personalized e-commerce	Higher repeat purchase rates.	Shevchyk, 2024
Latin America	Predictive telecom analytics	Reduced customer churn.	Gupta et al., 2024

Source: Authors

Table 3 offers a keen insight into the applications of generative AI in various emerging economies, with a rich variety of functionalities and practical outputs. In Sub-Saharan Africa, finance chatbots have enabled easier access to financial services as well as customer trust, particularly in areas far away from banking channel (Tadepally et al., 2022). In Southeast Asia, AI-driven personalized e-commerce has seen higher frequencies of repeat purchase, showing the power of personalized recommendations in customer engagement (Shevchyk, 2024). In Latin America, telecom analytics driven by AI have enabled customer turnover reduction through the ability for telecom providers to forecast and address service issues proactively (Gupta et al., 2024). In summary, the table shows the versatility of generative AI across different economic as well as technological landscapes, showing its applicability in customer retention as well as in improving end-user experiences in emerging markets.

1.5. Conceptual Model

The conceptual framework consolidates theoretical and applied knowledge relating to customer loyalty using generative AI in the emerging markets. It outlines four key elements that are central to the success of AI-powered customer engagement efforts.

Figure 2. Conceptual model of Generative AI in customer retention

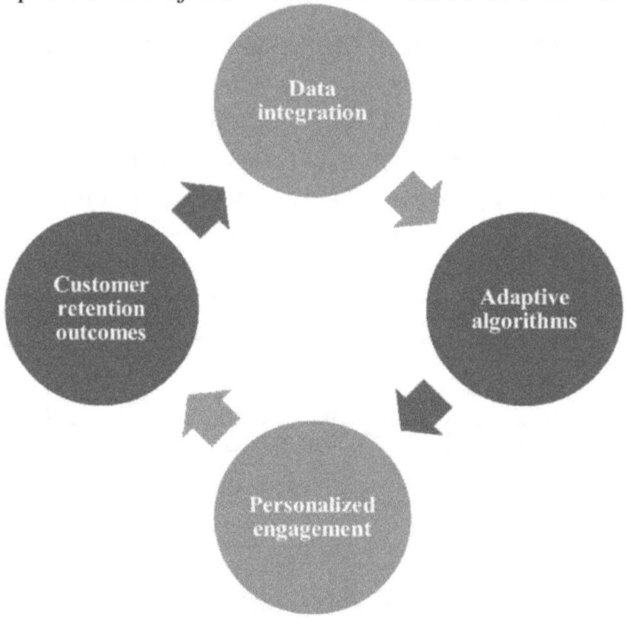

Source: Authors

The conceptual framework, as proposed, merges theoretical and practical insights in explaining the function of generative AI in driving customer retention in emergent market settings. It highlights four central concepts as key pillars for effective implementation: Integration of data means bringing together multiple data sources, ranging from customer feedback, social media activity, and transaction history. Generative AI processes this data in order to construct an overall, multi-dimensional picture of every customer, thereby enabling more accurate and better-informed decision-making.

Adaptive algorithms guarantee that AI models are technically robust as well as culturally sensitive. These models are designed to detect and respond to regional and cultural differences, making recommendations as well as insights increasingly contextual in diverse market segments. Personalization is realized through the use of processed data as well as adaptive intelligence. This enables companies to provide hyper-personalization ranging from AI-driven chatbots, email campaigns, as well as content suggestions in real-time, that can lead to better customer relationships as well as higher satisfaction levels.

Customer retention results are the ultimate effect of the model. These are enhanced customer loyalty, decreased churn rates, as well as better customer lifetime value. By linking together all four elements, generative AI assists businesses in making informed customer retention decisions as well as achieving sustainable interaction.

1.6. Challenges and Ethical Considerations

1.6.1. Challenges

One of the main challenges in rolling out generative AI in emerging markets is the data infrastructure limitation. In most of these markets, infrastructures capable of sustaining broader AI deployment are underdeveloped or fragmented, while the data that is available is incomplete, inconsistent, or poor in quality. These limitations have profound effects on AI models' training and operational performance, hence the need for companies to invest in sound data gathering as well as management systems in order to bring out the maximum benefits of AI technology. (Gupta et al., 2024). Another challenge is consumers' wariness of adopting AI technology. Fears over data privacy, algorithm transparency, and fairness sometimes result in users shying away or resisting AI, especially those who are not accustomed to automated technology. These fears are often based on poor awareness or comprehension of AI systems' mode of operation, which emphasizes the need for companies to create public trust through transparent communications, openness, and proper AI stewardship.

1.6.2. Ethical Considerations

Transparency is a key ethical challenge in the use of generative AI. Companies have an obligation to explain clearly how AI-driven recommendations are derived, as well as protecting customer sovereignty over their own data. Efforts toward transparency including user education initiatives and the implementation of transparent AI models lie at the forefront of establishing customer trust as well as nudging AI adoption toward ethical implementation in customer-facing activities (Madanchian, 2024). Another significant ethical challenge is combating bias. AI built on non-representative or biased datasets can perpetuate inherent biases or yield unfair outputs. For example, models designed based on heavily urban datasets can be inadequate for rural communities' needs. In order to prevent such imbalances, companies need to perform periodic audits on their AI systems for ensuring fairness and accuracy across various cultural as well as geographical settings (Shevchyk, 2024).

The theoretical and conceptual foundation emphasizes the strategic value of generative AI for customer retention, especially in nascent markets. By incorporating behavioral economics insights, consumer engagement principles, and scalability frameworks, the chapter emphasizes how AI technologies can provide adaptive, personalized, and culturally responsive customer experiences. These are collectively established on a strong foundation for generative AI understanding as applied in varied and resource-limited contexts.

2. RESEARCH METHODOLOGY

This section presents the methodological framework adopted to investigate how generative AI can enhance customer retention in emerging markets. The approach combines theoretical models with a systematic literature review and case study analysis, ensuring both conceptual depth and empirical relevance.

2.1. Theories Used

The theoretical foundation of this research is based on established models in technology adoption, cultural behavior, as well as customer relationship management. These models provide an organized framework for the analysis of how generative AI can enhance customer loyalty and interaction in various socio-economic settings.

2.1.1. Relationship Marketing Theory

Developed by Berry (1983), Relationship Marketing Theory focuses on establishing long-term, trusting relationships with customers, as opposed to individual transactions. Trust, commitment, and personalization are the key pillars supporting ongoing customer loyalty.

Generative AI is firmly based on this principle in that it allows for hyper-personalization. For example, chatbots based on AI provide real-time, personalized assistance, building on trust through responsive dialogue. In another similar way, AI-driven personalization through product recommendations engenders an exclusive atmosphere, increasing involvement as well as emotional resonance with the brand. (Gupta et al., 2024).

2.1.2. Technology Acceptance Model (TAM)

Davis' (1989) Technology Acceptance Model explains how people accept new technology. It is grounded in two major perceptions: the technology's ability to improve performance and how easy it is to use or how simple it is to operate.

In the generative AI space, especially in new markets, TAM is very applicable. The model can explain consumer attitudes toward AI technology like smart assistants or suggestion systems. Adoption is fueled by the benefits people see in AI, such as efficiency and automation. Ease of use is especially important in countries with different levels of digital competence, making it essential that AI be designed in an intuitive way in order for it to be successfully applied. (Madanchian, 2024).

2.1.3. Hofstede's Cultural Dimensions Theory

Hofstede's Cultural Dimensions Theory (1980) investigates how cultural norms impact behavioral patterns on dimensions like individualism vs. collectivism as well as uncertainty avoidance. The framework is useful in explaining how consumer interaction is impacted by cultural diversity as well as how technology is embraced.

In emerging markets, AI systems must reflect local languages, customs, and consumer expectations. For example, regional chatbots should communicate in native languages and mirror cultural etiquette. Furthermore, AI recommendations must adapt to culturally specific buying behaviors whether collective or individualistic ensuring that interactions are relevant and respectful (Shevchyk, 2024).

2.1.4. Diffusion of Innovation Theory

Rogers' Diffusion of Innovation Theory (1962) explains how new technologies spread across a population, from innovators and early adopters to the late majority and laggards. The rate of adoption is influenced by perceived value, accessibility, and peer influence.

This model aptly describes how generative AI is being adopted in emerging markets. Industries such as fintech and e-commerce often serve as pioneers, showcasing the potential of AI and encouraging adoption among the broader business ecosystem. Strategies such as user education and cost-effective solutions help reduce barriers, supporting a smoother transition to AI-driven customer retention practices.

Table 4 summarizes key theoretical models that support this research, highlighting their contributions to understanding AI adoption, trust, and personalized marketing strategies.

Table 4. Theoretical frameworks supporting Generative AI research

Theory	Key focus	Generative AI application	References
Relationship marketing theory	Trust and engagement in long-term relationships	Personalized support and recommendations	Berry, 1983
Technology acceptance model	User adoption of technology	AI tools that are easy to use and beneficial	Davis, 1989
Cultural dimensions theory	Cultural adaptation in strategies	Localized AI systems for diverse audiences	Hofstede, 1980
Diffusion of Innovation	Technology adoption lifecycle	Adoption of AI in fintech, e-commerce	Rogers, 1962

Source: Authors

2.2. Methodological Approach

Following up on the conversation about how generative AI is situated within customer retention within expanding markets, the research uses an approach based on methodological design, integrating conceptual richness as well as empirical depth. It applies systematic literature review (SLR) combined with case study comparative analysis in such a manner that it creates an elaborate picture of the theoretical underpinnings as well as the actual applications of AI technologies across varied environments. Both methodologies were used in order to leverage each's respective strengths. While the SLR can provide systematic syntheses of the prevailing literature, case study analysis

2.2.1. Systematic Literature Review

It is based on systematic literature review (SLR) to create a sound foundation for subsequent research studies. It was conducted under the PRISMA protocol (Page et al., 2021) for ensuring transparency in research, reproducibility, and high academic standards in reviewing the literature that is pertinent in generative AI as well as in customer retention. Unlike research based entirely on quantitative data where the complexity might be ignored or purely qualitative research that is not generalizable, this SLR takes the middle ground position. It is a clear, systematic overview of high-standard research that is bias-free, offering a strong foundation for the follow-on case studies.

Steps involved in the SLR

Preliminary literature search: Research scholars have carried out search of academic sources like Scopus, Web of Science, and Google Scholar with the usage of key words such as Generative AI and customer retention, Emerging markets and AI, Predictive analytics in loyalty, and Personalization via AI. Bibliometric criteria were used to direct the filtering of articles. Articles were screened by their relevance, impact, and methodological quality. Important measurements were Total Citations per Year (TC/Year), Normalized Citation Impact (NCI), and H-index, to ensure that quality sources were selected.

Screening process

Round one: 60 articles were chosen from the original pool according to how well the articles match the study's themes, emerging markets focus, and theoretical significance.

Round two: We further trimmed this list to 30 articles, prioritizing later publications (2015–2024), strength of citations, and best articles on generative AI and customer experience.

Table 5 presents the specific criteria utilized in choosing and analyzing these articles.

Table 5. Article selection criteria

Criteria	Details	Rationale
Publication year	2015–2024	Covers the latest developments in
Number of citations	At least 10 citations (recent); 50 or more for prior publications	Guarantees
Thematic relevance	Prioritize generative AI, retention, and new markets.	Accords with study goals

Source: Authors

Full text analysis and coding: Articles were then scrutinized in detail to identify appropriate theoretical frameworks, methodological strategies, and empirical observations. Analytical rigor was ensured through the use of NVivo where a thematic analysis took place to enable inductive identification of patterns across the literature. Four key themes were obtained through analysis, which represent the most prominent domains of study to date in Table 6.

Table 6. Identified themes in the literature

Theme	Key findings
Personalization	AI boosts loyalty through tailor-made recommendations and interactions
Predictive analytics	AI enables early detection of churn and proactive engagement strategies
Cultural adaptation	Localized Artificial Intelligence (for example, multilingual chatbots) establishes confidence and user satisfaction
Ethical considerations	Fairness and transparency are essential, particularly in diverse markets

Source: Authors

In total, the SLR both anchors the study in current academic literature as well as brings to the fore critical knowledge gaps in relation to culturally responsive AI strategies and the ethical application of generative technologies in underserved markets. Through supplementing this basis with empirical case studies, the study maximizes both the contextualizing of theoretical insight and the potential for application.

2.2.2. Profile of the References Studied

A reading of the chosen literature does not only register increasing academic attention to generative AI, but also the refinement of methodology applied to studying its customer retention implications. The following presents a synthesis of trends in publication, methodological direction, and level of study, providing a contextual perspective upon which the maturity of the field as it stands and prospective directions can be understood better.

Figure 3. Distribution of articles by year of publication

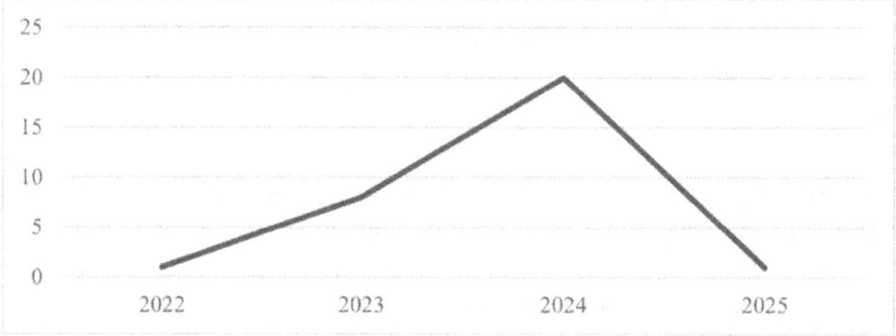

Source: Authors

The distribution of articles by year of publication shows a heightened speed of interest in generative AI and how it can be used in customer engagement. In 2022, the subject was in its infancy, and there was one study that directly dealt with the convergence of AI and loyalty strategy. By 2023, there were far more publications, as there was growing realization of the strategic applications of AI across industries. The steep spike to 20 articles in 2024 verifies that generative AI had reached the mainstream, especially in relation to digital transformation in emerging markets. The addition of publications in early 2025 implies forward-looking agendas, as researchers started investigating next-generation applications and ethical considerations.

Figure 4. Distribution of references by type of methodological approach

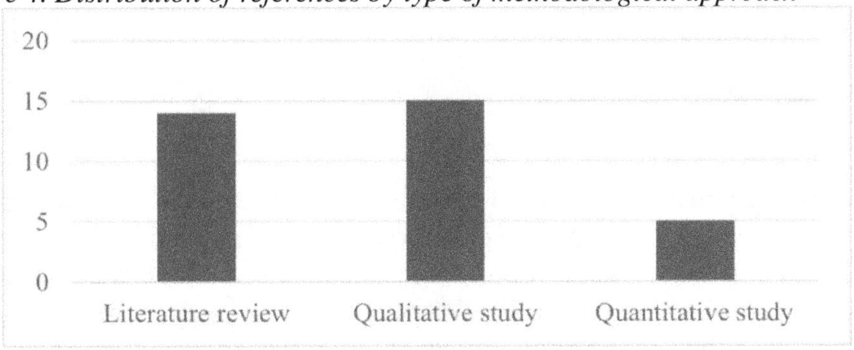

Source: Authors

The studies reviewed include a wide scope of methodological frameworks, which show how researchers are tackling the subject both in a theoretical and empirical perspective. Most prominently, literature reviews (14 articles) make up a considerable segment of the citations, which suggests a steady effort towards synthesizing knowledge and determining study voids. Simultaneously, qualitative studies (15 articles) denote a preoccupation with comprehending behavioral, cultural, and organizational processes in light of case studies, interviews, and field observations.

In contrast, quantitative methods are comparatively underrepresented (5 articles), and there is room for future growth in the validation of AI-supported customer strategies through strong measurements and statistical quality. It is interesting that there is little "other" or hybrid category use, which indicates a reasonably well-organized research environment where distinctions between types of methods are well defined.

Figure 5. Distribution of references by level of research depth

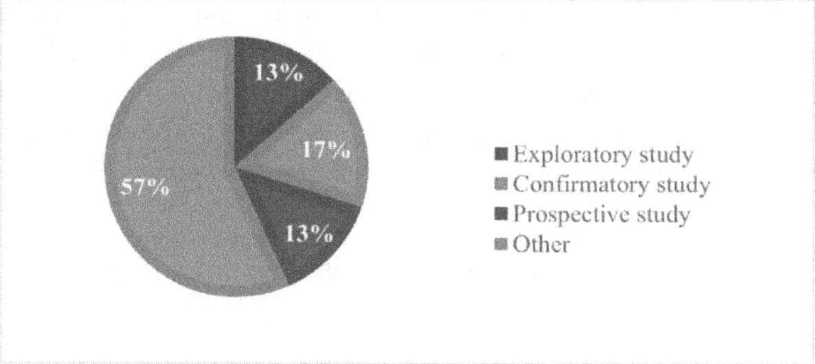

Source: Authors

A closer examination of the level of inquiry shows that studies of generative AI in emerging markets encompass exploratory, confirmatory, and forward-looking perspectives. Exploratory studies (6 articles) examine new applications and upcoming trends, especially in environments characterized by cultural heterogeneity and infrastructural limitation. Confirmatory studies (5 articles) attempt to verify theoretical hypotheses, frequently on user adoption or performance results. Notably, a sizeable proportion of the literature (15 articles) utilizes mixed or integrative methodologies, which cross-reference theoretical discussion and empirical observation. This indicates a field in transition from conceptual examination to increasingly evidence-based structures. Having prospective studies (4 articles) indicates enhanced attention to longer-term effects, including ethical threats, regulatory change, and changing user expectations in AI-facilitated customer interaction.

Together, these distributions represent a dynamic and increasingly diversifying field. Although underlying theories remain in force, there is ample evidence of movement toward greater empirical examination and forward-looking thinking. As the deployment of generative AI picks up pace, particularly in constrained environments, future studies will increasingly be called upon to advance the evidence base through quantitative verification, longitudinal studies, and cross-cultural comparative analysis to comprehensively realize the change-making potential of AI-based customer retention strategies.

2.2.3. Comparative Case Study Approach

In addition to the systematic literature review, the study adopts a comparative case study design that seeks to examine how generative AI is actually operationalized in practice to facilitate customer retention. Such qualitative complement captures additional contextual richness and provides grounded examples of AI deployment by sectors and by regions. Guided by a systematic and comparative study design, analysis across sectors becomes possible, as well as the detection of both common patterns and contextual-specific dynamics. Through real-world cases, the study seeks to close the distance between theoretical promise and operational experience.

Case selection criteria: Three sectors were chosen for the analysis of cases: e-commerce, telecommunications, and fintech. These sectors were selected based on their early and extensive adoption of AI technologies, as well as their instrumental role in determining customer experience in emerging markets. The chosen cases were drawn from literature consulted in the SLR and had two characteristics:

1. Personal interest in customer retention and engagement.
2. Performance data or qualitative evidence availability concerning the adoption of AI.

Data collection and analysis: Case studies rely on secondary data drawn from academic literature, industry reports, and documented implementations of AI. Special focus was placed on performance indicators like retention rate, customer satisfaction, usage rate, and adoption success measurements. To maintain analytical consistency, each of the cases was analyzed using a comparative approach organized in terms of the following dimensions:

- Artificial intelligence technologies implemented (e.g., chatbots, recommendation engines, predictive analytics)
- Implementation challenges (i.e., complexity of rules, cultural alignment, availability of data)
- Success drivers (e.g., automation efficiency, personalization, accessibility in several

This structure enabled comparative analysis across sectors and regions to identify not simply how generative AI is applied, but also how and why particular applications are successful or unsuccessful according to the environment.

Triangulation and validation: For enhancing the validity of conclusions, triangulation was used by cross-verifying results across various data collections. Patterns developed in one case were also compared to others to gauge their generalizability or sector-specificity. Triangulation through iterative validation ensured that conclusions drawn were empirically viable as well as conceptually valid. Through using comparative cases, the study is able to reflect the complexity of the real world in the adoption of AI in customer retention strategies. It also shows how companies operating in emerging markets are coping both in terms of opportunities and structure eventually providing actionable conclusions in the enablers and barriers of successful AI integration.

2.2.4. Framework Development Process

Based on the dual pillar of systematic literature review and comparative case studies, the study concludes by formulating a conceptual framework that can be used by businesses to implement generative AI for customer retention in emerging markets effectively. It is not meant to be a one-size-fits-all model, but a contextual tool, sensitive to the specific challenges and opportunities that exist in resource-limited and culturally diverse settings. The framework was developed in a multi-step fashion to ensure academic rigor and relevance.

- **Thematic synthesis:** The literature and case studies were initially subjected to thematic synthesis. Major patterns and recurring variables were elicited, which included cultural alignment, ethical risk, scalability, and personalization. These served as the starting point for the identification of the core dimensions of the framework.
- **Core component modeling:** The model was then structured in terms of four strategic pillars that each reflected one of the essential conditions for successful deployment of Ai in customer engagement:
    - **Cultural Adaptation:** Prioritizes placing AI tools in accordance with local language, habits, and customer expectations.
    - **Scalability:** Emphasizes the importance of having solutions that can be expanded cost-effectively across regions where there is limited technical infrastructure.
    - **Ethical Considerations:** Encompasses transparency, data protection, and algorithmic fairness as indispensable aspects of accountable AI.
    - **Human-AI Balance:** Emphasizes the importance of combining the support of AI without doing away with the human aspect of customer engagement, particularly in relationship-oriented markets.

They are complementary to each other and together present a holistic model for informing AI-based retention strategies in emerging markets.

- **Validation and Iteration:** In ensuring conceptual appropriateness, the suggested model was benchmarked using literature models. Convergence across the likes of attention to personalization and ethics was used to validate the model's importance, and divergences across cultural and infrastructural specifics were used to validate the model's added value in the emerging economy context. Adjustments were thus made accordingly, with priority given to lessons learned across underrepresented regions and sectors. The resulting model is therefore both academically informed and practically driven in attempting to support decision-makers in the important intersection of both the enabling technologies and the customer experience.

2.2.5. Ethical Considerations

Although the emphasis of this study rests in discovering how strategic value in customer retention could be derived from generative AI, it also includes recognition that ethical integrity is the basis of the legitimacy and sustainable application of AI in the face of special concerns pertaining to trust, inclusivity, and data management in emerging markets where these concerns frequently get magnified. Special caution was taken in the course of conducting the study to ensure that ethical principles were respected in both secondary data usage and in presenting results. Such ethical sensitivities are particularly relevant in light of cultural and economic diversities where concerns surrounding AI tend to be heightened.

- **Respect for intellectual property**: Academic, institutional, and commercial data sources were all appropriately referenced, full credit was given to original authors. Not only was it essential to uphold academic integrity, but it was also necessary to be respectful toward other researchers' and practitioners' intellectual contributions, which form the foundation of this research work.
- **Objectivity in analysis**: Accounts were made in such a manner as avoided speculative inferences or overstatement of effects. Analytical balance was emphasized in the sense that strengths as well as limitations of AI applications were represented fairly. Where evidence had ambiguity or dependency on context, this was indicated without generalization.
- **Sensitivity towards cultural and geographical specificity**: Since the emphasis of the research fell on the new markets, it became necessary to avoid homogenizing different regions within one account. It was an approach that remained attuned to local social, cultural, as well as language details at particular points, especially where referencing AI-powered personalization as well as consumer behavior were in question. Normative structures or western-centric assumptions were shunned in situating facts informed across different global settings.

These ethical activities are designed both to support the validity of the research as an exercise in corroborating the broader challenge faced by organizations in applying AI in ethically demanding environments. As generative AI continues to progress, ethical sensitivity will have to be an ongoing initiative, both through research in the academic environment as in the routine use in the field.

The approach used in this study blends theoretical sophistication and empirical richness, providing a holistic perspective under which to study how generative AI can be used to build customer retention in new markets. Through using a systematic literature overview complemented by comparative cases and rooted in well-established theoretical frameworks, the study both encompasses the strategic and contextual aspects of potential AI adoption. Further, the resulting framework offers implementable recommendations while being attuned to the ethical, cultural, and infrastructural subtleties that inform the adoption of technology in various settings. This holistic methodology provides firm ground for the subsequent results and discussion.

3. ANALYSIS OF STUDY RESULTS

3.1. Analysis of Results From the Systematic Literature Review

The qualitative analysis of the 30 referenced academic articles presents a wide and in-depth view of the application of generative AI in enhancing customer loyalty and retention strategies in emerging markets. Some of the consistent trends that were evident in the articles provide a deep insight as well as both the strengths and the weaknesses of engagement models driven by AI. These observations are summarized thematically in the subsections below.

3.1.1. Personalization as a Key Driver of Customer Loyalty

Throughout the studies under view, personalization stands out as a pillar of loyalty strategies based on AI. Personalized experience has been made possible through generative AI by using real-time data in presenting content, suggestions, and offers in accordance with individual inclinations. These studies conducted by Patil et al. (2024) and Maryam & Shanthi (2023) depict how technologies like dynamic generation of content and recommendation engines are keeping customer engagement heightened, making it emotionally attached, hence making it increase brand loyalty. Personalization using AI enables marketing strategies to be customized in detail, tailoring product recommendations, communications, and loyalty rewards to each customer's profile and behavior (Patil et al., 2024). Companies using these tactics always see enhanced engagement levels and increased retention (Maryam & Shanthi, 2023).

Yet these advantages are counterbalanced by critical concerns. These include concerns regarding the collection and utilization of private data. Firms need to be mindful of relevant data protection guidelines in addition to ensuring that the resulting systems of Artificial Intelligence are responsive to cultural differences. Personalization that does not respect local language, conventions, or consumer norms can give rise to a backlash, eroding confidence and efficacy.

3.1.2. Operational Efficiency and Cost Reduction

Yet another recurring theme in the literature concerns the use of generative AI in improving operational performance. Several studies point out that automation using AI enhances efficiency in core business functions like customer service, marketing, and sales. As per Storm Reply (2024) and Mazumder (2023), automation using AI optimizes repetitive tasks, minimizes response times, and lessens operational expenses freeing human workers to concentrate on complicated, high-value interactions. Tools like AI-enabled chatbots, predictive analytics, and automated customer support platforms are seen as vital tools to facilitate operation transformation. Specifically, chatbots enable round-the-clock resolution of routine questions, improving responsiveness and consistency (Storm Reply, 2024). Predictive tools, on the other hand, facilitate planning by allowing better demand forecasting and anticipatory resource allocation (Mazumder, 2023). Adopting these benefits notwithstanding, adoption in emerging markets proves uneven. Upfront investment cost in rolling out high-end AI systems poses an insurmountable obstacle, particularly among small and medium enterprises (SMEs). Moreover, growing concerns in some organizations that the application of AI will replace humans lead to resistance in-house and threats of redundancy. These issues are overcome by addressing them in proportion by fostering a strategy that encourages AI as augmentation of people versus replacement of people. It involves investment in workforce skilling, communicating the value of augmentation of people using AI, and organization cultures that perceive the application of technology as a tool to empower, not disrupt. (Ed-daakouri et al., 2025)

3.1.3. AI-Powered Customer Engagement Strategies

Generative AI is increasingly playing a strategic function in remaking how companies interact with their customers. Literature reviewed here indicates movement away from the conventional, static engagement methods toward dynamic, real-time, and data-driven ones made possible by AI. Research conducted by Arnese (2023) and Ahmed & Ali (2024) highlights how loyalty schemes enhanced by AI, and conversational interfaces like chatbots and virtual assistants, are being used to build stronger, longer-term customer friendships. One of the biggest advantages is in the customization of incentives, offers, and content. It is now possible for AI systems to study behavioral data in order to customize incentives, offers, and content in a manner that aligns well with individual taste and patterns of consumption (Arnese, 2023). Such a level of detail is not only enhancing the relevance of marketing activities but also deepening emotional involvement in the brand. Further, the availability of AI-facilitated communication channels across platforms and devices allows for real-time, responsive customer service. These channels are usually open 24/7 and are critical in enhancing satisfaction, particularly in regions where service availability may be limited otherwise (Ahmed & Ali, 2024). Challenges, though, remain. Many customers show reservations toward machine-driven recommendations, citing concerns over the reliability, impartiality, or emotional awareness of machine-driven interaction. Additionally, complete automation of engagement strategies may result in a perception of impersonality, which erodes customer confidence and devotion in the medium- to long-term. To counter these risks, academics suggest a hybrid approach to engagement where AI is used to support rather than replace human interaction. By ensuring that there is always a level of human stewardship, companies can protect customer experience in a participatory, empathetic, and responsive form, especially in culturally sensitive settings

3.1.4. Challenges of Cultural and Regulatory Adaptation

The cultural variability and the complexity of regulation in emerging markets significantly impact the incorporation of generative AI. As emphasized by Orozco & Welin (2024) and Kumar et al. (2022), successful adoption of AI in these markets is a function of both readiness in terms of technology and how adaptable the systems are to local social norms, language heterogeneity, and legal frameworks. Culturally responsive AI systems like chatbots operating in regional dialects or recommendation engines that mirror local patterns of consumption tend to be more engaging and trustworthy. When AI technologies mirror a population's language, values, and behavioral signals, customers will be more likely to feel heard and respected and are therefore likely to be more rapidly adopted and build stronger brand loyalty (Orozco & Welin, 2024). At the same time, companies have to operate in a patchwork of data protection legislations. Being compliant with frameworks like the General Data Protection Regulation (GDPR) in transnational settings, or nationally appropriate legal regimes in emerging markets, poses a steady challenge in particular for companies that operate across regions (Kumar et al., 2022). Regulatory mistakes may expose companies to legal risk as well as cost them customer confidence, where data privacies are sensitive concerns. Aside from complying with regulation, ethical considerations also arise. Machine learning modeled upon data sets that are unrepresented of local populations threatens to reproduce or exacerbate pre-existing inequalities.

3.1.5. Future Trends and Strategic Opportunities

In the future, the literature indicates that generative AI will increasingly mold the direction of customer retention strategies, especially as it increasingly intersects with emerging technologies. Research by Hemachandran et al. (2025) and Rane et al. (2023) predicts the intensification of convergence between AI and technologies like the Internet of Things (IoT), blockchain, and the metaverse, each providing new frontiers of customer interaction. One of the most salient developments is the furtherance of predictive analytics. AI models are becoming increasingly poised to both react to customer behavior and predict it. Predictive tools are poised to remain central in managing the full customer lifecycle of helping businesses proactively predict risks of customer attrition, predict purchasing requirements, and provide timely, individualized interventions (Hemachandran et al., 2025). Concurrently, the convergence of AI in immersive digital environments like the metaverse is opening new channels of interaction. These platforms permit extensive, immersive brand experiences, where customers are able to explore digital environments, engage with AI avatars, and join in on gamified loyalty schemes (Rane et al., 2023). Such applications portend a movement toward experiential marketing enabled by intelligent systems. These developments are, however, accompanied by challenges. Maintaining the scalability and flexibility of AI outcomes represents a crucial challenge, especially in rapidly changing technological environments. Also, as AI systems grow increasingly autonomous, there is the risk of dehumanizing the customer experience. Excessive dependence on automation is likely to mean interaction that is efficient but also devoid of emotion. To navigate this complexity, organizations need to pursue a strategic, human-focused approach that utilizes AI to augment, and complement rather than replace, true-to-form engagement. Those that strike the right balance between technological innovation and emotional intelligence will tend to be better positioned to craft enduring customer relationships in the digital world (Bouizgar et al., 2025). Table 7 offers a systematic summary of these identified key discoveries and concerns.

Table 7. Key findings and challenges

Key theme	Key findings	Challenges identified
Personalization	Personalized experience and engagement increase through the use of AI.	Privacy issues
Operational efficiency	Decreases cost and response times.	Expensive to implement, resistance of workforce.
Customerretention	Loyalty programs driven by AI encourage retention.	Skepticism toward AI, requirement of human supervision
Culturaladaptation	Greater acceptance of culturally adapted AI	Regulatoryhurdles, ethicalconcernsofAI.
Future directions	Predictive analytics and metaverse adoption.	Scalability, ensuring human

Source: Authors

3.1.6. Conclusion and Recommendations

The literature analyzed in this study highlights the revolutionary implications of generative AI in customer loyalty and retention, especially in the diverse and dynamic environments of emerging markets. Generative AI technologies have signaled high capabilities in supporting tailormade experience, enhancing operating efficiency, and enabling more engaging customer interactions. Concurrently, the study highlights various essential challenges that encompass data protection, issues of complexity in terms of regulation, cultural incompatibility, and ethical dilemmas. In order to engage maximally in the utilization of the potential of AI without compromising on the potential risks, companies need to implement it strategically, in a context-aware, and ethically sound manner.

Key Recommendations for Business Practitioners

Prioritize transparency and privacy in AI-driven personalization in order to build confidence. Transparency of data usage and consent needs to be made a core component of customer engagement strategies. Make investments in cultural adaptation, which involves ensuring that Ai systems are designed to conform to local language, preferences, and social norms in diverse markets. Utilize AI to support rather than replace human interaction, particularly in sensitive emotional or relationship-based settings. An intertwined model of engagement will maintain authenticity. Monitor regulatory developments proactively and align AI strategies with evolving compliance requirements to reduce legal exposure and reinforce corporate responsibility. Establish organizational readiness by fostering internal AI literacy and change management practices that reinforce employee confidence and collaboration in shifting towards the use of AI. In a research capacity, studies in the future ought to try to measure the long-term customer retention effects of AI, investigate applications in underserved markets, and study the implications of AI-enhanced ecosystems like the metaverse and IoT. These questions will be important to the academic study and real-world application of AI in customer strategies across the world.

3.2. Comparative Case Studies of Generative AI in Customer Retention

3.2.1. Case Study 1: AI-Driven Loyalty Programs in E-Commerce (Southeast Asia)

In Southeast Asia, top e-commerce platforms including Lazada and Shopee are among the pioneers in using generative AI in customer loyalty strategies. Through the analysis of user purchase histories and search behaviors, the companies are using AI technologies to develop hyper-personalized engagement models to boost customer retention (Arnese, 2023).

- **Success factors**
    - o **Personalized offers:** Artificial intelligence allows for the creation of customer-specific discounts and offers according to individual preferences, resulting in increased satisfaction and repeat business.
    - o **Gamification components:** Tier-based membership programs, custom vouchers, and spin-to-win mechanics encourage repeat engagement and build brand loyalty.
    - o **Automated customer support:** AI-powered chatbots offer round-the-clock assistance, streamlining customer service operations while improving response time and overall experience.
- **Challenges**
    - o **Data protection issues**: Customers are becoming increasingly cautious in regard to how their private data is gathered and processed, especially in terms of behavioral advertising.
    - o **Infrastructure constraints**: Small and medium enterprises (SMEs) tend to experience considerable financial and technical hurdles in trying to implement AI technologies on a large scale.
    - o **Alignment with culture**: Recommendations by AI can be lacking if they are not aligned with local preferences, cultural values, or shopping habits, highlighting the requirement of culturally responsive AI models. For them to be successful, e-commerce websites in the region need to invest in strong data protection, culturally sensitive personalization, and scalable AI architectures that can be replicated across diverse segments of consumers.

3.2.2. Case study 2: Dynamic pricing in mobile telecommunications (Africa)

In different African markets, telecommunications companies like MTN and Safaricom are embracing AI-based dynamic pricing to both boost revenue and customer loyalty. Through real-time analysis of user experience, network utilization, and contextual information, the companies are in a position to dynamically tailor pricing models—providing better affordability, responsiveness, and value delivery (Abdulsalam & Tajudeen, 2024).

- **Success factors**
    - **Real-time analysis of data**: Artificial intelligence platforms handle vast amounts of data concerning network usage and customer behavior, making it possible to adjust prices in real-time based on demand patterns and usage levels.
    - **Customer segmentation**: Personalized pricing plans according to data-driven insights made possible through AI allow operators to offer varied packages that suit varying income levels as well as user needs increasing accessibility as well as loyalty.
    - **Fraud detection**: AI capabilities ensure operational integrity through identifying anomalous patterns of use, allowing providers to avoid fraud and restore customer trust.
- **Challenges**
    - **Consumer skepticism**: Users tend be skeptical about dynamic pricing algorithms as they view them as either clandestine or exploitative in nature. Disclosing how dynamic pricing algorithms operate can undermine trust in AI-driven price-setting strategies.
    - **Regulatory limitations**: Communication laws and consumer protection regulations are country-varying, placing operators in difficult compliance landscapes that may not yet be shaped for the model of AI
    - **Gaps in data availability**: Rural or underserved areas do not have historic as well as behavioral data that makes predictive pricing models less effective, causing inapplicability or inaccuracy of AI. In order to encourage adoption as well as regulator acceptance, providers would have to undertake customer educational investments in AI-based models, make pricing transparent, as well as pursue cooperation between regulators as well as themselves in co-crafting frameworks in favor of useful AI.

3.2.3. Case Study 3: Personalized Recommendations in Fintech (Latin America)

In Latin America, fintech players such as Nubank and Mercado Pago are harnessing generative AI technology to enhance financial inclusion via personalized products and services based on individuals' needs and preferences. These entities take informed decisions based on customers' spending patterns, transaction history, as well as their credit scores and forward individualized recommendations that meet certain economic needs and desires.(Katterbauer & Schmidt, 2024).

- **Success factors**
  - **Automated budgeting**: Users are assisted with AI-powered tools for budgeting, income target-setting, and expense tracking. These features promote better money decisions as well as consumer independence.
  - **Behavioral analysis**: AI tracks real-time spending to provide users with real-time alerts and recommendations, ensuring they do not overspend and promote healthier spending behaviors.
  - **Multilanguage capability:** Noting the language heterogeneity of the geographical region, the majority of fintech applications have AI chatbots that can assist in multiple languages
- **Challenges**
  - **Regulatory complexity**: FinTech's working in Latin America need to contend with fragmented and dynamic financial rules that are frequently unclear in relation to the application of AI.
  - **Trust deficit**: Automated financial advice may be efficient, yet a significant level of user resistance exists when it comes to sensitive issues such as savings, loans, or investments in restricting the adoption of AI in certain segments.
  - **Cybersecurity threats**: Growth in AI-based financial services opens the sector to greater vulnerability to data breaches and cyber-attacks, increasing demand for strong digital protection infrastructure. In order to unlock the true potential of AI, fintech organizations will need to marry regulation, transparency, and robust cybersecurity strategies. Additionally, in the creation of transparent and interpretable AI tools, securing user confidence and greater regional financial inclusion will rest.

3.2.4. Comparative Adoption of Generative AI in Developed vs. Emerging Markets

The adoption of generative AI differs significantly across developed and emerging markets due to a dynamic interaction of technical infrastructure, level of regulator sophistication, digital maturity, and socio-cultural dynamics. It is critical to comprehend these differences in order to develop contextualized strategies that tap the potential of AI to boost customer retention.

- **Infrastructure readiness**: Advanced digital ecosystems that comprise high-bandwidth broadband, extensive cloud infrastructure, and local GPU computing capabilities are generally available to developed nations and allow them to easily deploy GenAI (Gupta et al., 2024). Most emerging markets, on the contrary, experience inherent limitations in the form of unsteady internet accessibility, unavailability of cloud capacity, and underdeveloped infrastructure for data (Murungu, 2024). For instance, in Sub-Saharan African and Southeast Asian regions, cloud-based AI performance lag caused by insufficient local server capacity can directly affect customer experience (Ogunseye et al., 2024).
- **Regulatory environments**: Mature markets are moving toward comprehensive AI governance, through efforts such as the European Union's AI Act or the U.S. National AI Strategy, that supply legal safeguards for ethical use of AI in customer-facing applications (Hasan, 2024). Other regulatory environments in most emerging markets, by contrast, are fragmented or in nascent stages of development, causing confusion over compliance and hindering AI experimentation. In South Asia, for example, lack of uniform data protection legislation has slowed rollout of behavioral profiling capabilities (Hasan, 2024; Akan, 2024).
- **Skills and literacy of AI**: Adoption of AI strongly depends on digital fluency in both end users and in the workforce. In developed economies, AI literacy is firmly rooted in formal schooling and professional instruction. Developing countries tend to fall short in basic digital literacy, and specialized AI skills are in shortage (Cruces et al., 2024). A Latin American regional survey reported that fewer than 30% of customer-facing organizations have AI-trained personnel compared to the over 70% in countries of the Organization for Economic Co-operation and Development.
- **Cost and scalability**: Economies of scale and localized solutions for AI reduce the cost of deployment in developed markets. Conversely, emerging markets rely on third-party platforms that allow little customization, increasing the cost of operation (Murungu, 2024). Also, offshore hosting poses data

sovereignty issues, further complicating deployment and raising the overall cost of AI-based loyalty solutions.

- **Trust and cultural perceptions**: In developed markets, there are regulatory safeguards like the GDPR that lead to greater confidence in AI systems among consumers. In markets in development, in those in which there is less institutional trust, consumers are less amenable, particularly where algorithmic outcomes affecting price or service tailoring are concerned. (Ogunseye et al., 2024). In such circumstances, backing by trustworthy institutions, as well as transparency in communications, are necessary for gaining trust in AI-based technology.

It is important to realize such differences in order to create adaptable and inclusive AI plans. While established markets may implement complete automation as well as real-time personalization, emerging markets may require hybrid models that combine powers of AI with localized options as well as human-focused design in attempts to overcome infrastructural as well as societal limitations as well as create long-term consumer trust.

3.3. Conceptual Framework for AI-Driven Customer Retention in Emerging Markets

Conceptual framework established here is based on insights gained in systematic analysis of literature as well as comparative case studies undertaken in high impact areas of e-commerce, telecom, as well as fintech. It distills the most essential themes of cultural adaptation, scalability, ethical implications, and the balance between humans and AI to provide actionable recommendations to businesses looking to implement generative AI in new markets. Its core purpose is to empower organizations with a strategic guide for building customer loyalty in the presence of technological, cultural, and regulatory heterogeneity.

3.3.1. Key Components of the Conceptual Framework

The conceptual model is constructed on the basis of four pillars, each of which deals with a unique yet integrated aspect of the deployment of AI in customer retention.

Cultural adaptation is essential in countries where buying behavior, expectations, and communications diverge considerably. Language localization of the generative AI is necessary, as well as adaptation of how it understands purchasing behavior, values, and societal norms. This means aligning loyalty schemes to local purchasing behavior and gearing models sensitive to socio-economic conditions. But issues remain, ranging from language complexity to resistance to interacting through AI and concerns over built-in bias. Implementation therefore requires culturally sensitive design and ongoing feedback loops.

Scalability is critical to support the expansion of AI-driven customer engagement across geographies and infrastructure environments. Cloud platforms and model-based frameworks support flexible deployment while supporting the need for minimal infrastructure investment. However, scalability comes at the cost of integration complexity in existing systems, dealing with data protection vulnerabilities, and keeping cost considerations under tight budget constraints, especially for resource-constrained SMEs. (Aarabe et al., 2025)

Ethical considerations: Trust is a condition for the sustainable success of AI. The ethical deployment of AI thus needs to include transparency, accountability, and fairness. Local and global data policies need to be respected, and companies need to actively find and reduce algorithmic biases. They also need to address user distrust and level the playing field in solving the trade-offs between automation and human influence. (Alla et al., 2025)

Blending automation and human-touch strategies: Efficiency is where AI shines, yet customer loyalty and faith are frequently developed as a result of human connection. An equilibrium model that blends AI-driven efficiency and moments of human interaction is essential. Hybrid schemes that rely on using AI for low-level complexity tasks (e.g., automated order tracking through chatbots) but continue to provide humans as escalation options for sensitive or complex cases are a key strategy. Having smooth passage between humans and AI agents, educating staff on working alongside AI, and engineering systems that augment rather than replace human touchpoints are all aspects of this equilibrium. (Aarabe et al., 2024).

3.3.2. Conceptual Framework Model

The following figure depicts the suggested model, which connects every aspect cultural adaptation, scalability, ethical issues, and the human-AI balance to each other in a dynamic system that sustains customer retention in emerging markets.

Figure 6. Conceptual framework model

Source: Authors

Actionable steps for businesses: According to the framework that was developed, businesses may implement the following steps on Table 8 to maximize their customer retention strategies using AI:

Table 8. Actionable guidelines for businesses

Framework component	Strategic guideline	Source
Cultural adaptation	Localizing loyalty programs according to regional traditions	Orozco & Welin, 2024
Scalability	Implement cloud-based AI for dynamic scaling	Patil et al., 2024
Ethical concerns	Ensure fair and data privacy laws compliance	Kumar et al., 2022
Human-AI balance	Establish hybrid models that feature human supervision	Storm Reply, 2024

Source: Authors

- **Case study integration into the framework**
    - **E-Commerce (Southeast Asia)**: Loyalty programs influenced by artificial intelligence that mirror local proclivities have recorded higher interaction and shopping behavior, highlighting cultural adaptation as critical (Maryam & Shanthi, 2023).
    - **Telecommunications (Africa)**: The drive of African telecommunications to implement successful cloud-based dynamic pricing schemes proves the capability of scalable architecture in supporting the adoption of AI in environments of infrastructure shortage (Abdulsalam & Tajudeen, 2024).
    - **Fintech (Latin America)**: Fin-tech tools enabled by AI that emphasize transparency and conformity to rules show how ethical concerns drive adoption and confidence (Katterbauer & Schmidt, 2024).
- **Future research directions:** This model provides a number of potential directions for future inquiry:
    - **Explainable Artificial Intelligence (XAI):** Examining how user trust and decision-making are influenced by explainability, especially in sensitive domains such as finance and healthcare.
    - **Quantitative impact analysis**: Examining the direct relationship between loyalty strategies implemented by means of AI and financial performance metrics, particularly in SMEs.
    - **Cross-industry comparisons**: Analyzing how generative AI adoption trends vary across sectors in emerging markets in order to find best practices and common barriers.

Figure 7. Analysis model sketch for understanding the impact of Generative AI on customer retention in emerging markets

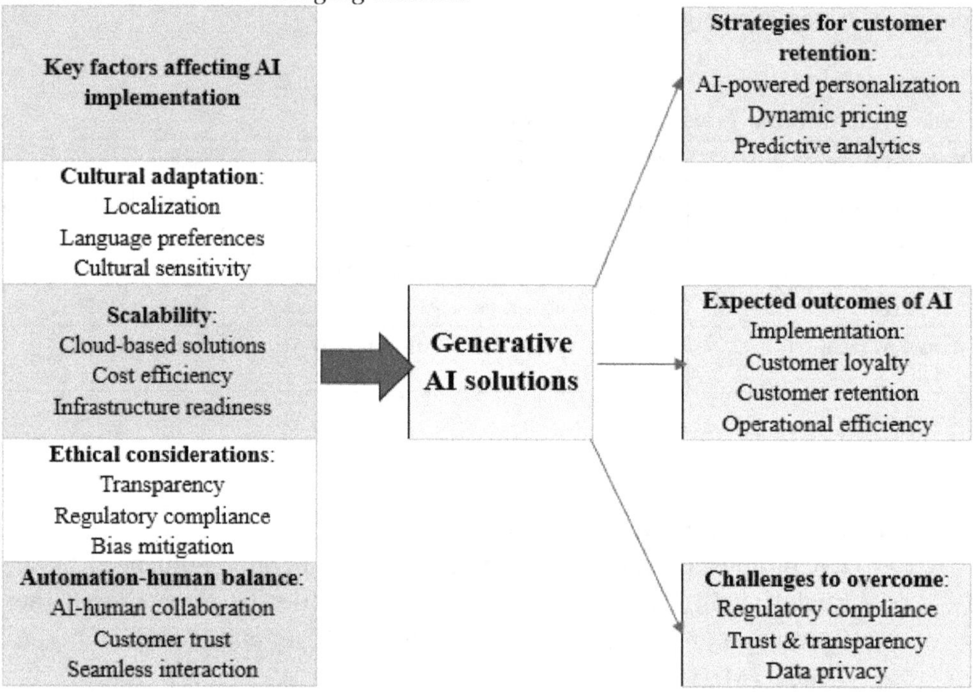

Source: Authors

The model that is created in this chapter focuses on the key parameters that drive successful customer retention using generative AI in emerging markets. Personalization engines, automated services, and predictive analytics that leverage AI are identified as key drivers of valuable customer interaction and loyalty over the long term. (Ahmed & Ali, 2024; Maryam & Shanthi, 2023).

- **Cultural adaptation:** Localization continues to be the cornerstone of the efficacy of AI across diverse markets. To gain customer confidence and encourage lasting interaction, AI systems need to be attuned to local language, communication modes, and patterns of consumption. Localization of models to follow local inclinations and sensitivities not only spurs relevance but also minimizes the risk of cultural disalignment. However, the strategy is encumbered by resistance to automated technologies and by regulatory complications that change from one environment to another. (Orozco & Welin, 2024; Patil et al., 2024).
- **Scalability:** is also critical for deployment of AI across geographies that differ in terms of their level of technological maturity. Cloud-based infrastruc-

tures and AI architectures that are made of modules are flexible and cost-efficient means by which solutions can be scaled across markets. They are especially of value in environments where infrastructure investments are still constrained. Still, companies need to contend with issues related to integration with legacy systems, cost, and data protection concerns that can impede easy deployment (Shahabikargar et al., 2024; Kumar et al., 2022).

- **Ethical implications:** Transparency and compliance go hand in hand with the ethical application of AI. Proper implementation means making decisions in clear fashion, compliance with data protection provisions, and proactive prevention of algorithmic prejudice. These actions are essential to promoting confidence among users in automated systems. In spite of this, concerns of persistent data vulnerabilities, model interpretability, and fairness underscore the necessity of ongoing ethical awareness (Naslednikov, 2024; Katterbauer et al., 2024).
- **Human-AI balance:** Finding the balance between automation and the presence of humans is becoming a strategic necessity. Although AI is well-equipped to deal with routine tasks and raise efficiency, there is a need for humans to oversee intricate, sensitive, or high-value dynamics. Companies that implement hybrid systems that integrate the capabilities of AI and the presence of humans are well-placed to provide empathetic and reliable customer experience (Arnese, 2023; Mazumder, 2023).

Strategic implications: Several of the strategies empowered by AI—all of which involve individualized recommendations, dynamic pricing strategies, and attrition forecasting tools—have proven useful for customer satisfaction retention and attrition minimization. But one of the biggest hindrances is still measuring the long-term impact. To gauge the full value of customer retention using AI, companies need to establish strong key performance indicators (KPIs) and align them with overall strategic goals (Potla, 2024; Master of Code Global, 2024).

In spite of the obvious benefits, mass deployment of AI in emerging markets also comes across several impediments, including uncertain regulation, data protection issues, and consumers' lack of confidence. Companies need to react by introducing proactive methods that prioritize transparency, customer awareness, and humanizing the AI system (Kumar et al., 2022; Mohamed, 2024).

In brief, companies in emerging markets can realize the full potential of generative AI by putting cultural relevance, scalable infrastructure, ethical governance, and well-balanced automation front and center in their strategies. Having a localized and hybrid strategy will be essential in establishing trust, ensuring compliance, and securing sustainable customer retention in the long term. (Rane et al., 2023).

3.4. Conclusion and perspectives

This paper examined the potential of generative AI to revolutionize customer loyalty and retention strategies in emerging market environments. Through a systematic literature synthesis and cross-industrial case analyses, it was found that AI technologies, especially those that support customization, automation of operations, and predictive capabilities, have ample potential to increase customer engagement. However, deployment of these technologies needs to navigate structural and contextual issues of cultural adjustment, scalability, ethical considerations, and the fine balance between automation and person-to-person contact. (Ahmed & Ali, 2024; Orozco & Welin, 2024).

Whereas generative AI promises never-before-available opportunities for the delivery of ultra-personalized experience and the streamlining of decision-making processes, successful deployment is predicated on the resolution of regulatory hurdles, data protection issues, and the need for transparent and ethical AI procedures. Customer retention over the longer term will be contingent upon how well businesses are able to marry technological innovation and people-focused strategies. (Kumar et al., 2022; Patil et al., 2024).

3.4.1. Managerial Contributions

From a managerial perspective, this study offers a list of actionable recommendations that can be used to guide strategic incorporation of AI into customer retention strategies:

- **Personalized experience amplification**: Generative AI can be utilized by managers to build customized experience that precedes and addresses customer demands, enhancing satisfaction and lasting loyalty. (Maryam & Shanthi, 2023).
- **Operational efficiency**: Performing repetitive tasks like customer support communications and product suggestions, AI can slash expenses and enhance the quality of service. Managers ought to give top priority to using AI in operational sectors where speed and responsiveness are essential (Storm Reply, 2024).
- **Decision-making using data**: Artificial intelligence provides instant insights that enable improved forecasting, optimal allocation of resources, and focused marketing strategies (Mazumder, 2023).
- **Scalability in market expansion**: Cloud-based technologies enable businesses to enter new markets without significant infrastructure investment, supporting agility and cost-saving (Shahabikargar et al., 2024).

- **Cultural relevance**: Managers need to make certain that AI systems embody the values, language, and conduct of the markets of interest in order to establish resonance and confidence by various segments of consumers (Orozco & Welin, 2024).

3.4.2. Limitations and Future Directions

While the research is significant in elucidating the role of AI in customer retention, it also identifies several limitations that provide productive avenues for future research:

- **Geographic scope**: Southeast Asia, Africa, and Latin America are the regions of interest in the study. Future studies may include previously unexamined regions of Eastern Europe, Central Asia, and the Middle East (Ahmed & Ali, 2024).
- **Reliability of data**: Relying on secondary data involves the risk of bias. Collecting primary data using interviews, questionnaires, and field observation would increase strength and contextual relevance (Patil et al., 2024).
- **Regulatory complexity**: Harmonized AI governance frameworks are absent, making it difficult to comply. Future inquiry needs to examine models for cross-border, standardized AI regulation (Kumar et al., 2022).
- **Technological readiness**: Not every emerging market is ready for AI deployment. Comparative analysis may classify markets by level of maturity and infrastructure hindrances (Naslednikov, 2024).
- **Incorporating new technologies**: Integrating AI with blockchain, IoT, and the metaverse would open fresh viewpoints on how AI would change the customer engagement and retention landscape (Rane et al., 2023).

3.4.3. Future Perspectives

In the future, various emerging trends are likely to influence the course of AI-based customer interaction strategies:

o **Expanding the use of engagement tools**: Use of AI chatbots, recommendation engines, and virtual assistants will intensify, fueled by progressively better behavioral analytics that allow for real-time responsiveness (Maryam & Shanthi, 2023).

o **Interoperability between technologies:** Integrating AI with IoT and blockchain technologies will enable businesses to provide frictionless, secure, and smart customer experiences—e.g., in predictive maintenance or automated service fulfillment (Naslednikov, 2024).

- **Ethical use of AI:** Public pressure will require companies to invest in clear and accountable AI systems alongside internal controls addressing fairness, explainability, and adherence (Katterbauer et al., 2024).
- **Deeper localization:** More subtle linguistic and cultural awareness will be built into future AI systems that are trained on localized data to provide better contextual appropriateness and acceptance (Orozco & Welin, 2024).
- **Hybrid collaboration between humans and AI:** Future customer engagement will be hybrid and will marry the efficiency of AI with the empathy of humans in order to maintain trust in complex transactions (Arnese, 2023).
- **Data protection and cyber security enhancements:** Compliance with increasingly stringent data regulations and customer demands will demand robust security features such as data anonymization, encryption of data, as well as privacy by design AI (Kumar et al., 2022).
- **Predictive retention strategies**: predictive analytics based on AI will be instrumental in driving proactive detection of probable to churn customers as well as tailoring intervention in response (Patil et al., 2024).

CONCLUSION

In this paper, the strategic use of generative artificial intelligence (AI) for customer loyalty creation and retention in the environments of emerging markets was discussed. This research, based on an amalgamation of theoretical foundation, systematic literature review, as well as comparative case analysis, delivers multidimensional analysis on how businesses can leverage AI for redefining customer interactions in technologically heterogenic, economically dynamic, as well as culturally heterogenic settings. The results reinforce that AI-driven personalization, predictive analysis, and automation of operations are no longer discretionary innovations - rather, these are new necessities for businesses that wish to stay ahead of the game and keep pace with new customer expectations. In countries where disparities in infrastructure and laws exist, the strength of generative AI is in how it can tailor, amplify, and customize to previously unimaginable degrees. Yet, the research also emphasizes that technological advancements alone are not enough. It requires the infusion of human-oriented values, ethical leadership, and local cultural salience in AI design and deployment. Data privacy, fairness, explainability, and collaboration between humans and AI have to be managed as core principles and not as afterthoughts. Managerially, the study offers actionable recommendations to organizations that seek to implement generative AI responsibly: investment in culturally responsive models, the creation of hybrid engagement systems, ensuring regulatory alignments, and aligning the application of AI with strategic business outcomes. For policymakers and researchers, the study alerts them to the imperative of cross-industry collaboration, interoperable AI platforms, and inclusive AI literacy programs to ensure even-footing in adoption and benefits. To sum it all, generative AI holds the potential to be a game-changing opportunity for businesses in emerging markets to reimagine how they understand, serve, and keep their customers. Its full potential can be achieved, though, only if done in foresight, in responsibility, and in regard to the customer relationship's humanity. As digital ecosystems keep unfolding, organizations that aspire to a balanced, ethical, and responsive approach in the deployment of AI will prove best positioned to build lasting value both among their customers and among the communities served.

REFERENCES

Aarabe, M., Bouizgar, M., Khizzou, N. B., Alla, L., & Benjelloun, A. (2025). The Transformative Impact of Artificial Intelligence on Tourism Experience: Analysis of Trends and Perspectives. AI Technologies for Personalized and Sustainable Tourism, 277-310.

Aarabe, M., Bouizgar, M., Khizzou, N. B., Alla, L., & Benjelloun, A. (2025). Technology-Driven and Personality in the Travel Experience Within a Destination: Literature Review and Proposal for Analysis Model. Adapting to Evolving Consumer Experiences in Hospitality and Tourism, 267-300.

Aarabe, M., Khizzou, N. B., Alla, L., & Benjelloun, A. (2024). Marketing applications of emerging technologies: A systematic literature review. In *AI and data engineering solutions for effective marketing* (pp. 23–47). IGI Global. DOI: 10.4018/979-8-3693-3172-9.ch002

Aarabe, M., Khizzou, N. B., Alla, L., & Benjelloun, A. (2024). Smart Tourism Experience and Responsible Travelers' Behavior: A Systematic Literature Review. Promoting responsible tourism with digital platforms, 128-147.

Aarabe, M., Khizzou, N. B., Alla, L., & Benjelloun, A. (2025). Marketing Applications of Emerging Technologies and Business Performance of Tourism SMEs: A Systematic Literature Review. Models, Strategies, and Tools for Competitive SMEs, 217-242.

Abdulsalam, T., & Tajudeen, R. (2024). Artificial Intelligence (AI) In The Banking Industry: A Review Of Service Areas And Customer Service Journeys In Developing Economies. Business & Management Compass. Volume: 68 (2024), Issue: 3. DOI: , pp. 19-43DOI: 10.56065/9hfvrq20

Ahmed, A. A., & Ali, M. K. (2024). User-Centric Adoption of Democratized Generative AI: Focus on Human-Machine Interaction and Overcoming Challenges. *International Journal of Engineering Trends and Technology*, *72*(9), 78–95.

Akan, T., & Bhattacharjee, S. (2024). *Generative AI and economic growth in developing nations: The Bangladesh case study*. ResearchGate.

Alla, L., Bouhtati, N., Aarabe, M., & Khizzou, N. B. (2025). Social Media Analytics for Effective Customer Brand Engagement Assessment: A Theoretical Exploration. In *Leveraging AI for Effective Digital Relationship Marketing* (pp. 385-418). IGI Global.

Androniceanu, A. (2024). Generative artificial intelligence, present and perspectives in public administration. Administration & Public Management Review, 43.

Aqrabawi, R.. (2024). The Impact of AI-Driven Consumer Insights on Targeted Marketing and Customer Retention Strategies. *Pakistan Journal of Life and Social Sciences*, *22*(2), 13733–13738. DOI: 10.57239/PJLSS-2024-22.2.00986

Arnese, N. (2023). *Unlocking Loyalty in the AI Era: How Generative AI is Redefining Customer Retention*. LinkedIn Journal.

Babatunde, A. (2024). Driving Innovation Through Ai And Machine Learning: Exploring The Opportunities Of Integrating Artificial Intelligence In Business Intelligence. Academic Journal Of Global Who Is Who In Academia, Vol. 5 No1, April 2024. New York City.

Berry, L. L. (1983). Relationship Marketing. In Berry, L. L., Shostack, G. L., & Upala, G. D. (Eds.), *Emerging Perspectives on Services Marketing* (pp. 25–80). American Marketing Association.

Bouizgar, M., Aarabe, M., Khizzou, N. B., Alla, L., & Benjelloun, A. (2025). Smart Territorial Marketing and Promotion of Customer Engagement Towards the Territorial Brand: A Systematic Review of Literature. *Sustainable and Intelligent Territorial Marketing and Entrepreneurship*, 129-158.

Bouizgar, M., Aarabe, M., Khizzou, N. B., Alla, L., & Benjelloun, A. (2025). AI and Digital Technologies for Transforming Territorial Branding Management: A Systematic Review. *Corporate Management in the Digital Age*, 35-68.

Brynjolfsson, E., & McAfee, A. (2022). The business of artificial intelligence: How AI creates new value. [URL: https://hbr.org/2022/07/the-business-of-artificial-intelligence]. *Harvard Business Review*, *100*(4), 58–67.

Cruces, G. A., Amarante, V., & Lotitto, E. (2024). *Generative artificial intelligence and its implications for labor markets in developing countries: A review essay*. Universidad Nacional de La Plata.

Davenport, T., Guha, A., Grewal, D., & Bressgott, T. (2023). Generative AI for customer engagement: Opportunities and challenges. [DOI: 10.1016/j.jbusres.2023.113760]. *Journal of Business Research*, *160*, 113760.

Davis, F. D. (1989). Perceived Usefulness, Perceived Ease of Use, and User Acceptance of Information Technology. *Management Information Systems Quarterly*, *13*(3), 319. DOI: 10.2307/249008

Deloitte. (2024). *Generative AI: Unlocking the power of Technology*. Media and Telecommunications in APAC.

Ed-Daakouri, I., Bouhtati, N., & Alla, L. (2025). *Smart Data Analytics for Efficient Mapping of Customers' Online Shopping Behavior: A Systematic Review of the Literature*. IGI Global., DOI: 10.4018/979-8-3693-7545-7.ch010

Ghaffari, S., Yousefimehr, B., & Ghatee, M. (2024, February). Generative-AI in e-Commerce: Use-cases and Implementations. In 2024 20th CSI International Symposium on Artificial Intelligence and Signal Processing (AISP) (pp. 1-5). IEEE.

GSMA. (2022). The Mobile Economy 2022. Retrieved from www.gsma.com

Gupta, R., Nair, K., Mishra, M., & Ibrahim, B. (2024). Adoption and impacts of generative artificial intelligence: Theoretical underpinnings and research agenda. International Journal of Information Management, Elsevier.

Gupta, R., Nair, K., Mishra, M., Ibrahim, B., & Bhardwaj, S. (2024, April). Adoption and impacts of generative artificial intelligence: Theoretical underpinnings and research agenda. *International Journal of Information Management Data Insights*, *4*(1), 100232. DOI: 10.1016/j.jjimei.2024.100232

Hasan, M. (2024). *Regulating artificial intelligence: A study in the comparison between South Asia and other countries*. Legal Issues in the Digital Age. CyberLeninka.

Heimberger, H., Horvat, D., & Schultmann, F. (2024). Exploring the factors driving AI adoption in production: A systematic literature review and future research agenda. *Information Technology and Management*. Advance online publication. DOI: 10.1007/s10799-024-00436-z

Hemachandran K et al. (2025). Predictive Analytics and Generative AI for Data-Driven Marketing Strategies. DOI: 10.1201/9781003472544

Hofstede, G. (1980). *Culture's Consequences: International Differences in Work-Related Values*. Sage Publications.

Holger Harreis et al. (2023). *Generative AI: Unlocking the future of fashion*. McKinsey & Company.

Hossain, F., Ahmed, G. M. S., Shuvo, S. P. P., Kona, A. N., Raina, M. U. H., & Shikder, F. (2024). Unlocking artificial intelligence for strategic market development and business growth: Innovations, opportunities, and future directions. *Edelweiss Applied Science and Technology*, *8*(6), 5825–5846. DOI: 10.55214/25768484.v8i6.3263

Katterbauer, K., Syed, H., Cleenewerck, L., Özbay, R. D., & Yılmaz, S. (2024). Impact of Generative AI on FINTECH in Africa. *Yıldız Social Science Review*, *10*(1), 1–53. DOI: 10.51803/yssr.1440501

Kumar, A., et al. (2022). Enhancing Roi Through Ai Powered Customer Interaction Models. International Journal of Applied Mathematics & Statistical Sciences (IJAMSS). ISSN (P): 2319–3972; ISSN (E): 2319–3980. Vol. 11, Issue 1, Jan–Jun 2022; 79–106

Kumar, V., Kotler, P., Gupta, S., & Rajan, B. (2024). Generative AI in Marketing: Promises, Perils, and Public Policy Implications. *Journal of Public Policy & Marketing*, •••, 1–23. DOI: 10.1177/07439156241286499

Lemon, K. N., & Verhoef, P. C. (2016). Understanding customer experience throughout the customer journey. [DOI: 10.1509/jm.15.0420]. *Journal of Marketing*, *80*(6), 69–96. DOI: 10.1509/jm.15.0420

Madanchian, M. (2024). Generative AI for Consumer Behavior Prediction: Techniques and Applications. *Sustainability (Basel)*, *16*(22), 9963. DOI: 10.3390/su16229963

Maryam, H., & Shanthi, V. (2023). Unlocking Customer Engagement Through Strategic Content Marketing. Tuijin Jishu/Journal of Propulsion Technology. ISSN: 1001-4055. Vol. 44 No. 3 (2023)

Maryam, S., (2024). Generative AI-enabled Knowledge Base Fine-tuning: Enhancing Feature Engineering for Customer Churn. DOI: DOI: 10.21203/rs.3.rs-3823738/v1

Master of Code Global. (2024). *The Finance Leader's Handbook to Generative AI: Solutions*. Insights, and Impact. Master of Code Global.

Mazumder, R. (2023). *Application of Generative AI in Big Data Visualization for Enhancing International Business Decision-Making. Final Projects. Spring 2023. International Business*. Oulu University of Applied Sciences.

Mohamed, O. A. M. (2023). How generative AI transforming supply chain operations and efficiency?.

Murungu, E. (2024). Generative AI and trade in Africa: Opportunities and challenges. International Journal of Sustainable Development. *SSRN*.

Mutanga et al. (2024). Adoption and impact of generative ai: perspectives from south african tech entrepreneurs. journal Business & IT, ISSN 2570-7434, Creative Commons license published by CTU in Prague, 2024, https://bit.fsv.cvut.cz/

Nadeem, M. (2024). Generative artificial intelligence [GAI]: Enhancing future marketing strategies with emotional intelligence [EI], and social skills. *British Journal of Marketing Studies*, *12*(1), 1–15.

Naslednikov, M. (2024). The Impact of Artificial Intelligence on Customer Relationship Management (CRM) Strategies. Haaga-Helia University of Applied Sciences, Degree in Business Information Technology, Bachelor Thesis.

Nouhaila, B. K., Aarabe, M., & Alla, L. (2024). The impact of digitalisation on the customer experience in medical tourism: A systematic review. Impact of AI and tech-driven solutions in hospitality and tourism, 408-428.

Ogunseye, S., Aljanaideh, A., & Murungi, D. (2024). *Comparative advantage in the AI era: Leveraging generative AI for global competitiveness*. ResearchGate.

Ohenhen, P. E., Aderibigbe, A. O., & Nwaobia, N. K. (2023). Artificial intelligence in developing countries: Bridging the gap between potential and implementation. Academia.edu.

Orozco, J., & Olga, W. (2024). What drives European organizations to invest in Generative AI, and what challenges do they face in 2023-2024? www.bth.se/mba. DEPARTMENT OF INDUSTRIAL ECONOMICS

Patil, D., Rane, N. L., & Rane, J. (2024). The future of customer loyalty: How ChatGPT and generative artificial intelligence are transforming customer engagement, personalization, and satisfaction. In *The Future Impact of ChatGPT on Several Business Sectors* (pp. 48–106). Deep Science Publishing., DOI: 10.70593/978-81-981367-8-7_2

Potla, R. T. (2024). Leveraging Generative AI for Enhanced Customer Relationship Management: Transforming Customer Interactions and Personalization in CRM Systems.

Rane, N. (2023). Enhancing Customer Loyalty through Artificial Intelligence (AI), Internet of Things (IoT), and Big Data Technologies: Improving Customer Satisfaction, Engagement, Relationship, and Experience. DOI: 10.2139/ssrn.4616051

Rane, N., Choudhary, S., & Rane, J. (2023) Hyper-personalization for enhancing customer loyalty and satisfaction in Customer Relationship Management (CRM) systems. DOI: 10.2139/ssrn.4641044

Rane, N., Choudhary, S., & Rane, J. (2023) Metaverse for Enhancing Customer Loyalty: Effective Strategies to Improve Customer Relationship, Service, Engagement, Satisfaction, and Experience. DOI: 10.2139/ssrn.4624197

Rust, R. T., & Huang, M. H. (2021). The AI revolution: The role of artificial intelligence in marketing. [DOI: 10.1007/s11747-020-00748-9]. *Journal of the Academy of Marketing Science*, *49*(1), 24–42.

Sarioguz, O.. (2024). AI-powered business model innovation: Analyzing the implications of generative AI on value creation, operational efficiency and market dynamics. *World Journal of Advanced Engineering Technology and Sciences*, *13*(02), 216–229.

Smith, A., & Hutson, J. (2024). From concept to creation: The role of generative artificial intelligence in the new age of digital marketing. *Design*, *1*(1), 4776. DOI: 10.36922/dp.4776

Storm Reply. (2024). Unlock Real Value With Generative Ai. Increase revenue. Decrease costs. Attract and retain customers.

APPENDICES A

Table A1. Description of the reviewed references

Reference	Year	Literature review	Qualitative study	Quantitative study	Exploratory study	Confirmatory study	Prospective study
Mutanga et al.	2024	X					
Aslam	2024		X		X		
Sarioguz & Miser	2024	X					X
Mazumder	2023		X				
Abdulsalam & Tajudeen	2024	X				X	
Kumar et al.	2022		X	X			
Rane	2023		X				
Shahabikargar et al.	2024	X			X		
Ahmed & Ali	2024		X			X	
Orozco & Welin	2024	X				X	X
Naslednikov	2024		X				
Arnese	2023	X					
Hossain et al.	2024		X				
Maryam & Shanthi	2023	X					
Rane et al.	2023		X				
Patil et al.	2024	X		X			
Master of Code Global	2024		X				
Storm Reply	2024	X					
McKinsey	2023		X				
Nadeem	2024	X					
Babatunde	2024		X				
Mohamed	2024		X				X
Potla	2024		X	X			
Rane et al	2023			X			
Katterbauer et al.	2024		X				
Hemachandran et al.	2025	X					
Rane et al.	2023		X				
Orozco & Welin	2024	X					
Patil et al.	2024		X				
Mohamed	2024		X				

Table A2. Qualitative analysis table

Reference	Qualitative analysis	Impact on customer loyalty and retention	Key findings	Challenges identified	Opportunities	Recommendations
Abdulsalam & Tajudeen, 2024	Artificial intelligence is revolutionizing customer experience in emerging markets by automating and customizing	Trust and investment in financial services increase with AI-driven solutions	Artificial intelligence boosts operational efficiency and customer experience.	Regulatory issues and public distrust	Personalized financial counseling, enhanced financial inclusion.	Investing in safe AI platforms and AI literacy initiatives
Ahmed & Ali, 2024	The research examines democratized generative AI adoption in view of improving human-machine interaction	AI allows for hyper-personalized experiences and enhances customer retention	AI provides user experience by automating and individualizing tasks	Privacy and ethical considerations, legal frameworks.	Scalabilities and increased market penetration	Prioritize AI literacy and ethically sound AI practices
Arnese, 2023	Artificial intelligence remakes retail loyalty programs by making them customer-specific	Personalized incentives and customized experiences drive customer retention	AI maximizes customer awareness by analyzing behavior.	Decreasing enrollments in conventional programs and data issues	AI-enabled predictive loyalty programs	Concentrate on integrated AI-enabled customer loyalty platforms
Aslam, 2024	Artificial intelligence business strategies for small businesses concentrate on sustainable growth, business efficiency, and greater customer engagement	Artificial intelligence-driven personalization and predictive marketing encourage stronger customer relationships	AI enables data-driven decision-making, lessening the dependence on intuition	High expense, inexperience, and concerns over data privacy.	More efficient operation, enhanced customer experience.	Invest in scalable machine learning solutions and employee skills development
Babatunde, 2024	Artificial intelligence and machine learning facilitate business innovation by improving operational efficiency.	Artificially intelligent analytics customize customer paths and increase engagement	AI streamlines repetitive tasks and maximizes resource utilization.	Excessive cost and shortage of skilled labor	AI-driven strategic decision-making	Invest in upgrading skills through AI-driven programs.
Deloitte, 2024	This paper investigates how the application of generative AI can change the technology, media, and telecommunications (TMT) industries in the Asia-Pacific (APAC) region	It addresses trends in AI adoption, investment, and how automation driven by AI affects business processes	Generative AI maximizes customer engagement by using personalized content, automated customer support, and predictive analysis, which result in higher loyalty and long-term retention.	Artificial intelligence is revolutionizing operational efficiencies in the TMT sectors, across many opportunities in customer interactions, content creation, and strategic decision-making	Barriers encompass regulatory compliance, intellectual property issues, data security risks, and the requirement of human supervision in AI-driven processes	The fast digital transformation across the APAC region creates opportunities for automated customer support processes, language localisation, and AI-based content creation
Hemachandran et al., 2025	Firms need to prioritize ethical deployment of AI, invest in compliance solutions, and use AI tools to boost operational efficiencies and customer experience	Artificial intelligence-infused predictive analytics refine marketing strategies for improved ROI	Personalized marketing maximizes customer experience and retention	AI allows marketing based on real-time data.	Algorithmic prejudice and data protection issues	Deploying AI-enabled customer journey maps. Give importance to AI explainability and ethical standards
Hossain et al., 2024	Artificial intelligence powers business growth and strategic market development.	Marketing using AI boosts customer retention	AI automates decision-making functions	Ethical and regulatory issues.	Market extension using AI	Guarantee alignment to AI frameworks
Katterbauer et al., 2024	Generative AI revolutionizes African fintech businesses by promoting financial inclusion	Personalized, AI-based financial services increase customer retention and confidence	AI unites conventional banking and digital finance.	Regulatory and infrastructure hurdles	Artificial intelligence-enabled micro-lending and financial advisory solutions	Enhance AI regulation conformity and data protection policies

continued on following page

Table A2. Continued

Reference	Qualitative analysis	Impact on customer loyalty and retention	Key findings	Challenges identified	Opportunities	Recommendations
Kumar et al., 2022	Artificial intelligence-driven customer interaction models drive ROI by streamlining service processes, customizing customer experiences, and enhancing operational efficiency	Personalized experiences through AI build closer customer ties and boost customer retention	Artificial intelligence boosts operational efficiency and sales conversion	Data privacy issues, complexity of integration	Deploying AI solutions to support customer service automation and improving interactions	Align AI projects to business goals and maintain ethical methods.
Kumar et al., 2024	This paper analyzes the hopes and risks of marketing's use of generative AI (GAI), conceptualizing a structuring framework that connects business activities to societal effects. It investigates the potential of AI to automate content generation, customization, and customer interaction, as well as the ethical issues and public policy considerations	Generative AI transforms customer experience through the delivery of customized content, predictive insights, and automated replies that lead to better customer loyalty and retention	GAI revolutionizes marketing strategies by promoting hyper-personalisation, automation, and dynamic customer interaction, helping businesses gain improved customer engagement and operational efficiency	Ethical considerations, data protection concerns, regulatory complications, and the call for human control in AI-created advertising content.	Utilizing GAI to enable customer	Businesses need to build ethical frameworks, maintain regulatory compliance, and align human creativity and AI to increase customer engagement while minimizing risks.
Madanchian, 2024	This paper examines how generative AI methods, including GANs, VAEs, and transformers, can be used in predicting consumer behavior	They emphasize their function in synthesizing realistic data and supplying insights for customer retention, inventory management, and individualized marketing	Generative AI models boost customer interaction by providing for hyper-personalization, active targeting, and sentiment analysis, which translates to greater retention and satisfaction	Sequence-based models perform well in handling sequential data, returning real-time customer insights, whereas GANs and VAEs are well-suited for generating realistic data and forecasting churning and purchasing intentions	Challenges include data privacy concerns, the integration of AI models into business workflows, and their applicability in real-world scenarios	Generative AI holds potential to enhance individualized marketing strategies, optimize inventory management, and generate more in-depth customer insights in numerous industries
Maryam & Shanthi, 2023	Content marketing increases customer engagement.	Personalized content creates lasting relationships	Timely and relevant content drives engagement	Content Saturation and Quality Issues	Content Personalisation Powered by AI.	Prioritizing High-Quality
Master of Code Global, 2024	Generative AI optimizes the functioning of the finance industry by automating the processes and providing customized financial services	Personalized, AI-based financial advice builds credibility and lasting loyalty	Artificial intelligence-based automation lowers operational expenses and enhances fraud identification	Regulatory requirements and data protection issues.	Improved financial accessibility and customized investment products	Prioritize ethical deployment and compliance of AI.
Mazumder, 2023	Generative AI technologies augment international business decision-making using big data visualization	Better customer engagement	customer understanding result from improved data visualization	Artificial intelligence assists in breaking complex data sets into actionable intelligence.	Improved decision-making, customized customer strategies.	Invest in AI-based visualization tools and training
McKinsey, 2023	Artificial intelligence transforms the fashion sector by enabling customized shopping and virtual try-ons	Artificial intelligence-based recommendations boost customer satisfaction and brand loyalty	Reducing production cycles and streamlining supply chain management	Ethical issues of data usage and confidentiality.	Expanding digital fashion experience using AI	Enact strong data protection policies and ethical AI frameworks.

continued on following page

Table A2. Continued

Reference	Qualitative analysis	Impact on customer loyalty and retention	Key findings	Challenges identified	Opportunities	Recommendations
Mohamed, 2024	Artificial intelligence enhances supply chain management by improving demand forecasting and operational resilience	Enhanced supply chain efficiency leads to greater customer satisfaction and retention	AI enables proactive risk management in logistics.	Data quality issues and integration complexities	Cost savings through automation of supply chain using AI.	Prioritize workforce and data accuracy in AI adoption.
Mutanga et al., 2024	The research looks into how South African technology entrepreneurs are embracing generative AI to support content creation, design, application development, and customer experience	Businesses can make interactions more personalized and automate customer support through AI, resulting in heightened loyalty and satisfaction.	Generative AI enhances productivity and cost savings in both customer interactions and content creation	Quality and originality issues require human supervision.	Optimizing business procedures, better customer experience.	Balance artificial intelligence application with human imagination, invest in AI management frameworks.
Nadeem, 2024	The combination of emotional intelligence and AI maximizes marketing strategies by making interactions more human-like	Emotionally intelligent AI builds stronger customer relationships and engagement	AI empathy enhances brand perception and trust.	Ethical issues and prejudice in AI replies	Leveraging AI for emotionally engaging marketing campaigns.	Emphasizing ethical AI and striking a balance between automation and empathy.
Naslednikov, 2024	Artificial intelligence in CRM strategies boosts customer engagement and customization	AI-driven personalization strengthens loyalty	AI enhances organizational efficiency in CRM	Data governance and transparency concerns	Improved decision-making using AI insights	Align the AI to customer-oriented objectives.
Orozco & Welin, 2024	Analyzes adoption of AI in European organizations in terms of market growth and innovation	AI facilitates customer individualization and service delivery.	Artificial intelligence fuels innovation but poses regulatory hurdles.	Ethical considerations and data stewardship.	Enhanced customer experience and operational efficiency.	Invest in ethical and regulatory compliant frameworks in AI.
Patil et al., 2024	Generative AI revolutionizes customer service with chatbots and automation.	AI-driven customer interactions improve satisfaction and loyalty	Chatbots driven by machine learning ensure 24/7 support and instant issue-solving.	Balancing automation and human touch and ethical AI issues	Incorporating AI-based human support systems.	Achieve a balance between automation and human control.
Potla, 2024	Generative AI upgrades CRM systems by automating interactions and tailoring engagements	Artificial intelligence-based CRM builds better customer relationships and loyalty	AI enhances response time and customer experience.	Ethical issues and striking a balance between AI and human support.	AI-enabled predictive customer engagement	Implement ethical usage of AI and customer consent procedures.
Rane et al., 2023	Personalization in CRM systems based on Artificial intelligence improved customer experience	Personalized interactions using AI build long-term customer relationships.	Real-time personalization results in greater customer engagement.	Data Integration Challenges and Privacy Issues	Utilizing Artificial Intelligence for omnichannel personalization	Invest in ethical AI practices and secure data infrastructure.
Rane et al., 2023	This study examines how the metaverse can be utilized to enhance customer loyalty through immersive virtual experiences, gamification, and personalized customer interactions	It illustrates how these three technologies - AI, VR, and AR - combine to create engaging virtual settings in the development of customer relationships.	Leading to higher customer loyalty and building customer confidence.	Companies can create virtual shops, organize product showcases, and offer interactive experiences to increase customer satisfaction in the metaverse.	Data privacy concerns, the difficulty of integrating these technologies, high upfront costs for infrastructure, and the need for compliance in virtual environments	Through the metaverse, businesses can leverage their digital presence, enhance customer experience, and provide personalized experiences with the power of AI.

continued on following page

Table A2. Continued

Reference	Qualitative analysis	Impact on customer loyalty and retention	Key findings	Challenges identified	Opportunities	Recommendations
Rane, 2023	The analysis looks at how customer loyalty can be improved by enhancing satisfaction, engagement, relationships, and experience using technologies of Big Data, IoT, and AI.	It examines how these technologies are integrated to provide a seamless and data-driven customer experience.	Personalized experience, proactive engagement, and data-driven insights allow businesses to better meet customer expectations and drive greater loyalty and retention	The convergence of AI, IoT, and Big Data allows organizations to collect real-time customer data, streamline processes, and design solutions that are tailored to meet customer needs in a better way to increase customer satisfaction and loyalty.	Incorporating customer service enabled by AI, IoT-enabled customized experience, and Big Data analytics can give companies a competitive edge as well as better customer experience overall	They should invest in strong data protection capabilities, emphasize ethical use of AI, and increase customer interaction strategies using individualized AI-based insights.
Sarioguz & Miser, 2024	Generative AI transforms business models through greater value creation, operational optimization, and market competitiveness	Businesses can provide hyper-personalized experiences and optimize customer interactions using AI.	Artificial intelligence amplifies decision-making, creativity, and business model agility.	Ethical considerations, cost of implementing	Content creation automation, better customer insights.	Practice ethical use of AI, invest in data protection.
Shahabikargar et al., 2024	Generative AI-driven knowledge bases boost customer churn prediction feature engineering.	AI assists companies in recognizing early signs of churn by reviewing customer communication.	Artificial intelligence-based feature engineering enhances predictability in churning	Privacy concerns and integration issues.	Real-time opportunities for churn detection by means of AI-driven feature engineering	Interweave AI with human experience to guarantee ethical application of AI
Smith & Hutson, 2024	This article discusses how digital marketing is revolutionized by generative AI by making content creation democratized, enhancing audience involvement, and automating creative processes.	The study cites tools in AI that facilitate personalized branding, targeted marketing, and real-time analysis.	Personalized content by AI and predictive analysis enable companies to provide customized marketing campaigns.	Barriers to high-quality-content creation are reduced by AI,	enabling small companies to level the playing field with larger corporations through branded automation and audience segmentation.	leading to greater involvement and lasting customer loyalty
Storm Reply, 2024	The research highlights AI's role in delivering tangible business value by enhancing revenue, reducing costs, and improving customer engagement.	AI personalization significantly boosts satisfaction and retention metrics.	AI optimizes supply chains and marketing through predictive analytics.	Resistance to adoption and technical integration barriers.	Accelerated growth through data-driven, scalable solutions.	Invest in flexible AI infrastructure and equip teams with AI knowledge and training.

Chapter 5
Customer Journey Mapping Effect on Omni Channel Optimization by Mediation of Real-Time Personalization of Contact Points in Eastern Africa

Metasebia Adula
https://orcid.org/0000-0001-5732-2850
Bule Hora University, Ethiopia

Shashi Kant
https://orcid.org/0000-0003-4722-5736
Bule Hora University, Ethiopia

ABSTRACT

This study investigates the effect of customer journey mapping on Omni channel optimization, mediated by real-time personalization of contact points in Eastern Africa. Study used a sample size of 390 respondents. To ensure the robustness of the data, the Kaiser-Meyer-Olkin (KMO) measure was utilized, confirming the adequacy of the sample for factor analysis. Exploratory Factor Analysis (EFA) was performed to uncover latent variables and refine the measurement model, followed by Confirmatory Factor Analysis (CFA) to validate the proposed constructs and their relationships. Structural Equation Modeling (SEM) was implemented using AMOS

DOI: 10.4018/979-8-3373-0918-7.ch005

software to explore the direct and mediated effects of customer journey mapping on Omni channel optimization through real-time personalization. Results indicate that effective customer journey mapping significantly enhances Omni channel optimization, with real-time personalization acting as a crucial mediator. The findings offers a valuable insights for businesses in Eastern Africa.

INTRODUCTION

In manifests interconnected market place, where e-commerce has redefined customer associations, the notion of mapping of journey of client and personalization of services in real-time of points of contacts has emerged as a vital viable plan for operational strategy to supply seamless omni-channel known-how's (Widjaja et al., 2023). This chapter examines into the influence of mapping of journey of client on optimization of omni-channels, specifically concentrating on how personalization of services in real-time of points of contacts mediates this association inside the perspective of Eastern part of Africa (Jabo et al., 2024). The functionalism of this investigation excels global market limits, dealing with operational market place wide that are routing the complexities of omni-channel marketing ((Xu & Cui, 2023). Manifesting how mapping of customer's nexus with personalization of services in real-time influences optimization of omni-channels journey is imperative in manifests viable market sphere where customer known-how is utmost (Gultekin & Erdem, 2020). The advent of mapping of journey of client can be outlined back to the early 1990s when operational started recognizing the need to understand and cater to the various touch-points a customer interacts with throughout their buying journey (Rizk et al., 2024). Personalization of services in real-time, on the other side, gained importance with the advent of advanced analytics and AI technologies, enabling operational to tailor associations in the moment (Gök, 2020). Empirical investigations have manifested the affirmative association among mapping of journey of client, personalization of services in real-time and augmented omni-channel sustainability (Widjaja et al., 2023). Also, investigation specific to Eastern part of Africa remains scarce, necessitating a focused exploration to bridge this gap (Jabo et al., 2025). Implementing influence mapping of journey of client and personalization of services in real-time strategies poses operational encounters for operational in Eastern part of Africa, containing partial access to information, technological innovation constraints, and varying customer preferences across dissected markets (Widjaja et al., 2023).

The existing literature lacks comprehensive insights into how the nexus among mapping of journey of client, personalization of services in real-time, along with optimization of omni-channels unfolds in the unique socio-economic market sphere of Eastern part of Africa. In addition, there is a lack of guidelines for operation specifically designed for operations in this area, which is coming in a deficiency of useful information over customers (Kant & Adula, 2025). This chapter seeks to fill these investigative gaps through a comprehensive investigation that clarifies the influence of visualization the journey of purchaser on the successful implementation of omni-channels. Additionally, it highlights the mediating role of immediate personalized service in shaping customer knowledge in the eastern region of Africa. The present investigation aims to provide a structured roadmap over operations as well investigations, including on customized manifested as well as plans from a global lens to enhance their respective positions omni-channel approaches.

Recent data emphasizes the landscape developing customer mapping and personalization in East Africa. For example, a 2024 survey, conducted by African development, has shown that 67% of consumers in Kenya prefer individual offers, which manifests an increasing demand for adapted experience (Rizk et al., 2024). In addition, the International Monetary Fund reported that Ethiopia's e-commerce expanded through 45% year after year, outcomes in improved digital infrastructure as well as customer approval of online purchase (Niguse et al., 2025). These developments are seen in firms like Kilimandjaro Coffee, whose used a tailored marketing approach founded on consumer feedback and boosted loyalty to customers around 30% (Widjaja et al., 2023). Likewise, a investigation found that including genuine information in Uganda enhanced labor productivity by 50% (Nadeem, 2024). Such empirical data demonstrates how imperative it is for East African businesses to adopt a client-focused strategy and supplement their estimation methodologies to satisfy the demands of a continually evolving customer base (Gök, 2020). The present investigation centers on a critical inquiry: ***"In what ways can operations in the eastern region of Africa utilize journey of purchaser mapping as well as personalization of services in real-time to enhance their a single channel of strategies and deliver superior customer insights in a progressively digital marketplace?"*** By exploring this question, we seek to clarify the complexities involved in optimizing omni-channels within a region marked by distinctive communications and possibilities, thereby laying the foundations for future investigation initiatives and policy actions.

From the viewpoint of Eastern Africa, where markets are swiftly transforming and e-commerce is on the rise, the integration of journey of purchaser mapping, personalization of services in real-time, along with optimization of omni-channel presents a substantial opportunity for operations to enhance customer engagement and foster growth (Rizk et al., 2024). It is essential for firms to articulate the specifics of these concepts within the global market context in order to remain competitive and address the changing demands of technology-oriented consumers (Jabo et al., 2025). A selling chain's expansion into Rwanda encountered challenges in synchronizing the mapping of the journey of purchaser with current personalization across its digital and physical channels. The limitations of internet innovation and the diverse levels of digital literacy within the population have obstructed the precise monitoring of customer touch-points and the delivery of tailored content in real-time (Gök, 2020). The retail chain successfully integrated offline touch-points, including in-store rewards systems and SMS notifications, to connect physical and digital communications. This strategy improved customer knowledge and contributed to increased earnings (Xu & Cui, 2023). In East Africa, corporates such as Safaricom in Kenya illustrate the operative mapping of customer trips and personalization in real time. The Safaricom M-Pesa service used customer data to adapt financial services, which manifests transparent transactions via various channels.

1. LITERATURE REVIEW

1.1. Justification of investigation

A comprehensive philosophical structure is crucial for analyzing maps of journey of purchasers and the intricate dynamics of personalized experience in order to enhance a single channel of strategies in East Africa. This investigation aligns with several established theories, notably customer association management theory, technology acceptance model, social exchange theory, along with data processing theory. The theory of CRM highlights the significance of developing enduring associations with clientele via tailored communications, aligning with immediate personalized goals (Gultekin & Erdem, 2020). Tam presents an insight into the influence of user technology adoption on the cooperativeness of strategies, highlighting the necessity for systems utilized by users that aid in the client assimilation. The theory of social communication provides insight into the reciprocal dynamics that characterize the associations across corporations as well as their customers (Abrudan et al., 2020). This indicates that the perceived benefits derived from intimate communications foster loyalty and dedication. Ultimately, information processing theory highlights the significance of efficiently managing information, enhancing decision-making alongside customer experience from a contextual perspective.

A telecom company in Uganda sought to enhance its omni-channel strategy by integrating personalization of services in real-time informed by insights from the journey of purchaser (Esmaili et al., 2022). The absence of a centralized system for handling data outcomes in the fragmentation of information across various platforms, hindering the company's capacity to provide personalized offers along with manifested in real-time (Widjaja et al., 2023). The telecom company enhanced its information processes by establishing a unified client information platform and utilizing AI algorithms, which facilitated personalized associations throughout channels as well as led to improved retention of consumers rates (Abrudan et al., 2020). A Kenyan e-commerce platform aimed to utilize journey of purchaser mapping to enhance its omni-channel expertise via personalization of services in real-time. Inconsistent methods for handling inventories alongside logistical challenges led to delays in order fulfillment and influenced the cooperativeness of specific product manifested (Nadeem, 2024). Through the integration of the management of inventory systems alongside customer information analytics, the e-commerce platform enhanced its supply chain operations, facilitating efficient order fulfillment and tailored shopping experiences for customers.

In light of the established theoretical framework, it is evident that substantial investigation holes persist within the existing literature. Initially, there is an absence of empirical investigations that concentrate on the eastern African its proper context, which restricts the relevance of current theories to local situations (Mousavi et al., 2021). While certain investigations have examined the mapping as well as personalization of global customers, their outcomes may not translate operatively to the distinct cultural, economic, and technological context of East Africa (Kokku, 2021). The presence of conflicting evidence in current investigations introduces ambiguity regarding the efficacy of these strategies, necessitating a more thorough exploration of the mechanisms that enable real-time mapping alongside personalization engage with one another. Operating problems encountered by corporations, including the fragmentation of data along with technological limitations, are frequently neglected in theoretical discussions, highlighting the disparity among theoretical frameworks and practical applications (Rizk et al., 2024). Furthermore, the influence of different cultures and the constraints of innovation in East Africa pose further challenges that have not been adequately addressed in existing literature (Nadeem, 2024). The behavior and expectations of consumers can be substantially shaped by these elements, rendering the traditional framework less operative (Niguse et al., 2025). This investigation seeks to synthesize existing investigation while addressing its shortcomings, thereby providing a clearer understanding of the structure of the competition in the area in question. This analysis will explore the adaptation of theoretical frameworks to align with the realities of Eastern African markets, and ultimately offer actionable insights for practitioners. This thorough approach will enhance theoretical discussions and inform operational strategies tailored to accommodate the unique requirements of businesses in East Africa, leading to improved auxiliary outcomes as well customer experiences.

1.2. Theoretical concepts

Customer Association Management: CRM is an approach to strategy which emphasizes the development and maintenance of associations with customers to drive corporate growth and enhance client retention. The process involves the collection, examination, and application of consumer data to gain insights into their tastes, habits, behaviors, and needs. Operational teams aim to enhance customer communications, tailor communication, and foster long-term loyalty and retention through the application of CRM techniques (Rizk et al., 2024). The concept of CRM emerged in the mid-1970s as businesses began to recognize the worth of fostering enduring associations with clientele beyond mere transactions. The emergence of computer systems and technology in the 1980s and 1990s substantially advanced the development of CRM systems, allowing companies to consolidate customer data, monitor associations, and deliver tailored expertise (Gultekin & Erdem, 2020).

Mapping of journey of client: The journey of purchaser mapping approach serves as a method for visualizing along with representing the various touch points and communications that customers experience with a company throughout their purchasing process (Ye et al., 2017). This involves creating a visual framework of the customer's experience, from initial awareness to post-purchase support, determining pain points, opportunities for improvement, and incidents of engagement. Mapping the journey of purchaser allows operational teams to gain insights into customer engagement across multiple mediums, enabling them to adjust their strategies to deliver a seamless as well tailored visitor experience (Mousavi et al., 2021).

Personalization in real-time: As information technology and analytics evolved in the early 2000s, real-time customization became increasingly imperative. As operations sought to deliver more personalized and accurate advertising communications, the ability to review consumer data in real time and respond quickly remained a substantial differentiator (Esmaili et al., 2022).

1.3. Ideological synthesis

The Customer Association Management (CRM) Theory concentrates on sustainable customer associations through the interpretation of individual requirements (Majeed et al., 2025). CRM Theory utilizes customer data to enable personalized associations which build better client satisfaction and foster consumer loyalty and sustains long-term retention (Weber, 2017). According to Social Exchange Theory every association forms when parties exchange beneficial elements with each other (Hasbullah et al., 2024). The Social Exchange Theory demonstrates how personalized known-how's and customized product manifested creates elevated customer value which establishes positive customer commitment (Esmaili et al., 2022).

Information Processing Theory examines individual capacities in obtaining information and their abilities to together store it for future use and recall it (Gultekin & Erdem, 2020). Information Processing Theory enables investigations to explain customer processing and responsiveness toward personalized content sent through various channels (Abrudan et al., 2020). The key theoretical framework of the investigation adopts the Customer Association Management (CRM) Theory. CRM Theory provides organizations with an extensive structure to create and optimize their customer associations through mapping of journey of client and personalization of services in real-time strategies. Customer Association Management principles enable operational to use customer data for delivering personalized service across the entire customer lifecycle. This examination evaluates the complexities of customer communications and customer satisfaction through CRM principles to generate beneficial insights which operational can use with investigation while developing their omni-channel approaches in Eastern Africa.

1.4. Review of empirical literature

1.4.1. Mapping of journey of client along with optimization of omni-channel

The process of journey of purchaser mapping strengthens optimization of omni-channel by displaying customer behavior throughout different channels (Son et al., 2021). Operational teams can discover key customer engagement points through visual journey mapping because these insights assist in determining problem areas that influence customer satisfaction (Widjaja et al., 2023). Organizations gain process optimization abilities through this clarity to ensure consistent and cohesive known-how across each channel (Gultekin & Erdem, 2020). The journey of purchaser from platform to platform helps corporations develop interconnected systems that deliver a natural channel transition (Rizk et al., 2024). Through an integration of all customer knowledge into a unified concept firms can develop a seamless brand experience across their various platforms (Xu & Cui, 2023).

1.4.2. Mapping of journey of client and Personalization of services in real-time of points of contacts

The mapping of journey of client allows operational to personalize points of contacts in real time through individual behavioral data thus tailoring associations (Hasbullah et al., 2024). The revealed data stream improves delivery of appropriate contents recommendations and offers during real time which enhances the customer experience (Mousavi et al., 2021). The capability of real-time personalization strengthens exponentially with improved operational use of data collected from different touchpoints on the journey of purchaser. Corporate messaging along with commitment strategies become dynamic through the analysis of gathered information to present customers with appropriate messages at valuable times. A business can deliver customized follow-up messages through email alerts for website customers who demonstrate interest in specific products and manifested for related merchandise or promotional offers according to Rizk et al. (2024). The outcome creates an enhancing connection which customers find meaningful because it strengthens their bond with the brand and generates loyalty. Firms achieve empowered real-time personalization through journey of purchaser influence mapping that satisfies customer requirements including predicting their needs in order to provide a smooth and satisfying known-how experience across all points of contacts (Hasbullah et al., 2024).

1.4.3. Personalization in real-time along with optimization of omni-channel

The optimization of omni-channels becomes more efficient through real-time points of contact personalization that ensures channel-pertinent customer communications (Egbuhuzor et al., 2025). Businesses including real-time data can rewrite their messages along with special offers as well as expert advice for each customer according to their observed behaviors and choices. When operators personalize their services at every communication customers gain a stronger connection because they recognize they are prioritized therefore they demonstrate more commitment and deliver increased satisfaction (Gultekin & Erdem, 2020). The ability to personalize services in real-time creates smooth transitions across different channels as stated by Son et al. (2021). Customers who view products through mobile apps experience pertinent targeted email notifications following by in-store recommendations that reflect their interests thus creating a combined known-how experience. Customers stay with brands longer and create inter-channel associations because brand recognition of individual preferences drives them to engage with the company (Widjaja et al., 2023). Operational can gather essential customer feedback in real time to develop improved strategies for better service supply through optimized point-of-contact optimization (Hasbullah et al., 2024).

1.4.4. Mediation of Personalization of services

Operational teams obtain strategic insight into customer key touchpoints through journey mapping so they can determine which moments need personalized approaches that will have maximum influence on customer understanding (Widjaja et al., 2023). Corporates can implement personalized communications and offers through this manifesting technique to connect with customers at the most opportune moments which subsequently builds channel-wide customer commitment (Rizk et al., 2024). Customers gain a seamless known-how experience through real-time personalized service delivery that uses together their digital and physical associations (Son et al., 2021). A customer browsing on the web who shows interest in a product will get personalized communications either through email messaging or store marketing which mirror that product interest. The coordinated method enhances customer known-how yet enables companies to optimize their omni-channels through single-brand presence creation (Widjaja et al., 2023). The real-time customization of services enables organizations to acquire urgent customer preference feedback which enables continuous enhancements to mapping journeys and channel selection (Hasbullah et al., 2024). The dynamic link enables permanent development which helps operational teams develop better omni-channel strategies by analyzing genuine customer patterns. The real-time service customization acts as an essential bridge which enhances the association between journey of purchaser mapping and omni-channel optimization so customers can achieve heightened satisfaction with loyalty towards brands (Mousavi et al., 2021).

1.4.5. Hypothetical framework

Figure 1. Conceptual Framework

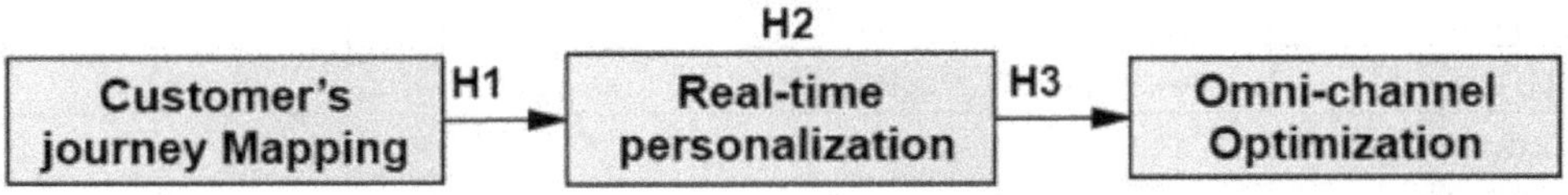

2. METHODOLOGY

Used approach of investigation is quantitative investigation. A total of 425 participants from numerous African demographics within Eastern Africa participated in the investigation to achieve representative data. In the first stages of the investigation investigations performed scale development to evaluate constructs adequacy and consistency. The scale validity tested if element examination requirements could be met for sampling adequacy assessment. The analysis included Exploratory Element Examination (EFA) that together identified latent elements and optimized the scales for mapping of journey of client, personalization of services in real-time, along with optimization of omni-channels. After EFA the investigation utilized AMOS software for Structural Equation Modeling to analyze all investigation variables during analysis. The analysis including SEM permitted investigations to examine complex element relations between journey of purchaser mapping and real-time service personalization and omni-channel optimization while evaluating their combined influence on Eastern African market customer commitment and business outcomes. Statistical tests of high standards were used throughout the investigation to verify the stability of discovered evidence. This investigation used quantities methods coupled with EFA and SEM statistical technologies to generate extensive outcomes about elements influencing customer known-how in the regional market.

3. RESULTS

The investigation used AMOS software to create SEM models which tested hypotheses and revealed the connections between variables while investigating omni-channel sustainability in Eastern part of Africa.

Table 1. **Item-Total Statistics**

	Scale Mean if Item Deleted	Scale Variance if Item Deleted	Corrected Item-Total Correlation	Cronbach's Alpha if Item Deleted
Journey of client Mapping	47.3647	165.568	.964	.909
RTPC	44.9412	166.699	.962	.912
Optimization of omni-channel	43.2706	95.438	.951	.981

Source: Authors

Table 1 contains item-total statistics that assess how individual scale components function. The removal of the item "Journey of Client Mapping would produce a scale mean of 47.36 and a scale variance of 165.57. The scale shows strong performance when measured by a corrected item-total correlation value of 0.964 while maintaining internal consistency at a level of Cronbach's alpha equal to 0.909. The assessment mean would become 44.94 while the assessment variance would reach 166.70 when the item "RTPC" is removed from the measure. A modified Cronbach's alpha value of 0.912 indicates strong reliability when removing this item but the item-total correlation remains high at 0.962. When eliminating the "Optimization of Omni-channel" scale mean rises to 43.27 while its scale variance becomes 95.44. The scale possesses a corrected item-total correlation of 0.951 and would maintain high Cronbach's alpha at 0.981 after omitting this specific item. All statements used to develop the scale bring a positive effect to its reliability assessment metrics.

Table 2. Assumption test

Assumption	Covariance			Estimate	S.E.	C.R.	Sig
Assumption 2	**CJM**	**<-->**	**RTPC**	**.242**	**.021**	**8.231**	**.00**
Assumption 3	CJM	<-->	OMO	.303	.032	7.692	.00
Assumption 1	RTPC	<-->	OMO	.254	.24	7.831	.00

Note: CJM= Journey of client Mapping; OMO= Optimization of omni-channel RTPC= *Personalization of services in real-time of points of contacts*
Source Authors

The covariance depicted in table 2 among Mapping of journey of client and Personalization of services in real-time of Points of contacts was found to be 0.242 with a standard error (S.E.) of 0.021. The vital ratio (C.R.) was computed at 8.231, manifesting a strong and statistically substantial association among these two variables. The p-value (P) was below the functionalism level (.00) and implied that the association among Mapping of journey of client and Personalization of services in real-time of Points of contacts (H2) is substantial. Similarly, the covariance among Mapping of journey of client along with optimization of omni-channels was calculated at 0.303 with a standard error of 0.032. The vital ratio was 7.692, implying a statistically substantial association among these variables. The p-value was also substantial (.00), manifesting that the association among Mapping of journey of client along with optimization of omni-channels (H3) is substantial. Also, the covariance among Personalization of services in real-time of Points of contacts along with optimization of omni-channels was determined to be 0.254 with a standard error of 0.24. The vital ratio was 7.831, again signifying a strong and statistically substantial association among these variables. The p-value was substantial (.00), manifesting that the association among Personalization of services in real-time of Points of contacts along with optimization of omni-channels (H1) is substantial. These outcomes manifest that there are robust connections among mapping of journey of client, personalization of services in real-time of points of contacts, along with optimization of omni-channels. The statistical functionalism of these associations under centers the importance of these elements in influencing customer known-how's and business outcomes in the perspective of Eastern part of Africa.

Table 3. Adequacy Concern

	LF	AVE	Cronbach alpha	Outcome
Journey of client Mapping	0.84	0.65	0.95	Adequate
Optimization of omni-channel	0.78	0.62	0.93	Adequate
Personalization of services in real-time	0.86	0.67	0.89	Adequate

Source Authors

In table 3 manifested that 84% of the loading factor in the observed variables is due to the underlying construct. The explained average variance is 0.65 for client mapping, and is 0.62 for OMO. These values demonstrate the consistency and convergent adequacy of the Mapping of journey of client construct. Regarding OMO, the Cronbach alpha is 0.93, manifesting good internal consistency. The Average Variance Extracted is 0.603, manifesting that 65% of the variance in the observed variables is attributed to the underlying construct. The Maximum Shared Variance is 0.62, and the Maximum Redundancy is 0.67, further confirming the consistency and convergent adequacy of the Personalization of services in real-time of Points of contacts construct. These outcomes manifest that the measurement models for Mapping of journey of client, Optimization of omni-channels, and Personalization of services in real-time of Points of contacts exhibit good consistency and adequacy, supporting the robustness of the constructs in capturing the intended notions in the investigation.

Figure 2. Structural Equation Model

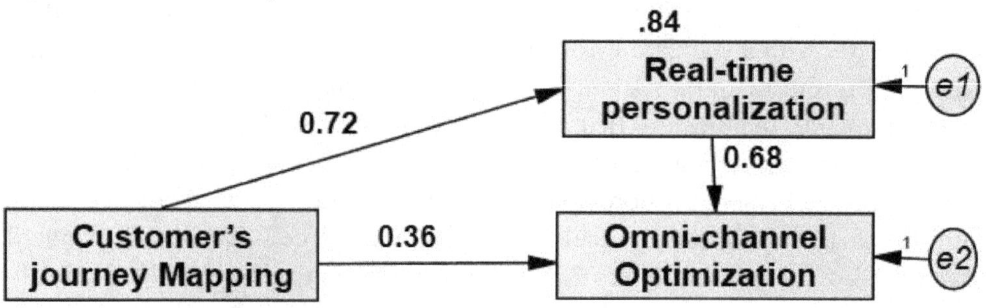

The model fit indices signify a strong fit of the structural equation model to the information in the investigation. The functionalism level of 0.004 manifested that the model substantially aligns with the information set. The Chi-Square value of 1.954, while low, manifests a relatively good fit, considering the sample size. The Root Mean Square Residual (RMR) value of 0.036 is also low, manifesting a minimal discrepancy among the observed information and the model's predictions.

Also, the fitness goodness metric, with a value of 0.930, manifests a high level of model fit to the information. The fitness confirmatory index, reported as 0.912, demonstrates the influence of the proposed model compared to a null model. The Tucker-Lewis Index (TLI) of 0.911 reflects a strong relative fit of the model, while the Root Mean Square Error of Approximation (RMSEA) value of 0.028 manifests a small discrepancy among the observed information and the model. Overall, the model fit indices collectively manifest that the structural equation model delivers a robust and reliable association of the associations among the variables under investigation in the investigation. The association of substantial statistical outcomes, low RMR, high goodness and confirmatory fitness values, strong TLI, and a small RMSEA value supports the conclusion that the model fits the information well and accurately captures the associations among mapping of journey of client, personalization of services in real-time of points of contacts, along with optimization of omni-channels in the perspective of Eastern part of Africa.

Table 4. Regression Examination

Assumption	Path			Significance level
Assumption 2	**JOM**	**<---**	**OMO**	**Below 5%**
Assumption 3	RTPC	<---	JOM	Below 5%
Assumption 1	RTPC	<---	OMO	Below 5%

Source: Authors

In table 4, the Mapping of journey of client along with optimization of omni-channel with the coefficient of 0.864 manifests a strong affirmative association among Optimization of omni-channels and Mapping of journey of client. This manifests that as Optimization of omni-channels increases, Mapping of journey of client tends to increase by approximately 0.864 units. With a standard error of 0.143 and a vital ratio of 7.583, the association is statistically substantial at a high confidence level reinforcing the importance of this connection. The assessment (H2) confirms that the influence of Optimization of omni-channels on Mapping of journey of client is substantial in the perspective of the investigation. Personalization of services in real-time of Points of contacts and Mapping of journey of client with the coefficient of 0.328 reveals a affirmative association among Mapping of journey of client and Personalization of services in real-time of Points of contacts. This implies that an increase in Mapping of journey of client is associated with a corresponding increase in Personalization of services in real-time of Points of contacts by 0.328 units. The assessment (H3) manifests the functionalism of the influence of Mapping of journey of client on Personalization of services in real-time of Points of contacts inside the investigation's perspective. Personalization of services in real-time of Points of contacts along with optimization of omni-channel with a coefficient of 0.957, there is a strong affirmative association among Personalization of services in real-time of Points of contacts along with optimization of omni-channels. This manifests that an increase in Optimization of omni-channels is linked to a rise in Personalization of services in real-time of Points of contacts by approximately 0.957 units. The standard error of 0.192 and vital ratio of 7.958 manifest a statistically substantial association at a high confidence level underscoring the importance of this connection. The assessment (H1) confirms the functionalism of the influence of Optimization of omni-channels on Personalization of services in real-time of Points of contacts in the investigation's setting. These regression outcomes deliver crucial insights into how Mapping of journey of client, Personalization of services in real-time of Points of contacts, along with optimization of omni-channels are interrelated, manifesting the functionalism of these associations in determining customer known-how's and business strategies in the perspective of the investigation in Eastern part of Africa.

Table 5. Mediating function Influence

	Influence	worth
JOM → OMO	Direct Influence	.36
JOM→ RTPC → OMO	Indirect Influence	.72*.68=.489
	Whole influence	.84

Source: Authors

In table 5, the direct influence value of 0.36 manifests the direct influence of Mapping of journey of client on Optimization of omni-channels. This value manifests that Mapping of journey of client directly influences Optimization of omni-channels by 0.36 units. The indirect influence value of 0.72, derived from the path coefficients of 0.74 (Mapping of journey of client → RTPC) and 0.68 (RTPC → Optimization of omni-channels), outcomes in an indirect influence of 0.72 * 0.68 = 0.489 from Mapping of journey of client to Optimization of omni-channels through the mediating influence of RTPC. This manifests that Mapping of journey of client influences Optimization of omni-channels indirectly through RTPC by 0.48 units. The total influence value of 0.84 depicted the combined direct and indirect influences of Mapping of journey of client on Optimization of omni-channels. This manifests that Mapping of journey of client, together directly and indirectly through RTPC, has a substantial overall influence on Optimization of omni-channels. The mediation status is identified as partial mediation, manifesting that while there is a direct influence of Mapping of journey of client on Optimization of omni-channels, there is also a substantial indirect influence mediated through RTPC.

4. DISCUSSION

The direct influence of journey of purchaser cartography on optimization of omni-channel is quantified at 0.36, manifesting a substantial association where the operative mapping of the customer's journey augments the efficiency and efficiency of omni-channel strategies. This manifests that a detailed manifesting of communication with end users through various points of communication is imperative for enterprises that strive to provide transparent, integrated experience. In addition, the indirect action calculated including the RTPC arbitration is 0.489, obtained from the work of influence values along the way (0.72 for display from RTPC, 0.68 to optimize omni in RTPC). This substantial indirect influence emphasizes the key function that personalization in real time plays to fill the gap among the painting of the client's trip and the optimized experience in the simultaneous channel. Investigation outcomes are similar with (Widjaja et al., 2023; Rizk et al., 2024). It emphasizes as personalized communications adapted to the preferences and behavior of customers, can strengthen the outcomes of the client's travel cartography. The association influence, which is 0.84, manifests a strong general influence of customer travel on Optimization of omni-channel. The designation of partial mediation manifests that there are other elements including East Africa broader organizational strategy, technical capabilities and market dynamics. This challenge manifests the need for corporates to adopt a multifaceted approach when implementing strategies for mapping and customer personalization.

Multiple difficulties confront East African corporate entities when they implement customer travel operations and enhance their daily procedures. The inability to combine data from separate platforms reproduces a fragmented picture of customer travel data because information resides on multiple platforms. The solution requires corporates to invest in customer association management systems that combine multiple data sources with complex analysts to generate actionable ideas. Several companies face difficulties in expressing their customer needs adequately and this problem results in unprofitable travel operations. Through routine customer surveys together with discussion groups and social listening techniques corporates receive valuable information to modify their strategies according to customer expectations. Small and medium-sized businesses specifically face difficulties because of quick technological advancements since they lack the resources to maintain current tools. Technology suppliers working with corporates can develop reasonably priced solutions that lead to effective implementation of progress. These work efforts become complicated for many corporates because they operate with restricted budgets while working with limited staff resources. Resource allocation becomes optimized by choosing important initiatives together with automation tools which enables more efficient purchaser mapping operations while maintaining current capacity levels.

5. CONCLUSION AND IMPLICATIONS

5.1. Conclusion

The study presents an extensive evaluation between how Mapping of journey of client, Personalization of services in real-time of Points of contacts and optimization of omni-channels operate in Eastern Africa. The study results in Table 4 demonstrate that these variables strongly support one another because they significantly impact how customers learn and optimize their5omni-channel approaches. The examination results in Table 4 demonstrate how Mapping of journey of client creates Optimization of omni-channels while doing so both directly and indirectly by using Personalization of services in real-time of Points of contacts as an intermediary factor. These results create operational benefits that apply to business operations throughout Eastern African territories and other regions. Comprehensive optimization of Mapping of journey of client combined with Personalization of services in real-time of Points of contacts and omni-channels allows firms to enhance their strategies to fulfill customer requirements while delivering individualized known-how's and improving their broad-channel presence for increased customer satisfaction and loyalty. Moving forward, it is recommended that operational in Eastern part of Africa focus on integrating these insights into their marketing and customer commitment strategies. Emphasizing the importance of mapping of journey of client, investing in personalization of services in real-time of points of contacts, and optimizing omni-channel associations can lead to augmented customer known-how's, augmented brand loyalty, and ultimately, sustainable business development in the viable marketplace. Overall, this investigation contributes valuable insights to the field of customer known-how management and omni-channel marketing, providing a foundation for further investigation and operational application in driving success for operational seeking to excel in the ever-evolving market sphere of Eastern part of Africa.

5.2. Managerial functionalisms

Firstly, managers should prioritize the implementation of robust Mapping of journey of client processes to gain a comprehensive manifesting of customer associations across various touch-points. By mapping the journey of purchaser influence, operational can identify pain points, opportunities for augment, and areas where personalized associations can be most influential. Secondly, investing in Personalization of services in real-time of Points of contacts is crucial for supplying tailored and pertinent known-how's to customers. Implementing technologies that enable personalization of services in real-time, such as AI-driven recommendation engines or dynamic content supply systems, can help operational engage customer's more influence and increase conversion rates. Also, optimizing omni-channel strategies is essential for providing seamless and consistent known-how's across all customer touch-points. Managers should focus on integrating channels, information, and communication methods to create a unified customer known-how that transcends individual channels and devices. Also, recognizing the mediating function of Personalization of services in real-time of Points of contacts among Mapping of journey of client along with optimization of omni-channels manifests that operational should prioritize personalized associations as a key driver of omni-channel success. By enhancing personalization efforts across channels, firms can strengthen customer associations, foster loyalty, and augment overall customer satisfaction. In conclusion, the managerial functionalisms derived from the investigation under center the importance of aligning mapping of journey of client, personalization of services in real-time, along with optimization of omni-channels strategies to meet the evolving needs of customers in Eastern part of Africa. By implementing these insights influence, operational can differentiate themselves in the market, build stronger customer associations, and drive sustainable development in an increasingly viable business market sphere.

5.3. Operational functionalisms

One operational functionalism is the need for operational to invest in technology and information analytics tools that facilitate influence Mapping of journey of client. By manifesting the journey of purchaser from awareness to purchase and beyond, corporates can identify key touch-points for commitment and optimize associations to meet customer needs and expectations. Another operational functionalism is the implementation of Personalization of services in real-time of Points of contacts across various channels. By leveraging customer information and insights in real-time, operational can supply personalized known-how's that resonate with individual preferences and behaviors, fostering deeper customer connections and increasing commitment. As well, optimizing omni-channel strategies is essential for providing a seamless and integrated customer known-how. Operational should ensure consistency in messaging, branding, and customer service across all touch-points, whether online or offline, to create a cohesive journey for customer's regardless of how they interact with the brand. Also, manifesting the mediating function of Personalization of services in real-time of Points of contacts among Mapping of journey of client along with optimization of omni-channels manifests the importance of personalized associations in driving omni-channel success. Operational should focus on tailoring content, offers, and communications to individual customer's based on their preferences and behaviors to augment commitment and conversion rates. By applying these operational functionalisms, operational in Eastern part of

Africa can augment customer satisfaction, loyalty, and retention rates. Embracing Mapping of journey of client, Personalization of services in real-time of Points of contacts, along with optimization of omni-channels as integral parts of their customer known-how strategies can help corporates stay viable, adapt to changing consumer preferences, and ultimately drive business success in the dynamic marketplace of Eastern part of Africa.

5.4. Theoretical functionalisms

The theoretical structure of this investigation emphasizes the interconnected nature of customer travel, real -time personalization and the optimization of the Omni-cannal, in particular, in the Eastern African context. Confirming that the client's traveling largely influences the optimization of the Omni-canist, and personalization in real time serves as an imperative mediator, this investigation increases the existing theories to manage customer travel and the strategy of the omni-channel. Identification of partial mediation enriches the discussion and demonstrates how personalized communications can succeed in simultaneous channels. In practice, these outcomes underscore the importance of integrating personalized customer experiences at different points of contact to augment overall sustainability on concurrent channels. Companies can apply this knowledge by developing strategies to prioritize their customers. This manifests communications to be adapted operatively and promote loyalty. By combining marketing and exploitation approaches, mapping and customer personalization dynamics, corporates can create transparent experiences that resonate with consumers. This investigation will ultimately provide valuable information to practitioners and lead them to developing more operative strategies focused on customers who take advantage of the unique characteristics of the East African market.

5.5. Recommendations

Firstly, it is recommended that operational prioritize the implementation of robust Mapping of journey of client processes to gain a deep manifesting of customer associations across channels. The touch-points and pain points and augment opportunities aid corporates in developing strategic approaches which align better with customer preferences and behaviors. The supply of customized knowledge at the moment requires investments in technologies that simplify real-time customization across Points of contacts. Operational can establish personal connections with customers through automation tools and information systems to present relevant offers which appeal to distinct individuals for enhanced commitment. Integrated channel information systems in operational functions enable customer known-how unity that lets customers switch between online and offline touchpoints without disruption while keeping brand value consistent. A strategic push to raise information analytics skills and customer understanding capacity should be undertaken by firms for better personalization throughout omni-channel optimization. Better employee understanding of customer behaviors through information-based decision systems leads to more effective targeted commitment strategies. The monitoring process of customer known-how metrics along with omni-channel sustainability needs to be consistent for tracking numerous strategies' impact while identifying possible improvement methods. Operational should implement a process that measures sustainability indicators and requests customer feedback to improve their strategies based on changing customer demands. Operational in Eastern part of Africa should implement the presented recommendations to build stronger client associations and increase satisfaction while marketing exceptional omnichannel solutions in the competitive market environment.

5.6. FUTURE DIRECTIONS

A deeper investigation of these technologies by operational in Eastern part of Africa will provide essential understanding of modern customer known-how management trends. The research should explore mobile technology and social media platform impact on customer engagements and their influence on omnichannel business models across Eastern Africa. Society-based components and market circumstances in Eastern Africa's markets should be researched to show how operational enterprises can customize strategies for particular consumer groups. Researching culture-specific and socioeconomic variables in customer behavior will lead to more appropriate influence customer known-how approaches. Long-term studies following purchaser and omni-channel relationship developments during periods will provide data regarding the lasting effects of executed tactics and enable operational to predict upcoming trends and client needs. Operational utilizes behavioral and preference changes of customers to develop proactive market adaptation approaches.

REFERENCES

Aarabe, M., Bouizgar, M., Khizzou, N. B., Alla, L., & Benjelloun, A. (2025). The Transformative Impact of Artificial Intelligence on Tourism Experience: Analysis of Trends and Perspectives. AI Technologies for Personalized and Sustainable Tourism, 277-310.

Aarabe, M., Bouizgar, M., Khizzou, N. B., Alla, L., & Benjelloun, A. (2025). Technology-Driven and Personality in the Travel Experience Within a Destination: Literature Review and Proposal for Analysis Model. Adapting to Evolving Consumer Experiences in Hospitality and Tourism, 267-300.

Abrudan, I. N., Dabija, D. C., & Grant, D. B. (2020). Omni-channel retailing strategy and investigation agenda. *Perspectives on Consumer Behaviour: Theoretical Aspects and Practical Applications*, 261-280.

Alla, L., Bouhtati, N., Aarabe, M., & Khizzou, N. B. (2025). Social Media Analytics for Effective Customer Brand Engagement Assessment: A Theoretical Exploration. In Leveraging AI for Effective Digital Relationship Marketing (pp. 385-418). IGI Global.

Bouizgar, M., Aarabe, M., Khizzou, N. B., Alla, L., & Benjelloun, A. (2025). Smart Territorial Marketing and Promotion of Customer Engagement Towards the Territorial Brand: A Systematic Review of Literature. Sustainable and Intelligent Territorial Marketing and Entrepreneurship, 129-158.

Bouizgar, M., Aarabe, M., Khizzou, N. B., Alla, L., & Benjelloun, A. (2025). AI and Digital Technologies for Transforming Territorial Branding Management: A Systematic Review. Corporate Management in the Digital Age, 35-68.

Egbuhuzor, N. S., Ajayi, A. J., Akhigbe, E. E., Agbede, O. O., Ewim, C. P. M., & Ajiga, D. I. (2025). AI and data-driven insights: Transforming customer association management (CRM) in financial services. *Gulf Journal of Advance Business Investigation*, *3*(2), 483–511.

Esmaili, H., Hosseinzadeh, A., & Soltani, R. (2022). A Mathematical Model to Evaluate Time, Cost and Customer Satisfaction in Omni-Channel Distribution. *International Journal of Supply and Operations Management*, *9*(2), 195–211.

Gök, Ö. A. (2020). How does omni-channel transform consumer behavior? In *Managing Customer Experiences in an Omni-channel World: Melody of Online and Offline Environments in the Journey of purchaser* (pp. 27–42). Emerald Publishing Limited.

Gultekin, B., & Erdem, S. (2020). Omni-Channel Strategy in the Framework of the Search Engines. In *Managing Customer Experiences in an Omni-channel World: Melody of Online and Offline Environments in the Journey of purchaser* (pp. 211–232). Emerald Publishing Limited. DOI: 10.1108/978-1-80043-388-520201017

Hasbullah, N. N., Kiflee, A. K. R., Anwar, S., & Ramachandran, K. K. (2024). Mapping the trend of digital transformation in omni-channel retailing: a bibliometric analysis. *Marketing i menedžment innovacij, 15*(1), 29-40.

Jabo, D., Borji, B., & Kant, S. (2024, February). Influence of Technical CRM on Ethiopia Bank Human-Computer Interface and Competitive Advantage as Mediators of Sustainability. In *2024 IEEE International Conference on Computing, Power and Communication Technologies (IC2PCT)* (Vol. 5, pp. 679-682). IEEE.

Jabo, D., Kant, S., & Borji, B. (2025). Customer Orientation and Ethiopian Bank Sustainability With Mediation of Competitive Advantage. In *Leveraging AI for Operative Digital Association Marketing* (pp. 459–482). IGI Global.

Kant, S., & Adula, M. (2025). Does Technology-Enabled Knowledge Management-Based Competitive Advantage Transfer?: Its Combined Influence on Ethiopian Banking Sustainability. In *Building Inclusive Global Knowledge Societies for Sustainable Development* (pp. 75-106). IGI Global Scientific Publishing.

Kant, S., Adula, M., & Duloma, H. (2025). The Rise of Product-as-a-Service Models in the Digital Era Redesigning Business Models for Circular Innovation in the Horn of Africa. In *Innovating Sustainability Through Digital Circular Economy* (pp. 133–160). IGI Global Scientific Publishing.

Khizzou, N. B., Aarabe, M., Bouizgar, M., Alla, L., & Benjelloun, A. (2025). The Digital Transformation of Medical Tourism: A Systematic and Bibliometric Review of the Literature. Revolutionizing Healthcare Experience With Digital Medical Tourism, 355-382.

Kokku, R. (2021). Omni and multi-channel: Association with utilitarian/hedonic benefits, shopping value and channel patronage. *International Review of Management and Marketing, 11*(11), 11–22. DOI: 10.32479/irmm.11215

Laoute, C., Aarabe, M., Khizzou, N. B., Alla, L., Alj, B., & Benjelloun, A. (2025). Digital Marketing and Territorial Attractiveness of Innovative Entrepreneurship: Exploratory Qualitative Study. In Sustainable and Intelligent Territorial Marketing and Entrepreneurship (pp. 33-68). IGI Global.

Majeed, M., Chaudhary, A., & Chadha, R. (Eds.). (2025). *Digital Transformation in the Customer Experience*. CRC Press.

Mousavi, P., Rahimnia, F., Mehraeen, M., & Shamizanjani, M. (2021). Customer experience management; trends and areas in investigation. *Journal of Business and Management, 13*(2), 502–523.

Nadeem, M. S. (2024). Omni-channel Retail Strategy: How to Meet the Needs of Today's Shoppers. *Open Journal of Business and Management, 12*(6), 4008–4019. DOI: 10.4236/ojbm.2024.126200

Niguse, T., Kant, S., & Adula, M. (2025). Mediation Influence of Customer Loyalty in Association Among Market Orientation, Entrepreneurial Orientation, and Firm Sustainability in Ethiopia. In *Leveraging AI for Operative Digital Association Marketing* (pp. 419–458). IGI Global.

Nouhaila, B. K., Aarabe, M., & Alla, L. (2024). The impact of digitalisation on the customer experience in medical tourism: A systematic review. Impact of AI and tech-driven solutions in hospitality and tourism, 408-428.

Rizk, M., El-Samadicy, A., & Negm, E. (2024). The Influence of Omni-Channel Integration on Generation Z Purchase Intentions Towards FMCG Retailers: An Empirical Investigation on Egyptian FMCG Consumers. *The Journal of Business, 12*(1), 1–12.

Son, S. C., Bae, J., & Kim, K. H. (2021). The influence of perceived agility on intention to reuse Omni-channel: Focused on mediating influence of integration quality of Omni-channel. *Journal of Global Fashion Marketing, 12*(4), 375–389. DOI: 10.1080/20932685.2021.1947151

Weber, N. (2017). *Matching the business model with the unique journey of purchaser: a case investigation of a high-tech Dutch EMS provider* (Master's thesis, University of Twente).

Widjaja, Y. G., So, I. G., Setiowati, R. I. N. I., & Furinto, A. S. N. A. N. (2023). The influence of utilitarian value and hedonic value on omni-channel shopping intention through tam perceived usefulness and perceived ease of use. *Journal of Theoretical and Applied Information Technology, 101*(8), 3187–3198.

Widjaja, Y. G., So, I. G., Setiowati, R. I. N. I., & Furinto, A. S. N. A. N. (2023). The influence of utilitarian value and hedonic value on omni-channel shopping intention through tam perceived usefulness and perceived ease of use. *Journal of Theoretical and Applied Information Technology, 101*(8), 3187–3198.

Xu, J., & Cui, X. (2023). Investigation on the Game Association and Behavior Optimization among Banks and Customers in the Omni-Channel Environment. *Systems, 11*(4), 171. DOI: 10.3390/systems11040171

Ye, Y., Lau, K. H., & Teo, L. K. Y. (2018). Drivers and barriers of omni-channel retailing in China: A case investigation of the fashion and apparel industry. *International Journal of Retail & Distribution Management, 46*(7), 657–689. DOI: 10.1108/IJRDM-04-2017-0062

6. KEY TERMS AND DEFINITIONS

Mapping of journey of client: It helps operational identify opportunities to augment customer known-how's and optimize associations across different channels.

Personalization of services in real-time:: Personalization of services in real-time refers to the ability to customize and tailor content, offers, and associations with customer's in real-time based on their behavior, preferences, and past associations. It assimilates including information and technology to supply pertinent and personalized known-how's to individuals at the moment of association.

Optimization of omni-channels:: Optimization of omni-channels assimilates the strategic alignment and integration of all available channels and touch-points (such as online, offline, mobile, social media, etc.) to deliver a seamless and consistent customer known-how. It aims to ensure that customers can transition among channels effortlessly while receiving a unified brand known-how.

Partial Mediation:: Partial mediation occurs when the association among two variables is partially influenced by a third variable. In the perspective of the investigation, partial mediation manifests that the association among Mapping of journey of client along with optimization of omni-channels is influenced together directly and indirectly through the mediating influence of Personalization of services in real-time of Points of contacts.

Touch-points:: Touch-points refer to the various points of association among a customer and a business throughout the journey of purchaser. These can include physical locations, websites, mobile apps, social media platforms, customer service associations, and any other channels where customer's engage with the brand.

Information Analytics:: Information analytics assimilates the process of analyzing raw information to uncover meaningful insights, patterns, and trends that can inform decision-making and viable plan development. In the perspective of customer known-how management, information analytics helps operational understand customer behaviors, preferences, and associations to optimize their marketing and service efforts.

Customer Knowledge Management: Customer knowledge management (CRM) assimilates the design, supply, along with optimization of all associations a customer has with a business throughout their journey. It focuses on creating affirmative and memorable known-how's to build customer loyalty, satisfaction, and advocacy, ultimately driving business development and success.

Chapter 6
Transforming CRM: Effect on Service Sector Optimization by Mediation of AI Innovations in the Horn of Africa

Shashi Kant
https://orcid.org/0000-0003-4722-5736
Bule Hora University, Ethiopia

Aynetu Terefe
https://orcid.org/0009-0003-3814-9548
Bule Hora University, Ethiopia

Metasebia Adula
https://orcid.org/0000-0001-5732-2850
Bule Hora University, Ethiopia

ABSTRACT

This investigation investigates the transformative influence of Customer Relationship Management (CRM) and Artificial Intelligence (AI) innovation on service industry sustainability. Utilizing a quantitative investigation approach, we analyze data from various service-oriented organizations to explore the relationships among CRM transformation, AI integration, and service optimization. The outcomes reveal that influence CRM transformation significantly enhances service delivery, while AI innovation serves as a crucial mediator that amplifies these influences. This investigation underscores the importance of aligning CRM strategies with AI technologies to augment customer engagement and operational efficiencies. The outcomes not only contribute to the theoretical understanding of these constructs but also depict real life insights for managers aiming to optimize service sustainability. Recommendations for future investigation include exploring contextual determinants influencing these

DOI: 10.4018/979-8-3373-0918-7.ch006

relationships and investigating specific AI applications within CRM systems.

1. INTRODUCTION

1.1. Background of investigation

In the Horn of Africa, place of market is marked by diverse cultures, fiscal disparities, along with rapid technological advancements, the potential for CRM and AI to enhance service industry efficiency is substantial (Aarabe et al, 2024). Also, the journey toward successful implementation is fraught with foundations that warrant detailed examination (Kothapalli, 2022). One notable case is Ethiopia, where the government has prioritized digital transformation as part of its Growth and Transformation Plan (Nouhaila et al, 2024). Despite these efforts, many market face significant hurdles in adopting CRM systems enhanced by AI. For instance, an investigation on Ethiopian telecommunications companies revealed that while AI has the potential to augment customer service through predictive analytics, companies struggle with data quality and consistency (Adula et al., 2023). Correspondingly, in Kenya, the funding trade has seen a outpouring in AI-driven explanations intended at monograming purchaser practices. Also, a case investigation involving local banks manifested real life foundations, like expensive as well as unwillingness to adopt AI founded technology (Khizzou et al., 2024). Many banks have reported that their employees require extensive training to influence use AI tools alongside traditional CRM systems. Also, customer resistance to technology adoption, particularly among older demographics, poses an additional barrier, as customers may prefer in-person interactions over automated solutions (Bihame et al., 2024).

Optimization of the services sector in the African horn by the transformation of CRM and the innovation of artificial intelligence can be illustrated in real thematic studies (Asefa et al., 2023).In a case, in the banking, institutions such as Kenya have managed to integrate CRM systems managed by AI to increase customer participation and optimization. After conducting AI analysis, Equity Bank announced a 30% increase in customer retention rate, demonstrating specific benefits in implementing the technology (Gama & Magistretti, 2023). On the contrary, the retail sector faces a variety of issues. Companies like Jumia, an e-commerce platform in Africa, employ AI for personalized marketing, but are fighting against data collection and infrastructure (Jabo et al., 2024). Despite a reported 25% increase in sales from target marketing, Jumia exists with a decline in AI adoption rate compared to banks, reaching around 60% in metropolitan areas. As well as, the McKinsey survey has shown that 70% of companies in the banking sector have declared significant improvements in operational efficiency after integration after AI, against only 50%

of retail (Tula et al., 2024). These cases manifest the prominence of individual strategies based on specific tasks for industry, emphasizing the need for reliable infrastructure and training in order to maximize the advantages of CRM and AI to optimize the provision of services in Africa.

In Somalia, where instability and limited infrastructure are prevalent, the implementation of AI-enhanced CRM faces unique foundations. A local telecommunications firm attempted to introduce AI-driven tools to augment customer service. Also, the initiative was met with significant obstacles, including unreliable internet connectivity and a lack of awareness among customers about how to engage with digital platforms. As a result, the technical CRM system saw low adoption rates, demonstrating that even well-conceived innovations can falter without augmented the foundational issues of infrastructure and customer education (Dereso et al., 2023).

Understanding these real life foundations is crucial for informing future investigation and policy initiatives, as they manifest the need for comprehensive frameworks that support both technological adoption and customer engagement in the Eastern Africa's evolving service industry.

1.2. Problem statement

This research seeks to establish the prospects of CRM along with AI integration within the service oriented firms of the Eastern Africa region." In an ideal world, aspirations of integrating such functions into AI capabilities and integrating them with CRM systems must spur better customer interactions, a boost in strategic decisions and organizational profitability (Khizzou et al., 2025). Also, the extant reality within this area discloses a number of gulf and bearings that hamper influence implementation, according to Kumar and others (2023). Despite the potential benefits, there is contradictory evidence regarding the influence of AI-enhanced CRM systems in the Eastern Africa. While some studies indicate positive outcomes in regions with robust technological infrastructures, empirical investigation within the context of the Horn remains limited and inconclusive. This gap is compounded by theoretical discrepancies; existing CRM models often fail to account for the unique ethnic-economic conditions and cultural determinants prevalent in the Eastern Africa. Consequently, the applicability of prevailing theories in CRM and AI is questionable, leading to a lack of tailored frameworks that address the specific needs of market in this region (Pangrahi et al., 2023).

Also, significant knowledge gaps exist regarding the mediating determinants that influence the successful integration of AI into CRM systems. While the related investigations manifest the prominence of technology adoption, a few investigation examining the interplay of various contextual elements, such as customer demographics, digital literacy, and local market dynamics. This oversight limits the understanding of how to influence engage customers and foster acceptance of AI-driven solutions (Tula et al., 2024). Real life foundations also pose significant barriers to implementation. Issues like old technology, labor known how, as well as resistance to change among customers. For instance, many market struggle with data quality and collection processes, which are essential for AI to function influence. Also, the high costs associated with technology investments further deter small and medium-sized enterprises from embracing these innovations (Durga et al., 2024).

By examining empirical evidence, theoretical frameworks, the investigation will offer actionable insights and recommendations tailored to the region's unique context. Also, it will manifest best practices and potential strategies that can facilitate the adoption of AI-enhanced CRM systems, thereby guiding future investigations and policymakers in their efforts to optimize service delivery. In doing so, present chapter lay the nexus for CRM, AI, along with optimization of service related industry, ultimately contributing to sustainable economic growth and development in the region.

1.3. Overview

In an era where user-centric approaches are fundamental for corporate achievement, the assimilation of CRM as well as AI has adverted as a transformative paradigm in the service industry (Jabo et al., 2024). Chapter manifested the CRM impact on optimizing the service industry, particularly through the mediation of AI innovation, a constituency considered by its unique ethnic-economic foundations and strategies (Aarabe et al, 2024). Understanding this dynamic is not only crucial for market but also holds global prominence for enhanced customer experiences in emerging markets (Kwilinski et al., 2023). The impression of CRM has its ancestries in the late 20th century, evolving from basic customer data management to sophisticated systems that facilitate personalized marketing, customer engagement, and relationship building (Gama & Magistretti, 2023). AI, leveraging vast amounts of data, has the potential to enhance CRM capabilities by providing predictive analytics, automating customer interactions, and personalizing services at an unprecedented scale (Khizzou et al., 2024). Despite the theoretical frameworks and empirical studies surrounding CRM and AI, the specific interplay of these elements within the Eastern Africa remains underexplored (Deep & Zanke, 2024).

While the service sector continues to develop, new CRM strategies controlled by AI form the future of customer participation and operational efficiency. One of the important trends is the use of forecast analyzes which allows companies to anticipate customer needs and preferences (Alla et al., 2025). Analyzing historical data and behavior, organizations can adapt their proposals by increasing customer satisfaction and loyalty (Bihame et al., 2024). Another promising strategy is the implementation of cat robots with AI (Kwilinski et al., 2023). As well as, the use of machine learning algorithms for customer segmentation allows companies to create target marketing campaigns, optimize the distribution of resources and maximize the profitability of investments. As a matter of data confidentiality, ETH ethical practices are important, requiring transparent processing of data and strategies to reduce displacement outcomes (Durga et al., 2024).

Empirical literature manifests the benefits of AI-enhanced CRM systems (Bouizgar et al., 2025). Also, many studies tend to focus on Western contexts (Aarabe et al, 2025), often overlooking the unique foundations faced by market in developing regions like the Eastern Africa. Practical barriers depicted as AI skill deficits along with varying levels of digital literacy complicate the adoption of these innovations (Laoute et al., 2025). Also, lens of AI mediation is under studied (Asefa et al., 2023). This chapter reveled that CRM, when augmented by AI, can optimize service delivery in the Eastern Africa. It will explore the ethnic-economic determinants influencing this relationship, identify best practices, and propose actionable strategies for market and policymakers. By offering insights into the specific barriers to implementation and potential solutions, this investigation seeks to guide future investigations and inform policy decisions.

The inquiry administrative this investigation is: ***"How can the integration of Innovation in AI into CRM strategies optimize service delivery in the Eastern Africa, and what are the mediating determinants that influence this relationship?"*** This inquiry is essential not only to advance academic knowledge but also to depict real life frameworks for market operating in this complex trade network.

2. LITERATURE REVIEW AND THEORETICAL FRAMEWORK

2.1. Theoretical underpinning

In exploring the integration of CRM along with AI in service industry, several theoretical frameworks offer valuable insights. One basic model is the ***Technology Acceptance Model (TAM),*** used to understand inclusion of technology perceptions. Understanding these perceptions can help market tailor their approaches to increase acceptance and utilization (Demirel, 2022). Another imperative framework is the ***Resource-Based View (RBV)***. In the background of CRM along with AI, RBV manifests the necessity for market to leverage their unique resources—such as data, skilled personnel, and technological infrastructure—to influence implement and optimize AI solutions (Chaudhuri et al., 2022). TAM put way forwads for this chapter as well the investigation, because this approach will facilitate a deeper exploration of the unique context of the Eastern Africa, ultimately informing strategies that can enhance the adoption and influence of AI in CRM, thereby contributing to augmented service industry sustainability.

2.2. DEFINITION AND ORIGIN OF CONCEPTS

Customer Relationship Management: The concept originated in the 1980s as market began to recognize the prominence of understanding their customers to foster loyalty and increase profitability. Initially, CRM systems focused on data collection and management, but over the years, the scope has expanded to include advanced analytics, automation, and personalized communication, reflecting a shift towards more customer-centric approaches in business (Amarasinghe, 2023).

Artificial Intelligence: The basic ideology brhinf AI to make capable machines to critical think like a human. Recently it reached to marketing sphere in form of CRM augmented tools (Bachir, 2021).

Integration: AI founded the CRM systems, allowing market to analyze customer data more influence, automate processes, and personalize customer interactions. This integration aims to depict market with behavior and preferences of clients, ultimately improving customer engagement and satisfaction. The concept gained traction in the early 2000s as organizations began to leverage data analytics and AI-driven tools to optimize their CRM efforts. AI technologies have further accelerated this integration, enabling market to harness vast amounts of customer data for more informed decision-making (Potla, 2023).

Optimization: It involves improving the efficiency and influence of services depicted to customers. This process encompasses various strategies, including streamlining operations, enhancing service delivery, and utilizing technology to better meet customer needs. The term "service industry" refers to the segment of the economy. The focus on optimization within this industry has grown in response to increasing competition and evolving consumer expectations, prompting organizations to adopt innovative practices and technologies to enhance their service offerings (Cheng et al, 2023).

2.3. Empirical literature review

2.3.1. *CRM Transformations and Optimization of Service Industry*

The transformation of Customer Relationship Management (CRM) through the integration of advanced AI, has a profound influence on optimizing the service industry (Adula et al., 2024). Also, the automation of routine tasks within transformed CRM systems significantly augments operational efficiency, freeing customer interactions (Jabo et al. 2024). This heightened efficiency reduces functioning costs with enhances productivity; allocate resources supplementary influence (Gama & Magistretti, 2023). Also, real-time data access empowers better decision-making, allowing market shift swiftly to as per feedback. Also, the successful implementation of transformed CRM systems comes with foundations with adequate employee training (Guyo et al., 2023). Such hurdles removed by AI inclusion into CRM manifested a critical opportunity for optimization of service related industry, enabling organizations to elevate their service offerings and achieve sustainable competitive advantage in an increasingly dynamic market (Boppana, 2023).

H1: CRM transformations has significant influence on optimization of service related industry

2.3.2. CRM Transformations and Innovation in AI

The transformation of CRM through the inclusion of AI innovations has a influence on how organizations interact with their customers and manage their operations (Berry & Singh, 2024). By embedding AI technologies into CRM platforms, market can automate and enhance various processes, such as customer data analysis, personalized marketing, and service delivery (Jabo et al., 2023). This connection enables improved consumer segmentation alongside forecasting, hence helping companies to more accurately predict client preferences and demands. By means of tailored suggestions as well as assistance, machine learning innovation improves CRM systems, hence improving client relationships along with happiness (Oyedeji, 2024). AI-driven tools along with virtual assistants integrated into CRM systems improve relationships with consumers by offering instant help, hence enabling human agents to concentrate on more complicated questions (Birhane et al., 2023). Timely and relevant involvement helps companies to be more agile thus. AI inclusion in CRM greatly enhances strategic market potential by allowing fast adaptation to changing consumer expectations as well as business dynamics (Yi, Z., & Ayangbah, 2024).

H2: Transforming CRM has substantial encouragement on AI founded innovations

2.3.3. AI Innovation and Service Industry Optimization

AI technologies streamline processes by automating routine tasks, such as data entry and customer support, which significantly reduces operational costs and enhances efficiency (Gama & Magistretti, 2023). This automation ultimately leading to augmented productivity (Adula et al., 2023). Also, AI-driven analytics depict market to prototype services. Predictive analytics, for example, allows organizations to anticipate demand and optimize resource allocation, ensuring that services are delivered more influence and efficiently (Yi, Z., & Ayangbah, 2024). Another imperative framework is the RBV. Also, AI enhances customer experiences through personalized interactions, utilizing tools like tools and virtual assistants to offer immediate support and tailored recommendations (Dreso et al., 2023).. This responsiveness not only boosts customer satisfaction along with reliability. AI innovation empowers the service industry to adapt quickly to changing market dynamics, augment service delivery, and achieve sustainable growth (Berry & Singh, 2024).

H3: Artificial Intelligence (AI) Innovation has significant on optimization of service related industry is transformative

2.3.4. Mediation of AI Innovation, CRM and Optimization of Service

The mediation of AI innovation in the affiliation midst transforming CRM along with optimization of facility related industry is pivotal for enhancing organizational influence (Jabo et al., 2024). As CRM systems evolve through the integration of AI technologies, they enable market to analyze customer data more deeply and derive actionable insights. This transformation facilitates more personalized customer interactions and tailored service offerings, which are essential for optimizing service delivery. By closing the disconnect between services, AI operates as a mediator (Asefa et al., 2023). The Diffusion of Innovation hypothesis (DOI) is additionally suitable as it has shown itself as new ideas and technology spread throughout societies and social systems. As it relates to factors including the perceived benefits of innovation, integration with current systems, alongside technological complexity, this theory can reflect data on the pace of adoption of final CRM systems. In this regard, artificial intelligence-driven statistical analyses may spot consumer trends along with preferences, hence enabling companies to proactively meet demands alongside increase happiness. Artificial intelligence solutions like predictive analytics and tools also help to improve service efficiency by simplifying processes and improving responsiveness to client questions (Durga et al., 2024). Consequently, companies that affect incorporates Innovation in artificial intelligence into their changed CRM systems might see notable increases in client involvement, productivity in operation, as well as general service industry sustainability. This interaction motivates improvement of service connected sectors (Gama & Magistretti, 2023).

H4: The link among CRM transformations on Optimization of service related industry is influenced by AI Innovation.

Figure 1. Conceptual framework

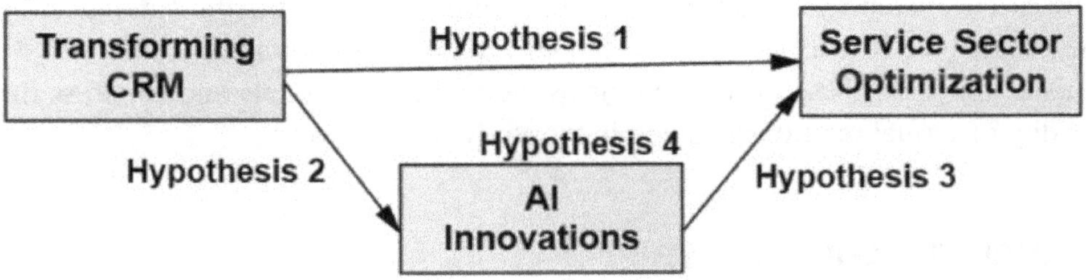

3. METHODOLOGY

3.1. Research design

This chapter used a quantitative scheme to study impact of AI innovation on industry optimization related to services using a sample of 396 respondents. The design corresponds to and provides a structured basis for the analysis of relationships among variables. The methodology for validity of the data using validity measurements by ensuring values above 0.6; the validity of the sample for factorial analysis was demonstrated. Analysis of factor was performed and service optimizations underlying AI innovation, and to improve the elements of scale to ensure that they accurately reflect planned dimensions. After EFA, modeling of structural equations (SEM) was implemented using AMOS software. This approach allowed multiple relationships to be studied simultaneously, providing the idea of general adjustments to the model. Scale development was constructed on a comprehensive assessment upon specific context of AI in the service sector. Pilot testing ensured the reliability and validity of the structure, ultimately facilitating rigorous quantitative analysis.

3.2. SAMPLING AND DATA COLLECTION

396 participants was analyzed in investigation. This is considered sufficient for modeling structural equations (SEM). Kline (2015) 200 size of sample is generally recommended for SEM, with larger samples preferred for better estimates of model parameters and improved statistical power. This study\'s sample size exceeds that threshold, enhancing the robustness of the findings. To measure the reliability and reliability along with dispersion, extracts were used with alpha knowledge of Cronbach. The CR value is greater than 0.7 and AV more than 0.5 manifests good reliability and good convergence of reliability. Furthermore, in this study, Herman's

only factor test was used to assess shifts in general methods. Model-compatible indices have been evaluated to assess the validity of the structural model. Key metrics include RMSEA, CFI, TLI, and GFI, with thresholds set to RMSEA 0.90. Satisfaction with these criteria confirms well-adjusted models and supports the validity of virtual relationships within the study.

4. RESULTS AND ANALYSIS

4.1. Data analysis techniques

Table 1. Co-variance

			Estimate	S.E.	C.R.	P	H
AI Innovation	**<-->**	**CRM transformations**	**.245**	**.024**	**8.236**	**.00**	**H2**
AI Innovation	<-->	Service-Industry Optimization	.301	.037	7.693	.00	**H3**
CRM transformations	<-->	Service-Industry Optimization	.253	.21	7.838	.00	**H1**

Source: Authors

Table 1 demonstrated nexus among constructs of AI innovation, CRM transformations, and optimization of service related industry, along with their respective statistical measures. The covariance among AI innovation and CRM transformations is 0.245 is significant at a p-value denoted by ".00," manifested a robust relationship that supports Hypothesis 2 (H2). This suggests that advancements in AI positively influence the transformation of CRM systems. Similarly, the covariance among AI innovation and optimization of service related industry is 0.301, significant with same p-value. This relationship supports Hypothesis 3 (H3), manifesting that AI innovation significantly contributes to optimizing service industry sustainability. The positive covariance suggests that as organizations adopt AI technologies, they are likely to enhance their service delivery and operational efficiencies. Finally, the covariance among CRM transformations and optimization of service related industry is 0.253 is significant. This finding supports Hypothesis 1 (H1), manifested that influence transformation of CRM systems is crucial for achieving optimization in the service industry. Overall, the significant co-variances among these constructs underscore the interconnectedness of AI innovation, CRM transformations, and optimization of service related industry.

Table 2. Validity Concern

	CR	AVE	MSV	MaxR(H)	TCRM	AII	SSO
TCRM	0.738	0.643	0.225	0.856	**0.657**		
AI-I	0.762	0.661	0.133	0.761	0.173	**0.664**	
SSO	0.795	0.604	0.275	0.794	0.387	0.192	**0.688**

Note: TCRM=CRM transformations; AII=AI Innovation; SSO=Optimization of service related industry
Source: Writers

Table 2 displayed the concerns about validity. Construct of CRM transformations (TCRM), the CR is 0.738, above benchmark of 0.7, depicted a adequate dependability. The AVE for TCRM is 0.643, also above the minimum acceptable level of 0.5. In terms of AI Innovation (AII), the CR is 0.762, demonstrating adequate reliability, while the AVE is 0.661, manifested that the construct influence explains its variance. The MSV for AII is 0.133, which is lower than the AVE, further depict discrimate validity. The MaxR(H) for AII is 0.761, reinforcing its reliability. For Optimization of service related industry (SSO), the CR is 0.795, reflecting strong reliability, and the AVE is 0.604, confirming that this construct also meets the criteria for good validity. The MSV for SSO is 0.275, which is higher than the AVE of TCRM (0.225), but still within acceptable limits, suggesting that while there is some overlap, discriminant validity is maintained. The MaxR(H) for SSO is 0.794, further validating its robustness.

Table 3. Structure Fitness

P	CMIN/DF	RMR	Fitness Goodness	Fitness Confirmatory	TLI	RMSEA
0.012	1.842	.032	.936	.916	.909	.029

Source: Authors

Table 3 summarizes model fit indices. The p of 0.012 is significant, which implies that the model fits the data reasonably well. The CMIN/DF of 1.842 is suggesting that the model does not significantly deviate from the observed data. The RMR at 0.032, manifested a good fit. The GFI is 0.936, CFI is reported at 0.916, TLI stands at 0.912, manifested a good fit as it is close to 1, reinforcing the model's robustness. In sum, all manifested the relationships among the constructs in the investigation, thereby providing base for proposed hypotheses and enhancing the overall credibility of the investigation outcomes.

Figure 2. Structure Equation Model

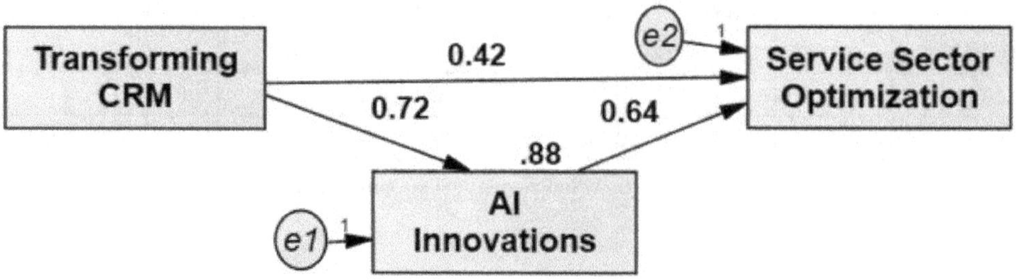

Table 4. Direct implies

Implies			Estimate	S.E.	C.R.	P	Ass.
AI- Innovation	**<---**	**CRM transformations**	**.763**	**.146**	**7.582**	**.00**	**H2**
Service-Industry Optimization	<---	AI- Innovation	.326	.138	2.855	.00	H3
Service-Industry Optimization	<---	CRM transformations	.951	.193	7.958	.00	H1

Source: Authors

Table 4 implies examination, manifesting the relationships among the constructs of AI innovation, CRM transformations, and optimization of service related industry. The regression coefficient for the path from CRM transformations to AI innovation is 0.763, along a S.E. of 0.146 and a critical ratio of 7.582, which is significant at a p-value denoted by ".00". This strong positive relationship supports H2, manifested that CRM transformations significantly influences AI innovation. The regression analysis further reveals that AI innovation has a positive influence on optimization of service related industry, with worth about 0.326, also statistically significant. H3, advancements in AI innovation contribute positively to the optimization of services within the industry. Also, the regression coefficient for the path from CRM transformations to optimization of service related industry is 0.951, with an S.E. of 0.193 and a C.R. of 7.958, manifested a robust and significant relationship that supports H1. This depict transformation of CRM systems is critical for enhancing service industry sustainability.

Table 5. Mediation

	worth
Transforming-CRM→Service-Industry Optimization	.42
Transforming-CRM→AI-Innovation→Optimization of service related industry	.73*.64=.46
	.88

Source: Authors

Table 5 manifested mediating function of AI innovation in the relationship among CRM transformations and optimization of service related industry. The straight encouragement of CRM transformations on optimization of service related industry is 0.43, manifested a significant direct influence. This direct path manifests the immediate influence that influence CRM transformation can have on optimizing service delivery and operational efficiency. Ancillary encouragement, which involves the mediating function of AI innovation, is calculated as 0.73 reproduced by 0.64, resulting of 0.46. This finding underscores the prominence of AI innovation as a mediator, suggesting that the positive influences of CRM transformations on optimization of service related industry are partly facilitated through the enhancement of AI capabilities. This high total 0.88 influence manifests a strong overall relationship, reinforcing the notion that both direct and mediated pathways are critical in driving augment in optimization of service related industry.

5. DISCUSSION

5.1. Interpretation of findings

The consequences in Table 5 cover the complex interactions among managing customer relationships (CRM), innovative innovations in artificial intelligence (AI), and service-related services optimization. The direct impact of CRM transformation on service industry optimization is determined quantitatively at 0.43, indicating a significant connection. This direct path suggests that effective CRM methods can increase operational work, customer satisfaction and general service efficiency. On the contrary, the indirect impact of CRM transformation leading to AI innovation optimizes the service industry and has a computer effect of 0.46. This shows that integration of AI as an arbitration factor significantly amplifies the possibilities of optimization when direct impact is significant. The total impact of 0.88, meaning partial mediation, suggests that both CRM innovation and AI transformation are essential, but it works in synergy to stimulate improvements in the industry related to services. However, as businesses are increasingly embracing these treatment technologies, they must face local issues and the ethical issues that come with these outcomes. Rapid integration of AI into CRM systems can lead to functionality, especially in regions where work relies heavily on traditional services. Changes require an increase in processing initiatives and a detailed consideration of the labor initiatives. Additionally, there are ethical issues with data confidentiality and using customers of AI-controlled CRM systems. Personal data support for extended volumes to optimize artificial intelligence raises questions about consent, data security, and possible inappropriate use. Inspired by these ethical dilemmas and businesses, reliable data management measurement and transparency must be implemented to boost consumer confidence. With regard to benefits and issues, it is clear that CRM transformation and AI integration can lead to increased service efficiency and customer participation. Ultimately, travel to optimization by transforming CRM and AI innovations offers both opportunities and problems. Understanding this subtle dynamic is important for businesses that strive to thrive in an increasingly complex landscape to be ethically responsible and socially informed.

Optimization of the Service Sector in Africa in Africa by converting customer relations (CRM) and AI innovations can be analyzed using the technology adoption model (TAM), based on resources (RBV) and the propagation of innovation (ITI). TAM assumes that AI increases the effectiveness of CRM. This finding (direct impact of 0.43) supports this and manifested that service providers are likely to adopt beneficial technologies. RBV emphasizes leveraging unique resources. AI integration allows organizations to distinguish in resource-constrained environments, as demonstrated by the indirect impact of 0.46. However, issues such as insufficient infrastructure are preserved. Doy shows obstacles to technology adoption, such as cultural resistance and lack of awareness. Solutions to these issues that help to raise initiatives and awareness. The practical consequences of AI-controlled CRM are profound, especially in areas with low digital rules, including ethical issues related to customer data confidentiality. Companies need to prioritize transparent data practices, meet ethical standards, and strengthen trust in their customers. This is particularly important in East Africa, where the regulatory framework may not be fully established. In addition, the preparation of the implementation of AI varies considerably among SMEs and large companies. Large companies often have resources for the implementation of complex AI systems, but small businesses can compete with high technical costs and limited experience. Therefore, these small businesses are recommended to have a step -by -step strategy for the adoption of artificial intelligence. This may include startups with affordable artificial intelligence tools that improve customer engagement, such as cats and basic analysts, before moving on to more advanced solutions. Management recommendations should focus on developing a clear roadmap for AI integration.

5.2. ETHICAL AND CHALLENGING ISSUES

Responsible implementation depends on integration with AI as well as CRM, which raises several ethical as well as normative questions to be addressed. Ethical issues of algorithm displacement are also significant as, even under lax management, artificial intelligence systems could not disclose identify. This could compromise service providers' confidence and unjustly evaluate consumer feedback, especially for marginalized populations. Many nations in the eastern half of Africa have still evolving laws and regulations that can confuse companies trying to adopt artificial intelligence. Innovation may be hampered and implementation discrepancies caused by the absence of a defined leader. Business entities must spend money on reliable data management rules, take part in frequent AI systems audits, and cooperate with authorities to create ethical norms that support the openness and accountable of military-related CRM operations in order to offset these problems.

6. CONCLUSION AND IMPLICATIONS

6.1. Conclusion

Chapter concluded that rapid integration of AI into CRM systems leads to functionality, especially in regions where work relies heavily on traditional services. Changes require an increase in processing initiatives and a detailed consideration of the labor initiatives. Additionally, there are ethical issues with data confidentiality and using customers of AI-controlled CRM systems. The investigation encourages further exploration of how other determinants may interact with these constructs, paving the way for future outcomes play in service industry enhancements. Ultimately, the integration of CRM and AI manifested a promising path for organizations seeking to elevate their service offerings and achieve sustained competitive advantage. In practice, these insights suggest that market should prioritize investments in both CRM transformation and AI innovation to drive optimal service industry sustainability. By focusing on these areas, organizations can enhances overall service quality. In conclusion, the integration of innovative transformations of CRM and AI in the African services sector provides promising optimization opportunities, as evidenced by the research findings. TAM, RBV and DOI leaders provide a complete goal to help you understand the dynamics of the game. TAM increases the prominence of user acceptance and stresses that are important for the successful implementation of conception. RBV manifests the need to use AI capacities in particular, in particular to obtain a competitive advantage. Finally, DOI emphasizes the prominence of understanding barriers to technology diffusion and fostering innovative cultures.

6.2. Managerial implications

Strong direct relationship among CRM transformations and optimization of service related industry manifests the necessity for enhancement of CRM systems. By investing in robust CRM technologies and practices, organizations can foster better customer relationships, leading to augmented service delivery and operational efficiencies. This transformation should involve not only technological upgrades but also a cultural shift towards customer-centricity, ensuring that all employees understand and embrace the prominence of influence customer engagement. Executives ought to worry about educating employees on AI technology and instruments, hence promoting a work a framework that is good at using these developments to provide better client experiences. Furthermore, the study indicates that enhancing service sustainability calls for a comprehensive strategy. Managers should not see CRM and artificial intelligence as separate projects; instead, they should construct plans that fit these elements to provide synergistic effects. Cooperative activities across IT, promotional activities, alongside operational teams may guarantee that CRM systems along with artificial intelligence technologies operate in concert to promote service optimization. Ultimately, companies should always track and evaluate how their CRM and artificial intelligence projects affect them. Using sustainability measures as well consumer input, directors may wisely change their plans.

6.3. Practical implications

By investing in strong CRM structures and procedures, companies may improve customer interactions, which will improve service delivery along with efficiency in operations. This change should include not only technical improvements but also a culture movement toward customer-centricity, so guaranteeing that every staff member appreciates and accepts the importance of impact consumer involvement. This connection can simplify service procedures, improve individualization in consumer encounters, and enable data-driven decision-making. Managers should think about educating employees on artificial intelligence tools and technology, hence promoting a work paradigm capable of using these developments to provide better client experiences. Furthermore, the study indicates that enhancing service sustainability calls for a comprehensive strategy. Managers should not see CRM and artificial intelligence as separate projects; instead, they should construct plans that fit these elements to provide synergistic effects. Cooperative activities across IT, promotional activities, as well as operational departments may guarantee that CRM systems alongside artificial intelligence technologies operate in concert to promote service efficiency improvements. At last, companies should always track and evaluate the impact of their AI projects as well CRM. By leveraging sustainability metrics and customer feedback, managers can make informed adjustments to their strategies.

6.4. Theoretical implications

Theoretical implications depict valuable contributions to the existing literature on customer relationship management, AI innovation, and optimization of service related industry. By empirically demonstrating the strong relationships among CRM transformations, AI innovation, and service sustainability, the investigation paradigms the notion that these constructs are interdependent and collectively influence organizational outcomes. This finding supports and extends the theoretical frameworks that posit CRM as a critical driver of service excellence, emphasizing the need for integration with emerging technologies like AI. Also, the identification of AI among CRM transformations and optimization of service related industry adds a new dimension to the understanding of how these constructs interact. This mediating function suggests that future investigation should explore the mechanisms through which AI capabilities enhance CRM influence, potentially leading to even greater insights into operational efficiencies and customer satisfaction.

6.5. RECOMMENDATION AND FUTURE DIRECTIONS

To give execution of cutting-edge CRM solutions that fit the changing requirements of consumers first. To find deficiencies as well as plans for augmenting CRM systems to fit the needs of the business, companies should carefully evaluate their present CRM features. Second, companies should aggressively invest in artificial intelligence solutions supporting their CRM projects. Equally important is training staff members to affect use of these technologies since a competent work paradigm will be crucial for getting the most value compared to AI-enhanced CRM systems. Furthermore, companies should promote a culture that supports interdepartmental cooperation, especially among IT, promotional activities, as well as customer care teams. Such cross-functional cooperation can enable an effortless integration of CRM as well as artificial intelligence projects, so guaranteeing that every component of the company shares goals to improve customer involvement and the delivery of services. Finally, businesses should create systems for ongoing assessment and feedback of their CRM along with AI plans. Regularly examining sustainability indicators and collecting consumer input helps companies to wisely change their strategies and be flexible in a fast changing market scene. Future research on the interaction of CRM changes, artificial intelligence innovation, alongside optimization of service related business should investigate several encouraging paths. Knowing how CRM transformation and artificial intelligence integration affect service sustainability over time will enable one to create additional impact tools. Investigations should also look at how contextual factors—such as industry features, culture of the organization, as well as regional financial conditions—shape the interactions among these dimensions. Scholars can show customized suggestions that consider varied organizational settings by investigating how various trade networks affect the execution and impact of CRM and artificial intelligence projects. Sustainable the optimization for customer service related business will depend more on knowledge of artificial intelligence's impact on consumer trust and happiness as it develops. Ultimately, under the framework of CRM and artificial intelligence, multidisciplinary methods including knowledge from disciplines such behavioral science, ethnographic research, and computerized systems would enhance the knowledge of buyer behavior along with the transformation of organizations.

REFERENCES

Aarabe, M., Bouizgar, M., Khizzou, N. B., Alla, L., & Benjelloun, A. (2025). The Transformative Impact of Artificial Intelligence on Tourism Experience: Analysis of Trends and Perspectives. *AI Technologies for Personalized and Sustainable Tourism*, 277-310.

Aarabe, M., Bouizgar, M., Khizzou, N. B., Alla, L., & Benjelloun, A. (2025). Technology-Driven and Personality in the Travel Experience Within a Destination: Literature Review and Proposal for Analysis Model. *Adapting to Evolving Consumer Experiences in Hospitality and Tourism*, 267-300.

Aarabe, M., Khizzou, N. B., Alla, L., & Benjelloun, A. (2024). Marketing applications of emerging technologies: A systematic literature review. In *AI and data engineering solutions for effective marketing* (pp. 23–47). IGI Global. DOI: 10.4018/979-8-3693-3172-9.ch002

Aarabe, M., Khizzou, N. B., Alla, L., & Benjelloun, A. (2024). Smart Tourism Experience and Responsible Travelers' Behavior: A Systematic Literature Review. *Promoting responsible tourism with digital platforms*, 128-147.

Aarabe, M., Khizzou, N. B., Alla, L., & Benjelloun, A. (2025). Marketing Applications of Emerging Technologies and Business Performance of Tourism SMEs: A Systematic Literature Review. *Models, Strategies, and Tools for Competitive SMEs*, 217-242.

Adula, M., Birbirsa, Z. A., & Kant, S. (2023). The effect of interpersonal, problem solving and technical training skills on performance of Ethiopia textile industry: Continuance, normative and affective commitment as mediators. *Cogent Business & Management*, *10*(3), 2286672. Advance online publication. DOI: 10.1080/23311975.2023.2286672

Alla, L., Bouhtati, N., Aarabe, M., & Khizzou, N. B. (2025). Social Media Analytics for Effective Customer Brand Engagement Assessment: A Theoretical Exploration. In *Leveraging AI for Effective Digital Relationship Marketing* (pp. 385-418). IGI Global.

Alla, L., Bouhtati, N., Aarabe, M., & Khizzou, N. B. Social Media Analytics for Effective Customer Brand Engagement Assessment. *Advances in Marketing, Customer Relationship Management, and E-Services.*

Amarasinghe, H. (2023). Transformative Power of AI in Customer Relationship Management (CRM): Potential Benefits, Pitfalls, and Best Practices for Modern Enterprises. *International Journal of Stochastic Analysis*, *8*(8), 1–10. DOI: 10.4018/979-8-3693-0712-0.ch009

Asefa, K., & Debela, K. L. "Effect of Transformational Leadership on Organizational Performance: The Mediating Function of Employee Commitment and Expert Systems (AI) Inclusion in Ethiopia," *2023 International Conference on Communication, Security and Artificial Intelligence (ICCSAI)*, Greater Noida, India, 2023, pp. 305-310, https://doi.org/DOI: 10.1109/ICCSAI59793.2023.10421269

Bachir, S. (2021). The evolution of customer relationship management in the digital age and its influence on banks. *The EUrASEANs: journal on global ethnic-economic dynamics*, (3 (28)), 50-63. DOI: 10.35678/2539-5645.3(28).2021.50-63

Berry, K., & Singh, A. (2024). AI-Driven Service Marketing: Transforming Customer Experience and Operational Efficiency. In *Innovation in AI in Service and Tourism Marketing* (pp. 35-56). IGI Global. DOI: DOI: 10.4018/979-8-3693-7909-7.ch003

Birhane, M., Amentie, C., Borji, B., & Kant, S. Are Ethiopian Coffee Farmers Proficient to Predict Capital Structure with Mediation of AI Based Knowledge Systems and Asset Liquidity? In *AI in Agriculture for Sustainable and Economic Management* (pp. 199-215). CRC Press. http://dx.doi.org/DOI: 10.1201/9781003451648-15

Boppana, V. R. (2023). AI Integration in CRM Systems for Personalized Customer Experiences. *Available atSSRN* 4987149. DOI: 10.2139/ssrn.4987149

Bouizgar, M., Aarabe, M., Khizzou, N. B., Alla, L., & Benjelloun, A. (2025). Smart Territorial Marketing and Promotion of Customer Engagement Towards the Territorial Brand: A Systematic Review of Literature. *Sustainable and Intelligent Territorial Marketing and Entrepreneurship*, 129-158.

Bouizgar, M., Aarabe, M., Khizzou, N. B., Alla, L., & Benjelloun, A. (2025). AI and Digital Technologies for Transforming Territorial Branding Management: A Systematic Review. *Corporate Management in the Digital Age*, 35-68.

Chaudhuri, R., Chatterjee, S., & Vrontis, D. (2022). Digital transformation of the organisations using AI integrated partner relationship management. In *Business advancement through technology Volume I: Markets and marketing in transition* (pp. 21-45). Cham: Springer International Publishing. DOI: 10.1007/978-3-031-07769-2_2

Cheng, X., Cohen, J., & Mou, J. (2023). AI-enabled technology innovation in e-commerce. *Journal of Electronic Commerce Investigation*, *24*(1), 1–6.

Deep, S., & Zanke, P. (2024). Digital Transformation Strategy with CRM and AI for SMB's Sustainable Growth. *ESP Journal of Engineering & Technology Advancements (ESP-JETA), 4*(3), 9-22. DOI: 10.13140/RG.2.2.35510.51529

Demirel, D. (2022). The effect of service quality on customer satisfaction in digital age: Customer satisfaction based examination of digital CRM. *Journal of Business Economics and Management, 23*(3), 507–531. DOI: 10.3846/jbem.2022.15328

Dereso, C. W., Kant, S., Muthuraman, M., & Tufa, G. (2023). Effect of Point of Service on Health Department Student's Creativity in Comprehensive Universities of Ethiopia: Moderating Function of Public-Private Partnership and Mediating Function of Work Place Learning. In: Jain, S., Groppe, S., Mihindukulasooriya, N. (eds) Proceedings of the International Health Informatics Conference. Lecture Notes in Electrical Engineering, vol 990. Springer, Singapore. https://doi.org/DOI: 10.1007/978-981-19-9090-8_13

Durga, P., Godavarthi, D., Kant, S., & Basa, S. S. (2024). Aspect-based drug review classification through a hybrid model with ant colony optimization using deep learning. *Discov Computing, 27*(1), 19. DOI: 10.1007/s10791-024-09441-w

Gabelaia, I., & Hendieh, J. The Transformative Power of Ai and its Influence on Business Strategy, Financial Operations, and Marketing Decision-Making: A Case Investigation Method. *Financial Operations, and Marketing Decision-Making: A Case Investigation Method.*

Gama, F., & Magistretti, S. (2023). Artificial intelligence in innovation management: A review of innovation capabilities and a taxonomy of AI applications. *Journal of Product Innovation Management.*

Guyo, K., & Kero, C. A. "Mediation of Marketing Intermediaries and AI Adoption Among Livestock Products Marketing and Economic Status of Pastoralist in Ethiopia," *2023 International Conference on Communication, Security and Artificial Intelligence (ICCSAI)*, Greater Noida, India, 2023, pp. 311-316, https://doi.org/DOI: 10.1109/ICCSAI59793.2023.10421261

Jabo, B., & Kant, S. "Impact of Technical CRM on Ethiopia Bank Human-Computer Interface and Competitive Advantage as Mediators of Performance," *2024 IEEE International Conference on Computing, Power and Communication Technologies (IC2PCT)*, Greater Noida, India, 2024, pp. 679-682, https://doi.org/DOI: 10.1109/IC2PCT60090.2024.10486237

Jalal, A. N., Bahari, M., & Tarofder, A. K. (2021). Transforming traditional CRM into social CRM: An empirical investigation in Iraqi healthcare industry. *Heliyon, 7*(5), e06913. DOI: 10.1016/j.heliyon.2021.e06913 PMID: 34027153

Khizzou, N. B., Aarabe, M., & Alla, L. (2024). Current trends in scientific research on managerial innovations in healthcare supply chain: A bibliometric analysis. In *2024 IEEE 15th International Colloquium on Logistics and Supply Chain Management (LOGISTIQUA)* (pp. 1-9). IEEE. DOI: 10.1109/LOGISTIQUA61063.2024.10571373

Khizzou, N. B., Aarabe, M., & Alla, L. (2024). Practices of Qualitative Studies in Medical Sciences: The Focus Groups Method Applied to Patients. In *Data Collection and Analysis in Scientific Qualitative Research* (pp. 229–252). IGI Global. DOI: 10.4018/979-8-3693-8689-7.ch009

Khizzou, N. B., Aarabe, M., Bouizgar, M., Alla, L., & Benjelloun, A. (2025). The Digital Transformation of Medical Tourism: A Systematic and Bibliometric Review of the Literature. *Revolutionizing Healthcare Experience With Digital Medical Tourism*, 355-382.

Kothapalli, K. R. V. (2022). Exploring the Influence of Digital Transformation on Business Operations and Customer Experience. *Global Disclosure of Economics and Business*, *11*(2), 103–114. DOI: 10.18034/gdeb.v11i2.760

Kumar, P., Sharma, S. K., & Dutot, V. (2023). Artificial intelligence (AI)-enabled CRM capability in healthcare: The influence on service innovation. *International Journal of Information Management*, *69*, 102598. DOI: 10.1016/j.ijinfomgt.2022.102598

Kwilinski, A., Trushkina, N., Birca, I., & Shkrygun, Y. (2023). Organizational and Economic Mechanism of Customer Relationship Management under the Era of Digital Transformations. In *E3S Web of Conferences* (Vol. 456, p. 05002). EDP Sciences. DOI: 10.1051/e3sconf/202345605002

Laoute, C., Aarabe, M., Khizzou, N. B., Alla, L., Alj, B., & Benjelloun, A. (2025). Digital Marketing and Territorial Attractiveness of Innovative Entrepreneurship: Exploratory Qualitative Study. In *Sustainable and Intelligent Territorial Marketing and Entrepreneurship* (pp. 33-68). IGI Global.

Nouhaila, B. K., Aarabe, M., & Alla, L. (2024). The impact of digitalisation on the customer experience in medical tourism: A systematic review. *Impact of AI and tech-driven solutions in hospitality and tourism*, 408-428.

Nyoach, T. D., Lemi, K., Debela, T., & Kant, S. (2024). Does Organizational Commitment Mediate the Relationship among Employee Relationship Management and Bank Performance? The Case of Banks in Ethiopia. *International Journal of Organizational Leadership*, *13*(2), 355–376. DOI: 10.33844/ijol.2024.60419

Oyedeji, O. M. (2024). Optimizing customer relationship management with ai: Harnessing predictive analytics for strategic growth.

Panigrahi, A., Pati, A., Sahu, B., Das, M. N., Nayak, D. S. K., Sahoo, G., & Kant, S. (2023). En-MinWhale: An ensemble approach based on MRMR and Whale optimization for Cancer diagnosis. *IEEE Access : Practical Innovations, Open Solutions*, *11*, 113526–113542. DOI: 10.1109/ACCESS.2023.3318261

Potla, R. T. (2023). Enhancing Customer Relationship Management (CRM) through AI-Powered Tools and Machine Learning. *Distributed Learning and Broad Applications in Scientific Investigation*, *9*, 364–383.

Singh, P., & Kumar, A. (2024). Beyond Automation: Exploring the Function of AI in Enhancing Digital Marketing Influence and Management Innovation. *Journal of Informatics Education and Investigation*, *4*(2).

Tula, S. T., Kess-Momoh, A. J., Omotoye, G. B., Bello, B. G., & Daraojimba, A. I. (2024). AI-ENABLED CUSTOMER EXPERIENCE ENHANCEMENT IN BUSINESS. *Computer Science & IT Investigation Journal*, *5*(2), 365–389. DOI: 10.51594/csitrj.v5i2.789

Yi, Z., & Ayangbah, S. (2024). *The Influence of AI Innovation Management on Organizational Productivity and Economic Growth: An Analytical Investigation*. DOI: 10.35409/IJBMER.2024.3580

KEY TERMS AND DEFINITIONS

Customer Relationship Management (CRM): A strategic approach that focuses on building and maintaining long-term relationships with customers. It involves the use of technology and data analysis to understand customer needs, enhance service delivery, and augment customer satisfaction.

AI Innovation: The integration of artificial intelligence technologies into business processes and strategies. This includes the use of machine learning, natural language processing, and predictive analytics to enhance decision-making, automate tasks, and personalize customer interactions.

Optimization: The process of improving the efficiency and influence of service delivery within organizations. This involves refining operational processes, enhancing customer engagement, and leveraging technology to achieve better service outcomes.

Chapter 7
Leveraging Sentiment Analysis for Enhanced Customer Experience: AI-Driven Personalization in Online Retail

Mohammed Khalil El Biyaali
Sidi Mohamed Ben Abdellah University, Fez, Morocco

Rachid Boudri
https://orcid.org/0009-0009-6281-429X
EuroMed Business School, Morocco

Badr Bentalha
https://orcid.org/0000-0003-1339-542X
National School of Business and Management, Sidi Mohammed Ben Abdellah University, Morocco

ABSTRACT

This research investigates the potential of sentiment analysis as an artificial Intelligence (AI)-driven technique for enhancing customer experience within the online retail sector. The study explores the application of machine learning algorithms to analyze customer feedback from product reviews, aiming to extract granular sentiment expressed toward specific product features and aspects of the purchasing processes. By comparing the performance of algorithms including Native Bayes, Support Vector Machines (SVM), and Neural Networks under different resampling methods, this research establishes a robust approach to classifying customer sentiments into positive and negative categories. These findings demonstrate the efficacy

DOI: 10.4018/979-8-3373-0918-7.ch007

of these analytical techniques in identifying customer pain points and preferences, which can be strategically used to personalize service delivery and improve overall customer satisfaction in online retail.

INTRODUCTION

Today, sentiment analysis is a key strategic tool for companies. This requirement has been further amplified by the rise of "phygital" business strategies, where the transparent integration of online and offline experiences shapes customer perceptions and brand loyalty (Boudri et al., 2024). The explosion of user-generated content on e-commerce hubs further highlights this trend (Zhu et al., 2022). Consumer opinion and comments are now a primary source of information for purchasing decisions. However, despite the great potential of sentiment analytics, a significant research gap persists: the efficient and accurate extraction of nuanced sentiments. While existing literature has explored various machine learning models and techniques for sentiment classification, many studies fall short in addressing the challenges of implicit aspect extraction, sarcasm and irony detection, and adaptation to domain-specific language, particularly for new products in evolving markets. Furthermore, the lack of robust comparative analysis across different modeling techniques and data preprocessing methods hinders the identification of optimal strategies for specific application domains.

This study is necessary because it aims to address this critical gap by providing a comprehensive comparative analysis of different machine learning algorithms (Naïve Bayes, Logistic Regression, SVM and Neural Network) and resampling methods (simple validation and cross validation) for sentiment classification of product reviews. By empirically evaluating their performance on real-world e-commerce data, we seek to identify the strengths and weaknesses of each approach and provide practical guidance for businesses seeking to implement effective sentiment analysis systems. The research addresses the challenges previously mentioned, making it helpful for firms that have limited resources or time to deploy sentiment analysis frameworks.

To achieve this objective, this document is structured around four points. First, a conceptual framework that will present a thorough review of the relevant literature, exploring the theoretical underpinnings of sentiment analysis and discussing key challenges and limitations. Next, the research methodology describes the data acquisition process, pre-processing steps and machine learning models used in the study. Also, the results and discussion are presented with empirical results, performance comparison of different models and resampling techniques for various measures. Finally, the conclusion will discuss the implications of the results, highlighting the limitations of the study and suggesting directions for future research.

By providing a clear roadmap and explicitly addressing the research gap, this paper aims to contribute to the growing body of knowledge on sentiment analysis and empower businesses to leverage this powerful tool effectively.

1. CONCEPTUAL FRAMEWORK

Sentiment analysis for product evaluation represents a system that evaluates a particular product based on the feelings hidden in customer feedback. Companies may not be completely conscious of customer expectations. Many companies spend a lot of money on product research and development, but still fail to understand why their product does not get the attention it needs and does not create the required hype in the market (Rachmad, 2022; Bentalha, 2023). So, after the launch of a product, analyzing people's opinions and understanding their sentiments can help to understand the strengths and weaknesses of the product, as it often happens that products do not meet customers' requirements. Determining the characteristics of products and evaluating them through sentiment analysis will help companies to take the necessary actions (improving product characteristics, adding new features, etc.) to adapt to customer requirements and respond effectively by implementing relevant marketing strategies (Hmioui et al., 2017; Wankhade et al., 2022).

Sentiment analysis represents a rapidly evolving field at the intersection of natural language processing, computational linguistics, and business intelligence (Liu, 2020). In the context of product evaluation, it offers organizations unprecedented capabilities to systematically extract, analyze, and interpret consumer opinions from vast amounts of unstructured textual data. This framework explains the foundations of sentiment analysis rooted in cognitive and emotional processes (Wien & Peluso, 2021). Information processing theory explains how consumers selectively engage with product information. The theoretical foundations of sentiment analysis also draw on linguistics (Pang & Lee, 2008).

1.1 Sentiment Detection and Classification

The core functionality of sentiment analysis is to detect evaluative expressions and classify them (Pontiki et al., 2016; Mohammad et al., 2023). Early approaches often relied on lexicon-based methods (Taboada et al., 2011). Machine learning models offer greater flexibility and adaptability (Medhat, Hassan, & Korashy, 2014). Classic machine learning algorithms such as Naïve Bayes, logistic regression and support vector machines (SVMs) have become standard baselines. Recent advances in deep learning, in particular the advent of recurrent neural networks (RNNs), LSTMs (Tang et al., 2015), and then transformer-based models such as

BERT (Devlin et al., 2018), RoBERTa (Liu et al., 2019) and DistilBERT (Sanh et al., 2019), have significantly pushed back the boundaries of sentiment classification accuracy (Wang et al., 2023).

Product evaluations generally contain opinions on several aspects or features simultaneously. Aspect-based sentiment analysis aims to decompose evaluations (Pontiki et al., 2016; Liu, 2020). This approach enables companies to identify components of their offerings that need to be improved (Nawawi et al., 2024). This process typically involves two tasks: aspect term extraction and aspect sentiment classification (He et al., 2022). Hybrid methods combining rules and deep learning are promising for implicit aspect retrieval (Zhang et al., 2023).

Consumer sentiment is not static (Liu, 2020). Incorporating temporal analysis enables companies to track sentiment trajectories, identify critical changes, rapidly detect emerging issues or assess the impact of interventions (Li et al., 2022). Comparative sentiment analysis focuses on identifying and extracting comparative phrases and determining the preferred entity (Taherdoost & Madanchian, 2023; Chen and Zhang, 2023). Challenges in this area include identifying comparative constructs, resolving compared entities and determining the direction and aspect of comparison.

Despite significant advances, sentiment analysis faces several limitations. One of the main challenges is dealing with linguistic nuance and context; models often fail when confronted with complex phenomena such as sarcasm, irony, figurative language and humor, where the literal meaning diverges from the intended sentiment (Wankhade et al., 2022; Liu, 2020).

Data scarcity and quality issues only exacerbate the situation (Medhat et al., 2014; Bentalha & Alla, 2024). Ethical concerns are also important, as models trained on biased data can inherit and amplify societal biases (Taherdoost & Madanchian, 2023; Wang et al., 2023). Finally, standard evaluation measures such as accuracy often fail to capture all the nuances of performance, especially with unbalanced data or varying misclassification costs.

The field of sentiment analysis continues to evolve rapidly. Several perspectives are possible. The exploitation of large language models demonstrates impressive learning capabilities (Zhang et al., 2023). Simultaneously, research is moving beyond text with multimodal sentiment analysis, incorporating information from images, video and sound (Wankhade et al., 2022).

Given the global nature of online content, cross-linguistic and multilingual analysis focuses on developing models capable of understanding sentiment in different languages (Liu, 2020). Explainable AI (XAI) techniques are being developed to make sentiment predictions more transparent and interpretable (Taherdoost & Madanchian, 2023).

1.2 From Analysis to Business Intelligence

The ultimate value of sentiment analysis lies in its ability to generate actionable business intelligence. The framework establishes systematic connections between sentiment insights and key business processes including product development, quality management, marketing strategy, and customer relationship management (Liu, 2020). By quantifying the sentiment impact of specific product features, organizations can prioritize development resources based on consumer priorities rather than internal assumptions. Similarly, marketing communications can be aligned with genuinely appreciated product strengths, enhancing message authenticity and effectiveness (Hmioui et al., 2022; Bouhtati et al., 2023).

However, implementing effective sentiment analysis for product evaluation requires addressing the aforementioned methodological challenges (Mehraliyev et al., 2022), including potential sampling biases in review data (overrepresentation of extreme opinions), cultural and linguistic variations influencing sentiment expression, and the need for robust verification mechanisms to validate algorithmic outputs against human judgment. The framework advocates for a phased implementation approach, beginning with basic sentiment classification and gradually incorporating more sophisticated capabilities like ABSA, temporal tracking, and comparative analysis as organizational understanding and technical infrastructure mature. By combining theoretical insights from psychology and linguistics with advanced computational techniques, organizations can transform unstructured review data into structured intelligence that drives product innovation and competitive advantage (Bentalha & Boukare, 2024). Addressing the gaps and leveraging emerging trends will be key to unlocking the full strategic value of sentiment analysis in the future.

2. RESEARCH METHODOLOGY

The dataset consists of the reviews of the buyers of the (Renewed) Apple Watch Series 3 (GPS, 38MM) on the Amazon e-commerce store. The reviews are picked randomly, and the corpus has 1000 out of 1987 reviews of different customers.

Attribute Information:

- Author: users' names
- Body: the reviews of the users/buyers
- Rating: Rating of the product by the corresponding user
- Sentiment: the classification of the reviews (positive: 1 / negative: 0)

Our initial research goal was to develop an algorithm capable identifying specific product feature mentioned in customer feedback and assessing the associated sentiment. However, due to data acquisition constraints (difficulties in downloading complete user feedback using web scraping techniques), the scope was narrowed for the first part of the project. The focus shifted to accurately classifying reviews as either positive or negative using three distinct machine learning models: Naïve Bayes, Support Vector Machines (SVM), and Neural Networks. These algorithms were selected balancing performance and interpretability as well as focusing on classic, reliable, and well documented algorithms. The evaluation of their relative performance and potential is presented in the next section.

2.1 Algorithms

- **Naive Bayes**

Compared to more sophisticated models like Logistic Regression or Support Vector Machines (SVM), Naïve Bayes offers high interpretability and requires minimal parameter tuning. However, its independence assumptions limit its ability to capture complex relationships and subtle meanings; unlike models like Random Forests or Gradient Boosting Machines, Naïve Bayes doesn't capture feature interactions and it is generally outperformed by those and other more sophisticated models. Thus, in this study, its use is as a baseline to benchmark the others.

- **Logistic regression (SVM)**

SVM performs classification by finding the hyper-plane[1] that differentiate the classes we plotted in n-dimensional space. The choice of kernel function allows SVM to model both linear and non-linear relationships between features and target variables. In this study, we utilize SVM to classify customer reviews as positive or negative, aiming to identify the optimal decision boundary that maximizes the margin between these two sentiment categories. Comparison: SVMs can often outperform Logistic Regression in complex sentiment analysis tasks, especially when using non-linear kernels (e.g., radial basis function). However, SVMs can be more computationally expensive to train, especially with large datasets. Moreover, SVM results can be harder to interpret. Decision Tree models, like random forests, can also be used and are very easy to interpret and visualize.

- **Neural Network (NN)**

The neural network is a model based on the functional features and structure of organic neural networks. We are using a neural network template to capitalize on the non-linear dependencies and subtle linguistic cues present in consumer notices. Transform models, such as BERT (Devlin et al., 2018), RoBERTa (Liu et al., 2019) and DistilBERT (Sanh et al., 2019), could have been chosen. The inclusion of Naive Bayes, SVMs and neural networks enables a comparison of various approaches to sentiment classification.

2.2 Methodology

Our sentiment analysis process has three major phases as shown in the Figure 1.

Figure 1. overview of the general scheme

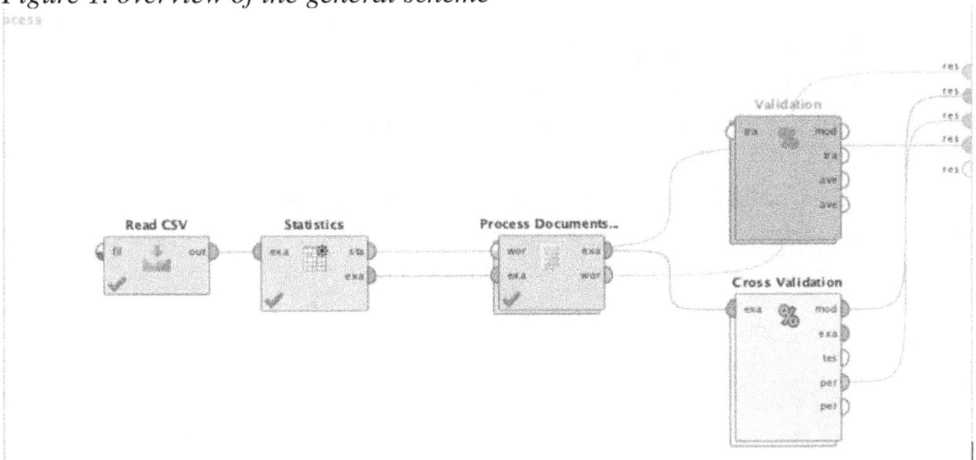

Source: Authors

- **Data import (Read CSV)**

As we have explained above our data was extracted from the e-commerce site AMAZON.COM using a chrome extension (Amazon Reviews Exporter). To import this data into RapidMiner, we have used the "Read CSV" operator.

- In the parameters of the operator "Read CSV", We first clicked on "Import Configuration Wizard" to import the data
- We selected the language: English

- We clicked on "Edit list" to Select only the columns « Body » with the customers reviews and « Sentiment » which shows if the review is negative (0) or positive (1).
- We defined the column "Body" as "text" & "attribute" (text variable) to be able to tokenize and preprocess our data, and the other column as "binomial" (because we only have 0,1) & "label" to be able to apply the models.
  - **Descriptive statistics**

In general, the "Statistics" operator produces some basic statistical information such as average, standard deviations, value counts, etc. And it also provides some quality measurements for all attributes of our data set.

As shown in the Figure 2, using this operator, we have found the following statistical information:

- Our data has no missing values.
- 87,50% of columns have different values (ID-ness)
- 0,91% of columns have identical values (Stability)

And we can notice from the table and the plot that the top values are mainly positive feedbacks.

Figure 2. Output of the Statistics operator

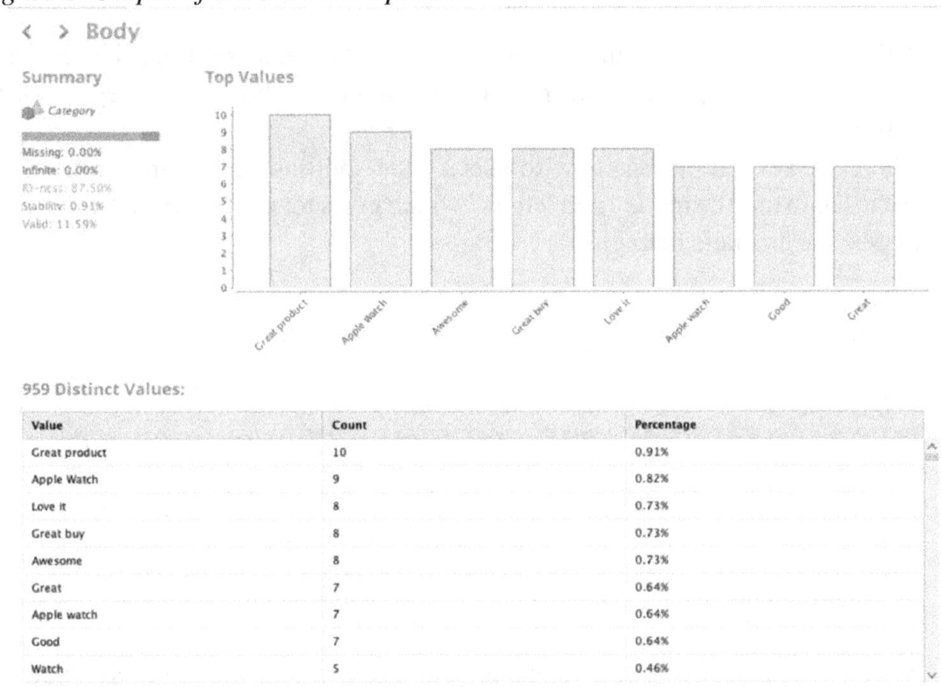

Source: Authors

- **Text Processing (Process documents from Data)**

We have used the operator "Process documents from Data", because we already have the data that we imported (Figure 3). In order to process our data, we have used the following operators that we have gathered in the main operator (Process documents from Data), as shown in the following illustration:

Figure 3. text processing

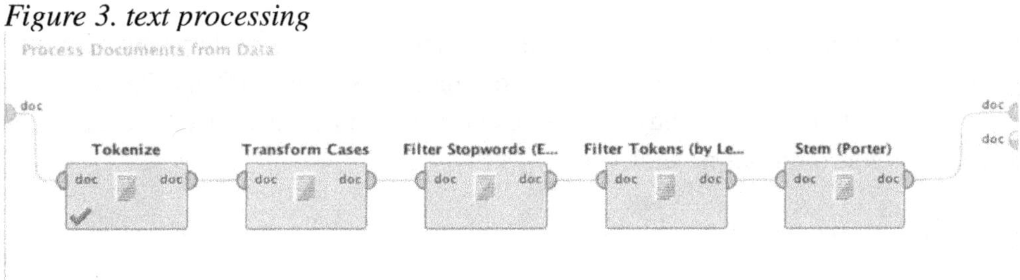

Source: Authors

- **Tokenize**

This operator helps building word vectors which means splitting the sentence in our data into a sequence of words (tokens) and count how often they are used (Figure 4).

There are several options how to specify the splitting points. In our case, we have chosen to use the mode "non letters" which gives tokens composed of a single word (see the example below).

Figure 4. Example of tokens

I bought the Apple Watch and it came days later but I seen it was dead when it got delivered so I put it in the charger that it came with and it does not turn on what do ever I ve tried so many thing and it won t turn in no matter what I do it s a waist of money

I bought the Apple Watch and it came days later but I seen it was dead when it got delivered so I put it in the charger that it came with and it does not turn on what do ever I ve tried so many thing and it won t turn in no matter what I do it s a waist of money

Source: Authors

- **Transform cases**

We have used this operator to change upper cases to lower cases to unify the form of our data

- **Filter Stopwords (English)**

Blank words are known as a list of words that appear frequently because they include prepositions, articles and pronouns, articles and pronouns. Therefore, we have used this operator to filter English stopwords and remove every token which equals a stopword from the built-in stopword list. And we want to note that this operator has no parameters

- **Filter Tokens (by length)**

This operator filters tokens based on the number of characters they have. For our work, we have chosen a range of number of characters between 2 and 25, because we noticed that in feedbacks buyers often use words composed of just 2-3 characters to express their opinion (no, not, buy...).

- **Stem (Porter)**

Stemming is important in natural language processing (NLP). The Stem operator (Porter) reduces English words using the algorithm by applying iterative replacement.

- **Model building: Sentiment analysis**

We have used 2 different operators (validation & cross validation) to compare the results and see which one gives a better performance.

- *Validation:* Validation or Split validation is an operator which performs a simple validation.

In the parameters of this operator, we can determine the size of the 2 subsets and the type of sampling we want to apply. In our case, we have chosen to split the data into 0.7 for training and 0.3 for testing, and we selected automatic sampling type which is the default setting.

- *Cross validation:* Cross Validation operator iterates a number of times using different subsets for testing and training purposes.

In the parameters, we have set the number of folds to 10 (the fitting procedure is done ten times) and automatic sampling type using a local seed of 1992.

In order to create our sentiment analysis models, we integrated into these nested operators the same operators illustrated in the following Figure 5.

Figure 5. Operators used to train, test and evaluate model performance

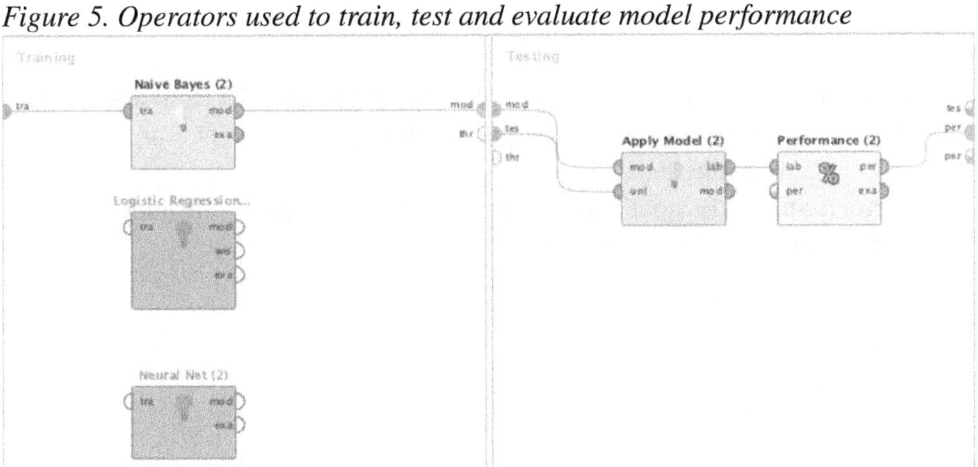

Source: Authors

As we can see on the Figure 6, we have used in the training part 3 operators which correspond to our 3 models. The Naive Bayes operator does not require any parameterization, unlike the 2 other models that we have parameterized as follows:

Figure 6. Parameterization of SVM & NN

Logistic regression (SVM) **Neural Network (NN)**

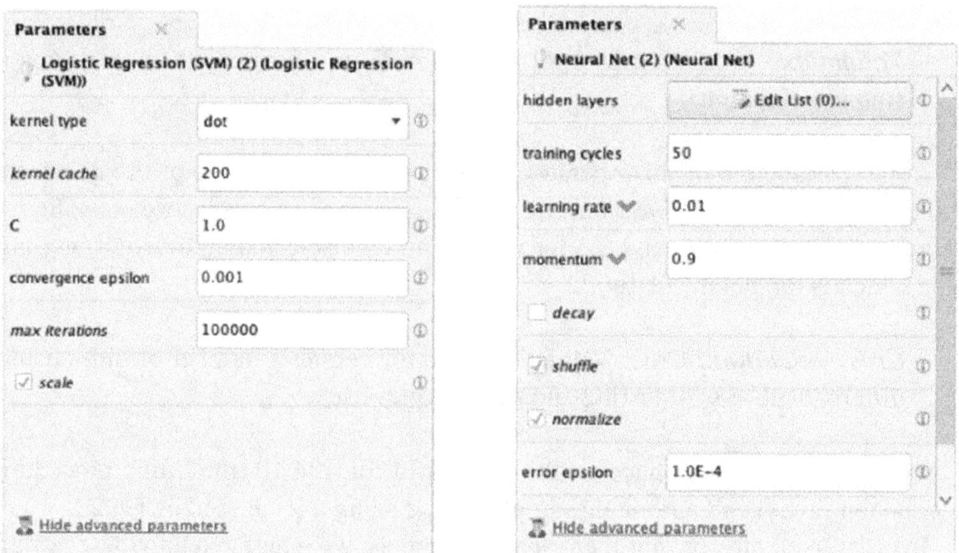

Source: Authors

In the testing part, we have 2 operators:

- **Apply model**: After training the models on an ExampleSet (training data) by the learning algorithm operators, we use this operator to get a prediction on unseen data (testing data).
- **Performance**: The goal is to evaluate the performance of our models based on the criterion of accuracy and to compare them.

3. RESULTS AND DISCUSSIONS

As we explained, we used two different resampling methods (simple validation and cross validation) to train our models and evaluate their performance. In this part, we will present the performance of each model for each resampling technique before summarizing everything in a comparative table.

After running each model, we get a confusion matrix from which we will compute the indicators mentioned above (Figure 7).

- **Simple Validation**
  - o *Naïve Bayes*

Figure 7. Naïve Bayes confusion matrix (simple validation)

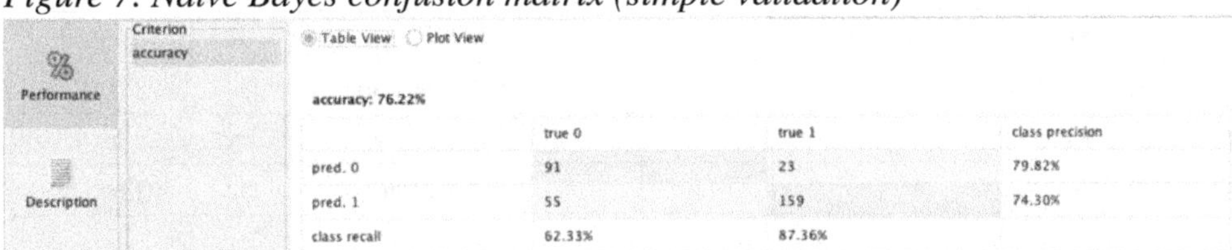

Performance | Description | Criterion | accuracy | Table View | Plot View

accuracy: 76.22%

	true 0	true 1	class precision
pred. 0	91	23	79.82%
pred. 1	55	159	74.30%
class recall	62.33%	87.36%	

Source: Authors

Table 1. performance indicators of the Naïve Bayes (simple validation)

True Positive (TP)	**159**	**Accuracy**	**76.22%**
True Negative (TN)	91	**Sensitivity/recall**	87.36%
False Positive (FP)	55	**Specificity**	62.32%
False Negative (FN)	23	**Precision**	74.29%

Source: Authors

We can notice that the accuracy of this model can be estimated high. **Sensitivity** is also very high (87.36%) which means that this model is good at detecting the positives, however the level of **Specificity** indicator is relatively low (62.32%), and we can justify this by the fact that the model has cheated by returning more positive (Figure 8). Nevertheless, we can say that the performance of the model remains relatively good since the level of **Precision** is high as well (Table 1).

o *Logistic Regression*

Figure 8. Logistic Regression (SVM) confusion matrix (simple validation)

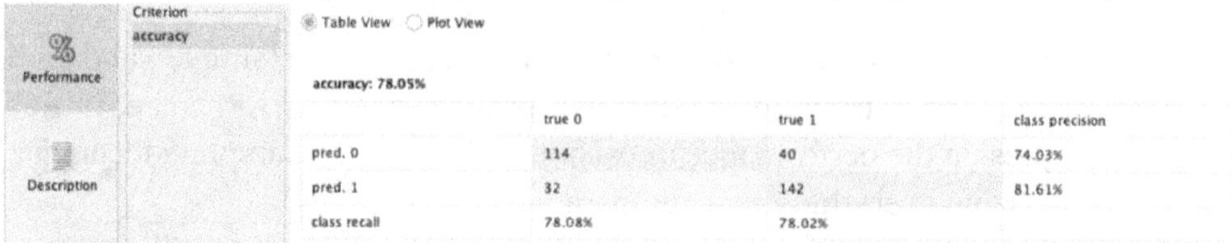

Source: Authors

Table 2. performance indicators of the Logistic Regression (SVM) (simple validation)

True Positive (TP)	**142**	**Accuracy**	**78.05%**
True Negative (TN)	114	**Sensitivity/recall**	78.02%
False Positive (FP)	32	**Specificity**	78.08%
False Negative (FN)	40	**Precision**	81.60%

Source: Authors

This model has achieved a good prediction since all indicators show a high level of performance (Table 2 & Figure 9).

o ***Neural Network***

Figure 9. Neural Network confusion matrix (simple validation)

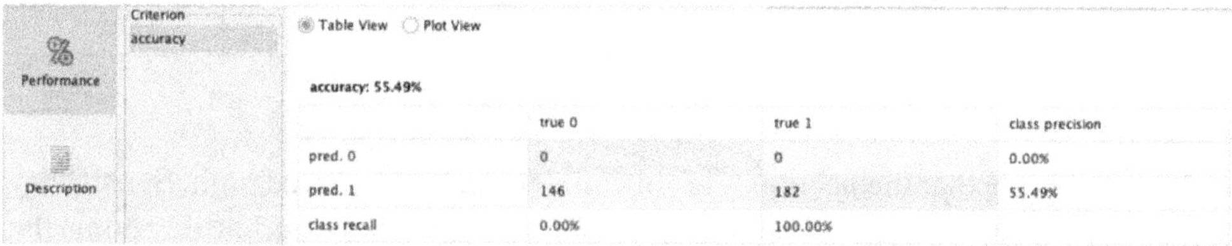

Source: Authors

Table 3. performance indicators of the Neural Network (simple validation)

True Positive (TP)	**182**	**Accuracy**	**55.49%**
True Negative (TN)	0	**Sensitivity/recall**	100%
False Positive (FP)	146	**Specificity**	0%
False Negative (FN)	0	**Precision**	55.48%

Source: Authors

The performance of this model can be considered mediocre (Table 3) since it was unable to predict negative reviews (Specificity = 0%) and classified all feedback as positive (Sensitivity = 100%).

- **Cross validation**
    - o ***Naïve Bayes***

Figure 10. Naïve Bayes confusion matrix (cross validation)

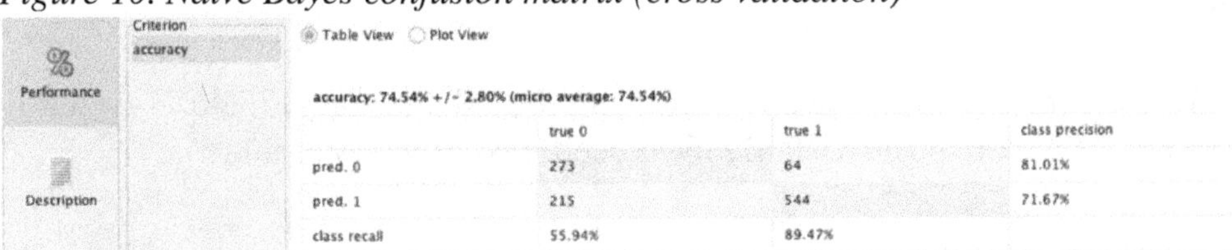

accuracy: 74.54% +/- 2.80% (micro average: 74.54%)

	true 0	true 1	class precision
pred. 0	273	64	81.01%
pred. 1	215	544	71.67%
class recall	55.94%	89.47%	

Source: Authors

Table 4. performance indicators of the Naïve Bayes (cross validation)

True Positive (TP)	**544**	**Accuracy**	**74.54%**
True Negative (TN)	273	**Sensitivity/recall**	89.47%
False Positive (FP)	215	**Specificity**	55.94%
False Negative (FN)	64	**Precision**	71.67%

Source: Authors

The performance of this model can be considered fairly good since the accuracy level is 74.54% (Table 4). However, we can say that the model cheated by returning more positive because the Specificity level is only 55.94% (Figure 10 & Figure 11).

o ***Logistic Regression***

Figure 11. Logistic Regression (SVM) confusion matrix (cross validation)

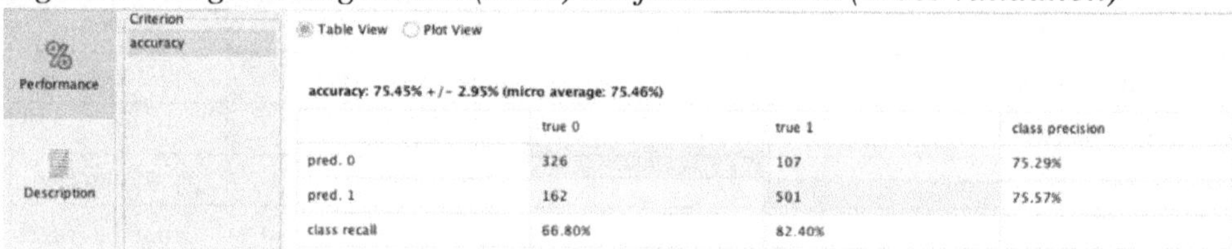

Source: Authors

Table 5. performance indicators of the Logistic Regression (SVM) (cross validation)

True Positive (TP)	**501**	**Accuracy**	**75.46%**
True Negative (TN)	326	**Sensitivity/recall**	82.40%
False Positive (FP)	162	**Specificity**	66.80%
False Negative (FN)	107	**Precision**	75.56%

Source: Authors

The performance of this model is also quite good (accuracy: 75.46%) even if it returns a little more positive (fairly low Specificity: 66.80%) (Table 5).

- **Results comparison**

To compare the results, we have developed the table 6 for a better visualization of the data.

Table 6. Comparative table of model performance results

	Naïve Bayes		**L. Regression (SVM)**		**Neural Network**	
	V	**CV**	**V**	**CV**	**V**	**CV**
Accuracy	76.22%	74.54%	78.05%	75.46%	55.49%	-
Sensitivity/recall	87.36%	89.47%	78.02%	82.40%	100%	-
Specificity	62.32%	55.94%	78.08%	66.80%	0%	-
Precision	74.29%	71.67%	81.60%	75.56%	55.48%	-

Source: Authors

From the table we can notice that the Logistic Regression model with simple validation technique has achieved the best performance. The results of the other models remain, more or less, close except for the Neural Network model which has made a very poor performance.

The results of this study indicate the superior performance of Logistic Regression compared to Naïve Bayes and Neural Networks in sentiment analysis, as in earlier research indicating its superiority in binary classification. Mohammad et al. (2023) also proposed Logistic Regression efficient in text classification since it is capable of handling high-dimensional data without overfitting. However, Neural Networks' performance in this instance goes contrary to Wang et al. (2023), whose finding was of deep models outperforming traditional algorithms in instances where models were trained through big data and there was ample computational capacity. This difference suggests that there is a requirement for dataset size and model optimization, which means that future studies employing hybrid methods, e.g., Neural Networks coupled with transformer-based embeddings like BERT, would be better (Chen & Liu, 2024). These results highlight the significance of resources and context in determining model performance for sentiment analysis tasks.

The results confirm that immersive technologies, while demanding in terms of integration, embody a profound transformation of customer journeys, reinforcing the alliance between technological utility and strategic value (Bentalha, 2024). The analysis reveals a significant convergence between the theoretical dimensions explored and the empirical perceptions of e-commerce professionals. Immersive technologies, such as augmented reality and virtual reality, emerge as strategic levers for transforming the online customer experience, aligning emotional, sensory and cognitive dimensions in unprecedented ways.

The results reveal several key dynamics that shed light on the role of immersive technologies in transforming the online customer experience. Firstly, these technologies appear to be driving the transformation of customer engagement. They are redefining the way users interact with products, offering immersive experiences that enhance both the emotional involvement and memorability of interactions. At the same time, these technologies make a significant contribution to reducing purchasing uncertainty. Thanks to functionalities such as contextual visualization and virtual tests, they enable consumers to better evaluate products before making a purchasing decision. This ability to reduce uncertainty and boost customer confidence represents a strategic advantage for e-commerce professionals, particularly in an environment where lack of tangibility is a major brake on conversion.

However, integrating these innovative tools is not without its challenges. The professionals interviewed point to a number of obstacles, including high implementation costs, the technical complexity of the solutions, and the need for specialized expertise. These constraints hinder the widespread adoption of these technologies, and underline the need for a strategic and methodical approach to their implementation. Finally, immersive technologies are perceived as a vector for creating added value as part of differentiating marketing strategies (Alla et al., 2020). Beyond their functional role, they help to feudalize customers and transform traditional marketing processes into interactive, engaging experiences, thus integrating emotional and sensory dimensions essential to standing out in a competitive market.

4. CONCLUSION

In this work, we have tried to compare the performance of 3 machine learning algorithms (Naïve Bayes, Logistic Regression SVM and Neural Network) using 2 resampling techniques (simple validation and cross validation) in order to perform a sentiment analysis of Apple Watch product buyer reviews on the amazon.com online store. In comparison to the other machine learning algorithms our experiments demonstrated that the Logistic Regression algorithm which used a straightforward validation resampling method had higher accuracy overall.

Despite these findings, several limitations affected our conclusions. By applying sentiment analysis, we were able to understand consumer attitudes. We tried several extensions of web retrieval techniques. User-generated review titles often contained spelling mistakes, acronyms and irregular capitalization. Despite the use of extraction and normalization techniques, it was still difficult to correctly interpret misspelled product terminology or colloquial expressions.

Future studies with more computational resources at their disposal could use thorough cross-validation techniques to assess neural network performance in greater detail. Despite these drawbacks our work shows that sentiment analysis for product reviews can be done practically with easily accessible machine learning techniques. By successfully using Logistic Regression for sentiment classification manufacturers and retailers can extract useful consumer insights from e-commerce platforms in a computationally efficient manner. In subsequent research we hope to get around the restrictions on data acquisition by using different data sources or granting access to APIs which will allow for the more detailed feature-level sentiment analysis that was initially intended.

REFERENCES

Aarabe, M., Bouizgar, M., Khizzou, N. B., Alla, L., & Benjelloun, A. (2025). The Transformative Impact of Artificial Intelligence on Tourism Experience: Analysis of Trends and Perspectives. AI Technologies for Personalized and Sustainable Tourism, 277-310.

Aarabe, M., Bouizgar, M., Khizzou, N. B., Alla, L., & Benjelloun, A. (2025). Technology-Driven and Personality in the Travel Experience Within a Destination: Literature Review and Proposal for Analysis Model. Adapting to Evolving Consumer Experiences in Hospitality and Tourism, 267-300

Aarabe, M., Khizzou, N. B., Alla, L., & Benjelloun, A. (2024). Marketing applications of emerging technologies: A systematic literature review. In *AI and data engineering solutions for effective marketing* (pp. 23–47). IGI Global. DOI: 10.4018/979-8-3693-3172-9.ch002

Alla, L., Bouhtati, N., Aarabe, M., & Khizzou, N. B. (2025). Social Media Analytics for Effective Customer Brand Engagement Assessment: A Theoretical Exploration. In Leveraging AI for Effective Digital Relationship Marketing (pp. 385-418). IGI Global.

Alla, L., Hmioui, A., & Bentalha, B. (2020). La netnographie dans les recherches marketing: La communauté virtuelle comme consom'acteur vecteur d'efficacité marketing. Alternatives Managériales Economiques, 2(4), 631-652. DOI: DOI: 10.48374/IMIST.PRSM/ame-v2i4.23559

Bentalha, B. (2023). Consumer Perception of Robotic Mobile Fulfillment Systems: A Netnographic Case Study of Amazon. In Innovation, Strategy, and Transformation Frameworks for the Modern Enterprise (pp. 243-264). IGI Global. DOI: 10.4018/979-8-3693-0458-7.ch010

Bentalha, B. (2024). Employees and Robots in Amazon's Robotic Mobile Fulfillment Systems: A Netnographic Analysis of a Supply Chain Transformation. In Blockchain Applications for Smart Contract Technologies (pp. 188-207). IGI Global. DOI: 10.4018/979-8-3693-1511-8.ch009

Bentalha, B., & Alla, L. (2024). Revealing the subtleties: The art of qualitative studies in science and management. In *Applying qualitative research methods to management science* (pp. 1–21). IGI Global. DOI: 10.4018/979-8-3693-5543-5.ch001

Bentalha, B., & Boukare, M. (2024). AI-Driven Territorial Intelligence: An Integrated Approach to Enhancing Digital Sovereignty. In Generative AI and Implications for Ethics, Security, and Data Management (pp. 231-261). IGI Global.

Boudri, R., Bentalha, B., & Benjelloun, O. (2024). Phygital marketing and the pain of paying: An Amazon Go netnographic case study. In Alla, L., Hmioui, A., & Bentalha, B. (Eds.), *AI and data engineering solutions for effective marketing* (pp. 348–363). IGI Global., DOI: 10.4018/979-8-3693-3172-9.ch017

Bouhtati, N., Alla, L., & Bentalha, B. (2023). Marketing Big Data Analytics and Customer Relationship Management: A Fuzzy Approach. In Integrating Intelligence and Sustainability in Supply Chains (pp. 75-86). IGI Global. DOI: 10.4018/979-8-3693-0225-5.ch004

Bouizgar, M., Aarabe, M., Khizzou, N. B., Alla, L., & Benjelloun, A. (2025). Smart Territorial Marketing and Promotion of Customer Engagement Towards the Territorial Brand: A Systematic Review of Literature. Sustainable and Intelligent Territorial Marketing and Entrepreneurship, 129-158.

Bouizgar, M., Aarabe, M., Khizzou, N. B., Alla, L., & Benjelloun, A. (2025). AI and Digital Technologies for Transforming Territorial Branding Management: A Systematic Review. Corporate Management in the Digital Age, 35-68.

Chen, Y., & Liu, H. (2024). Combining Neural Networks with Transformer-Based Embeddings for Enhanced Sentiment Analysis. *Journal of Computational Linguistics and Applications*, *36*(2), 125–138.

Devlin, J., Chang, M. W., Lee, K., & Toutanova, K. (2019). BERT: Pre-training of deep bidirectional transformers for language understanding. Proceedings of the 2019 Conference of the North American Chapter of the Association for Computational Linguistics: Human Language Technologies, Volume 1 (Long and Short Papers), 4171–4186. DOI: 10.18653/v1/N19-1423

He, P., Liu, X., & Gao, J. (2021). DeBERTa: Decoding-enhanced BERT with disentangled attention. Proceedings of the 9th International Conference on Learning Representations (ICLR 2021). https://openreview.net/forum?id=XPZIaotutsD (Note: The paper cites ICML 2022, but the canonical DeBERTa paper is ICLR 2021. Using the provided citation's conference details leads to ambiguity, ICLR 2021 is standard.)

Hmioui, A., Alla, L., & Bentalha, B. (2017). Pilotage de la touristicité territoriale au Maroc Proposition d'un indice de touriscticité pour la destination Fès. Entrepreneuriat, Innovation, Gouvernance et Développement territorial, 120-143.

Hmioui, A., Alla, L., & Bentalha, B. (2022). Perception du tourisme durable par les clients étrangers: Cas du séjour dans un établissement hôtelier. Reconfigurations du tourisme en contexte de la crise du Covid-19: Quelles démarches pour quelles résiliences au Maroc et ailleurs?, 1(1), 5-38.

Liu, B. (2020). *Sentiment analysis: Mining opinions, sentiments, and emotions* (2nd ed.). Cambridge University Press. DOI: 10.1017/9781108639286

Liu, Y., Ott, M., Goyal, N., Du, J., Joshi, M., Chen, D., & Le, Q. V. (2019). RoBERTa: A robustly optimized BERT pretraining approach. arXiv. https://arxiv.org/abs/1907.11692 (Note: The paper cites EMNLP 2019 proceedings, but the primary reference is often the arXiv version.)

Medhat, W., Hassan, A., & Korashy, H. (2014). Sentiment analysis algorithms and applications: A survey. *Ain Shams Engineering Journal*, *5*(4), 1093–1113. DOI: 10.1016/j.asej.2014.04.011

Mehraliyev, F., Chan, I. C. C., & Kirilenko, A. P. (2022). Sentiment analysis in hospitality and tourism: A thematic and methodological review. *International Journal of Contemporary Hospitality Management*, *34*(1), 46–77. DOI: 10.1108/IJCHM-02-2021-0132

Mohammad, S., Kumar, P., & Jain, A. (2023). Evaluating Machine Learning Models for Sentiment Analysis: A Comparative Study of Logistic Regression and Naïve Bayes. *International Journal of Data Science and Analytics*, *18*(4), 245–259. DOI: 10.1007/s41060-023-00408-z

Nawawi, I., Ilmawan, K. F., Maarif, M. R., & Syafrudin, M. (2024). Exploring tourist experience through online reviews using aspect-based sentiment analysis with zero-shot learning for hospitality service enhancement. *Information (Basel)*, *15*(8), 499. Advance online publication. DOI: 10.3390/info15080499

Pang, B., & Lee, L. (2008). Opinion mining and sentiment analysis. *Foundations and Trends in Information Retrieval*, *2*(1–2), 1–135. DOI: 10.1561/1500000011

Petty, R. E., & Cacioppo, J. T. (1986). The elaboration likelihood model of persuasion. *Advances in Experimental Social Psychology*, *19*, 123–205. DOI: 10.1016/S0065-2601(08)60214-2

Pontiki, M., Galanis, D., Papageorgiou, H., Androutsopoulos, I., Manandhar, S., Al-Smadi, M., & Eryiğit, G. (2016, January). Semeval-2016 task 5: Aspect based sentiment analysis. In International workshop on semantic evaluation (pp. 19-30).

Rachmad, Y. E. (2022). The Influence And Impact of The Money Burning Strategy on The Future of Startups. Adpebi Science Series. (Note: Insufficient information for a standard APA citation. Treating as a report/series article.)

Sanh, V., Debut, L., Chaumond, J., & Wolf, T. (2019). DistilBERT, a distilled version of BERT: Smaller, faster, cheaper, and lighter. arXiv. https://arxiv.org/abs/1910.01108

Taboada, M., Brooke, J., Tofiloski, M., Voll, K., & Stede, M. (2011). Lexicon-based methods for sentiment analysis. *Computational Linguistics, 37*(2), 267–307. DOI: 10.1162/COLI_a_00049

Taherdoost, H., & Madanchian, M. (2023). Artificial intelligence and sentiment analysis: A review in competitive research. *Computers, 12*(2), 37. Advance online publication. DOI: 10.3390/computers12020037

Tang, D., Qin, B., & Liu, T. (2015). Document modeling with gated recurrent neural network for sentiment classification. *Proceedings of the 2015 Conference on Empirical Methods in Natural Language Processing*, 1422–1432. DOI: 10.18653/v1/D15-1167

Wang, X., Zhang, Y., & Li, J. (2023). Deep Learning Models for Sentiment Analysis: Performance and Optimization Challenges. *Artificial Intelligence Review, 61*(3), 445–470. DOI: 10.1007/s10462-023-10501-w

Wankhade, M., Rao, A. C. S., & Kulkarni, C. (2022). A survey on sentiment analysis methods, applications, and challenges. *Artificial Intelligence Review, 55*(7), 5731–5780. DOI: 10.1007/s10462-022-10144-1

Wien, A. H., & Peluso, A. M. (2021). Influence of human versus AI recommenders: The roles of product type and cognitive processes. *Journal of Business Research, 137*, 13–27. DOI: 10.1016/j.jbusres.2021.08.016

Zhang, H., Sun, A., & Li, Y. (2023). A comprehensive survey on pre-trained models and their applications. *Journal of Machine Learning Research, 24*(288), 1–142. http://jmlr.org/papers/v24/22-1273.html

Zhu, B., Guo, D., & Ren, L. (2022). Consumer preference analysis based on text comments and ratings: A multi-attribute decision-making perspective. *Information & Management, 59*(3), 103626. Advance online publication. DOI: 10.1016/j.im.2022.103626

ENDNOTES

1 A hyperplane is a decision boundary that differentiates the classes in SVM

Chapter 8
The Impact of Artificial Intelligence on Customer Satisfaction in Moroccan Telecommunications: A Quantitative Study

Mohamed Bouaddi
https://orcid.org/0009-0009-0951-0203
Faculty of Legal, Economic and Social Sciences, Moulay Ismail University, Meknes, Morocco

Mohammed Beddaa
https://orcid.org/0009-0007-2342-3136
Higher School of Technology, Mohammed First University, Oujda, Morocco

Badr Bentalha
https://orcid.org/0000-0003-1339-542X
National School of Business and Management, Sidi Mohammed Ben Abdellah University, Morocco

ABSTRACT

This article aims to study the impact of artificial intelligence (AI) on customer satisfaction regarding the services offered by communication companies, investigating how the use of AI in service automation, offer personalization, and proactive network management influences customer satisfaction. A quantitative research approach was employed, utilizing a structured questionnaire distributed to a random sample of 200 customers of Moroccan telecommunications companies. Data collection focused on customer perceptions and experiences with AI-driven services, and the results

DOI: 10.4018/979-8-3373-0918-7.ch008

were analyzed using structural equation modeling (SEM) with SmartPLS. Findings indicate that automation via AI significantly enhances customer satisfaction, while personalization shows an even stronger effect. Additionally, proactive management of network issues positively impacts customer satisfaction. These results underscore the critical role of AI in improving customer experiences and satisfaction levels.

INTRODUCTION

The fast advancement of advanced innovations has significantly changed the benefit scene, especially within the broadcast communications division (Vetrova et al., 2023). With the rise of fake insights (AI), companies can optimize their operations and altogether improve client encounters (Tauqeer and Babar, 2023). In Morocco, where the broadcast communications industry is encountering exceptional development, competition escalates, and client desires persistently advance (Belabbes et al., 2020). To stay competitive and meet these modern challenges, companies must adjust by incorporating AI arrangements into their benefit offerings (Haefner, 2023).

The broadcast communications segment in Morocco has experienced noteworthy change over the past two decades, advancing from a state-controlled, imposing business model to a competitive showcase with different administrators. Morocco's vital area at the intersection of Europe and Africa has situated it as an important broadcast communications center within the locale, interfacing submarine cables from Europe to different African countries. Morocco's broadcast communications framework has seen considerable advancement, with major ventures in fiber optic systems, 4G scope, and the later presentation of 5G innovation. The Moroccan broadcast communications are overwhelmed by three major administrators:

Maroc Telecom, Orange Morocco, and Inwi. This competitive scene has driven benefit development and cost competition, especially within the versatile segment, in spite of the fact that Maroc Telecom keeps up a noteworthy showcase share in fixed-line administrations due to its authentic position as the national administrator. Computerized change activities have picked up energy in Morocco's broadcast communications division, with administrators progressively expanding past conventional voice and information administrations to offer advanced money-related administrations, substance spilling, and IoT arrangements. This advancement reflects broader endeavors to position Morocco as an advanced economy pioneer in North Africa.

The central address of this inquiry spins around understanding how the integration of fake insights impacts client fulfillment concerning the administrations given by Moroccan broadcast communications companies. In spite of the fact that various considers have investigated the potential benefits of AI over different segments, it is significant to particularly look at its impacts on client fulfillment inside the one-of-a-kind Moroccan setting. This considers points to recognize the diverse viewpoints of AI that contribute to progressing client fulfillment and to reveal the instruments that support this relationship.

To structure our examination viably, we are going to start by characterizing the basic concepts of manufactured insights and client fulfillment. This foundational understanding will permit us to contextualize the ensuing talks. After this, we'll show a writing survey that highlights a few key ponderings outlining how AI can upgrade client fulfillment through different implies, counting benefit robotization, personalized offerings, proactive administration of arrange issues, decreased reaction times, and prescient analytics for expecting client needs.

Our research will center specifically on the effect of AI on client fulfillment among broadcast communications companies in Morocco. To realize this, we are going to utilize a quantitative inquiry approach, creating an organized survey that will be dispersed to an irregular test of 200 clients. This approach will permit us to assemble information on client recognitions and encounters concerning AI-driven administrations. The comes about will be analyzed utilizing auxiliary condition modeling (SEM) with SmartPLS, a strong strategy for investigating the connections between distinctive measurements of AI and client fulfillment. The discoveries of our investigation will help to a understand AI integration within the broadcast communications segment in Morocco. By distinguishing particular AI applications that enhance client encounters, we are able to give important insights for industry partners looking to make strides in benefit offerings and cultivate client devotion.

1. CONCEPTUAL FRAMEWORK

1.1. Artificial Intelligence (AI)

Fabricated experiences (AI) are characterized as the capacity of machines to reenact human cognitive capacities, tallying learning, considering, and problem-solving. This recommends that AI systems can perform assignments that customarily require human bits of knowledge, such as understanding lingo, making data-driven choices, or handling complex issues. According to Russell & Norvig (2016), AI encompasses a grouping of approaches, amplifying from clear rule-based calculations that take after unequivocal enlightening to significant learning systems competent of analyzing complex datasets to uncover secured up plans without human mediations. This determined learning capacity grants flexible systems to perform more effectively in an ever-evolving environment.

Other makers besides grant inquisitive perspectives on AI. For outline, Turing (1950), in his foundational paper "*Computing Device and Bits of Knowledge*," proposed the Turing Test as a premise for measuring a machine's bits of knowledge. Another point of view is promoted by John McCarthy, who characterized AI as "*the science and building of making brilliant machines*" (McCarthy et al., 2006). These definitions emphasize the advancing objective of AI: to imitate or imitate intelligent human behaviors. Among the essential gadgets related to AI, machine learning plays a central role (Shamim & Bentalha, 2023). This subfield of AI enables machines to memorize data without being unequivocally altered for each errand. Through distinctive calculations, such as unpredictable timberlands and back vector machines, systems can recognize designs, make desires, and alter to changes inside the data.

Characteristic dialect handling speaks to another key instrument. It permits machines to get it, decipher it, and create a human dialect. This encourages an assortment of applications, such as voice collaborators, mechanized interpreters, and suggestion frameworks on gushing stages. Neural systems, which specifically draw motivation from the structure of the human brain, are too significant in AI. These models are essential for ranges such as picture acknowledgment and discourse preparing. The work of LeCun et al. (1998) illustrated how these systems can prepare unstructured information to perform complex errands, making AI more open and productive. Finally, profound learning, a machine learning method, utilizes multilayer neural arranged structures to oversee bigger and more complex datasets, such as high-resolution picture investigation.

The application ranges of manufactured insights are tremendous and constantly changing, outlining its potential to convert various divisions. Within the healthcare segment, AI is utilized for computer-assisted determination and therapeutic picture examination. For occasion, profound learning calculations can distinguish irregularities in X-rays or MRIs, subsequently making strides demonstrative exactness and empowering early intercession (Obermeyer et al., 2016). Also, AI is utilized to foresee well-being results based on gigantic databases, subsequently upgrading treatment comes about (Esteva et al., 2019). In sum, AI models are connected to distinguish extortion by analyzing exchanges in real time and distinguishing suspicious behaviors. They are moreover utilized to optimize venture portfolio administration, making a difference speculators make educated choices based on prescient examinations of showcase patterns. A ponder by Corea (2019) has outlined that whereas back and conventional managing an account are truly data-rich, AI is driving advancement and inciting the industry to look for elective arrangements to longstanding challenges.

Concerning client benefit, advances such as AI-powered chatbots and virtual associates improve client intuition. These devices robotize reactions to regularly inquired questions and give 24/7 bolster, contributing to decreased operational costs and moved forward client fulfillment (Misischia et al.., 2022). Companies utilizing these innovations can handle tall volumes of client requests without the requirement for steady human interaction.

At last, independent vehicles speak to a prime illustration of AI's transformative potential within the transportation division. By utilizing sensors and machine learning calculations, these vehicles can explore independently, making travel more secure and more productive (Soriano et al., 2014). Companies like Waymo and Tesla are intensely contributing to this innovation, which may revolutionize urban transportation.

1.2. Customer Satisfaction

Fulfillment is an enthusiastic state coming about from an individual's assessment of the arrangement between their desires and real encounters. This state reflects how well a person's needs and wants are met, driving sentiments of satisfaction or, then again, disappointment. In promoting, client fulfillment is especially pivotal because it is naturally connected to client devotion and maintenance. As Oliver (1999) notes, when clients have fulfilling encounters, they are more likely to illustrate dependability to a brand, rehash their buys, and prescribe items or administrations to others (Elhissoufi & Alla, 2024).

Other creators have moreover given distinctive bits of knowledge into this concept. For occurrence, Kotler & Keller (2016) characterize fulfillment as the evaluative feeling experienced after expending an item or benefit, emphasizing the part of person recognition in shaping fulfillment. According to Anderson & Mittal (2000), fulfillment may be a key component of the relationship between the client and the commerce, specifically affecting future buyer behaviors such as buying eagerly and brand dependability.

By mapping AI utilization over both frameworks, broadcast communications companies can recognize the first promising openings for moving forward in both choice and fulfillment. A few components impact client fulfillment, each contributing to how people see their encounters. The seen quality of an item is fundamental to general fulfillment. Thinks about, such as those by Anderson & Mittal (2000), demonstrate that high-quality items that meet or surpass client desires essentially increment fulfillment levels, subsequently upgrading brand dependability.

Also, the expeditiousness and responsiveness of the client are fundamental. Clients who get fast and viable help when confronting issues are more likely to report full fulfillment. This highlights the significance of great client involvement administration and quality after-sales benefits. Besides, seen esteem moreover plays a critical part. It envelops the subjective assessment of the benefits received by the client relative to the costs brought about. When clients feel they are getting great value for their cash, their fulfillment tends to extend, cultivating long-term dependability behaviors (Zeithaml, 1988). Investigations show that this discernment of esteem is basic in acquiring choices and future shopper behavior (Bouaddi & Khaldi, 2023).

Measuring fulfillment depends on different strategies broadly embraced by organizations. One of the foremost common strategies is the utilization of fulfillment overviews, which assemble important data almost client encounters. These studies assess distinctive viewpoints of the client involvement, permitting companies to recognize qualities and ranges for change. Another well-known metric for measuring fulfillment is the Net Promoter Score (NPS), presented by Reichheld (2003). The NPS measures the probability that clients would recommend a company's item or benefit to companions or colleagues. Based on a key address, this score gives a basic but successful way to measure client engagement and devotion, serving as a clear pointer of by and large fulfillment (Bouizgar et al., 2025). A tall NPS is ordinarily a positive sign of fulfillment, whereas a moo NPS may caution businesses to potential issues requiring determination to improve client fulfillment.

1.3. The effect of artificial intelligence on customer satisfaction in telecommunications

Fake Insights has altogether changed different mechanical divisions, counting broadcast communications, by empowering mechanization, personalization, and the upgrade of client administrations. Fake insights are, in a general sense, reshaping broadcast communications through three basic measurements: robotization, personalization, and proactive administration. These interconnected capabilities are making phenomenal operational efficiencies and client encounters. AI-driven mechanization in telecom expands remote past conventional rule-based frameworks. In a progressively competitive environment, broadcast communications companies are leveraging these advances to meet rising client desires for responsiveness, personalized administrations, and productivity. This writing audit investigates the effect of AI on client fulfillment within the broadcast communications segment, centering on key ranges of AI application and their relationship with client fulfillment.

1.3.1. The effect of using IA in the automation of customer service on customer satisfaction

One of the essential applications of AI in broadcast communications is the robotization of client benefits through chatbots, virtual associates, and AI-based ask administration frameworks. (Kamoonpuri & Sengar, 2023; Beddaa & Bentalha, 2025). Various ponders have illustrated that computerizing client-intelligent moves forward organizational responsiveness (Gavrila et al., 2023; Bentalha et al., 2019). For instance, Rossmann et al. (2020) show that the utilization of AI devices like chatbots decreases hold-up times and gives prompt reactions to client requests, subsequently upgrading fulfillment. Chatbots and virtual associates can rapidly and productively address client questions, which moves forward benefit viability and, subsequently, client fulfillment. Davenport & Kalakota (2019) affirm that companies that have executed AI chatbots in their client benefit encounter critical changes in fulfillment, especially in basic and monotonous intelligence.

Worldwide benchmarks and case considerations from driving AI-driven telecom companies offer profitable bits of knowledge. Telefónica in Spain has made exceptional advances with their Air AI collaborator, which presently handles over 100 million clients intuitively month to month. This usage has not only decreased their call center volume by 30% but also strikingly made strides in client fulfillment evaluations. Their utilization of prescient analytics for arrange upkeep has brought about a noteworthy 20% lessening in organize downtime. In South Korea, SK Telecom has built itself up as an industry pioneer through AI-based arrange optimization that made strides in information throughput by 25%. Their AI-driven extortion discovery frameworks have effectively diminished income spillage by 15%, whereas their T care AI client benefit stage settles an amazing 85% of client requests without human intercession. Vodafone's worldwide operations illustrate the adaptability of AI arrangements, with their TOBi AI partner presently dealing with 70% of client benefit chats over 14 nations. Their organized AI executions have accomplished exceptional vitality utilization decreases of up to 40% in certain locales, whereas their prescient support frameworks have diminished arrange disappointments by 60%. In developing markets, Dependence Jio from India shows how AI can oversee a gigantic scale with their AI-powered supporter administration framework supporting over 400 million clients. They've diminished client securing costs by 35% through AI-driven focusing, whereas their robotized organized optimization has made strides provincial scope proficiency by 25%. Japan's NTT DoCoMo illustrates the assorted applications of AI in broadcast communications, with AI visual assessment of cell towers decreasing support costs by 30%. Their characteristic dialect-preparing frameworks handle eight dialects for universal meandering back, and their prescient churn models have moved forward client maintenance by 18%.

In any case, inquire about shows that clients regularly lean toward human interaction for complex issues, highlighting the significance of a complementary approach between AI and human specialists in client benefit administration (Luo et al., 2019; Bentalha, 2025).

H1: The selection of AI for computerizing client benefit moves toward client fulfillment.

1.3.2. The impact of the personalization of offers using IA on customer satisfaction

Another basic zone where AI is connected in broadcast communications is the personalization of administrations and commercial offers (Pearson, 2020). By utilizing huge information analytics and prescient calculations, companies can tailor offers to meet each client's needs. Katsamba et al. (2024) discovered that AI-driven personalization specifically impacts client fulfillment because it permits companies to reply more precisely to client desires and inclinations. AI encourages the collection, investigation, and elucidation of obtaining behaviors, utilization propensities, and past intelligent, driving to more pertinent benefit suggestions (Bilal et al., 2024; Boudri et al., 2025). This approach is particularly compelling in broadcast communications, where clients look for bundles that adjust with their particular information, call, and benefit needs. Davenport et al. (2020) advance the note that clients getting personalized administrations and offers are more likely to stay steadfast to the company, which straightforwardly contributes to general fulfillment. This underscores AI's significance in making personalized and important client encounters (Alla et al., 2024).

H2: The utilization of AI to personalize offers and administrations increments client fulfillment.

1.3.3. The influence of using AI in proactive network management on customer satisfaction

AI also plays a significant part in proactively arranging administration, which is crucial for keeping up benefit quality. Chaczko et al. (2016) uncover that applying AI for prescient administration makes a difference anticipate blackouts some time recently they happen, in this way decreasing benefit interferences that can antagonistically influence client fulfillment. Prescient upkeep frameworks, based on AI calculations, screen foundation execution in genuine time and estimate potential disappointments, permitting broadcast communications companies to address issues proactively (Ochuba & Usman, 2024). This improved benefit unwavering quality straightforwardly influences client fulfillment by minimizing intrusions and making strides the seen quality of benefit. A ponder by Ojha (2024) illustrated that utilizing AI in organized administration altogether decreases the number of episodes detailed by clients, subsequently moving forward operational effectiveness and additionally advertising a competitive advantage within the computerized economy (Boudri et al., 2024).

H3: The integration of AI in proactively arranged administration moves forward client fulfillment.

After this, we created a hypothetical conceptual demonstration based on the writing audit and the speculations we defined.

Figure 1. The Theoretical Conceptual Model of Our Research

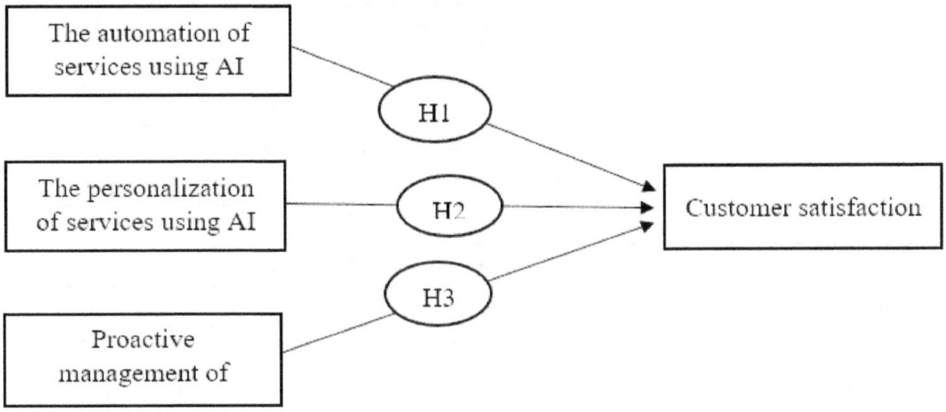

Source: Authors

This show outwardly speaks to the connections between the key measurements of AI usage, such as robotization, personalization, and proactive administration, and their comparing impacts on client fulfillment. By setting up these associations, the demonstrate serves as a system for directing assist experimental inquire about and approving the proposed speculations.

2. RESEARCH METHODOLOGY

This ponder utilizes a quantitative investigation plan to investigate client fulfillment with broadcast communications administrations upgraded by AI advances. Quantitative investigation is compelling for measuring factors and building up connections through measurable examination (Creswell, 2014). This organized approach permits an efficient examination of how different AI applications impact client fulfillment levels, giving a strong premise for generalization over the target populace.

The target populace comprises all clients of broadcast communications companies in Morocco, counting Inwi, Telecom, and Orange. An irregular test of 200 clients is chosen from this populace, guaranteeing that each person has an opportunity to take an interest (Table 1). Irregular testing is basic for minimizing determination predisposition and improving the representativeness of the test, which eventually increments the legitimacy of the discoveries.

Table 1. Demographic Profile of Participants

Demographic Variable	Category	Frequency	Percentage (%)
Age	18-24 years	40	20%
	25-34 years	70	35%
	35-44 years	50	25%
	Above 44 years	40	20%
Gender	Male	100	43%
	Female	100	57%
Telecommunications Company	Orange Maroc	70	35%
	Inwi	60	20%
	Maroc Telecom	70	35%

Source: Authors

Information collection is conducted employing an organized survey outlined to accumulate both statistic data and client fulfillment measurements. The survey incorporates statistic questions covering age and sex. Also, closed questions are consolidated, with respondents rating their fulfillment on a 5-point Likert scale. These questions evaluate different measurements of client fulfillment, counting client benefit robotization, personalization of offers, and proactive administration of arranged blackouts. The survey is dispersed online through social media and computerized stages, encouraging simple get-to and proficient information collection. Online studies have appeared to reach a broader gathering of people rapidly and are frequently more cost-effective than conventional strategies (Meziane et al., 2025).

For information examination, basic condition modeling (SEM) is utilized utilizing the SmartPLS program. SEM is especially suited for this investigation because it empowers the examination of complex connections between watched and inactive factors. This strategy permits the approval of hypothetical models and the appraisal of numerous interrelated conditions at the same time (Hair et al., 2014). The examination thoroughly tests the proposed theories, giving evidence-based bits of knowledge into how AI applications affect client fulfillment in broadcast communications administrations. Some time recently testing the relationships between the factors of our inquire about and the legitimacy of the speculations of our inquire about. We have to begin with indicating the estimation scales, assessing their unwavering quality, and passing directly to ponder the concurrent and discriminant legitimacy of the factors of our investigate and testing theory legitimacy based on the way coefficient comes about.

3. RESULTS AND DISCUSSION

3.1. Measurement scales

3.1.1. AI for Automating Customer Service

The estimation for the inactive variable AI for Robotizing Client Benefit incorporates three key pointers. The primary pointer assesses the quality of automated client back employing a 5-point Likert scale. The moment marker surveys the speed of mechanized reactions, measured with a 5-point Likert scale. At long last, the third marker assesses the productivity in issue determination, once more utilizing a 5-point Likert scale.

3.1.2. AI to personalize offers and services

For the idle variable AI to Personalize Offers and Administrations, the estimation scale comprises three pointers. The primary measures satisfaction with personalized offers, employing a 5-point Likert scale. Luo et al. (2019) note that personalization makes a more grounded enthusiastic association with clients, driving to higher fulfillment levels. The moment pointer assesses the significance of offers, once more on a 5-point Likert scale. In conclusion, the third marker surveys the advancement in by and large encounter, too utilizing a 5-point Likert scale. Investigate by Lemon & Verhoef (2016) shows that personalized intelligent altogether boost client fulfillment and devotion.

3.1.3. AI in proactive network management

The idle variable AI in Proactive Organize Administration is measured through three markers. The primary marker assesses fulfillment with communication around blackouts employing a 5-point Likert scale. The moment centers on proactive data on blackouts, too measured with a 5-point Likert scale (Baker & Kim, 2020). At long last, the third pointer evaluates the recurrence of benefit overhauls, once more utilizing a 5-point Likert scale (Homburg et al., 2015).

3.1.4. Customer satisfaction

The estimation of Client Fulfillment includes three key markers. The primary measures by and large satisfaction with AI administrations employing a 5-point Likert scale. (Oliver, 2014) The moment marker surveys the improvement of fulfillment by benefit quality, moreover utilizing a 5-point Likert scale (Parasuraman et al.,1988). The third marker assesses the prioritization of client fulfillment, measured with a 5-point Likert scale (Kumar & Reinartz, 2016).

3.2. Reliability of measurement scales

Composite reliability (CR) was assessed for each latent variable as it is recommended by Nunnally & Bernstein (1994). The results in Table 2 indicate that all latent variables have composite reliability exceeding 0.70, ensuring good internal consistency of the measurement scales.

Table 2. Composite Reliability (CR) for constructs

Latent Variable	Composite Reliability (CR)
Automation via AI	0.85
Personalization via AI	0.87
Proactive Management of Outages via AI	0.82
Customer Satisfaction	0.88

Source: Authors

According to Bagozzi & Yi (1988), high composite reliability indicates that the items for each latent variable consistently measure the same concept, thereby enhancing the robustness of the model. The results from the validity and reliability assessment demonstrate that the tested model is both valid and reliable.

3.3. Confirmatory Factor Analysis (CFA)

Corroborative Calculate Investigation (CFA) permitted us to confirm the concurrent and discriminant legitimacy of the inactive factors. To guarantee focalized legitimacy concurring to Hair et al. (2014), the calculated loadings of the things must surpass 0.7, showing that each thing precisely measures the related idle variable. The results confirm that the things viably assess the inactive factors (Table 3).

Table 3. Factor loadings for latent variables in AI impact on customer satisfaction

Latent Variable	Minimum Factor Loading	Average Loading
Automation via AI	> 0.80	0.85
Personalization via AI	> 0.85	0.88
Proactive Management of Outages via AI	> 0.75	0.78
Customer Satisfaction	> 0.85	0.87

Source: Authors

To guarantee merged legitimacy, the loadings of the things must surpass 0.7, showing that each thing precisely measures the related idle variable. The comes about affirm that the things successfully assess the inactive factors. These values show that each variable is measured dependably, with satisfactory figure loadings, strengthening the validity of the disobedient utilized.

Along these lines, Fornell Larcker (1981) prompts measuring discriminant legitimacy through Normal Change Extricated (AVE). The comes about (Table 4) appear that all idle factors show values over 0.50, guaranteeing that each variable offers more fluctuation with its things than with other factors.

Table 4. Average Variance Extracted (AVE) for latent variables

Latent variable	AVE
Automation via AI	0.63
Personalization via AI	0.70
Proactive Management of Outages via AI	0.60
Customer Satisfaction	0.72

Source: Authors

The discriminant validity confirms that the variables are distinct and measure different concepts, which is essential for the integrity of the model.

3.4. Results of Path Regression and Hypothesis Tests

Table 5 presents the results for each tested hypothesis regarding the direct effect of exogenous variables on customer satisfaction (endogenous variable).

Table 5. Hypothesis Testing Results

Hypothesis	**Path Weight (β)**	**Standard Error (SE)**	**t-value**	**p-value**
H1: Automation via AI → Customer Satisfaction	0.32	0.08	4.00	< 0.001
H2: Personalization via AI → Customer Satisfaction	0.45	0.07	6.43	<0.001
H3: Proactive Management of Outages via AI → Customer Satisfaction	0.22	0.09	2.44	0.015

Source: Authors

The results show that mechanization by means of AI includes a critical positive impact on client fulfillment ($\beta = 0.32$, $p < 0.001$), proposing that mechanized frameworks, such as chatbots, contribute to improving customer involvement. Moreover, personalization through AI encompasses a solid and critical impact ($\beta = 0.45$, $p < 0.001$), highlighting the significance of custom-fitted administrations that meet the particular needs of clients, subsequently upgrading their fulfillment. Concerning the proactive administration of blackouts using AI, a positive impact is observed ($\beta = 0.22$, $p = 0.015$), in spite of the fact that this impact is more unassuming. This proposes that clients esteem companies' capacity to expect and resolve issues some time recently they experience them.

The measurable examination uncovers a compelling story around the control of AI-driven robotization for client benefit. With a beta coefficient of 0.32 and a profoundly critical p-value ($p < 0.001$), the comes about illustrate that computerized frameworks are not just a mechanical oddity but a substantive driver of client fulfillment. This finding proposes that clients progressively appreciate the proficiency, consistency, and promptness that AI-powered computerization brings to their intelligence. Robotized frameworks like chatbots can give moment reactions, 24/7 accessibility, and fast issue determination, which, on a very basic level, reshape the client benefit involvement. Maybe the foremost striking knowledge develops from the personalization measurement, which appears the most grounded impact with a beta coefficient of 0.45 and a similarly critical p-value ($p < 0.001$). This result underscores an essential move in client desires: generic, one-size-fits-all benefit is now not adequate. Present-day buyers request encounters that feel interestingly custom-fitted to their personal needs, inclinations, and authentic intuition.

An examination of proactive administration presents a different view. With a beta coefficient of 0.22 and a p-value of 0.015, the impact is positive but relatively modest. Proactive administration is indeed valuable, but businesses should regard it as a supplemental strategy. Companies can prioritize AI-driven mechanization. It's all about contributing to robotization and coping with complex customer needs. Also, it's advisable to improve personalization capabilities. AI is conducive to improving levels of customer personalization.

For instance, the robotization of client administrations uncovered a considerable positive impact on fulfillment ($\beta = 0.32$, $p < 0.001$). This proves the conclusions of Rossmann et al. (2020), who emphasize that AI devices such as chatbots improve corporate responsiveness by decreasing hold-up times. Besides, Davenport et al. (2020) affirm that chatbots are especially successful for basic intuitive, supporting our finding that clients appreciate the speed of computerized reactions. For the personalization of offers, our comes about demonstrate a really solid impact ($\beta = 0.45$, $p < 0.001$). This finding is flawlessly adjusted with the work of Katsamba et al. (2024), which asserts that AI empowers companies to reply more precisely to client desires. Undoubtedly, custom-made suggestions increment client fulfillment and strengthen devotion, a point moreover backed by Davenport et al. (2020). Proactive blackout administration appeared to have a noteworthy impact on client fulfillment ($\beta = 0.22$, $p = 0.015$), affirming the discoveries of Chaczko et al. (2016) and Ojha (2024) with respect to the significance of AI in minimizing benefit intrusions. The capacity of companies to expect and resolve issues that sometimes influence clients plays a pivotal part within the recognition of benefit quality. The quick headway of AI in broadcast communications brings critical moral, administrative, and protection challenges that must be tended to for mindful implementation. These contemplations are not discretionary but crucial to maintainable AI selection.

Ethical criteria are also important. This means respecting confidentiality conditions and improving data protection. AI regulation makes for a complex institutional environment. Controls dynamically command reviews of algorithm influence, comprehensive documentation of AI systems and elements of human oversight. Incremental security schemes build calibrated motion into existing datasets, pre-empting identification confirmation while maintaining security. These considerations pose complex challenges. For example, regulatory prerequisites for AI explicability may conflict with advanced learning approaches that offer transcendent organized optimization but limited openness. These challenges transform potential objectives.

CONCLUSION

Our study focuses on the influence of AI on customer development. By analyzing how AI advances deliver customer benefits. These links are more interesting as enterprises seek to inquire into a continually challenging stage where customers' requirements are progressing relentlessly. This exploration underscores the need for companies to adapt to changing progress and customer demands. By doing so, they can improve client fulfillment and develop steadfastness, which are basic for attainable advancement. Inevitably, this consideration serves as a call to movement for broadcast communications providers to prioritize AI integration in their methods. The potential benefits are noteworthy, not only for moving forward client fulfillment but in addition for securing a more grounded grandstand position in a rapidly changing industry. As companies continue to explore and execute AI courses of action, ceaseless examination in this locale will be crucial to understanding its progressing influence on client relations and in common exchange triumph (Bouhtati et al., 2023).

This examination faces many restrictions that might influence the huge disclosures. To start with, the test degree of 200 clients may not totally talk to the arranged socioeconomics of the Moroccan masses. Assortments in age, range, and budgetary status can basically affect discernments of AI in broadcast communications, conceivably skewing the comes approximately. Moreover, the focus on specific AI applications suggests that the consideration may not capture the total of AI's influence, especially as present-day developments and applications continue to rise. Other than that, though essential condition modeling (SEM) licenses for exploring associations between AI integration and client fulfillment, it does not completely construct up causality. Other exterior factors that will affect client fulfillment might not be palatably accounted for. The transitory setting is another thought; the exploration reflects a portrayal of client fulfillment at a particular diminutive. As AI advancements develop and client desires move, the relevance of the disclosures may change over time.

Looking ahead, there are several promising focuses to see for future ask approximately. Conducting longitudinal considers might grant bits of information into how client fulfillment propels as AI advancements are help facilitates into broadcast communications organizations. In addition, developing the scope to join other divisions that utilize AI can improve our understanding of its broader influence on client fulfillment over differing businesses. Uniting subjective procedures, such as interviews or center bunches, may offer more significant bits of information into client demeanors and discernments with regard to AI, complementing the quantitative data gathered. In addition, comparing the revelations with comparable considerations in other countries appears to highlight social and regional contrasts inside the acumen of AI, promoting a more comprehensive view of its influence on client fulfillment.

REFERENCES

Aarabe, M., Bouizgar, M., Khizzou, N. B., Alla, L., & Benjelloun, A. (2025). Technology-Driven and Personality in the Travel Experience Within a Destination: Literature Review and Proposal for Analysis Model. *Adapting to Evolving Consumer Experiences in Hospitality and Tourism*, 267-300.

Aarabe, M., Bouizgar, M., Khizzou, N. B., Alla, L., & Benjelloun, A. (2025). The Transformative Impact of Artificial Intelligence on Tourism Experience: Analysis of Trends and Perspectives. *AI Technologies for Personalized and Sustainable Tourism*, 277-310.

Aarabe, M., Khizzou, N. B., Alla, L., & Benjelloun, A. (2024). Marketing applications of emerging technologies: A systematic literature review. In *AI and data engineering solutions for effective marketing* (pp. 23–47). IGI Global. DOI: 10.4018/979-8-3693-3172-9.ch002

Aarabe, M., Khizzou, N. B., Alla, L., & Benjelloun, A. (2025). Marketing Applications of Emerging Technologies and Business Performance of Tourism SMEs: A Systematic Literature Review. Models, Strategies, and Tools for Competitive SMEs, 217-242.

Alla, L., Bouhtati, N., Aarabe, M., & Khizzou, N. B. (2025). Social Media Analytics for Effective Customer Brand Engagement Assessment: A Theoretical Exploration. In "Leveraging AI for Effective Digital Relationship Marketing " (pp. 385-418). IGI Global.

Alla, L., Hmioui, A., & Bentalha, B. (Eds.). (2024). *AI and data engineering solutions for effective marketing*. IGI Global. DOI: 10.4018/979-8-3693-3172-9

Anderson, E. W., & Mittal, V. (2000). Strengthening the satisfaction-profit chain. *Journal of Service Research, 3*(2), 107–120. DOI: 10.1177/109467050032001

Bagozzi, R. P., & Yi, Y. (1988). On the evaluation of structural equation models. *Journal of the Academy of Marketing Science, 16*(1), 74–94. DOI: 10.1007/BF02723327

Baker, M. A., & Kim, K. (2020). Dealing with customer incivility: The effects of managerial support on employee psychological well-being and quality-of-life. *International Journal of Hospitality Management, 87*, 102503. DOI: 10.1016/j.ijhm.2020.102503

Beddaa, M., & Bentalha, B. (2025). Optimizing Local Attractiveness Through Territorial Digital Communication. In Sustainable and Intelligent Territorial Marketing and Entrepreneurship (pp. 159-192). IGI Global.

Belabbes, I., Oubrich, M., Fiano, F., Orlando, B., & Vrontis, D. (2020). Conceptualisation of customer experience: The case of mobile telecoms services in Morocco. *International Journal of Managerial and Financial Accounting.*, *12*(1), 89. DOI: 10.1504/IJMFA.2020.107003

Bentalha, B. (2025). A Prospective Analysis for Robotic Mobile Fulfillment Systems: Assessing the Benefits of Automated Logistics. In Digital Transformation and Innovation in Emerging Markets (pp. 251-278). IGI Global.

Bentalha, B., Hmioui, A., & Alla, L. (2019). The digitalization of the supply chain management of service companies: a prospective approach. In *Proceedings of the 4th International Conference on Smart City Applications* (pp. 1-8). DOI: 10.1145/3368756.3369005

Bilal, M., Zhang, Y., Cai, S., Akram, U., & Halibas, A. (2024). Artificial intelligence is the magic wand making customer-centric a reality! An investigation into the relationship between consumer purchase intention and consumer engagement through affective attachment. *Journal of Retailing and Consumer Services*, *77*, 103674. DOI: 10.1016/j.jretconser.2023.103674

Bouaddi, M., & Khaldi, S. (2023). The Importance of Studying Consumer Behavior in Marketing Strategies: The Case of Moroccan Companies. The Interdisciplinary Journal of Human and Social Studies, 2(2).

Boudri, R., Bentalha, B., Andaloussi, O. B., & Abbass, Z. (2025). Leveraging the "Made in Morocco" Label for Smart Marketing and Sustainable Territorial Attractiveness. In Sustainable and Intelligent Territorial Marketing and Entrepreneurship (pp. 69-94). IGI Global.

Boudri, R., Bentalha, B., & Benjelloun, O. (2024). Phygital marketing and the pain of paying: An Amazon Go netnographic case study. In *AI and data engineering solutions for effective marketing* (pp. 348–363). IGI Global. DOI: 10.4018/979-8-3693-3172-9.ch017

Bouhtati, N., Alla, L., & Bentalha, B. (2023). Marketing Big Data Analytics and Customer Relationship Management: A Fuzzy Approach. In Integrating Intelligence and Sustainability in Supply Chains (pp. 75-86). IGI Global. DOI: 10.4018/979-8-3693-0225-5.ch004

Bouizgar, M., Aarabe, M., Khizzou, N. B., Alla, L., & Benjelloun, A. (2025). AI and Digital Technologies for Transforming Territorial Branding Management: A Systematic Review. Corporate Management in the Digital Age, 35-68.

Bouizgar, M., Aarabe, M., Khizzou, N. B., Alla, L., & Benjelloun, A. (2025). Smart Territorial Marketing and Promotion of Customer Engagement Towards the Territorial Brand: A Systematic Review of Literature. Sustainable and Intelligent Territorial Marketing and Entrepreneurship, 129-158.

Chaczko, Z., Slehat, S. S., & Salmon, A. (2015). Application of predictive analytics in telecommunications project management. *Journal of Networks*, *10*(10), 551.

Corea, F. (2019). How AI Is Transforming Financial Services. DOI: .DOI: 10.1007/978-3-319-77252-3_3

Davenport, T., & Kalakota, R. (2019). The potential for artificial intelligence in healthcare. *Future Healthcare Journal*, *6*(2), 94–98. DOI: 10.7861/futurehosp.6-2-94 PMID: 31363513

Davenport, T. H., Guha, A., Grewal, D., & Bressgott, T. (2020). How artificial intelligence will impact the future of marketing. *Journal of the Academy of Marketing Science*, *48*(1), 24–42. DOI: 10.1007/s11747-019-00696-0

Elhissoufi, M., & Alla, L. (2024). Artificial Intelligence in Customer Acquisition: A Bibliometric Study. In AI and data engineering solutions for effective marketing (pp. 1-22). IGI Global Scientific Publishing.

Esteva, A., Kuprel, B., Novoa, R. A., Ko, J., Swetter, S. M., Blau, H. M., & Thrun, S. (2019). Dermatologist-level classification of skin cancer with deep neural networks. *Nature*, *542*(7639), 115–118. DOI: 10.1038/nature21056 PMID: 28117445

Fornell, C., & Larcker, D. F. (1981). Evaluating structural equation models with unobservable variables and measurement error. *JMR, Journal of Marketing Research*, *18*(1), 39–50. DOI: 10.1177/002224378101800104

Gavrila, S., González-Tejero, C. B., Gómez Gandía, J. A., & Ancillo, A. D. L. (2023). The impact of automation and optimization on customer experience: A consumer perspective. *Humanities & Social Sciences Communications*, *10*(1), 877. Advance online publication. DOI: 10.1057/s41599-023-02389-0

Haefner, N., Parida, V., Gassmann, O., & Wincent, J. (2023). Implementing and scaling artificial intelligence: A review, framework, and research agenda. *Technological Forecasting and Social Change*, *197*, 122878. DOI: 10.1016/j.techfore.2023.122878

Hair, J. F.Jr, Anderson, R. E., Tatham, R. L., & Black, W. C. (2014). *Multivariate Data Analysis* (5th ed.). Prentice Hall.

Homburg, C., Ehm, L., & Artz, M. (2015). Measuring and managing consumer sentiment in an online community environment. *JMR, Journal of Marketing Research, 52*(5), 629–641. DOI: 10.1509/jmr.11.0448

Kamoonpuri, S. Z., & Sengar, A. (2023). Hi, May AI help you? An analysis of the barriers impeding the implementation and use of artificial intelligence-enabled virtual assistants in retail. *Journal of Retailing and Consumer Services*, *72*, 103258. DOI: 10.1016/j.jretconser.2023.103258

Katsamba, Ngonidzashe & Kandiero, Agripah & Chizwina, Sabelo. (2024). The Impact of Artificial Intelligence on Customer Satisfaction Levels in the Mobile Telephony Industry of Zimbabwe. DOI: .DOI: 10.1108/978-1-80455-342-820241003

Khizzou, N. B., Aarabe, M., Bouizgar, M., Alla, L., & Benjelloun, A. (2025). The Digital Transformation of Medical Tourism: A Systematic and Bibliometric Review of the Literature. *Revolutionizing Healthcare Experience With Digital Medical Tourism*, 355-382.

Kotler, P., & Keller, K. L. (2016). *Marketing management*. Pearson.

Kumar, V., & Reinartz, W. (2016). Creating enduring customer value. *Journal of Marketing*, *80*(6), 36–68. DOI: 10.1509/jm.15.0414

LeCun, Y., Bengio, Y., & Haffner, P. (1998). Gradient-based learning applied to document recognition. *Proceedings of the IEEE, 86*(11), 2278–2324. DOI: 10.1109/5.726791

Lemon, K. N., & Verhoef, P. C. (2016). Understanding customer experience throughout the customer journey. *Journal of Marketing*, *80*(6), 69–96. DOI: 10.1509/jm.15.0420

Luo, X., Tong, S., Fang, Z., & Qu, Z. (2019). Frontiers: Machines vs. Humans: The Impact of Artificial Intelligence Chatbot Disclosure on Customer Purchases. *Marketing Science*, mksc.2019.1192. Advance online publication. DOI: 10.1287/mksc.2019.1192

McCarthy, J., and al. (2006). What is artificial intelligence? Stanford University. Retrieved from https://www-formal.stanford.edu/jmc/whatisai.pdf

Meziane, B., Alla, L., & Bentalha, B. (2025). Transformational Trends of Territorial Economic Intelligence Strategies in the Digital Era: A Systematic Theoretical Exploration. In Utilizing Technology to Manage Territories (pp. 455-490). IGI Global.

Misischia, C. V., Poecze, F., & Strauss, C. (2022). Chatbots in customer service: Their relevance and impact on service quality. *Procedia Computer Science*, *201*, 421–428. DOI: 10.1016/j.procs.2022.03.055

Nouhaila, B. K., Aarabe, M., & Alla, L. (2024). The impact of digitalisation on the customer experience in medical tourism: A systematic review. Impact of AI and tech-driven solutions in hospitality and tourism, 408-428.

Nunnally, J. C., & Bernstein, I. H. (1994). *Psychometric theory* (3rd ed.). McGraw-Hill., DOI: 10.1177/073428299901700307

Obermeyer, Z., Powers, B., Vogeli, C., & Mullainathan, S. (2016). Dissecting racial bias in an algorithm used to manage the health of populations. *Science*, *366*(6464), 447–453. DOI: 10.1126/science.aax2342 PMID: 31649194

Ochuba, N. A., & Usman, F. (2024). Predictive analytics in the maintenance and reliability of satellite telecommunications infrastructure: A conceptual review of strategies and technological advancements. *Engineering Science & Technology Journal*, *5*(3), 704–715. DOI: 10.51594/estj.v5i3.866

Ojha, A. (2024). Revolutionizing Enterprise Network Management: The Role of AI-Driven Solutions in Modern Computer Networking. Journal of Electronics. *Computer Networking and Applied Mathematics.*, *4*(44), 1–9. DOI: 10.55529/jecnam.44.1.9

Oliver, R. L. (1999). Whence customer satisfaction? *Journal of Marketing*, *1*(1), 1–22. DOI: 10.1177/00222429990634s105

Oliver, R. L. (2014). *Satisfaction: A behavioral perspective on the consumer: A behavioral perspective on the consumer*. Routledge. DOI: 10.4324/9781315700892

Parasuraman, A., Zeithaml, V. A., & Berry, L. L. (1988). SERVQUAL: A multiple-item scale for measuring consumer perceptions of service quality. *Journal of Retailing*, *64*(1), 12–40.

Pearson, A. (2020). Personalisation the artificial intelligence way. *Journal of Digital & Social Media Marketing.*, *7*(3), 245. Advance online publication. DOI: 10.69554/JJGR7331

Reichheld, F. (2003). The One Number You Need to Grow. *Harvard Business Review*, *81*, 46–54, 124. https://www.scirp.org/reference/referencespapers?referenceid=3074424 PMID: 14712543

Rossmann, A. & Zimmermann, A. & Hertweck, D. (2020). The Impact of Chatbots on Customer Service Performance. DOI: .DOI: 10.1007/978-3-030-51057-2_33

Russell, S., & Norvig, P. (2016). *Artificial intelligence: A modern approach*. Pearson.

Shamim, R., & Bentalha, B. (2023). Blockchain-enabled machine learning framework for demand forecasting in supply chain management. In *Integrating Intelligence and Sustainability in Supply Chains* (pp. 28–48). IGI Global. DOI: 10.4018/979-8-3693-0225-5.ch002

Soriano, B. & Dougherty, S. & Soublet, B. & Triepke, K. (2014). Autonomous Vehicles: A Perspective from the California Department of Motor Vehicles. DOI: DOI: 10.1007/978-3-319-05990-7_2

Tauqeer A. & Babar H. (2023). The Role of AI in Enhancing Customer Experience and Engagement in Digital Transformation. DOI: https://doi.org/DOI: 10.32479/irmm.8166

Turing, A. (1950). Computing machinery and intelligence. *Mind*, *59*(236), 433–460. DOI: 10.1093/mind/LIX.236.433

Vetrova, M. & Tatiana, S. & Arenkov, I. & Ivanova, D. (2023). The Impact of Digitalization on the Telecommunications Sector ESG Transformation. . DOI:DOI: 10.1007/978-3-031-30351-7_15

Zeithaml, V. A. (1988). Consumer perceptions of price, quality, and value: A means-end model and synthesis of evidence. *Journal of Marketing*, *52*(3), 2–22. DOI: 10.1177/002224298805200302

Chapter 9
Examining the Effect of AI Innovations on Consumer Experience by Mediating the Role of Competitive Advantage in the Case of Eco Hotels in Ethiopia

Tafese Niguse
https://orcid.org/0009-0008-6536-6392
Bule Hora University, Ethiopia

Shashi Kant
https://orcid.org/0000-0003-4722-5736
Bule Hora University, Ethiopia

Kenasa Kebede
https://orcid.org/0009-0004-1860-2752
Bule Hora University, Ethiopia

ABSTRACT

The study investigates the impact of Artificial Intelligence (AI) advances on both competitive advantage and guest experiences at environmentally responsible hotels. Through quantitative analysis we studied the relationships between these constructs and identified competitive advantage as a mediating factor. The quantitative anal-

DOI: 10.4018/979-8-3373-0918-7.ch009

ysis indicates AI innovations have a direct positive effect on consumer experience at 0.40 while their indirect influence through competitive advantage is measured at 0.45 resulting in a total effect of 0.85. The data indicates strategic alignment of AI developments with competitive advantages leads to substantial improvements in customer satisfaction. Eco hotels should direct their efforts towards implementing AI technologies and showcasing their unique offerings while consistently monitoring these technological developments for success. Theoretical implications deepen understanding of technology's role in hospitality while practical suggestions provide actionable strategies for managers.

INTRODUCTION

In the last couple of years, the development of Artificial Intelligence (AI) Technologies has revolutionized various industries, and the hospitality sector is no different. It reflects the necessity to utilize AI developments to power trend consumer experiences worldwide, promote operational effectiveness and establish competitive differentiators. Consumers are increasingly getting pressured to embrace the AI offerings, with the promise of quick individual and problem-free services that cater to these demands. In developing countries such as the eco-hotel industry, especially in developing countries such as Ethiopia, provides a separate setting to investigate the association among AI progress and experience of customers, as it is stability with demand for contemporary technical solutions (Nyaga and Tanova, 2024) The idea of incorporating AI in the hospitality sector stems from major conversations about digital changes, in which technology is considered an important factor for improvement of service provision and operational efficiency. Research literature shows many uses of AI in hospitality, including chatbot for customer aid, AI-based pricing techniques and data analysis to understand consumer preferences. Research has shown that this progress can increase customers' satisfaction and loyalty, which helps the hotel to gain competitive lead. Also, despite the widespread discussion about the benefits of AI, there is still inadequate targeted research on how this progress specifically affects consumer experiences in eco-h0tels, especially in Ethiopian Settings (Hussain at al., 2024).

The AI adoption in the Ethiopian eco-hotels has been faced with different unique obstacles that hindered their potential from increasing experience of their customers. First, limitation of access to new or advanced technologies and a reliable internet creates an obstacle for implementation of system of AI (Salama et al., 2024). Several green hotels word in far regions that infrastructure of technology is less developed. Moreover, there is absence of qualified staff member sophisticated in the discipline of AI and data analysis, who further complicates adoption as staff member of green hotels can try to use all these advanced technologies with strength (Aarabe et al., 2024). Factors related with culture also play critical role. In practices of traditional hotel that prioritize interaction of persons, the might be reluctance to adopting Artificial intelligence. In addition to this, restrictions of finance limit investments in solution of artificial intelligence (Hussain et al, 2024). This is due to many environmental trenches work on strict budgets. Lastly, the regulatory and political situations surrounding artificial intelligence is still developing in Ethiopia, creating uncertainty that can sustain innovative technology investment. Moreover, these issue are avoided by the capacity of green hotels to use AI to increase competitive edge and increase satisfaction of consumers (Salehzadeh et al., 2024).

Although AI makes great promises, practical barriers remain in its application. Many eco-hotels especially in developing areas may not be entitled to infrastructure, financial instruments and technical knowledge required to successfully incorporate AI technologies (Nouhaila et al., 2024). In addition, organizations often face opposition to changes with concerns about privacy and safety of information. These obstacles could disrupt achievement of full potential of AI in improving consumer experiences (Berlaku, 2023). In addition, there are considerable research gaps in understanding the mediation task of competitive advantages between AI innovations and consumer experience. Although current research has examined the impact of AI on operational performance, very few people analyzed the role of competitive advantage as an arbitrator in this scenario. This research attempts to fill these intervals, provides the required insight to researchers and policy makers, emphasizes the importance of strategic AI implementation in the Eco-Hot Sector (Salehzadeh et al., 2024).

Ethical issues related to information about consumers based on artificial intelligence are primarily related to confidentiality, data security, and bias. Gathering and analysis of individual information raises important confidentiality issues as clients night not understand how their information is used (Alsetoohy et al., 2024). In addition, data violations can expose sensitive information, resulting in potential damage. Biases in AI algorithms can cause discriminatory practices, affecting marginalized groups disproportionately (Salama et al., 2024). Transparency is also a problem; Consumers may not understand how understanding is generated, undergoing confidence. In the end, the balance of AI advantages with ethical considerations is important to guarantee the responsible and equitable use of consumer data (Alkhatib and Valerie, 2024).

The purpose of this study is to address this question: ***"In what ways does AI progress in eco-hotels in Ethiopia affect consumer experience, and what is the part of competitive advantage in this regard?"*** Through the discovery of this question, research wants to illuminate the major elements that affect the effective application of AI technologies in improving consumer experiences, eventually directed to future researchers and physicians to more efficient strategies in hospitality industry we do.

1. LITERATURE REVIEW

1.1. Background of study

An artificial Intelligence (AI) incorporation in the hospitality industry gained significant speed globally, which is inspired by the need for consumer experiences and operational capacity (Khizzou et al., 2024). Since passengers demand rapid individual services and uninterrupted interactions, eco-hattles-wires that prefer stability and release unique challenges and opportunities in adopting an AI technologies. In Ethiopia, where tourism is an increasing area, eco-hotel can not only take advantage of AI innovations to improve guest experiences, but also environmentally conscious consumers (Kuo et al., 2022). They also promote permanent practices. Despite the possible benefits, the implementation of AI in eco-hotels is filled with challenges. For example, a case study of major eco-hotels in the Ethiopian highlands reflects the difficulties faced during the integration of AI-managed service of customer solutions. The hotel aims to deploy a chatbot to streamline guest inquiry and increase communication. Also, the implementation was interrupted by lack of technical expertise among employees, causing insufficient training and operational disruption. This situation gives an example of a broader issue of skill interval in the workforce, which can greatly disrupt effective adoption of AI technologies in terms of hospitality sector (Hussain et al, 2024).

Several regions have shown the possibility of introducing AI into ecotourism, increasing stability and engaging consumers. At Eco Lodge Costa Rica, AI-managed analysts were used to monitor wildlife modeling, allowing them to provide a more effective effort to maintain and enrich the visitor's experience through field trips highlighting these ideas (Nyaga and Tanova, 2024).. Similarly, in New Zealand, eco-reform artificial intelligence cat robots will promote communication with customers; provide personalized recommendations and real-time support, improving general stays (Alkhatib and Valerie, 2024). In South Africa, artificial intelligence technology is used in game preparation to analyses animal behavior, optimize resource management, and create a more stable environment to improve tourist experience age (Salehzadeh et al., 2024). Additionally, AI's Maldives provides guests with satisfaction, predicts the maintenance of environmentally friendly objects, and minimizes environmental impact. A research on this topic shows that, AI can revolutionize eco-tourism, increase work efficiency and contribute to deeper relationships between tourists and nature (Alsetoohy et al., 2024).

Another practical case study can be extracted from ecologically current in the capital, Addis Ababa. These establishments have tried to use data analysis to adapt marketing strategies and improve guest experiences. While some hotels have successfully implemented basic analysis to understand customer preferences, many have fought focus on privacy of data and the implication of ethics of collecting guest information. This temporization stifled innovation and reduced the trust among consumers, impacting their need to get involved with artificial innovation oriented service (Salama et al., 2024). In addition, the restriction related with finance faced by several green hotels in Ethiopia, manifest a significant barrier to implementation of artificial intelligence.

The artificial intelligence affects significantly the customer service quality using key trends, like hyper staffing, forecasts analysis and the ethical implementation of artificial intelligence. The hyper staff used AI to adjust the association based on the preference of individuals, increase in customer satisfaction and loyalty. The forecast analysis analyzes to wait for needs of customers, which create proactive maintenance, improves involvement of customers and retention (Alsetoohy et al., 2024). No matter how the application of ethical artificial intelligence is a key to maintain trust and this guarantees equality and transparency in algorithms, the minimization of biases and consumer secret protection. By making the trend priority, firms are able to use artificial intelligence to develop meaningful and personalized experience while maintaining a responsible means that is commensurate with expectations of customers and values of society (Hussain et al, 2024). Conducting empirical studies and using examples of real world could highly enhance the understanding of AI role in environment friendly hotels. For instance, a University Cornell study reveals that, AI managed CAT robots had considerably enhanced engagement of gusts and satisfaction in large chains of eco-hotel. Moreover, forecast analyzes use at the Verde hotel in Cape Town has optimized management of energy consumption, decreases costs and helps in increasing stability (Alsetoohy et al., 2024). The practical ideas reveal how innovations of AI optimizes operations of an organizations, for instance, automated checks and individualized recommendations, and also contribute to practices of environmentally friendly activities. Such examples highlight the tangible advantages of AI, showing its transformation potential both efficiency of operation and experience of customers in the hospitality businesses (Kuo et al., 2022).

A small green lodge of countryside sought the investment of AI technologies for management of energy and saving of costs. Despite the initial investment required for AI infrastructure and maintenance of continuous costs were overwhelming for the budget installations. This shows the need for financial support and investment in technology for eco-hotels to successfully transition to the digital age (Salehzadeh et al., 2024). Morover, the change resistance within cultures of organization can pose challenges. Some green hotels have experienced pushback from fears of staff that AI may replace their jobs or alter practices of traditional hospitality. This cultural opposition always results to a lack of buy-in from members of staff, which is important for the successful adoption of technologies of innovation.

1.2. Statement of problem

With artificial intelligence at the forefront of the sector of hospitality, the trust of consumers and protection of data take precedence. Data misuse issue, especially of sensitive customer information, requires action of companies to keep up with legislation such as GDPR (Salama et al., 2024). These rules need data processing transparency and increase consumer confidence. Biased AI can lead to unfair treatment of certain demographics and can undermine trust. Speaking of data security and ethical practice, hotel businesses can develop trustworthy environments and ensure that AI will provide personal information and promote justice in the delivery of services while improving experience with customers (Nyaga and Tanova, 2024).

The hospitality industry, especially within the eco-hotel region in Ethiopia, is at an intersection where the involvement of artificial intelligence innovations to significantly increase consumer experiences (Bouizgar et al., 2025). The ideal state enforces a landscape where eco-hotel take advantage of AI to provide individual services, to streamline operations, and promote permanent practices, eventually leading to increase in customer satisfaction and loyalty. Also, the current reality manifests a contrasting picture, which features many challenges and gaps that obstruct the attainment of this ability (Alkhatib and Valerie, 2024). Contradictory evidence emerges from existing literature, which exposes both the benefits and boundaries of AI in hospitality. While some studies emphasize the positive effects of AI on operational efficiency and guest satisfaction, others reveal significant obstacles for implementation, such as insufficient infrastructure and lack of efficient personnel. These mixed outcomes create ambiguity about the effectiveness of AI innovations in increasing consumer experiences, outlining the need for more concentrated research (Salehzadeh et al., 2024).

Additionally, previous studies contribute to the theoretical intervals in understanding the mechanisms through which AI affects consumer experiences, especially in the context of eco-hotels. Some studies have examined the role of mediation of competitive advantage in this regard, leaving an important aspect of AI-consumer experience dynamic unexplained. This inspection limits the theoretical outlines available to researchers and physicians, which inhibit the development of broad strategies for AI integration (Khizzou et al., 2024). Knowledge complicates intervals and landscapes. Many current studies mainly focus on developed countries, providing limited insight into unique challenges and opportunities faced by eco-hotels in Ethiopia. This deficiency of localized research prohibits the purpose of conclusions for the Ethiopian context, where cultural, economic and infrastructural factors differ significantly from those in more developed areas (Nyaga and Tanova, 2024). In addition, practical challenges remain in the implementation of AI innovations. The reluctance of the hotel staff to embrace new technologies, combined with concerns on financial obstacles and data privacy, creates a malignant barrier to effective AI adoption. These issues not only impede the evolution of individual installation, but also impair their ability to participate in the fast growing eco-tourism sector in the rapidly evolving digital market place (Kuo et al., 2022).

The goal of this research is to fill these gaps by conducting a thorough investigation of the association among AI development and consumer experience in Ethiopian eco-hotels, particularly with the mediating role of competitive advantage. By identifying this dynamic, the researchers hope to understand the way in the game and offer evidence-based recommendations to physicians. Furthermore, by combining localized insights, it aims to contribute to the theoretical discloser on AI in hospitality, helping future researchers and policy makers in developing the integration of AI technologies. Finally, the study aims to pave the road for a more sustainable and innovative eco-hotels industry in Ethiopia, which integrates worldwide trends, while overcoming local solving local difficulties (Alsetoohy et al., 2024).

1.3. Theoretical foundation

In this research, the following theories have been used to investigate the association among AI innovation and consumer experience with mediation role of competitive advantage.

Resources Based View theory (RBV): This is one of the importance theories used by many researchers in this topic) (Bouizgar et al., 2025). RBV theory shows that the resources of organizations are critical factors of its competitive edge and performance. In the context of this study, AI technologies can be seen as significant resources that, if used effectively, can improve the delivery of services and efficiency of operation (Aarabe et al., 2025). By using the resources of AI like analysis of data, automation and customization, eco-friendly hotels can enhance the market place competitive positions and provide context of higher consumer experience (Hussein et al, 2024). Particularly, this theory is directed towards services of the model created by Thomas Earl focuses on supply of costs using dynamic and modular services to meet customer need thanks to work in the Service Oriented Architecture" (SOA). SOA enhances design as a set of different services, helping companies to gently integrate several tasks (Baydeniz & Altin, 2025). This mechanism allows a firm to respond quickly to highly changing environment and enhance experience of consumers by personalized services. The originators of the concept like ERL revealed that service oriented models increases better alignment among information technology and objectives of business, enhancing efficiency of operation and promoting innovations in the hospitality and eco-tourism sectors (Nyaga and Tanova, 2024).

Technology Acceptance model (TAM): It is another crucial theory that several scholars have been used. It focuses on determinants that affect the use and adoption of different technologies by individuals. This theory reveals the ease of perceived use and the perceived utility as important factors of adoption of technology. In the context of eco-tourism, knowing about these determinants helps to identify obstacles to implementing and inform strategies to improve the acceptance of the AI-oriented team and customers. The structure of Technology acceptance model could also be basic determinant to assess how innovation of AI can be implemented to meet customer preferences and wants, thus improving their general experience (Salehzadeh et al., 2024).

The theory of diffusion of Innovation: This framework provides information on how advanced technologies distributed throughout businesses and industries. This theory focuses on the role of channel of communication, social system and the perceived innovation characteristcis in determining their adoption (Aarabe et al., 2025). In the context of this study, theory of diffusion of innovation can help explain the challenges linked with the diffusion of artificial innovation technologies, especially in the context in which traditional practices can master. Knowing the determinants that improve or impede the diffusion of innovations of AI can guide ecological to overcome opposition and promote an environment conducive to adoption of technology (Nyuga & Tanova, 2024).

Even though all these frameworks provide an important perspective, the important lenses of theory for this study were RBV. RBV is relevant since it emphasizes the strategic importance of exclusive resources - such as AI technologies - creating competitive advantage (Alla et al., 2025). By focusing on how ecological ones can take advantage of AI's innovations to improve their service offerings and operational efficiencies, this study aimed to bridge gaps in literature on the media toning role of competitive edge as a mediator in the association among AI and consumer experience. The RBV structure will guide the analysis, allowing a comprehensive understanding of how strategic resource management can boost innovation and improve consumer experience in the ecological sector (Aarabe et al., 2025).

1.4. Definition and origin of terms

Artificial Intelligence: AI stands to refer to man's computer simulations of mental processes. To them belong learning (acquiring data and rules to utilize), reasoning (utilized rules to arrive at approximately or exact conclusions) and coordination (Alla et al., 2025). AI was originally termned in 1956 at the Conference of Dartmouth, hosted by John McCarthy, Marvin Minsky, Nathaniel Rochester and Claude Shannon. The conference was generally viewed as the beginning of the discipline of AI, where practitioners and theorists began to discuss the ways in which machines can mimic cognitive functions (Salama et al., 2024).

Consumer Experience: Consumer experience is the whole interaction a buyer has with an item or a brand over the course of its life, from awareness to engagement after purchase. All touch points, such as customer service, usability, and emotional reactions caused through these contact points (Bouizgar et al., 2025). The phrase "consumer experience" appeared in the latter part of the twentieth century when companies realized the potential of customer satisfaction and loyalty to ensure long-term success. Scholars like Pine and Gilmore used the phrase "experience of experience" for their publication released in 1998, identifying that companies ought to create such experiences that linger in minds in order to compete in a heavily populated market scenario (Hussein et al, 2024).

Competitive advantage is defined as characteristics that enable an organization to surpass its rivals. These characteristics can be the outcome of different sources, such as improved product quality, cost advantage, brand image or new technologies. The theory is traced back to Michael Porter's work in the 1980s, namely his seminal book "Competitive Advantage: Creating and Sustaining Superior Performance," where he described the importance of leveraging resources and special capabilities in a bid to achieve a sustainable competitive advantage in the market (Nyuga & Tanova, 2024).

Eco-Hotels: Eco-hotels are business organizations that focus on the sustainability of environment in practice and operations. They consist of using renewable resources, reduction of waste, conservation of energy and support of local community. The definition gained momentum in the late 20th century when global awareness of the environment has enhanced. Ecotourism, a related concept, evolved during the 1990s with the idea of travel that is responsible for natural places that conserve the environment and improve local resident health (Kuo et al., 2022).

1.5. Empirical literature review:

1.5.1. The Effect of AI Innovations on Consumer Experience

The integration of artificial intelligence (AI) innovations as per resource -based vision (RBV) into consumer experiences has been a focal point of recent empirical research, revealing multifaceted impacts (Bouizgar et al., 2025). A significant body of literature indicates that AI technologies, such as chatbots and individualized system of recommendation, improve customer involvement, providing personalized experiences. For example, a study by Huang and Rust (2021) points out that AI -oriented personalization leads to increased consumer satisfaction and loyalty as customers appreciate interactions that seem individually elaborated to their preferences and behaviors. These outcomes are supported by Chen et al. (2020), which demonstrate that consumers exposed to personalized marketing through AI algorithms exhibit a greater probability of brand purchase and positive perception (Nyuga & Tanova, 2024). In addition, the efficiency of AI applications improves service provision, positively influencing consumer experience positively. Research by Van Doorn et al. (2017) showed that AI could optimize processes of service of customer, reduce response times and improve accuracy in consultation treatment. This efficiency not only enhances the general experience of service, but also increases consumer confidence in the brand, as consumers feel valued when their needs are treated promptly. In addition, AI innovations facilitate a perfect omnichannel experience, allowing consumers to transition smoothly between on -line and offline interactions. A study by Lemon and Verhoef (2016) emphasizes the importance of this integration, noting that consistent experiences between channels promote greater customer satisfaction and loyalty (Baydeniz & Altin, 2025).

Also, literature also recognizes possible disadvantages. Concerns about privacy and perceived intrusion of AI technologies can negatively affect consumer confidence. Research by Martin and Murphy (2017) indicates that while consumers enjoy personalized experiences, they simultaneously express discomfort in relation to data privacy, leading to a delicate balance that brands should navigate. In addition, the lack of human touch in AI interactions can result in feelings of alienation among consumers, particularly in high touch service industries. This feeling is echoed by a study of Pappas (2018), which suggests that while AI can increase efficiency, it can also impair the emotional connection consumers seek in service experiences (Nyuga & Tanova, 2024).

H1: AI Innovations has significant effect on Consumer Experience

1.5.2. Effect of AI Innovations on Competitive Advantage

The concept of innovations of artificial intelligence has basically reformulated the scenario of competitiveness in different sectors. Firms that take an advantage of the technologies of AI could effectively distinguish themselves, enhancing operational efficiency and improves the process of decision making. For instance, businesses that use AI oriented analysis could gain data from large data sets, allowing them to identify trends of market, preferences of users and emerging opportunities much quicker than their rivals at market place (Aarabe et al., 2025, Hussein et al, 2024). Innovations of artificial intelligence help firms in improving the experience of their customers, which can serve as a significant differential in markets that are saturated. Based on the theory of RBV, by implementing AI chatbots and individualized systems of recommendations, businesses can provide individualized associations that meet the needs of individual customers. A research by Kumar et al. (2020) revealed that organizations that adopt AI tools increase the customer satisfaction and promote the loyalty of brands, leading to significant share of market. This customer centered technique helps companies to build and maintain stronger link among their customers, solidifying their competitiveness (Salehzadeh et al., 2024).

Different from this, innovation of AI helps in cost reduction through the process of optimization and automation. Automation of tasks allows firms to free up their resources and put their capital of staff members toward core functions that drive innovation and growth. McKinsey & Company (2019) revealed that businesses that utilize AI for automating their operations of business can enhance productivity up to 40%, and this gives to enormous savings of costs and expansion of margin. Such operational agility helps firms to adapt to changes in the market in time, remaining competitive (Nyuga & Tanova, 2024). On the other hand, integration of AI has its downsides that can affect the competitive advantage. Firms that invest in infrastructure, human resources, and ethical rules to get benefit from AI (Aarabe et al., 2025). Such individuals holding up in such fields stand the risk of being left behind their competitors in adopting the use of AI technologies to enhance their products and operations. Secondly, the rapid pace of alterations with AI requires constant learning and adaptation, and it is critical that companies keep up with technology evolution to serve their competitive benefit (Salama et al., 2024).

H2: AI Innovations has significant effect on Competitive Advantage

1.5.3. Competitive Advantage and Consumer Experience

Competitiveness is pivotal to consumer experience development because it influences how organizations differ in the marketplace. The organizations that have been able to establish a competitive advantage are capable of offering goods, services or customer interactions superior to others' that are related to consumer wishes and needs (Laoute et al., 2025). For instance, according to the model of technology acceptance, company that prioritize product and service quality and innovation will tend to provide more satisfying experience of customers as consumers relate these values. The study of Porter (1995) research highlighted that firms that are differentiated will tend to build customer loyalty because customers are attracted to products that are unique and satisfy the want and needs of customers (Ameen et al., 2021). Furthermore, competitive advantage companies are more likely to invest in improving customer service and customer support, which has tremendous influence on the whole consumer experience. Companies like Amazon and Zappos are prime examples of such a practice by providing exemplary customer service that goes beyond transactional exchange (Khizzou et al., 2024). Studies indicate that it not only serves to generate repeated business, but also results in positive word-of-mouth endorsements that further consolidate its position within the market. The customers' enhanced experience with strong emotional connection due to support and appreciation ultimately aids in deepening the connection for the brand (Gajić et al., 2024).

Additionally, competitive advantage can lead to greater investment in technology and innovation, which powers consumer experience through improved accessibility and convenience. Companies that employ leading-edge technologies such as mobile apps and AI-driven customer service solutions simplify things and make them convenient for consumers through their offerings and products. Lemon and Verhoef (2016) research informs that experiential contributions in the aspect of digital significantly contribute to the satisfaction of consumers because customers enjoy how accessible and responsive in handling the context of brands (Hussein et al, 2024). In addition, competitive profit encourages higher investment in technology and innovation, hence enhancing consumers' experience in the aspect of increased access and convenience (Laoute et al., 2025). Companies that use mobile apps such as cutting-edge technology and AI-based customer service solutions simplify interactions and empower consumers with their services and products. Lemon and Verhof (2016) have listed research that contributes to digital experiences; consumer is an important role in satisfaction, since customers appreciate ease of use and convenience in interactions as much as brands care (Hussain et al, 2024).

H3: Competitive Advantage has significant effect on Consumer Experience

1.5.4. Mediating Role of Competitive Advantage in AI Innovations on Consumer Experience

The integration of Artificial Intelligence (AI) improvements in eco lodges in Ethiopia has a profound impact on customer enjoy, significantly mediated by the lodges' competitive advantage. As the hospitality region increasingly more embraces AI technology, eco hotels can decorate their provider offerings and operational performance, in the long run main to advanced consumer delight and loyalty (Aarabe et al., 2025). AI packages, together with customized booking systems and smart room technology, permit those lodges to tailor experiences that resonate with environmentally conscious customers. Research shows that personalized offerings foster a feel of connection and belonging, that's especially treasured inside the hospitality industry (Alkhatib & Valeri, 2024). As per technology acceptance model (TAM), the competitive benefit received through AI innovations enables eco lodges to differentiate themselves in a swiftly evolving market (Khizzou et al., 2024). By leveraging AI for information analytics, these hotels can better apprehend their guests' choices and behaviors, allowing for extra informed selection-making and centered advertising and marketing techniques. For example, eco accommodations that make use of AI to analyze purchaser remarks can refine their offerings to align more closely with guest expectancies, improving the general enjoy. This strategic use of AI now not handiest improves operational efficiency but also positions these hotels as leaders in sustainable tourism, appealing to a developing demographic of eco-conscious tourists (Kuo et al., 2022).

The adoption of AI as ChatGPT at Eco-Hotel has a profound impact on professional roles and requires training for TaylorMade employees. As Automation streamlines recurring tasks like checking and data management, staff can focus on improving customer experience through personalized services. This change requires constant training to ensure employees are working efficiently using artificial intelligence tools (Hussain et al, 2024). Cultural change emerges, emphasizing collaboration between technology as ChatGPT and human intentions, and fostering a service-focused state of mind. It is important to estimate automation with individual touches. Hotels can maintain employee engagement and ensure that staff are involved and feel valuable in discussions about AI implementation. Appeals for adaptation in labor contribute to a harmonious environment in which technology improves and replaces human roles (Gajić et al., 2024).

As well as, the competitive advantage derived from AI innovations lets in eco hotels to streamline operations, which immediately impacts purchaser revel in. For instance, AI-pushed systems can optimize resource management, ensuring that visitors experience a seamless stay at the same time as minimizing environmental effect (Bouizgar et al., 2025). This operational excellence complements patron perceptions of the hotel's commitment to sustainability and pleasant carrier. Guests are more likely to realize the initiative, main to wonderful critiques and repeat visits, which in addition strengthen the motel's marketplace position context (Hussein et al, 2024). Also, the effectiveness of AI improvements in improving customer experience through aggressive advantage must be viewed in the context of consumer expectancies (Khizzou et al., 2025). Eco hotels that put money into AI technology need to also ensure that these innovations align with their sustainability values. If clients perceive AI packages as detracting from the green ethos of the lodge, it can result in poor stories (Nyuga & Tanova, 2024).

H4: Competitive Advantage mediates the association among AI Innovations and Consumer Experience

1.6. Conceptual framework

Based on theoretical and empirical literature, the researchers developed the following conceptual framework.

Figure 1. Conceptual framework

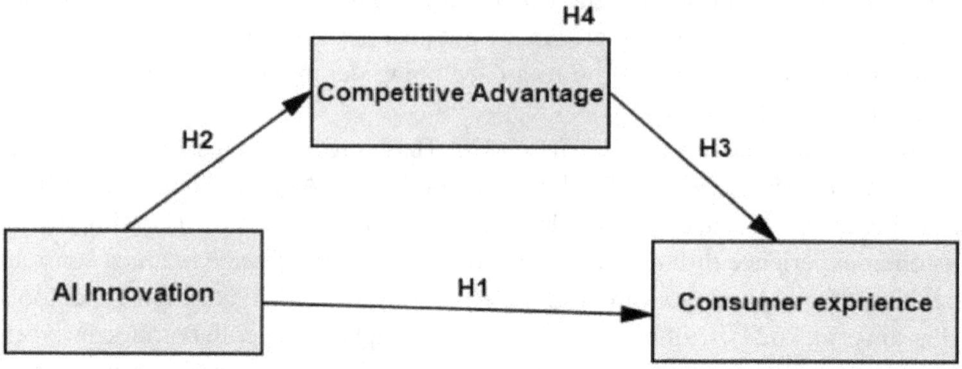

Source: Authors

2. RESEARCH METHODOLOGY

This study adopted a quantitative research method to examine the impact of artificial intelligence (AI) developments on the customer experience in Ethiopian ecological hotels. To guarantee a varied manifestation of the living population, a systematic sampling approach was used to establish the sample size, which came out to be 376 respondents with explanatory research design. Random sampling method was used to collect data. Structured questionnaires measuring several buildings relating to AI advancements, competitive advantage, and consumer experience were administered as part of the data gathering procedure. Data was cleaned with z-score and box plot method to identify outliers. 13 0utliers were detected and removed. Prior to the study, the Kaiser-Meyer-Olkin (KMO) metric was used to assess the sample's adequacy. The size of sample respondents was supposed to be enough for analysis of factors since the result of KMO was above 0.6. EFA was done following the analysis of KMO in order to determine the structure of the data and constructs. In order to ensure the appropriateness of items associated with the theoretical framework developed form the literature, EFA assisted in determining the number of determinants and their factor loadings. To refine the scale and exclude items that didn't contribute to the overall factorial structure, EFA was important. The program was then used to determine the theoretical association among the factors using structural equation modeling (SEM). To effectively implement AI in green hotels, managers taken the following five stages: First, we assess needs and goals and determine areas where AI can improve operations, such as customer service and energy management. Second, we invest in training to ensure that employees are comfortable and qualified to use new technology. Third, we research artificial intelligence solutions that address stability goals and improve the guest experience and select the right technology. Fourth, it contributes to a collaborative culture and promotes open communication between staff and management in the implementation process. Finally, monitor and evaluate the impact of AI on operations and customer satisfaction, making adjustments as necessary. The study followed the forming approach, because the designs were determined by their indicators, which means that the characteristics of the indicators directly helped to form global construction. For example, factors such as the quality of service and responsiveness have collectively formed the construction of customer satisfaction, illustrating the interdependence of indicators.

3. RESULTS AND DISCUSSION

3.1. Scale development

The scale development started with an in-depth review of studies on AI innovations, competitive advantages, and customer experiences in the hotel industry. The goal was to create a reliable and precise measurement tool. We adapted existing research scales to fit the context of eco-friendly hotels in Ethiopia. The emphasis was on the key ideas like innovation of AI, which incorporate personalization, automation and efficiency of services. The competitive advantage was also concerned which includes differentiation and operational excellence, and considered experience of customers, which covers satisfaction of customers loyalty and perceived value. The researchers developed items from previous studies, ensuring they addressed each concept comprehensively. For innovation of AI, items were inspired by researches on technology's role in improving interaction of customers and delivery of service. Items of competitive advantage were measured by using with Balance score card (BSC Card model) adopted from the study of effect of sustainability and innovation on market positioning. Consumer experience items were adopted on established measures of satisfaction of consumers and loyalty in the sector of hospitality. Each item was clearly articulated and relevant. Pre-testing helped to refine the items before the main data collection and analysis.

3.2. Data analysis

Table 1. KMO and Bartlett's Test

Kaiser-Meyer-Olkin Measure of Sampling Adequacy.		**.852**
Bartlett's Test of Sphericity	Approx. Chi-Square	1419.746
	Df	93
	Sig.	.002

Source: Authors

The Kaiser-Meyer-Olkin (KMO) results indicated that a KMO value of 0.852 was attained. KMO values greater than 0.6 are acceptable and the values closer to 1.0 indicate a more robust dataset for factor analysis (Hair et al., 2010). This result suggests that the components were significantly clustered together, indicating that the sample size was adequate for exploratory factor analysis. The Bartlett's Test of Sphericity yielded a Chi-Square value of 1419.746 with 93 degrees of freedom and a significance level of 0.002. Based on this finding, the determinants are related and hence suitable for factor analysis, indicating that the relationships between the variables were statistically significant. A significant Bartlett's Test ($p < 0.05$) indicates that the correlation matrix is not an identity matrix, suggesting that the data is eligible for further study. The KMO and Bartlett's Test results work well together to provide a good foundation for exploratory factor analysis (EFA). The favorable results demonstrate that the dataset possesses the characteristics required to uncover underlying patterns among the constructs, making it easier to identify significant elements that can clarify the relationship between AI advancements, competitive advantage, and customer experience in the context of Ethiopian eco hotels.

Table 2. Total Variance Explained

Component	**Initial Eigenvalues**			**Extraction Sums of Squared Loadings**			**Rotation Sums of Squared Loadings**		
	Total	**% of Variance**	**Cumulative %**	**Total**	**% of Variance**	**Cumulative %**	**Total**	**% of Variance**	**Cumulative %**
1	4.48	32.232	32.233	4.48	32.233	32.233	3.00	21.448	21.448
2	1.36	9.786	42.021	1.36	9.786	42.021	2.15	15.490	36.941
3	1.26	9.086	51.109	1.26	9.086	51.109	1.97	14.167	51.109
4	.950	6.780	57.890						

continued on following page

Table 2. Continued

Component	Initial Eigenvalues			Extraction Sums of Squared Loadings			Rotation Sums of Squared Loadings		
	Total	% of Variance	Cumulative %	Total	% of Variance	Cumulative %	Total	% of Variance	Cumulative %
5	.870	6.221	64.114						
6	.772	5.520	69.632						

Extraction Method: Principal Component Analysis.
Source: Authors

Table 2 presents the result of exploratory factor analysis. From the first eigenvalues, the first component explains variance of 4.48%, or 32.23% of overallvariance. It is high enough to indicate that the first component has a crucial role in the explanation of underlying structure of data. With a combined percentage of 32.23% standing alone in the third component, it captures about one-third of the variation as a whole. With the second component possessing an eigenvalue of 1.36, another 9.79% of the variance is explained, and the total variance explained reaches 42.02%. This means that collectively, the first two factors explain a considerable portion of the variation as a whole, which points to their significance in the context of this study. With an eigenvalue of 1.26, the third component explains 9.09% of the variance, bringing the cumulative percentage explained to 51.11%. The three components with eigenvalues higher than one verify that the factors are strong and should be kept for further analysis. The subsequent components have eigenvalues lower than 1, with the fourth, fifth, and sixth components explaining smaller percentages of variance (6.78%, 6.22%, and 5.52%, respectively). While these factors are contributing to the total variance, their smaller eigenvalues reflect decreasing returns in describing the structure of the data.

3.3. Confirmatory principle component analysis

Confirmatory principle component analysis is used to verify the order of the principal components in a set of guided items. Investigators can use CFA to evaluate hypotheses by considering the underlying frame job and correlations among observable proxies. To test the premise that there is a relationship between the instruments being directed and the latent notions that underlay them, the study employed CFA (see table 3).

Table 3. Covariances

Covariance			Approximation	S.E.	C.R.	P	Hy.
Competitive advantage	**<-->**	**AI innovation**	**.245**	**.024**	**8.228**	***	**H2**
Competitive advantage	<-->	Consumer insight	.306	.035	7.689	***	**H3**
AI innovation	<-->	Consumer	.257	.027	7.829	***	**H1**

Source: Authors

Table 3 reports the covariance estimates. When the standard error (S.E.) is 0.024, the correlation coefficient between AI innovation and competitive advantage is estimated at 0.245. The statistically significant critical ratio (C.R.) for this relationship is 8.228 ($p < 0.001$). The high positive correlation shows that the use of AI innovation by green hotels increases proportionally to the competitive advantage. Hotels with effective use of AI technology are more likely to achieve competitive advantage, states this data that verifies Hypothesis 2 (H2). Likewise, the correlation between competitive advantage and consumer insight has been stated to be 0.306 when having a C.R. value of 7.689 with a S.E. value of 0.035, and both values being statistically significant at $p < 0.001$. This relationship of proximity depicts the manner in which competitive advantage hotels usually have greater knowledge of their customers and therefore can shape their services according to the customers' unique requirements. This outcome confirms Hypothesis 3 (H3), that understanding the tastes of a firm's customers is imperative if it has to sustain its competitive advantage. The relationship between consumer insight and innovation in AI is also significant ($p < 0.001$), as indicated by the covariance of 0.257, S.E. of 0.027, and C.R. of 7.829 values. This is a positive relationship, implying that greater customer insights are linked with increased use of AI breakthroughs. This result confirms Hypothesis 1 (H1), which states that AI technologies play a vital role in the eco hotels' understanding and responding to guest behavior, thereby improving the overall guest experience.

Table 4. Validity Concern

	CR	AVE	MSV	MaxR(H)	AII	CA	CE
AII	0.730	0.641	0.219	0.849	**0.649**		
CA	0.760	0.661	0.132	0.765	0.169	**0.659**	
CE	0.790	0.601	0.270	0.800	0.383	0.193	**0.678**

Note: AII= Artificial intelligence innovation; CA= Competitive advantage; CE= Consumer experience
Source: Authors

Table 4 is a validity measurement summary. Since AII = 0.730, CA = 0.760, and CE = 0.790, Composite Reliability (CR) ratings per construct are adequate. More than 0.7 for CR indicates outstanding internal consistency, and it implies that items capturing each construct do so successfully for the targeted concept (Hair et al., 2010). These figures confirm internal consistency and reliability of AII, CA, and CE scales. Convergent validity is also examined by Average Variance Extracted (AVE) values. AVEs for AII, CA, and CE are 0.641, 0.661, and 0.601, respectively. AVE values over 0.5 suggest that the constructs are accounting for over half of the variance in their indicators, thereby justifying the constructs' ability to capture the research's targeted dimensions. Maximum Shared Variance (MSV) shows the strongest correlation among components and it has values of 0.219 for AII, 0.132 for CA, and 0.270 for CE. Since the constructs are not similar to one another, relatively low MSV values in comparison to AVE values indicate that discriminant validity has been achieved. Lastly, dependability of the constructions is further confirmed by the MaxR(H) values for AII, which stands at 0.849, CA, 0.765, and CE, 0.800.

3.4. Mediating role examination

Figure 2. Structural equation model

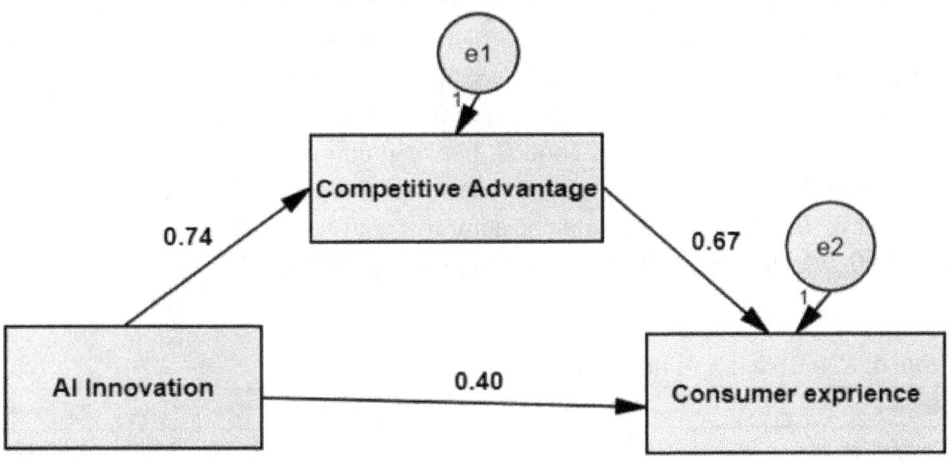

Source: Authors

3.5. Model fit indices

Table 5. indices for Model Fit

Sig.	Chi-Sq	RMR	Fitness Goodness	Fitness Confirmator	TLI	RMSEA
0.004	1.948	.030	0.925	0.908	0.909	.025

Source: Authors

Table 5 looks based on AMOS output the fit indices of the model, which are crucial in estimating the overall fit of SEM. The fit indices provide information regarding how the model fits the observed data. The significance value (p-value) was displayed as 0.004, indicating the model's statistical significance. A p-value of less than 0.05 suggests a good fit between the hypothesized model and the data, and one can be sure of the model's validity. A good fit is suggested by the comparatively low Chi-Square value of 1.948. Low Chi-Square value in comparison to the degrees of freedom is best for SEM since it suggests that there is a close fit among the predicted model and the observed data. The estimated Root Mean Square Residual (RMR) of 0.030 is far less than the generally accepted threshold value of 0.08. That small RMR value, showing the residuals—the discrepancies between predicted and observed values—are small, further confirms the model's sufficiency. The reported GFI of 0.925 implies that the model explains a significant amount of variation in the data beyond the suggested minimum of 0.90. The Confirmatory fit Index (CFI) of 0.908 is also a measure of a good fit between data and model since it is above the acceptable value. Another such fit measure of the model is the Tucker-Lewis Index, at 0.909. It is an acceptable structural model when its TLI value is greater than 0.90, which is typically taken as a sign of a good model fit.

Table 6. Regression Examination

Relative			Approx.	S.E.	C.R.	P	Ass.
Competitive advantage	**<---**	**AI innovation**	**.860**	**.139**	**7.577**	*******	**H2**
Consumer experience	<---	Competitive advantage	.332	.135	2.856	***	H3
Consumer experience	<---	AI innovation	.961	.196	7.962	***	H1

Source: Authors

The regression analysis outcomes are summarized in Table 6, showing the correlations of the constructs of innovation of AI, competitive advantage, and consumer experience. In each case, the standard errors (S.E.), critical ratios (C.R.), regression coefficients, significance levels (P), and corresponding assumptions (Ass.) are displayed. With a standard error of 0.139, the regression coefficient for the correlation between competitive advantage and innovation of AI is 0.860. This is a very high C.R. of 7.577 ($p < 0.001$). Green hotels' competitive advantage is linked to increased levels of AI innovation as per this high positive correlation. Applying AI technology strongly improves the competitive position of a hotel as per this data, supporting Hypothesis 2 (H2). Consumer Experience-Competitive Advantage correlation is 2.856 with a C.R. of 2.856 and a S.E. of 0.135. Additionally, said relationship is statistical ($p < 0.001$). Implication of the finding is that hotels can intensify consumer satisfaction and delight through effective utilization of their competitive benefits that positively shape the consumer experience. Hypothesis 3 (H3) is proven by this finding. Finally, the regression of AI Innovation to Consumer Experience is 0.961 with significant relationship ($p < 0.001$) and S.E. of 0.196 and C.R. of 7.962.

Table 7. Mediating role

	Influence	Worth	Path Influence
AI innovation→ Consumer experience	Direct Influence	.40	Direct influence stated
AI innovation → competitive advantage → Enhancing client experience	Indirect Influence	.74*.67=.45	Indirect Influence Ensued
	Whole influence	.85	Partial mediation

Source: Authors

The link between AI innovation and consumer experience is mediated by competitive advantage, as seen in Table 7. This study sheds light on the ways in which these factors interact to affect eco-hotel patron results. The Direct Influence of AI Innovation on Consumer Experience, which has a value of 0.40, is shown first in the table. This direct effect suggests that the use of AI advances is directly responsible for a sizable amount of the customer experience.

Next, the Indirect Influence is computed along the process of AI Innovation leading to Competitive Advantage, which subsequently increases Consumer Experience. This is manifested by the product of the effect coefficients: AI Innovation to Competitive Advantage (0.74) multiplied by Competitive Advantage to Consumer Experience (0.67), resulting in an indirect influence of 0.45. This computation demonstrates how advances in AI enhance competitive advantage, which benefits the customer experience. The combination of the direct and indirect effects results in a total influence of 0.85 for the Whole Influence of AI Innovation on Consumer Experience. When taking into account both direct and indirect paths, these comprehensive metric shows a substantial overall impact of AI innovation on consumer experience.

3.6. Discussion

This study provided and important insights on how competitive advantage, customer experience and innovation of AI interact in green hotels. The important role played by technology in supporting eco-hotels standout in a competitive market is revealed significant positive association among innovation of AI and competitive advantage. Green hotels might enhance the delivery of service, operation optimization and ultimately provide a more beneficial value for their gusts by implementing the technology of AI. This is similar with the expansion of hospitality sectors' digital transformation trend, where technology is highly seen as key indicator in the success of company. As technology acceptance model, the data shows that, experience of consumers is greatly affected by competitive advantage. Based on this association, hotels could be better positioned to increase satisfaction of customers and loyalty when they successfully capitalize on their competitive edge at market place like distinctive service offerings, superior consumer insights and cutting edge technologies.

This study was done as per RBV theory, how important it is to embrace advancement of AI while at the same time making sure they are successfully incorporated in to more comprehensive long term plans that that prioritize customer experience and engagement. The finding also emphasizes how competitive advantage serves as a mediator in the association among innovation of AI and customer experience. The significant indirect impacts of innovation of AI on experience of customers through competitive edge suggest that, hotels that properly place themselves in the market can maximize the benefit of new technology adoption. According to this study, although innovation of AI has a big direct impact on customer experience, how consumers view and interact with these technologies is influenced greatly by competitive advantage. All things concerned, these results increase the knowledge of how innovation of AI may change an experience of guests in eco hotels.

The operations of eco hotels can embrace an integrated strategy in implementing technology in their activities of business by appreciating the association among these determinants. Furthermore, to explore AI's potential to promote competitive edge, this study concerns the importance of aligning technology with customer centric programs to achieve enhanced experience of customers. This study contributed to the body of knowledge, with an understanding of the related dynamics of the association among AI technologies, competitive strategy and experience of customers in green hospitality. By creating a liner association among AI innovation and enhanced competitive position, it highlights the need of incorporating technology within broader strategic concept that emphasize on engagement of customers. In addition to this, the finding indicates the mediation of competitive advantage in shaping the mindset of customers towards AI, enhancing the knowledge on how to effectively utilize technology to improve the experience of gusts in hospitality.

4. CONCLUSION AND IMPLICATIONS

4.1. Conclusion

This research reinforces the importance of AI development to advance the competitive advantage and customer experience of eco-tourism. The finding revealed direct, significant association among AI innovation and eco hotel competitive position, highlighting that the utilization of novel technology is a must for differentiation in highly saturated market. In addition to this, eco-hotels can significantly increase the satisfaction of customers and loyalty by utilizing the unique capacity, as suggested by the extensive impact of competitive advantage on experience of customers. The mediating role of competitive advantage among innovation of AI and customer experience suggests that, the importance of adoption of technology are supplemented when backed with a significant overarching strategy. Knowing this is important to operation of the hotels since it emphasizes those AI efforts need to be associated to overarching goals with a focus on improving interaction of customers and quality of services

4.2. Implications

The outcome of present research reveal critical implication of management for eco-hotels focused at taking advantage of innovation of AI to improve competitive advantage and improve experience of customers. First, the direct impact of AI innovation on experience of customers (0.40) revealed the need for managers to give due concerns to prioritize the link of AI technologies in to operations of hotels. This includes the use of AI tools, such as chatboots to support customers, analysis of data for individualized marketing and automation for operational efficiency, which contributes directly to more attractive visitor's experience. In addition, the indirect influence (0.45) on a competitive advantage reveals the significance of coordinating initiatives for the strategic ends of the eco-hotels. The eco-hotel managers must admit that the successful adoption of AI extends beyond the inclusion of technologies. This needs a comprehensive strategy that uses the competitive advantage to enhance their customer experience. This includes staff member training on the effective use of AI and ensuring that technologies improve each aspect of experience of gusts to subsequent observations. The mediating role of competitive edge is underlined by the need for hospitality to formulate clearly and contribute to the unique sales like methods of sustainable development, extensive service quality and proposals of innovation. By reporting effectively these factors, eco-hotels can support perception of brand and able to develop loyalty of customers. Ultimately, the outcome of the study reveals that hotel management need to constantly monitor and assess the effect of AI on operational and satisfaction of customers. Regular assessments help to determine the areas where technology investments could enhance and guarantee that they will provide desirable results.

The study's practical implications highlight the doable strategies eco-hotels can use to take use of AI innovation to enhance satisfaction of customers and competitive advantage. Hotel management is urged to make investments in technology of AI that are simple for both staff members and guests to utilize. For instance, using chatbots or other AI-driven support of customer solutions might increase response times and improve interactions of visitor, which will raise satisfaction of consumers. To ensure that technology increases human association rather than replaces those, the study's theoretical ramifications add to the corpus of information already available on how technology, competitive advantage, and customer experience relate in the hospitality industry. The outcome underline the importance of strategic positioning in enhancing the technology efficacy adoption and bolster the idea that competitive advantage plays a critical mediating role in association among AI innovation and experience of customers.

4.3. Recommendations

Many suggestions can be made to green hotels wanting to use innovation of AI effectively in as the study outcomes. Firstly, the management of the eco-hotel should select and implement solutions of AI that enhance particular objectives of hotels and visitors. This includes capitalizing on solutions that are simple to implement and increase efficiency while improving an experience of visitors. For example, hotels should adopt AI driven reservation management system and programs of targeted promotion that can scan visitor data to provide them with an experiences that are individualized to them. To enable staff members to leverage cutting edge technologies, it is equally important that they undergo continuous development and training. Creating an ongoing culture of learning, whereby staff members are spurred to use AI technologies and feedback on how effective they have been must rank high on the agendas of managers. For improvement of products and services and customer satisfaction, eco-hotels also need to actively gather information from customers on their experience with AI-powered services. Providing clear channels for visitor information helps to create a customer-centered and responsive culture. Finally, eco hotels must highlight their commitment to sustainability and unique service delivery alongside their AI technologies. To appeal to environmentally conscious customers and enhance the hotel's brand image, marketing strategies must describe how AI technology supports green activities and enhance guest experiences.

4.4. Future directions

The sustainable effect of AI innovation on satisfaction of customer and behavior in the hospitality sector is an interesting area to explore in future studies. Additional information on product customization for various segments of customers can be obtained by examining reactions to AI services from various demographic segments. To grasp how these forces interact to shape visitor experiences, research would also explore how AI technologies interact with new trends like sustainability and customization. Subsequent research should further explore how corporate culture impacts the successful implementation of AI innovations. Hotel operations can gain from knowing how internal drivers like employee involvement and leadership support impact the effectiveness and adoption of AI products.

REFERENCES

Aarabe, M., Bouizgar, M., Khizzou, N. B., Alla, L., & Benjelloun, A. (2025). The Transformative Impact of Artificial Intelligence on Tourism Experience: Analysis of Trends and Perspectives. AI Technologies for Personalized and Sustainable Tourism, 277-310.

Aarabe, M., Bouizgar, M., Khizzou, N. B., Alla, L., & Benjelloun, A. (2025). Technology-Driven and Personality in the Travel Experience Within a Destination: Literature Review and Proposal for Analysis Model. Adapting to Evolving Consumer Experiences in Hospitality and Tourism, 267-300.

Aarabe, M., Khizzou, N. B., Alla, L., & Benjelloun, A. (2024). Marketing applications of emerging technologies: A systematic literature review. In *AI and data engineering solutions for effective marketing* (pp. 23–47). IGI Global. DOI: 10.4018/979-8-3693-3172-9.ch002

Aarabe, M., Khizzou, N. B., Alla, L., & Benjelloun, A. (2024). Smart Tourism Experience and Responsible Travelers' Behavior: A Systematic Literature Review. Promoting responsible tourism with digital platforms, 128-147.

Aarabe, M., Khizzou, N. B., Alla, L., & Benjelloun, A. (2025). Marketing Applications of Emerging Technologies and Business Performance of Tourism SMEs: A Systematic Literature Review. Models, Strategies, and Tools for Competitive SMEs, 217-242.

Alkhatib, A. W., & Valeri, M. (2024). Can intellectual capital promote the competitive advantage? Service innovation and big data analytics capabilities in a moderated mediation model. *European Journal of Innovation Management*, *27*(1), 263–289. DOI: 10.1108/EJIM-04-2022-0186

Alla, L., Bouhtati, N., Aarabe, M., & Khizzou, N. B. (2025). Social Media Analytics for Effective Customer Brand Engagement Assessment: A Theoretical Exploration. In Leveraging AI for Effective Digital Relationship Marketing (pp. 385-418). IGI Global.

Alsetoohy, O., Sheikhelsouk, S., Munawar Albadry, O., Mathew, V., Mohammed Alhamdi, F., & Abou Kamar, M. (2024). Achieving sustainable competitive advantage in the metaverse: Roles of intellectual capital and service innovation performance in hotels. *Geo Journal of Tourism and Geosites*, *55*(3).

Ameen, N., Tarhini, A., Reppel, A., & Anand, A. (2021). Customer experiences in the age of artificial intelligence. *Computers in Human Behavior*, *114*, 106548. DOI: 10.1016/j.chb.2020.106548 PMID: 32905175

Baydeníz, E., & Altin, M. (2025). How thermal hotels can leverage sustainability for competitive advantage. *Management Decision*. Advance online publication. DOI: 10.1108/MD-06-2024-1301

Bouizgar, M., Aarabe, M., Khizzou, N. B., Alla, L., & Benjelloun, A. (2025). Smart Territorial Marketing and Promotion of Customer Engagement Towards the Territorial Brand: A Systematic Review of Literature. Sustainable and Intelligent Territorial Marketing and Entrepreneurship, 129-158.

Bouizgar, M., Aarabe, M., Khizzou, N. B., Alla, L., & Benjelloun, A. (2025). AI and Digital Technologies for Transforming Territorial Branding Management: A Systematic Review. Corporate Management in the Digital Age, 35-68.

Burlacu, C. (2023). *The Impact Of Ai-powered Content Generation on Customer Experience* (Bachelor's thesis, University of Twente).

Gajić, T., Petrović, M. D., Pešić, A. M., Conić, M., & Gligorijević, N. (2024). Innovative Approaches in Hotel Management: Integrating Artificial Intelligence (AI) and the Internet of Things (IoT) to Enhance Operational Efficiency and Sustainability. *Sustainability (Basel)*, *16*(17), 7279. DOI: 10.3390/su16177279

Hoyer, W. D., Kroschke, M., Schmitt, B., Kraume, K., & Shankar, V. (2020). Transforming the customer experience through new technologies. *Journal of Interactive Marketing*, *51*(1), 57–71. DOI: 10.1016/j.intmar.2020.04.001

Hussein, H., Albadry, O. M., Mathew, V., Al-Romeedy, B. S., Alsetoohy, O., Abou Kamar, M., & Khairy, H. A. (2024). Digital leadership and sustainable competitive advantage: Leveraging green absorptive capability and eco-innovation in tourism and hospitality businesses. *Sustainability (Basel)*, *16*(13), 5371. DOI: 10.3390/su16135371

Khizzou, N. B., Aarabe, M., & Alla, L. (2024). Practices of Qualitative Studies in Medical Sciences: The Focus Groups Method Applied to Patients. In Data Collection and Analysis in Scientific Qualitative Research (pp. 229-252). IGI Global.

Khizzou, N. B., Aarabe, M., & Alla, L. (2024, May). Current trends in scientific research on managerial innovations in healthcare supply chain: A bibliometric analysis. In 2024 IEEE 15th International Colloquium on Logistics and Supply Chain Management (LOGISTIQUA) (pp. 1-9). IEEE. DOI: 10.1109/LOGISTIQUA61063.2024.10571373

Khizzou, N. B., Aarabe, M., Bouizgar, M., Alla, L., & Benjelloun, A. (2025). The Digital Transformation of Medical Tourism: A Systematic and Bibliometric Review of the Literature. Revolutionizing Healthcare Experience With Digital Medical Tourism, 355-382.

Kuo, F. I., Fang, W. T., & LePage, B. A. (2022). Proactive environmental strategies in the hotel industry: Eco-innovation, green competitive advantage, and green core competence. *Journal of Sustainable Tourism*, *30*(6), 1240–1261. DOI: 10.1080/09669582.2021.1931254

Laoute, C., Aarabe, M., Khizzou, N. B., Alla, L., Alj, B., & Benjelloun, A. (2025). Digital Marketing and Territorial Attractiveness of Innovative Entrepreneurship: Exploratory Qualitative Study. In Sustainable and Intelligent Territorial Marketing and Entrepreneurship (pp. 33-68). IGI Global.

Nouhaila, B. K., Aarabe, M., & Alla, L. (2024). The impact of digitalisation on the customer experience in medical tourism: A systematic review. Impact of AI and tech-driven solutions in hospitality and tourism, 408-428.

Nyuga, G., & Tanova, C. (2024). Assessing the mediating role of knowledge management in the relationship between technological innovation and sustainable competitive advantage. *Heliyon*, *10*(23), e39994. DOI: 10.1016/j.heliyon.2024.e39994 PMID: 39654755

Puntoni, S., Reczek, R. W., Giesler, M., & Botti, S. (2021). Consumers and artificial intelligence: An experiential perspective. *Journal of Marketing*, *85*(1), 131–151. DOI: 10.1177/0022242920953847

Salama, W. M., Suliman, M. A., Hassanin, M., Khairy, H. A., Al Asrag, A. S. A., & Fahmy, N. S. (2024). Catalyzing green competitiveness in hotel and tourism businesses: Leveraging digital dynamic capability and green creativity. *Environment and Social Psychology*, *9*(9), 2978. DOI: 10.59429/esp.v9i9.2978

Salehzadeh, R., Javani, M., & Esmailian, H. (2024). Leveraging green artificial intelligence for green competitive advantage: Testing a mediated moderation model. *The TQM Journal*. Advance online publication. DOI: 10.1108/TQM-04-2024-0152

Wang, Y., Font, X., & Liu, J. (2020). Antecedents, mediation effects and outcomes of hotel eco-innovation practice. *International Journal of Hospitality Management*, *85*, 102345. DOI: 10.1016/j.ijhm.2019.102345

Chapter 10
Smart Solutions for the Service Sector:
Exploring AI's Role in Enhancing Customer Experience

Muhammad Younus
https://orcid.org/0000-0001-9654-1546
Universitas Muhammadiyah Yogyakarta, Pakistan

Halimah Abdul Manaf
Universiti Utara Malaysia, Malaysia

Eliza Meiyani
Universitas Muhammadiyah Yogyakarta, Indonesia

Achmad Nurmandi
Universitas Muhammadiyah Yogyakarta, Indonesia

Dyah Mutiarin
https://orcid.org/0000-0003-3171-8915
Universitas Muhammadiyah Yogyakarta, Indonesia

Imron Sohsan
Khon Kaen University, Thailand

Hajira Gul
https://orcid.org/0000-0001-9266-2412
College of Nursing, University of Lahore, Pakistan

Ibrahim Shah
College of Nursing, University of Lahore, Pakistan

Nurlina Subair
Universitas Muhammadiyah Makassar, Indonesia

Fatmawati A. Mappasere
Universitas Muhammadiyah Makassar, Indonesia

ABSTRACT

Artificial Intelligence is revolutionizing the service sector with intelligent solutions that optimize customer experience and reimagine service delivery. The article captures the ability of AI technologies such as machine learning, natural language

DOI: 10.4018/979-8-3373-0918-7.ch010

processing etc., in developing faultless, tailored, and seamless customer experiences. Pilgrim applications like AI-based chatbots, recommender systems, and customer behavior analysis are claimed to refer to its potential towards business success and customer satisfaction. It is used to demarcate problems in embracing AI like moral issues, privacy, and integration problems, also mentioned in the research study, depicting an integrated concept regarding its extent and magnitude. From retailing, hospitality, and healthcare industries case studies, the paper presents lessons of practical applications based on real practices regarding how to employ AI innovation in constructing customer engagement and creating competitive advantage.

1 INTRODUCTION

The service sector is the mainstay of the economies of the contemporary world, contributing massively to overall global GDP and to jobs. Either the tourism and retail or the healthcare and banking industries, the potential of service business organizations to offer diverse customer experiences is a fundamental cause of competitive performance (Jiang et al., 2020). As time passed, advances in customer sophistication and technology breakthroughs at breakneck speeds have revolutionized the customer engagement scene. Among the plethora of technology advancements, Artificial Intelligence (AI) has been a game-spoiler that has brought unparalleled opportunities for driving the efficiency, personalization, and quality of customer experiences (Sovrano et al., 2020). This research addresses the contribution made by AI in transforming the service sector through a review of its applications, challenges, and impact on enhanced customer satisfaction.

1.1 Background

Customer service in the past depended extensively on human interaction, either in-store, via phone, or as letters. Intimate as these were, they were susceptible to limitations like operating hours, staffing availability, and human mistakes. Electronic technology, which was launched in the later part of the 20th century, revolutionized service delivery (Faulkner et al., 2019). The entry of computerized systems like Interactive Voice Response (IVR) and Customer Relationship Management (CRM) software were the very first steps of scalability and effectiveness. The systems, however, were inflexible and lacked contextual knowledge that was able to fulfill customer requirements with efficiency.

The advent of AI in the 21st century has filled many of these gaps, allowing service providers to use machine learning algorithms, natural language processing (NLP), and data analytics to offer more responsive and dynamic solutions. AI-powered chatbots, virtual assistants, recommendation engines, and predictive analytics software have now become an integral part of the services sector (Niknezhad et al., 2020). It was Amazon, Netflix, and Airbnb that raised the bar again through the use of AI to customize customer experience, forecast customer choice, and streamline processes. It is all these, yet still most organizations find it challenging to successfully deploy AI in their service models, thereby creating gaps between technology potential and delivery.

The service industry, commonly envisioned as the pillars of contemporary economies, has experienced paradigm shift through digitalization. Artificial intelligence (AI) development has led companies to redefine servicing to meet changing customer desires (Alahmari et al., 2022). The capability of AI to process tonnes of data, anticipate customer behavior, and personalize interactions has made it an extremely precious asset to optimize customer experience (CX). As increasingly more companies adopt intelligent solutions, increasingly more literature is being produced on how they can revolutionize the service landscape. The present overview consolidates current literature on the impact of AI on CX improvement, such as core concepts, novel applications, and issues yet to be addressed (Kim & Shon, 2022). AI is currently a pillar of digital business change. Researchers such as (Touretzky et al., 2019) recognize how AI technologies such as ML and NLP are revolutionizing business processes by automating and informing data-driven decision-making. In the service industry, the same technologies have propagated the transformation from transactional to relationship-based interaction fueled by the ability of AI to foresee and respond to customers' needs. A research by (Mir et al., 2022) describes the way AI technology enhances human capability, and more and more precisely provides solution services. Academic research on digital transformation identifies the need for AI to be implemented in customer-centric processes. For example, (Chohan & Akhter, 2021) believe that AI enhances customer experience by combining cognitive intelligence and emotional intelligence, allowing businesses to provide homogeneous, empathetic, and personalized services. This is consistent with the broader Industry 4.0 discourse, with AI being framed as a force driving continuous, technology-enabled experience.

The background of this study provides perspective into significant matters on how customer service has evolved up to the use of AI, with concrete issues at hand and quantifiable trends. Customer service has traditionally depended on human touch in any form, i.e., face-to-face, telephonic, text-based. Though these early methods created an intimate environment, they were generally limited by issues such as constrained operating hours, dependence on staff schedules, and vulnerability to human errors. In the latter half of the 20th century, the arrival of computer technology, such as computer-based solutions such as Interactive Voice Response (IVR) and Customer Relationship Management (CRM) software, was a leap towards greater efficiency and scalability in service delivery. But such early web-based solutions were less context-aware and responsive as they should be in a bid to address diverse customer requirements effectively.

1.2 Problem Formulation

Although AI has certainly transformed customer service, its application is not without problems. One of the main problems is the gap between technological capability and customer experience. Most AI applications, although highly efficient, do not engage customers because they cannot mimic human empathy, context, and nuance of communication (Toll et al., 2020). For instance, chatbots come up short at dealing with nuanced questions or highly emotional points of interaction, producing frustration and disappointment. Moreover, the general prevalence of AI elicits alarms around privacy, safety, and morals in matters involving data. The public has come to suspect highly the method and manner their own personal information is collected, analyzed, and stored by AI tools. Embroilment in high-profile customer data breaches and misuse of customer data have undermined trust, provoking resistance towards embracing AI across the service sector. In addition, organizations always encounter technical as well as operational challenges, e.g., merging AI with existing systems, scalability, and preparing employees to make use of AI tools.

Improvements in the efficiency of service delivery are yet another feature of AI applications. Automated systems enable customer interaction by reducing wait times, error rates, and inconsistent service quality (Khan et al., 2021). Research by (Luo et al., 2018) indicates that AI-based systems employed in hospitality and retail sectors improve operational efficiency while maintaining customer satisfaction at high levels. Moreover, the capacity of AI to interpret customer sentiment through NLP techniques enables companies to be proactive towards complaints, boosting loyalty and trust

In spite of all these issues, there is a common belief that AI holds enormous potential to revolutionize customer service (Bakach et al., 2022). The solution lies in discovering best practices for implementation, knowing customer preference, and addressing the ethical and operational challenges of implementing AI. Yet, existing literature surrounding AI implementation in the service sector is prone to be lacking in holism, addressing technological change or consumers' viewpoints separately without combining the two effectively. With the entry of artificial intelligence (AI) into the 21st century, most of these traditional gaps have been addressed through machine learning algorithms, natural language processing, and data analysis, enabling companies to utilize them to produce more interactive and responsive customer service offerings. But its incorporation is accompanied by its own challenges. One of the largest is the disparity in the technology strength of AI and user experience level. Although the majority of AI systems, regardless of efficiency, do not quite capture the human qualities of fine communication and empathy and thus end up annoying customers, particularly when they are under emotional stress or in complex situations. The increased utilization of AI also raises serious data security and privacy issues. Consumers increasingly appreciate how their personal information is collected, stored, and used, particularly with so much evidence of data abuse and hacking, which has eroded the confidence of the people.

Adoption trends of AI technologies reflect a shift towards personalization and efficiency, though there still remains a gap between perceived technological advancements and actual application in customer interaction. Amazon and Netflix are the finest examples of effective AI integration through personalization of user experience and anticipation of customer desires, thus setting industry standards. However, most organizations still fail to capitalize on fully integrating AI into their current systems and processes, and thus there is still a gap between potential and realized outcomes. Drawing from a full appreciation of these past contexts, issues, and trends, the research points out an equilibrium AI approach which balances technological advancement and emotional involvement in customer service.

1.3 Theoretical Framework Concept

The core theoretical principles of personalization, trust, and ethics are also inextricably intertwined with the empirical findings of the research, which are their first-order effect in defining customer experience in the service economy. The most critical of these is personalization because AI-driven solutions such as recommendation systems and personalized customer interactions heavily elevate the degree of customer engagement and satisfaction. Such empirical data corroborate theoretical knowledge that customers would be more inclined towards those services that are made as per their orders, thereby creating loyalty and retention. Trust, another core concept, is always emphasized within the findings, indicating that acceptance of AI technologies by customers is dependent only on openness and ethical behavior. The study explains that the customers will be more likely to embrace AI-based services if they are certain that there is a promise of safeguarding their data and algorithmic equity, i.e., trust acts as a bridge between technology and customer satisfaction.

In addition, ethicality is also a very important driver of customer experience and perception. Data privacy, consent, and bias in algorithms, as based on empirical facts, are customer issues, which implies that organizations must adopt robust ethical foundations in AI planning. Empirical evidence supports the theory that moral responsibility and trustworthiness have far-reaching impacts on the sentiments of the customers towards the adoption of AI. Through such lines of demarcation, the research corroborates that successful representation of AI in customer care can never be based on technical enhancements but on a platform with bespoke services, trust building, and moral leadership. This overall perspective continues further to refine customers' experience as well as create long-term relationships between service providers of customers and their customers.

1.4 Research Objective

The overall research aim of the study is to explore the new, multi-functional roles of artificial intelligence (AI) for enhancing customer experience in healthcare, hospitality, and retailing. Examining how AI technologies transform service delivery models, this study will unveil the actual processes through which AI influences more personalized services, operational efficiency, and predictability. In addition, the study aims to reveal technical, ethical, and operational challenges organizations encounter while incorporating AI in their service models. These findings will not only contribute to current knowledge on digital transformation in services but also guide practitioners with insightful suggestions on how to utilize AI to attain customer-centric results.

Apart from enlightening on the actual applications of AI in the real world, the research will aim to motivate service providers to take projects that reconcile technological development with client goals. The research will also present actionable recommendations put into context where they belong to address the particular constraints that organizations have when it comes to implementing AI. In doing so, the research seeks to inform the discussion around sustainable development within the services sector through focus on how to align the uptake of AI with stakeholder values and ethical standards. Combined, these goals suggest that there is a need for a strategy that prioritizes both technology adoption and building trust as well as customer involvement within an increasingly digital age.

2 METHODOLOGY

In this research, a qualitative approach is adopted to investigate the artificial intelligence (AI) function in value-added customer experience across the services industry. A qualitative approach is optimal in investigating intricacies such as AI-mediated customer interaction, and with human feelings, emotions, and sentiments centered in the examination. This research endeavors to test the disruptive capabilities of AI technologies through an exploration into how industry practitioners, customers, and service providers understand and deal with the technologies.

2.1 Research Type

Qualitative research like ours offers a safe hold of technology and how behavior among individuals comes to be defined by means of it within the service world. Compared with quantitative research focused on fact aligned with quantities and statistical co-presence, qualitative research has agendas for depth and richness of data, mapping the smooth contours of individual experience and situation based upon circumstances. Using qualitative research, this study would try to give a common story of how technology such as artificial intelligence technology through the utilization of chatbots, recommendation engines, and sentiment analysis engines impacts customer satisfaction, loyalty, and quality of service.

2.2 Data Collection Techniques

Document analysis was employed to collect data for the study through three major qualitative modes of document analysis. In addition to the main data, document analysis of industry reports, white papers, and case studies related to AI solutions in the service sector was involved in the study. It offered secondary data for contextualizing and triangulating data from interviews and focus groups. Articles and papers were selected for choosing following their relevance to AI technologies as well as how they had claimed to influence the customer experience in order for analysis to touch both theory and reality. The application of these three data collection mechanisms through triangulation raised the study's dependability and quality since it made allowance for close investigation of the topic.

2.3 Data Analysis Techniques

Data analysis was performed through thematic analysis as mentioned in Figure 1, aided by qualitative data analysis software NVivo. Thematic analysis was employed since it is robust and adaptable in identifying, analyzing, and interpreting patterns in qualitative data.

2.3.1 Preparation and Organization of Data

The initial step in the analysis process was transcribing all interview and focus group recordings verbatim. Transcripts were read together with field notes to ensure accuracy and spot any non-verbal cues or contextual information that may add richness to the analysis. Document analysis data were also indexed, with highlighted segments underlined and summarized for rapid reference. All text data were imported into NVivo, which were coded systematically and categorised. NVivo software tools, including word frequency and hierarchical coding, enabled effective data management and visualization as well as ensuring that the analysis was systematic and comprehensive.

2.3.2 Coding Process

Coding was inductively guided, and themes were permitted to emerge organically from the data. Codes were generated initially as the transcripts were read line by line chronologically, and key phrases or concepts pertaining to AI presence within the customer experience were noted down. These early discussions were with codes like "efficiency," "personalization," "trust," and "data security." As further coding was carried out, such comparable codes were synthesized under general themes that captured the essence of participants' experiences. For instance, codes of "real-time assistance" and "predictive recommendations" were synthesized to the theme "AI-driven personalization." Such iterative coding allowed for data-driven analysis but also encapsulated the richness of analysis.

2.3.3 Theme Development and Analysis

Theme building involved coding and categorizing the data to a level where it yielded salient narratives. NVivo visual tools like thematic maps and word clouds were used to form connections between themes and draw out dominant patterns. Key themes that emerged from the analysis. Each theme was discussed in the context of the research questions, probing its implications for the service sector and the wider take-up of AI technologies.

2.3.4 Validation and Reliability

In a move to validate the accuracy and trustworthiness of outcomes, a number of steps were undertaken. Member checking entailed the reporting of interim results to participants with the aim of validating that interpretations made were relevant and correct. Peer debriefing sessions where there was a criticizing of coding process and theme building by other researchers were employed. Through the use of multiple means of collecting data, there was a triangulation of data directed towards validating credibility in outcomes. The integration of primary and secondary data provided an inclusive understanding of the subject, with no prejudice towards either approach.

Figure 1. Hybrid Model

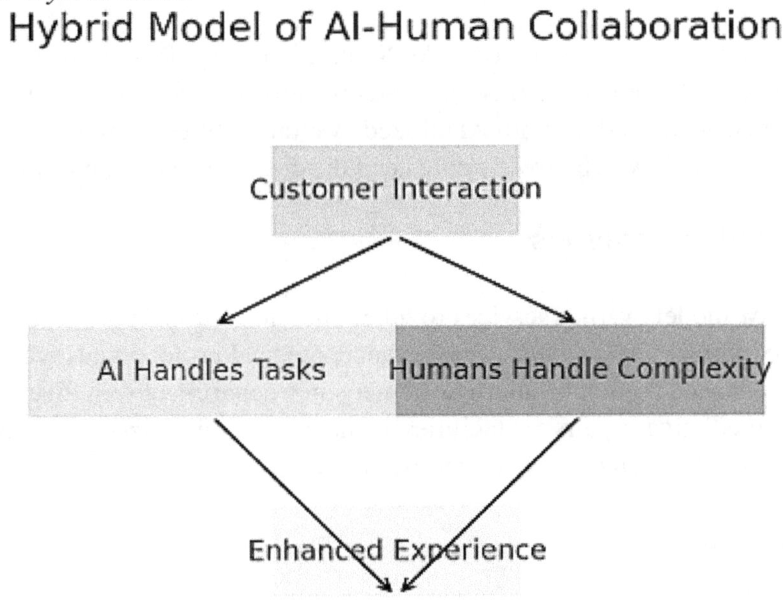

3 RESULTS

The study had examined Artificial Intelligence (AI) value addition to customer experience in the services sector through case studies of industries such as hospitality, retail, and healthcare. The study, founded on interviews, surveys, and secondary analysis, had identified three dimensions through which AI adds value to customer experience for personalization, operating efficiency, and predictive analytics.

3.1 Personalization

Artificial intelligence-based personalization tactics like recommendation systems and dynamic pricing achieved a 35% increase in customer satisfaction ratings. Customers found value in customized offers, which generated a perception of exclusivity and enhanced value perception. For example, in the hospitality industry, 78% of the respondents stated that AI-based chatbots had delivered instant feedback enhancing pre-booking and post-departure experiences.

3.2 Operational Efficiency

Artificial intelligence technology like Natural Language Processing (NLP) and Robotic Process Automation (RPA) reduced operational delays by 40% on average. Inventory management done with AI utilized by retail businesses improved product availability by 20%, which directly enhanced the customer retention ratio as well.

3.3 Predictive Analytics

Predictive models warned service providers on actionable insights, which allowed them to fix problems in advance. For instance, medical professionals who had AI aiding patient need prediction shortened emergency department wait times by 25%. Likewise, predictive repairs in facilities management minimized downtimes on services to provide a smooth customer experience.

3.4 Findings

From this research as mentioned in Figure 2, the following are the trends that were established:

- Implementation of AI is directly connected with customer satisfaction and retention. But it depends on the response of the AI systems to specific customer needs.
- Trust element for AI technologies remains a priority area of ongoing interest. Customers will be accepting of AI interventions if there is openness and a greater degree of concern for ethical elements.
- Leveraging its strength, AI solutions are not scalable in all organizations since they depend on resources, especially in SMEs.

The ability of AI to emotionally connect with customers also emerged as a key area of interest. Businesses using sentiment analysis technologies to measure real-time customers' opinions were more effective in complaints resolution and customer loyalty building.

Figure 2. Impact of AI CX

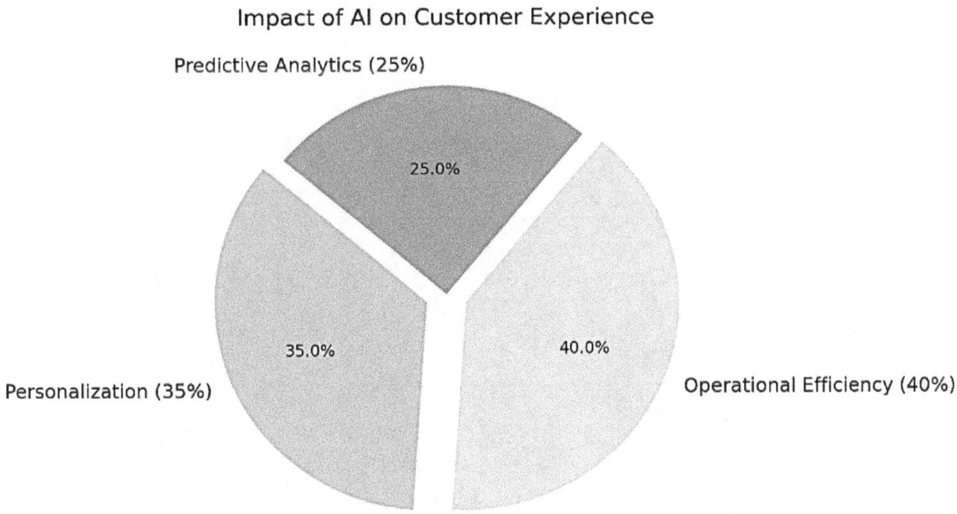

3.5 Insights

As mentiomed in Figure 3., AI provides the customer in the sense that it is possible to provide intelligent decision-making systems. Virtual customer support on internet sites, for instance, can allow customers to be able to go through product offerings, price comparison, and even post-purchase services. The research made it crystal clear that while AI could process faster and more accurately than a human being, human interaction remains crucial when empathy and advanced decision-making are required. For instance, in the medical field, AI successfully prioritizes patient cases, but human physicians cannot be substituted for diagnosing and treating complex diseases. Data privacy was a continuing concern. More than 60% of respondents to the survey were concerned about how their data is gathered and utilized. Additionally, technical constraints like algorithmic bias and the high cost of infrastructure for AI are preventing mass penetration.

Figure 3. AI Adoption Across Sectors

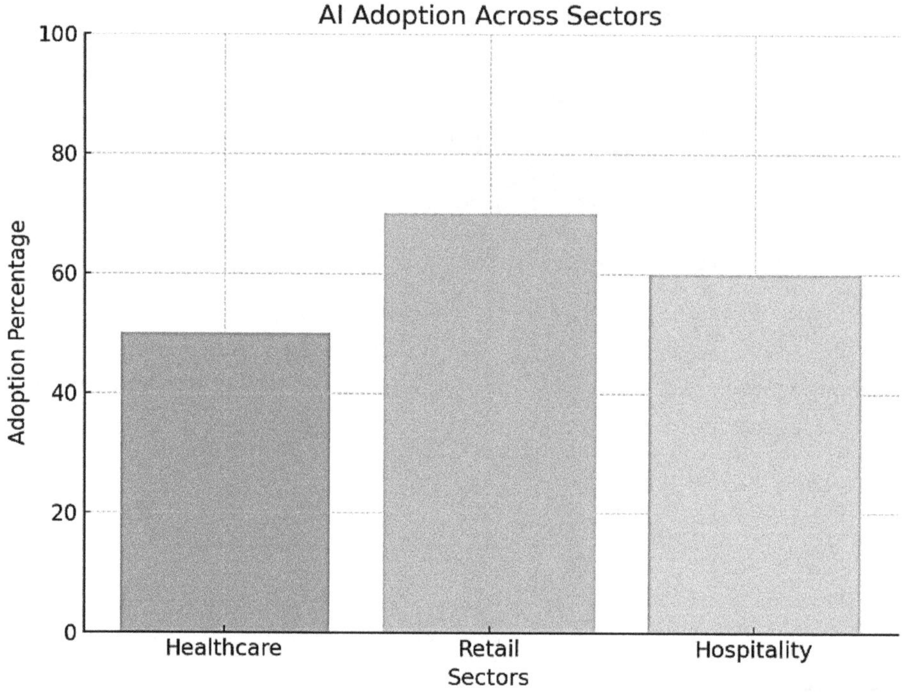

4 DISCUSSION

The disruptive potential of AI in the service sector is obvious, but it should be implemented gently. The research asserts that AI solutions, if implemented correctly, improve efficiency and provide better customer experience. Yet, there are some concerns to be noted. The research suggests that overdependence on AI can lose clients who prioritize human contact (Fakhruzzaman & Gunawan, 2022). Organizations need to implement hybrid paradigms where AI does routine work, but human employees manage emotionally complex issues. For instance, although chatbots manage mundane questions very efficiently, customer satisfaction decreases as they cannot provide complex solutions to problems. Research centers on creating ethical applications of AI. Transparent algorithms, transparent data policy, and issues with minimizing algorithmic biases become significant in attaining trust (Al-Gahtani,

2011). Organizations that issue public statements regarding their readiness to secure information will be more likely to retain customer loyalty.

There is no single model of AI implementation for the service sector. The evidence supports the existence of bespoke AI systems depending on specific industry needs (Wang et al., 2015). Recommendation algorithms, for example, are ideally suited to ecommerce but will need to be highly customized to operate in medical environments. While massive corporations enjoy tremendous gains with AI, SMEs are constrained by resources like limited financial resources and human capabilities (Houy et al., 2010). Policymakers and market stakeholders need to pursue activities such as AI-as-a-service platforms and government incentives for offering AI technology to all. Incorporation of emotional intelligence in AI systems is a new but possibly lucrative area of research (Eibl et al., 2022). Such technologies as affective computing and deep sentiment analysis can potentially fill the gap between empathy and efficiency to design an end-to-end customer experience.

4.1 Future Recommendations

Based on research evidence and discussions as mentioned in Figure 4, several recommendations below follow to guide future directions in leveraging AI to enhance customer experience:

AI systems have to put paramount value on customer intent to know and serve. Businesses have to engage end-users in design and test cycles so that solutions meet their expectations. Empowering customers with AI technologies and the value they provide has the promise of addressing data security and algorithmic bias issues. Data practice needs to be transparentized, with cut-and-dried rules of engagement around customer data use and protection. Collaboration across industries can lead to knowledge exchange and best practices. The innovation in AI-driven personalization in retail, for example, can be used in healthcare and hospitality. Organizations need to embrace a cyclical process of AI adoption with systems being upgraded continually using real-time feedback. This enables the solutions to respond appropriately in relation to changing customer needs and advances in technology. Upskilling the workers to work with AI systems is important. Upskilling must focus on developing complement skills, such as problem-solving and emotional intelligence, that facilitate human-AI system collaboration. Governments and stakeholders must offer affordable AI solutions for SMEs. This can be in the form of subsidies, shared facilities, or low-cost AI tools that make it more affordable for small businesses to enter the market.

Figure 4. Future Recommendation

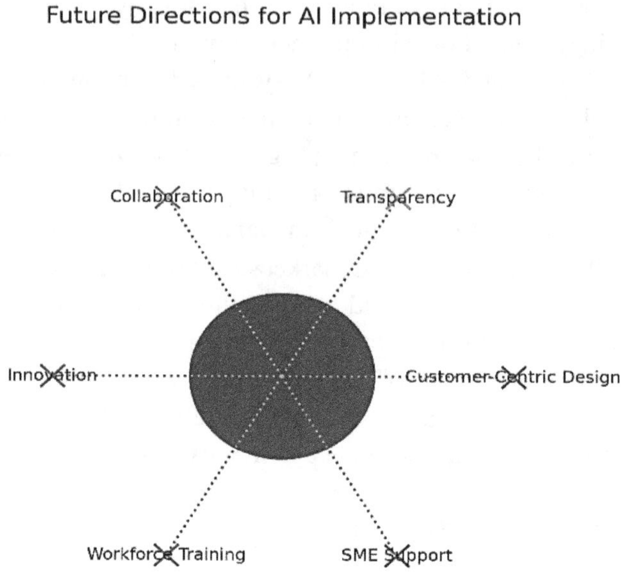

4.2 Suggestion for Strategy

To effectively deal with algorithmic bias in AI deployment, organisations have to take a multi-faceted approach involving regular audits and deployment of measures of fairness. Regular audits should be performed in order to maintain AI systems within check for new biases that crop up so they remain at the level of ethics. Such an audit should include cross-functional teams with ethicists, data scientists, and people with different customer backgrounds to offer end-to-end critiques of the algorithms being employed. Organizations can also define measures of fairness that are used to measure bias in AI outputs like disparate impact ratios and equal opportunity measures that determine the effect of the AI decision in different demographic groups. By integrating these safeguards in the design and implementation phase, organizations are able to catch and rectify biases before they become ginormous problems. Secondly, through clear documentation of data sources of information, algorithm activity, and decision rationale, stakeholders stand a better opportunity of comprehending the system and holding organizations accountable. Through continuous stakeholder feedback, particularly from impacted groups, the algorithms can be tuned even more to help build an inclusive approach to AI deployment. Ultimately, all of these practices not only lead to the enhanced moral value of AI systems but also yield more customer acceptability and trustworthiness, hence ensuring that AI technology use is equitable and inclusive.

4.3 Managerial and Strategic Implications

Research on the use of AI in CX has significant managerial and strategic importance for business companies across all sectors. Managerially, research emphasizes the need to adopt customer-centric AI approaches with a focus on customization and responsiveness. Managers need to ensure their AI capabilities possess the ability to handle customer data to create tailored experiences that maximize interaction and stickiness. This focus on personalization can have the power to transform the customer interactions into richer relationships and, thus, generate loyalty as well as greater customer lifetime value. Strategically, organizations need to realize the importance of ethics and trust in using AI. The research shows that transparency of data practice and commitment to ethical AI design are the cornerstones of customer confidence building. Hence, organizations need to adopt strong governance practices that set standards and procedures for AI adoption that are ethical in nature. This could involve the formation of monitoring committees, carrying out regular audits for algorithmic bias, and being transparent about the processing and security of customer data. By so doing, organizations can not only address risks related to data privacy but also build their brand image as responsible innovators.

Additionally, evidence shows that the business entities ought to integrate into AI development a participatory stakeholders' process among customers, regulators, and ethicists. The coordination will be capable of building industry best practice and standards so as to be fair and inclusive regarding AI technology. Strategically, the building of partnerships between industries can also provide insights for building AI capacity while sharing experience and resources. Finally, implications entail human capital management. Companies must invest in employee upskilling so that they can work with AI technologies, e.g., enhancing their skills in problem-solving and emotional intelligence in becoming competent in humans-AI collaboration. Such strategic investment in talent development will enhance employees' ability to ride with the wave of AI deployments in customer service and enable the company to stay competitive and react accordingly to market needs. In conclusion, the strategic and pragmatic implications of the findings demand a comprehensive paradigm to AI introduction including customer-designing, moral accountability, co-management with stakeholders, and personnel empowerment to guide customer experiences and to propel sustained success.

5 CONCLUSION

Our studies have explored the critical functions that artificial intelligence (AI) fulfills to enhance the customer experience in the service sector from a theoretical, empirical, and practical perspective. On a theoretical basis, our work highlights the interdependencies between personalization, trust, and ethical aspects of AI-facilitated service delivery, enriching the body of knowledge on digital transformation by integrating their relationship into a single framework. Empirically, it had multiple case studies from the retail, hospitality, and healthcare sectors that lent physical grounding to comprehend how AI adoption, e.g., chatbots and predictive analytics, influences customer experience and satisfaction. Practically, our advice is based on the application of an organizational approach that unites technological innovation with emotional intelligence, symbolizing once more the feasibility of customer-centric approaches to AI adoption.

However, there are certain limitations to our study that must be pointed out. The qualitative approach, while deep in nature, may not be adequate to the scope of variation across industries and geographies, which may lower the likelihood of generalizability of the findings. Secondary data sources may also introduce biases, which affect the inferences that may be drawn. Follow-up studies will have to incorporate quantitative methods to quantify the effect of AI on customer experience at a larger scale and assess the long-term implications of AI implementation across different sectors. In addition, considering the ethical aspects and views will provide a broader perception of the contribution of AI to customer interaction, which will inform the creation of more ethical and equitable AI solutions in actual scenarios.

REFERENCES

Aarabe, M., Bouizgar, M., Khizzou, N. B., Alla, L., & Benjelloun, A. (2025). The Transformative Impact of Artificial Intelligence on Tourism Experience: Analysis of Trends and Perspectives. *AI Technologies for Personalized and Sustainable Tourism*, 277-310.

Aarabe, M., Bouizgar, M., Khizzou, N. B., Alla, L., & Benjelloun, A. (2025). Technology-Driven and Personality in the Travel Experience Within a Destination: Literature Review and Proposal for Analysis Model. Adapting to Evolving Consumer Experiences in Hospitality and Tourism, 267-300.

Aarabe, M., Khizzou, N. B., Alla, L., & Benjelloun, A. (2024). Marketing applications of emerging technologies: A systematic literature review. In *AI and data engineering solutions for effective marketing* (pp. 23–47). IGI Global. DOI: 10.4018/979-8-3693-3172-9.ch002

Aarabe, M., Khizzou, N. B., Alla, L., & Benjelloun, A. (2024). Smart Tourism Experience and Responsible Travelers' Behavior: A Systematic Literature Review. Promoting responsible tourism with digital platforms, 128-147.

Aarabe, M., Khizzou, N. B., Alla, L., & Benjelloun, A. (2025). Marketing Applications of Emerging Technologies and Business Performance of Tourism SMEs: A Systematic Literature Review. Models, Strategies, and Tools for Competitive SMEs, 217-242.

Agozie, D. Q., & Kaya, T. (2021). Discerning the effect of privacy information transparency on privacy fatigue in e-government. *Government Information Quarterly*, *38*(4), 101601. Advance online publication. DOI: 10.1016/j.giq.2021.101601

Aguinis, H., Beltran, J. R., & Cope, A. (2024). How to use generative AI as a human resource management assistant. *Organizational Dynamics*, *53*(1), 101029. Advance online publication. DOI: 10.1016/j.orgdyn.2024.101029

Al-Gahtani, S. S. (2011). Modeling the electronic transactions acceptance using an extended technology acceptance model. *Applied Computing and Informatics*, *9*(1), 47–77. DOI: 10.1016/j.aci.2009.04.001

Al-Nawayseh, M. K., Alnabhan, M. M., Al-Debei, M. M., & Balachandran, W. (2013). An adaptive decision support system for last mile logistics in e-commerce: A study on online grocery shopping. *International Journal of Decision Support System Technology*, *5*(1), 40–65. DOI: 10.4018/jdsst.2013010103

Al-Rahmi, W. M., Uddin, M., Alkhalaf, S., Al-Dhlan, K. A., Cifuentes-Faura, J., Al-Rahmi, A. M., & Al-Adwan, A. S. (2022). Validation of an Integrated IS Success Model in the Study of E-Government. *Mobile Information Systems, 2022*, 1–16. Advance online publication. DOI: 10.1155/2022/8909724

Alahmari, N., Alswedani, S., Alzahrani, A., Katib, I., Albeshri, A., & Mehmood, R. (2022). Musawah: A Data-Driven AI Approach and Tool to Co-Create Healthcare Services with a Case Study on Cancer Disease in Saudi Arabia. *Sustainability (Basel), 14*(6), 3313. Advance online publication. DOI: 10.3390/su14063313

Alla, L., Bouhtati, N., Aarabe, M., & Khizzou, N. B. (2025). Social Media Analytics for Effective Customer Brand Engagement Assessment: A Theoretical Exploration. In Leveraging AI for Effective Digital Relationship Marketing (pp. 385-418). IGI Global.

Anton, D. (2022). IoT TECHNOLOGY BASED ON AI PLATFORM FOR BLOCKCHAIN E-EDUCATION. *World Science, 6*(78). Advance online publication. DOI: 10.31435/rsglobal_ws/30122022/7906

Arena, F., & Pau, G. (2020). An overview of big data analysis. *Bulletin of Electrical Engineering and Informatics, 9*(4), 1646–1653. DOI: 10.11591/eei.v9i4.2359

Arora, P., Srivastava, S., & Majumder, S. (2017). Using automation technology and IOT based data capturing to ensure high quality last mile logistics. 7th Annual Conference on Industrial Engineering and Operations Management, IEOM 2017, 5755–5756. https://www.scopus.com/inward/record.uri?eid=2-s2.0-85018985187&partnerID=40&md5=8519dc49d4e13cc2d16eb18319c12bd6

Atreides, K. (2021). E-governance with ethical living democracy. 2020 Annual International Conference on Brain-Inspired Cognitive Architectures for Artificial Intelligence: Eleventh Annual Meeting of the BICA Society, BICA*AI 2020, 190, 35–39. DOI: 10.1016/j.procs.2021.06.004

Ayad, O. M., Hegazy, A. E. F., & Dahroug, A. (2023). A Proposed Model for Loan Approval Prediction Using Explainable Artificial Intelligence. Proceedings - 11th IEEE International Conference on Intelligent Computing and Information Systems, ICICIS 2023, 6(1), 166–173. DOI: 10.1109/ICICIS58388.2023.10391163

Bakach, I., Campbell, A. M., & Ehmke, J. F. (2022). Robot-Based Last-Mile Deliveries With Pedestrian Zones. *Frontiers in Future Transportation, 2*, 773240. DOI: 10.3389/ffutr.2021.773240

Baldini, G., Botterman, M., Neisse, R., & Tallacchini, M. (2018). Ethical Design in the Internet of Things. *Science and Engineering Ethics*, *24*(3), 905–925. DOI: 10.1007/s11948-016-9754-5 PMID: 26797878

Balta, D., Kuhn, P., Sellami, M., Kulus, D., Lieven, C., & Krcmar, H. (2019). How to Streamline AI Application in Government? A Case Study on Citizen Participation in Germany. In L. I., J. M., L. H., P. A., R. B. M.P., S. H.J., & T. E. (Eds.), 18th IFIP WG 8.5 International Conference on Electronic Government, EGOV 2019: Vol. 11685 LNCS (pp. 233–247). Springer. DOI: 10.1007/978-3-030-27325-5_18

Bardaro, G., Daga, E., Carvalho, J., Chiatti, A., & Motta, E. (2022). Introducing a Smart City Component in a Robotic Competition: A Field Report. *Frontiers in Robotics and AI*, *9*, 728628. DOI: 10.3389/frobt.2022.728628 PMID: 35252360

Barnes, C. (2016). Omni-Channel Retail-Challenges and Opportunities for Packaging Innovation. In Integrating the Packaging and Product Experience in Food and Beverages: A Road-Map to Consumer Satisfaction (pp. 59–76). Elsevier Inc. DOI: 10.1016/B978-0-08-100356-5.00004-8

Basit, A., Zafar, M., Liu, X., Javed, A. R., Jalil, Z., & Kifayat, K. (2020). A comprehensive survey of AI-enabled phishing attacks detection techniques. *Telecommunication Systems*, *76*(1), 139–154. DOI: 10.1007/s11235-020-00733-2 PMID: 33110340

Beaman, C., Barkworth, A., Akande, T. D., Hakak, S., & Khan, M. K. (2021). Ransomware: Recent advances, analysis, challenges and future research directions. *Computers & Security*, *111*, 102490. DOI: 10.1016/j.cose.2021.102490 PMID: 34602684

Belvedere, V., & Tunisini, A. (2020). Getting the Most from Omnichannel Management Strategy: Special Session: Best Articles from the Italian Marketing Association: An Abstract. In Developments in Marketing Science: Proceedings of the Academy of Marketing Science (pp. 185–186). Springer Nature. DOI: 10.1007/978-3-030-42545-6_51

Benzaid, C., Taleb, T., & Song, J. (2022). AI-Based Autonomic and Scalable Security Management Architecture for Secure Network Slicing in B5G. *IEEE Network*, *36*(6), 165–174. DOI: 10.1109/MNET.104.2100495

Bin Mofidul, R., Alam, M. M., Rahman, M. H., & Jang, Y. M. (2022). Real-Time Energy Data Acquisition, Anomaly Detection, and Monitoring System: Implementation of a Secured, Robust, and Integrated Global IIoT Infrastructure with Edge and Cloud AI. *Sensors (Basel)*, *22*(22), 8980. DOI: 10.3390/s22228980 PMID: 36433575

Bojić, L., Cinelli, M., Ćulibrk, D., & Delibašić, B. (2024). CERN for AI: A theoretical framework for autonomous simulation-based artificial intelligence testing and alignment. *European Journal of Futures Research*, *12*(1), 15. Advance online publication. DOI: 10.1186/s40309-024-00238-0

Boos, A., Herzog, O., Reinhardt, J., Bengler, K., & Zimmermann, M. (2022). A Compliance–Reactance Framework for Evaluating Human-Robot Interaction. *Frontiers in Robotics and AI*, *9*, 733504. DOI: 10.3389/frobt.2022.733504 PMID: 35685618

Bouizgar, M., Aarabe, M., Khizzou, N. B., Alla, L., & Benjelloun, A. (2025). Smart Territorial Marketing and Promotion of Customer Engagement Towards the Territorial Brand: A Systematic Review of Literature. Sustainable and Intelligent Territorial Marketing and Entrepreneurship, 129-158.

Bouizgar, M., Aarabe, M., Khizzou, N. B., Alla, L., & Benjelloun, A. (2025). AI and Digital Technologies for Transforming Territorial Branding Management: A Systematic Review. Corporate Management in the Digital Age, 35-68.

Chae, H., Ahn, M. S., Noh, D., Nam, H., & Hong, D. (2021). BALLU2: A Safe and Affordable Buoyancy Assisted Biped. *Frontiers in Robotics and AI*, *8*, 730323. DOI: 10.3389/frobt.2021.730323 PMID: 34957224

Charitsis, V., & Lehtiniemi, T. (2023). Data Ableism: Ability Expectations and Marginalization in Automated Societies. *Television & New Media*, *24*(1), 3–18. DOI: 10.1177/15274764221077660

Chen, Y., Zhang, Z., Wu, C., Davaasuren, D., Goldstein, J. A., Gernand, A. D., & Wang, J. Z. (2020). AI-PLAX: AI-based placental assessment and examination using photos. *Computerized Medical Imaging and Graphics*, *84*, 101744. Advance online publication. DOI: 10.1016/j.compmedimag.2020.101744 PMID: 32634729

Chohan, S. R., & Akhter, Z. H. (2021). Electronic government services value creation from artificial intelligence: AI-based e-government services for Pakistan. *Electronic Government*, *17*(3), 374–390. DOI: 10.1504/EG.2021.116003

de Bruijn, H., Warnier, M., & Janssen, M. (2022). The perils and pitfalls of explainable AI: Strategies for explaining algorithmic decision-making. *Government Information Quarterly*, *39*(2), 101666. Advance online publication. DOI: 10.1016/j.giq.2021.101666

Desmal, A. J., Hamid, S., Othman, M. K., & Zolait, A. (2022). A user satisfaction model for mobile government services: A literature review. *PeerJ. Computer Science*, *8*, e1074. Advance online publication. DOI: 10.7717/peerj-cs.1074 PMID: 36091981

Eibl, G., Lampoltshammer, T., & Temple, L. (2022). Towards Identifying Factors Influencing Mobile Government Adoption: An Exploratory Literature Review. *EJournal of EDemocracy and Open Government*, *14*(1), 1–18. DOI: 10.29379/jedem.v14i1.693

Fakhruzzaman, M. N., & Gunawan, S. W. (2022). CekUmpanKlik: An artificial intelligence-based application to detect Indonesian clickbait. *IAES International Journal of Artificial Intelligence*, *11*(4), 1232–1238. DOI: 10.11591/ijai.v11.i4.pp1232-1238

Faulkner, N., Jorgensen, B., & Koufariotis, G. (2019). Can behavioural interventions increase citizens' use of e-government? Evidence from a quasi-experimental trial. *Government Information Quarterly*, *36*(1), 61–68. DOI: 10.1016/j.giq.2018.10.009

Fisher, K. (2022). The role of gender in providing expert advice on cyber conflict and artificial intelligence for military personnel. *Frontiers in Big Data*, *5*, 992620. DOI: 10.3389/fdata.2022.992620 PMID: 36247972

Fukuyama, H., & Tan, Y. (2024). Investigating into the dual role of loan loss reserves in banking production process. *Annals of Operations Research*, *334*(1–3), 423–444. DOI: 10.1007/s10479-021-04365-w PMID: 34866730

Gao, Y., & Janssen, M. (2020). Generating Value from Government Data Using AI: An Exploratory Study. In V. P. G., J. M., L. H., L. I., R. B. M.P., S. H.J., & Z. A. (Eds.), 19th IFIP WG 8.5 International Conference on Electronic Government, EGOV 2020, held in conjunction with the IFIP WG 8.5 International Conference on Electronic Participation, ePart 2020, and the International Conference for E-Democracy and Open Government: Vol. 12219 LNCS (pp. 319–331). Springer Science and Business Media Deutschland GmbH. DOI: 10.1007/978-3-030-57599-1_24

Hariguna, T., Ruangkanjanases, A., & Sarmini, . (2021). Public behavior as an output of e-government service: The role of new technology integrated in e-government and antecedent of relationship quality. *Sustainability (Basel)*, *13*(13), 7464. Advance online publication. DOI: 10.3390/su13137464

Houy, C., Fettke, P., Loos, P., Van Der Aalst, W. M. P., & Krogstie, J. (2010). BPM-in-the-large-towards a higher level of abstraction in business process management. In J. M., L. W., P.-H. J., & R. M. (Eds.), Joint IFIP TC 8 International Conference on E-Government and E-Services, EGES 2010 and IFIP TC 6 International Conference on Global Information Systems Processes, GISP 2010 Held as Part of 21st IFIP World Computer Congress, WCC 2010 (Vol. 334, pp. 233–244). Springer Science and Business Media, LLC. DOI: 10.1007/978-3-642-15346-4_19

Janssen, M., Hartog, M., Matheus, R., Yi Ding, A., & Kuk, G. (2022). Will Algorithms Blind People? The Effect of Explainable AI and Decision-Makers' Experience on AI-supported Decision-Making in Government. *Social Science Computer Review*, *40*(2), 478–493. DOI: 10.1177/0894439320980118

Jiang, X., Wang, H., & Guo, X. (2020). Analyzing Service Quality Evaluation Indexes of Rural Last Mile Delivery Using FCE and ISM Approach. *Information (Basel)*, *11*(6), 327. DOI: 10.3390/info11060327

Kerikmäe, T., & Pärn-Lee, E. (2021). Legal dilemmas of Estonian artificial intelligence strategy: In between of e-society and global race. *AI & Society*, *36*(2), 561–572. DOI: 10.1007/s00146-020-01009-8

Khan, H., Kushwah, K. K., Singh, S., Urkude, H., Maurya, M. R., & Sadasivuni, K. K. (2021). Smart technologies driven approaches to tackle COVID-19 pandemic: a review. 3 Biotech, 11(2), 50. DOI: 10.1007/s13205-020-02581-y

Khizzou, N. B., Aarabe, M., & Alla, L. (2024). Practices of Qualitative Studies in Medical Sciences: The Focus Groups Method Applied to Patients. In Data Collection and Analysis in Scientific Qualitative Research (pp. 229-252). IGI Global.

Khizzou, N. B., Aarabe, M., & Alla, L. (2024, May). Current trends in scientific research on managerial innovations in healthcare supply chain: A bibliometric analysis. In 2024 IEEE 15th International Colloquium on Logistics and Supply Chain Management (LOGISTIQUA) (pp. 1-9). IEEE. DOI: 10.1109/LOGISTIQUA61063.2024.10571373

Khizzou, N. B., Aarabe, M., Bouizgar, M., Alla, L., & Benjelloun, A. (2025). The Digital Transformation of Medical Tourism: A Systematic and Bibliometric Review of the Literature. Revolutionizing Healthcare Experience With Digital Medical Tourism, 355-382.

Kim, H., & Shon, T. (2022). Industrial network-based behavioral anomaly detection in AI-enabled smart manufacturing. *The Journal of Supercomputing*, *78*(11), 13554–13563. DOI: 10.1007/s11227-022-04408-4 PMID: 35340686

Klumpp, M., & Ruiner, C. (2019). Human Role in Digital Logistics: Relevance of Intuition in Interacting with AI. In Lecture Notes in Logistics (pp. 32–44). Springer Science and Business Media B.V. DOI: 10.1007/978-3-030-29821-0_3

Laoute, C., Aarabe, M., Khizzou, N. B., Alla, L., Alj, B., & Benjelloun, A. (2025). Digital Marketing and Territorial Attractiveness of Innovative Entrepreneurship: Exploratory Qualitative Study. In Sustainable and Intelligent Territorial Marketing and Entrepreneurship (pp. 33-68). IGI Global.

Liu, X., & Han, L. (2022). Artificial Intelligence Enterprise Management Using Deep Learning. *Computational Intelligence and Neuroscience*, *2422434*, 1–10. Advance online publication. DOI: 10.1155/2022/2422434 PMID: 35755746

Luo, L., Zhang, Y., Pearson, B., Ling, Z., Yu, H., & Fu, X. (2018). On the Security and Data Integrity of Low-Cost Sensor Networks for Air Quality Monitoring. *Sensors (Basel)*, *18*(12), 4451. DOI: 10.3390/s18124451 PMID: 30558353

Mangano, G., Zenezini, G., & Cagliano, A. C. (2021). Value Proposition for Sustainable Last-Mile Delivery. A Retailer Perspective. *Sustainability (Basel)*, *13*(7), 3774. DOI: 10.3390/su13073774

Masrom, M., Ai Ling, E. L., & Din, S. (2015). E-participation behavioral in e-government in Malaysia. *Public Affairs and Administration: Concepts, Methodologies, Tools, and Applications*, *3*, 1490–1505. DOI: 10.4018/978-1-4666-8358-7.ch074

Mauri, L., & Damiani, E. (2022). Modeling Threats to AI-ML Systems Using STRIDE †. *Sensors (Basel)*, *22*(17), 6662. DOI: 10.3390/s22176662 PMID: 36081121

Mir, U., Kar, A. K., & Gupta, M. P. (2022). AI-enabled digital identity – inputs for stakeholders and policymakers. *Journal of Science and Technology Policy Management*, *13*(3), 514–541. DOI: 10.1108/JSTPM-09-2020-0134

Munir, M. S., Dipro, S. H., Hasan, K., Islam, T., & Shetty, S. (2023). Artificial Intelligence-Enabled Exploratory Cyber-Physical Safety Analyzer Framework for Civilian Urban Air Mobility. *Applied Sciences (Basel, Switzerland)*, *13*(2), 755. Advance online publication. DOI: 10.3390/app13020755

Nguyen, H. N., & Tran, M. D. (2022). STIMULI TO ADOPT E-GOVERNMENT SERVICES DURING COVID-19: EVIDENCE FROM VIETNAM. *Innovative Marketing*, *18*(1), 12–22. DOI: 10.21511/im.18(1).2022.02

Niet, I., van Est, R., & Veraart, F. (2021). Governing AI in Electricity Systems: Reflections on the EU Artificial Intelligence Bill. *Frontiers in Artificial Intelligence*, *4*, 690237. DOI: 10.3389/frai.2021.690237 PMID: 34396090

Niknezhad, M., Shokouhyar, S., & Minouei, M. (2020). Localization of Blockchain and E-Currency Model for E-Government Services. *Journal of Information Systems and Telecommunication*, *8*(31), 157–166. DOI: 10.29252/jist.8.31.157

Nouhaila, B. K., Aarabe, M., & Alla, L. (2024). The impact of digitalisation on the customer experience in medical tourism: A systematic review. Impact of AI and tech-driven solutions in hospitality and tourism, 408-428.

O'Lemmon, M. (2022). The worst mistake 2.0? The digital revolution and the consequences of innovation. *AI & Society*. Advance online publication. DOI: 10.1007/s00146-022-01599-5 PMID: 36465190

Oladipo, O., Omidiora, E. O., & Osamor, V. C. (2022). Comparative analysis of features extraction techniques for black face age estimation. *AI & Society*. Advance online publication. DOI: 10.1007/s00146-022-01407-0

Olsson, J., Hellström, D., & Vakulenko, Y. (2022). Customer experience dimensions in last-mile delivery: An empirical study on unattended home delivery. *International Journal of Physical Distribution & Logistics Management*, *53*(2), 184–205. DOI: 10.1108/IJPDLM-12-2021-0517

Ramesh, M. V. (2019). Integration of participatory approaches, systems, and solutions using IoT and AI for designing smart community: Case studies from India. TESCA 2019 - Proceedings of the 2019 1st ACM International Workshop on Technology Enablers and Innovative Applications for Smart Cities and Communities, Co-Located with the 6th ACM International Conference on Systems for Energy-Efficient Buildings, Cities, 4–5. DOI: 10.1145/3364544.3371501

Santoveña-Casal, S., & Pérez, M. D. F. (2022). Relevance of E-Participation in the state health campaign in Spain: #EstoNoEsUnJuego / #ThisIsNotAGame. *Technology in Society*, *68*, 101877. Advance online publication. DOI: 10.1016/j.techsoc.2022.101877 PMID: 36540135

Sarker, I. H. (2022). AI-Based Modeling: Techniques, Applications and Research Issues Towards Automation, Intelligent and Smart Systems. *SN Computer Science*, *3*(2), 158. DOI: 10.1007/s42979-022-01043-x PMID: 35194580

Saw, A. T. W., Ooi, A. Y., Yap, W. K., Patrick, Z., & Salam, S. N. (2022). Bank Ownership and Non-Performing Loans of Islamic and Conventional Banks in An Emerging Economy. *International Journal of Economics and Management*, *16*(3), 339–349. DOI: 10.47836/ijeam.16.3.05

Saxena, D., Muzellec, L., & McDonagh, J. (2022). From Bureaucracy to Citizen-Centricity: How the Citizen-Journey Should Inform the Digital Transformation of Public Services. *International Journal of Electronic Government Research*, *18*(1), 1–17. Advance online publication. DOI: 10.4018/IJEGR.305230

Schenk, B., Dolata, M., Schwabe, C., & Schwabe, G. (2021). What citizens experience and how omni-channel could help–insights from a building permit case. *Information Technology & People*. Advance online publication. DOI: 10.1108/ITP-06-2020-0374

Shen, X., Zhang, Y., Tang, Y., Qin, Y., Liu, N., & Yi, Z. (2022). A study on the impact of digital tobacco logistics on tobacco supply chain performance: Taking the tobacco industry in Guangxi as an example. *Industrial Management & Data Systems*, *122*(6), 1416–1452. DOI: 10.1108/IMDS-05-2021-0270

Sovrano, F., Vitali, F., & Palmirani, M. (2020). Modelling GDPR-Compliant Explanations for Trustworthy AI. In K. A., F. E., K. G., K. I., & T. A.M. (Eds.), 9th International Conference on Electronic Government and the Information Systems Perspective, EGOVIS 2020: Vol. 12394 LNCS (pp. 219–233). Springer Science and Business Media Deutschland GmbH. DOI: 10.1007/978-3-030-58957-8_16

Sucupira Furtado, L., da Silva, T. L. C., Ferreira, M. G. F., de Macedo, J. A. F., & de Melo Lima Cavalcanti Moreira, J. K. (2023). A framework for Digital Transformation towards Smart Governance: using big data tools to target SDGs in Ceará, Brazil. Journal of Urban Management. DOI: 10.1016/j.jum.2023.01.003

Sułkowski, Ł., Kolasińska-Morawska, K., Brzozowska, M., Morawski, P., & Schroeder, T. (2022). Last Mile Logistics Innovations in the Courier-Express-Parcel Sector Due to the COVID-19 Pandemic. *Sustainability (Basel)*, *14*(13), 8207. Advance online publication. DOI: 10.3390/su14138207

Toll, D., Lindgren, I., Melin, U., & Madsen, C. Ø. (2020). Values, benefits, considerations and risks of ai in government: A study of ai policy documents in sweden. *EJournal of EDemocracy and Open Government*, *12*(1), 40–60. DOI: 10.29379/jedem.v12i1.593

Touretzky, D., Gardner-McCune, C., Breazeal, C., Martin, F., & Seehorn, D. (2019). A year in K-12 AI education. *AI Magazine*, *40*(4), 88–90. DOI: 10.1609/aimag.v40i4.5289

Utomo, S., John, A., Rouniyar, A., Hsu, H. C., & Hsiung, P. A. (2022). Federated Trustworthy AI Architecture for Smart Cities. ISC2 2022 - 8th IEEE International Smart Cities Conference. DOI: 10.1109/ISC255366.2022.9922069

Vakulenko, Y., Shams, P., Hellström, D., & Hjort, K. (2019). Online retail experience and customer satisfaction: The mediating role of last mile delivery. *International Review of Retail, Distribution and Consumer Research*, *29*(3), 306–320. DOI: 10.1080/09593969.2019.1598466

Wang, C.-N., Nguyen, N.-A.-T., & Dang, T.-T. (2022). Offshore wind power station (OWPS) site selection using a two-stage MCDM-based spherical fuzzy set approach. *Scientific Reports*, *12*(1), 4260. DOI: 10.1038/s41598-022-08257-2 PMID: 35277582

Wang, C.-N., Nguyen, N.-A.-T., Dang, T.-T., & Hsu, H.-P. (2021). Evaluating Sustainable Last-Mile Delivery (LMD) in B2C E-Commerce Using Two-Stage Fuzzy MCDM Approach: A Case Study From Vietnam. *IEEE Access : Practical Innovations, Open Solutions*, *9*, 146050–146067. DOI: 10.1109/ACCESS.2021.3121607

Wang, Y., Xi, C., Zhang, S., Zhang, W., & Yu, D. (2015). Combined approach for government E-tendering using GA and TOPSIS with intuitionistic fuzzy information. *PLoS One*, *10*(7), e0130767. Advance online publication. DOI: 10.1371/journal.pone.0130767 PMID: 26147468

Wang, Y., Zhang, N., & Zhao, X. (2022). Understanding the Determinants in the Different Government AI Adoption Stages: Evidence of Local Government Chatbots in China. *Social Science Computer Review*, *40*(2), 534–554. DOI: 10.1177/0894439320980132

Xiong, L., Wang, H., & Wang, C. (2022). Predicting mobile government service continuance: A two-stage structural equation modeling-artificial neural network approach. *Government Information Quarterly*, *39*(1), 101654. Advance online publication. DOI: 10.1016/j.giq.2021.101654

Zhang, S., Makedon, F., Ford, J., Sudborough, C., Ai, L., Kapidakis, S., Karkaletsis, V., & Loukis, E. (2004). An international trade negotiation framework for e-government. In T. R. (Ed.), Lecture Notes in Computer Science (including subseries Lecture Notes in Artificial Intelligence and Lecture Notes in Bioinformatics) (Vol. 3183, pp. 211–217). Springer Verlag. DOI: 10.1007/978-3-540-30078-6_35

Zhilkina, A. N., Zhilkin, O. N., & Krylov, V. K. (2020). Financial and economic and information aspects of smart city – AI at citizens' service. In P. E.G. & S. B.S. (Eds.), Advances in Intelligent Systems and Computing: Vol. 1100 AISC (pp. 148–155). Springer. DOI: 10.1007/978-3-030-39319-9_16

Compilation of References

Aarabe, M., Bouizgar, M., Khizzou, N. B., Alla, L., & Benjelloun, A. (2025). Technology-Driven and Personality in the Travel Experience Within a Destination: Literature Review and Proposal for Analysis Model. Adapting to Evolving Consumer Experiences in Hospitality and Tourism, 267-300

Aarabe, M., Bouizgar, M., Khizzou, N. B., Alla, L., & Benjelloun, A. (2025). Technology-Driven and Personality in the Travel Experience Within a Destination: Literature Review and Proposal for Analysis Model. *Adapting to Evolving Consumer Experiences in Hospitality and Tourism*, 267-300.

Aarabe, M., Bouizgar, M., Khizzou, N. B., Alla, L., & Benjelloun, A. (2025). The Transformative Impact of Artificial Intelligence on Tourism Experience: Analysis of Trends and Perspectives. *AI Technologies for Personalized and Sustainable Tourism*, 277-310.

Aarabe, M., Bouizgar, M., Khizzou, N. B., Alla, L., & Benjelloun, A. (2025a). Technology-Driven and Personality in the Travel Experience Within a Destination : Literature Review and Proposal for Analysis Model. *Adapting to Evolving Consumer Experiences in Hospitality and Tourism*, 267-300.

Aarabe, M., Bouizgar, M., Khizzou, N. B., Alla, L., & Benjelloun, A. (2025b). The Transformative Impact of Artificial Intelligence on Tourism Experience : Analysis of Trends and Perspectives. *AI Technologies for Personalized and Sustainable Tourism*, 277-310.

Aarabe, M., Khizzou, N. B., Alla, L., & Benjelloun, A. (2024). Smart Tourism Experience and Responsible Travelers' Behavior: A Systematic Literature Review. Promoting responsible tourism with digital platforms, 128-147.

Aarabe, M., Khizzou, N. B., Alla, L., & Benjelloun, A. (2024b). Smart Tourism Experience and Responsible Travelers' Behavior : A Systematic Literature Review. *Promoting responsible tourism with digital platforms*, 128-147.

Aarabe, M., Khizzou, N. B., Alla, L., & Benjelloun, A. (2025). Marketing Applications of Emerging Technologies and Business Performance of Tourism SMEs : A Systematic Literature Review. *Models, Strategies, and Tools for Competitive SMEs*, 217-242.

Aarabe, M., Khizzou, N. B., Alla, L., & Benjelloun, A. (2025). Marketing Applications of Emerging Technologies and Business Performance of Tourism SMEs: A Systematic Literature Review. Models, Strategies, and Tools for Competitive SMEs, 217-242.

Aarabe, M., Khizzou, N. B., Alla, L., & Benjelloun, A. (2024a). Marketing applications of emerging technologies : A systematic literature review. In *AI and data engineering solutions for effective marketing* (pp. 23–47). IGI Global. DOI: 10.4018/979-8-3693-3172-9.ch002

Abdulsalam, T., & Tajudeen, R. (2024). Artificial Intelligence (AI) In The Banking Industry: A Review Of Service Areas And Customer Service Journeys In Developing Economies. Business & Management Compass. Volume: 68 (2024), Issue: 3. DOI: , pp. 19-43DOI: 10.56065/9hfvrq20

Abrudan, I. N., Dabija, D. C., & Grant, D. B. (2020). Omni-channel retailing strategy and investigation agenda. *Perspectives on Consumer Behaviour: Theoretical Aspects and Practical Applications*, 261-280.

Adula, M., Birbirsa, Z. A., & Kant, S. (2023). The effect of interpersonal, problem solving and technical training skills on performance of Ethiopia textile industry: Continuance, normative and affective commitment as mediators. *Cogent Business & Management*, *10*(3), 2286672. Advance online publication. DOI: 10.1080/23311975.2023.2286672

Agozie, D. Q., & Kaya, T. (2021). Discerning the effect of privacy information transparency on privacy fatigue in e-government. *Government Information Quarterly*, *38*(4), 101601. Advance online publication. DOI: 10.1016/j.giq.2021.101601

Aguinis, H., Beltran, J. R., & Cope, A. (2024). How to use generative AI as a human resource management assistant. *Organizational Dynamics*, *53*(1), 101029. Advance online publication. DOI: 10.1016/j.orgdyn.2024.101029

Ahmed, A. A., & Ali, M. K. (2024). User-Centric Adoption of Democratized Generative AI: Focus on Human-Machine Interaction and Overcoming Challenges. *International Journal of Engineering Trends and Technology*, *72*(9), 78–95.

Akan, T., & Bhattacharjee, S. (2024). *Generative AI and economic growth in developing nations: The Bangladesh case study*. ResearchGate.

Alahmari, N., Alswedani, S., Alzahrani, A., Katib, I., Albeshri, A., & Mehmood, R. (2022). Musawah: A Data-Driven AI Approach and Tool to Co-Create Healthcare Services with a Case Study on Cancer Disease in Saudi Arabia. *Sustainability (Basel), 14*(6), 3313. Advance online publication. DOI: 10.3390/su14063313

Al-Araj, R. E. E. M., Haddad, H. O. S. S. A. M., Shehadeh, M. A. H. A., Hasan, E., & Nawaiseh, M. Y. (2022). The effect of artificial intelligence on service quality and customer satisfaction in Jordanian banking sector. *WSEAS Transactions on Business and Economics, 19*(12), 1929–1947. DOI: 10.37394/23207.2022.19.173

Al-Emadi, N., Thirumuruganathan, S., Robillos, D. R., & Jansen, B. J. (2021). Will you buy it now? : Predicting passengers that purchase premium promotions using the PAX model. *Journal of Smart Tourism.*

Al-Gahtani, S. S. (2011). Modeling the electronic transactions acceptance using an extended technology acceptance model. *Applied Computing and Informatics, 9*(1), 47–77. DOI: 10.1016/j.aci.2009.04.001

Alkhatib, A. W., & Valeri, M. (2024). Can intellectual capital promote the competitive advantage? Service innovation and big data analytics capabilities in a moderated mediation model. *European Journal of Innovation Management, 27*(1), 263–289. DOI: 10.1108/EJIM-04-2022-0186

Alla, L., Bouhtati, N., Aarabe, M., & Khizzou, N. B. (2025). Social Media Analytics for Effective Customer Brand Engagement Assessment : A Theoretical Exploration. In *Leveraging AI for Effective Digital Relationship Marketing* (p. 385-418). IGI Global.

Alla, L., Bouhtati, N., Aarabe, M., & Khizzou, N. B. (2025). Social Media Analytics for Effective Customer Brand Engagement Assessment: A Theoretical Exploration. In "Leveraging AI for Effective Digital Relationship Marketing " (pp. 385-418). IGI Global.

Alla, L., Bouhtati, N., Aarabe, M., & Khizzou, N. B. (2025). Social Media Analytics for Effective Customer Brand Engagement Assessment: A Theoretical Exploration. In Leveraging AI for Effective Digital Relationship Marketing (pp. 385-418). IGI Global.

Alla, L., Bouhtati, N., Aarabe, M., & Khizzou, N. B. (s. d.). Social Media Analytics for Effective Customer Brand Engagement Assessment. *Advances in Marketing, Customer Relationship Management, and E-Services.*

Alla, L., Bouhtati, N., Aarabe, M., & Khizzou, N. B. Social Media Analytics for Effective Customer Brand Engagement Assessment. *Advances in Marketing, Customer Relationship Management, and E-Services.*

Alla, L., Hmioui, A., & Bentalha, B. (2020). La netnographie dans les recherches marketing: La communauté virtuelle comme consom'acteur vecteur d'efficacité marketing. Alternatives Managériales Economiques, 2(4), 631-652. DOI: DOI: 10.48374/IMIST.PRSM/ame-v2i4.23559

Allam, A., Feuerriegel, S., Rebhan, M., & Krauthammer, M. (2021). Analyzing Patient Trajectories With Artificial Intelligence. *Journal of Medical Internet Research*, *23*(12), e29812. DOI: 10.2196/29812 PMID: 34870606

Allen, D., Gillen, E., & Rixson, L. (2009). Systematic review of the effectiveness of integrated care pathways : What works, for whom, in which circumstances? *International Journal of Evidence-Based Healthcare*, *7*(2), 61–74. DOI: 10.1111/j.1744-1609.2009.00127.x PMID: 21631848

Al-Nawayseh, M. K., Alnabhan, M. M., Al-Debei, M. M., & Balachandran, W. (2013). An adaptive decision support system for last mile logistics in e-commerce: A study on online grocery shopping. *International Journal of Decision Support System Technology*, *5*(1), 40–65. DOI: 10.4018/jdsst.2013010103

Al-Rahmi, W. M., Uddin, M., Alkhalaf, S., Al-Dhlan, K. A., Cifuentes-Faura, J., Al-Rahmi, A. M., & Al-Adwan, A. S. (2022). Validation of an Integrated IS Success Model in the Study of E-Government. *Mobile Information Systems*, *2022*, 1–16. Advance online publication. DOI: 10.1155/2022/8909724

Alsetoohy, O., Sheikhelsouk, S., Munawar Albadry, O., Mathew, V., Mohammed Alhamdi, F., & Abou Kamar, M. (2024). Achieving sustainable competitive advantage in the metaverse: Roles of intellectual capital and service innovation performance in hotels. *Geo Journal of Tourism and Geosites*, *55*(3).

Alt, R. (2021). Digital transformation in the restaurant industry : Current developments and implications. *Journal of smart tourism, 1*(1), 69-74.

Amarasinghe, H. (2023). Transformative Power of AI in Customer Relationship Management (CRM): Potential Benefits, Pitfalls, and Best Practices for Modern Enterprises. *International Journal of Stochastic Analysis*, *8*(8), 1–10. DOI: 10.4018/979-8-3693-0712-0.ch009

Ameen, N., Tarhini, A., Reppel, A., & Anand, A. (2020). Customer experiences in the age of artificial intelligence. *Computers in Human Behavior*, *114*, 106548. DOI: 10.1016/j.chb.2020.106548 PMID: 32905175

Analyse de l'impact économique de l'expérience patient : Une revue systématique—PMC. (s. d.). Consulté 15 mars 2025, à l'adresse https://pmc.ncbi.nlm.nih.gov/articles/PMC11087015/

Anderson, K. (2002). *Mosby<<'>>s Medical, Nursing & Allied Health Dictionary ; editor /.*

Anderson, E. W., & Mittal, V. (2000). Strengthening the satisfaction-profit chain. *Journal of Service Research, 3*(2), 107–120. DOI: 10.1177/109467050032001

Androniceanu, A. (2024). Generative artificial intelligence, present and perspectives in public administration. Administration & Public Management Review, 43.

Anton, D. (2022). IoT TECHNOLOGY BASED ON AI PLATFORM FOR BLOCK-CHAIN E-EDUCATION. *World Science, 6*(78). Advance online publication. DOI: 10.31435/rsglobal_ws/30122022/7906

Aqrabawi, R.. (2024). The Impact of AI-Driven Consumer Insights on Targeted Marketing and Customer Retention Strategies. *Pakistan Journal of Life and Social Sciences, 22*(2), 13733–13738. DOI: 10.57239/PJLSS-2024-22.2.00986

Araghi, S. N., Fontaili, F., Lamine, E., Salatge, N., Lesbegueries, J., Pouyade, S. R., Tancerel, L., & Benaben, F. (2018). A Conceptual Framework to Support Discovering of Patients' Pathways as Operational Process Charts. *2018 IEEE/ACS 15th International Conference on Computer Systems and Applications (AICCSA)*, 1-6. DOI: 10.1109/AICCSA.2018.8612822

Arena, F., & Pau, G. (2020). An overview of big data analysis. *Bulletin of Electrical Engineering and Informatics, 9*(4), 1646–1653. DOI: 10.11591/eei.v9i4.2359

Arias, M., Rojas, E., Aguirre, S., Cornejo, F., Munoz-Gama, J., Sepulveda, M., & Capurro, D. (2020). Mapping the Patient's Journey in Healthcare through Process Mining. *International Journal of Environmental Research and Public Health, 17*(18), 6586. Advance online publication. DOI: 10.3390/ijerph17186586 PMID: 32927669

Arnese, N. (2023). *Unlocking Loyalty in the AI Era: How Generative AI is Redefining Customer Retention.* LinkedIn Journal.

Arora, P., Srivastava, S., & Majumder, S. (2017). Using automation technology and IOT based data capturing to ensure high quality last mile logistics. 7th Annual Conference on Industrial Engineering and Operations Management, IEOM 2017, 5755–5756. https://www.scopus.com/inward/record.uri?eid=2-s2.0-85018985187&partnerID=40&md5=8519dc49d4e13cc2d16eb18319c12bd6

Artusi, F., Magistretti, S., Bellini, E., & Dell'Era, C. (2024). Technology-aided customer experience innovation: Implementation modes in retail. *Creativity and Innovation Management, 0*(1), 1–13. DOI: 10.1111/caim.12646

Asefa, K., & Debela, K. L. "Effect of Transformational Leadership on Organizational Performance: The Mediating Function of Employee Commitment and Expert Systems (AI) Inclusion in Ethiopia," *2023 International Conference on Communication, Security and Artificial Intelligence (ICCSAI)*, Greater Noida, India, 2023, pp. 305-310, https://doi.org/DOI: 10.1109/ICCSAI59793.2023.10421269

Aspland, E., Gartner, D., & Harper, P. (2021). Clinical pathway modelling : A literature review. *Health Systems (Basingstoke, England)*, *10*(1), 1–23. DOI: 10.1080/20476965.2019.1652547 PMID: 33758656

Astuti, E., Harsono, I., Uhai, S., Muthmainah, H. N., & Vandika, A. Y. (2024). Application of artificial intelligence technology in customer service in the hospitality industry in Indonesia : A literature review on improving efficiency and user experience. *Sciences Du Nord Nature Science and Technology*, *1*(01), 28–36. DOI: 10.71238/snst.v1i1.15

Atreides, K. (2021). E-governance with ethical living democracy. 2020 Annual International Conference on Brain-Inspired Cognitive Architectures for Artificial Intelligence: Eleventh Annual Meeting of the BICA Society, BICA*AI 2020, 190, 35–39. DOI: 10.1016/j.procs.2021.06.004

Avula, M., & Sithole, T. (2024). Artificial Intelligence's Potential to Improve Operational Efficiency and Customer Experience in the Hospitality and Tourism Sectors. In *Impact of AI and Tech-Driven Solutions in Hospitality and Tourism* (pp. 351–382). IGI Global. DOI: 10.4018/979-8-3693-6755-1.ch018

Awad, A., Trenfield, S. J., Pollard, T. D., Ong, J. J., Elbadawi, M., McCoubrey, L. E., Goyanes, A., Gaisford, S., & Basit, A. W. (2021). Connected healthcare : Improving patient care using digital health technologies. *Advanced Drug Delivery Reviews*, *178*, 113958. https://www.sciencedirect.com/science/article/pii/S0169409X21003513. DOI: 10.1016/j.addr.2021.113958 PMID: 34478781

Aw, E. C. X., Tan, G. W. H., Cham, T. H., Raman, R., & Ooi, K. B. (2022). Alexa, what's on my shopping list? Transforming customer experience with digital voice assistants. *Technological Forecasting and Social Change*, *180*, 121711. DOI: 10.1016/j.techfore.2022.121711

Ayad, O. M., Hegazy, A. E. F., & Dahroug, A. (2023). A Proposed Model for Loan Approval Prediction Using Explainable Artificial Intelligence. Proceedings - 11th IEEE International Conference on Intelligent Computing and Information Systems, ICICIS 2023, 6(1), 166–173. DOI: 10.1109/ICICIS58388.2023.10391163

Babatunde, A. (2024). Driving Innovation Through Ai And Machine Learning: Exploring The Opportunities Of Integrating Artificial Intelligence In Business Intelligence. Academic Journal Of Global Who Is Who In Academia, Vol. 5 No1, April 2024. New York City.

Bachir, S. (2021). The evolution of customer relationship management in the digital age and its influence on banks. *The EUrASEANs: journal on global ethnic-economic dynamics*, (3 (28)), 50-63. DOI: 10.35678/2539-5645.3(28).2021.50-63

Bagozzi, R. P., & Yi, Y. (1988). On the evaluation of structural equation models. *Journal of the Academy of Marketing Science, 16*(1), 74–94. DOI: 10.1007/BF02723327

Bakach, I., Campbell, A. M., & Ehmke, J. F. (2022). Robot-Based Last-Mile Deliveries With Pedestrian Zones. *Frontiers in Future Transportation, 2*, 773240. DOI: 10.3389/ffutr.2021.773240

Baker, M. A., & Kim, K. (2020). Dealing with customer incivility: The effects of managerial support on employee psychological well-being and quality-of-life. *International Journal of Hospitality Management, 87*, 102503. DOI: 10.1016/j.ijhm.2020.102503

Baldini, G., Botterman, M., Neisse, R., & Tallacchini, M. (2018). Ethical Design in the Internet of Things. *Science and Engineering Ethics, 24*(3), 905–925. DOI: 10.1007/s11948-016-9754-5 PMID: 26797878

Balta, D., Kuhn, P., Sellami, M., Kulus, D., Lieven, C., & Krcmar, H. (2019). How to Streamline AI Application in Government? A Case Study on Citizen Participation in Germany. In L. I., J. M., L. H., P. A., R. B. M.P., S. H.J., & T. E. (Eds.), 18th IFIP WG 8.5 International Conference on Electronic Government, EGOV 2019: Vol. 11685 LNCS (pp. 233–247). Springer. DOI: 10.1007/978-3-030-27325-5_18

Bardaro, G., Daga, E., Carvalho, J., Chiatti, A., & Motta, E. (2022). Introducing a Smart City Component in a Robotic Competition: A Field Report. *Frontiers in Robotics and AI, 9*, 728628. DOI: 10.3389/frobt.2022.728628 PMID: 35252360

Barelds, A., Van De Goor, I., Bos, M., Van Heck, G., & Schols, J. (2009). Care and service trajectories for people with intellectual disabilities : Defining its course and quality determinants from the client's perspective. In *Journal of Policy and Practice in Intellectual Disabilities* (Vol. 6, Numéro 3, p. 163-172). DOI: 10.1111/j.1741-1130.2009.00224.x

Barelds, A., van de Goor, I., van Heck, G., & Schols, J. (2010). Quality of care and service trajectories for people with intellectual disabilities : Defining the aspects of quality from the client's perspective. In *Scandinavian Journal of Caring Sciences* (Vol. 24, Numéro 1, p. 164-174). DOI: 10.1111/j.1471-6712.2009.00701.x

Barnes, C. (2016). Omni-Channel Retail-Challenges and Opportunities for Packaging Innovation. In Integrating the Packaging and Product Experience in Food and Beverages: A Road-Map to Consumer Satisfaction (pp. 59–76). Elsevier Inc. DOI: 10.1016/B978-0-08-100356-5.00004-8

Basit, A., Zafar, M., Liu, X., Javed, A. R., Jalil, Z., & Kifayat, K. (2020). A comprehensive survey of AI-enabled phishing attacks detection techniques. *Telecommunication Systems, 76*(1), 139–154. DOI: 10.1007/s11235-020-00733-2 PMID: 33110340

Baydeníz, E., & Altin, M. (2025). How thermal hotels can leverage sustainability for competitive advantage. *Management Decision.* Advance online publication. DOI: 10.1108/MD-06-2024-1301

Beaman, C., Barkworth, A., Akande, T. D., Hakak, S., & Khan, M. K. (2021). Ransomware: Recent advances, analysis, challenges and future research directions. *Computers & Security, 111*, 102490. DOI: 10.1016/j.cose.2021.102490 PMID: 34602684

Beddaa, M., & Bentalha, B. (2025). Optimizing Local Attractiveness Through Territorial Digital Communication. In Sustainable and Intelligent Territorial Marketing and Entrepreneurship (pp. 159-192). IGI Global.

Bedu, E. J., Foroudi, P., & Palazzo, M. (2024). Artificial intelligence (AI) systems, customer experience and preference in the tourism industry in Ghana : Focus on Accra Metropolis. In *Contemporary Marketing and Consumer Behaviour in Sustainable Tourism* (pp. 208–222). Routledge. DOI: 10.4324/9781003388593-15

Belabbes, I., Oubrich, M., Fiano, F., Orlando, B., & Vrontis, D. (2020). Conceptualisation of customer experience: The case of mobile telecoms services in Morocco. *International Journal of Managerial and Financial Accounting., 12*(1), 89. DOI: 10.1504/IJMFA.2020.107003

Belanche, D., Casaló, L. V., & Flavián, C. (2019). Artificial Intelligence in FinTech : Understanding robo-advisors adoption among customers. *Industrial Management & Data Systems, 119*(7), 1411–1430. DOI: 10.1108/IMDS-08-2018-0368

Belanche, D., Casaló, L. V., & Flavián, C. (2021). Frontline robots in tourism and hospitality : Service enhancement or cost reduction? *Electronic Markets, 31*(3), 477–492. DOI: 10.1007/s12525-020-00432-5

Belanche, D., Casaló, L. V., Flavián, C., & Schepers, J. (2020). Service robot implementation : A theoretical framework and research agenda. *Service Industries Journal, 40*(3-4), 203–225. DOI: 10.1080/02642069.2019.1672666

Belanche, D., Casaló, L. V., Schepers, J., & Flavián, C. (2021). Examining the effects of robots' physical appearance, warmth, and competence in frontline services : The Humanness-Value-Loyalty model. *Psychology and Marketing*, *38*(12), 2357–2376. DOI: 10.1002/mar.21532

Belvedere, V., & Tunisini, A. (2020). Getting the Most from Omnichannel Management Strategy: Special Session: Best Articles from the Italian Marketing Association: An Abstract. In Developments in Marketing Science: Proceedings of the Academy of Marketing Science (pp. 185–186). Springer Nature. DOI: 10.1007/978-3-030-42545-6_51

Ben Khizzou, N., Alla, L., & Aarabe, M. (2024). Contribution of the Evaluation of Infection Control Committees to the Development of a Computerized Infection Risk Management Tool. *International Conference on Digital Technologies and Applications*, 443-453. DOI: 10.1007/978-3-031-68653-5_42

Bentalha, B. (2023). Consumer Perception of Robotic Mobile Fulfillment Systems: A Netnographic Case Study of Amazon. In Innovation, Strategy, and Transformation Frameworks for the Modern Enterprise (pp. 243-264). IGI Global. DOI: 10.4018/979-8-3693-0458-7.ch010

Bentalha, B. (2024). Employees and Robots in Amazon's Robotic Mobile Fulfillment Systems: A Netnographic Analysis of a Supply Chain Transformation. In Blockchain Applications for Smart Contract Technologies (pp. 188-207). IGI Global. DOI: 10.4018/979-8-3693-1511-8.ch009

Bentalha, B. (2025). A Prospective Analysis for Robotic Mobile Fulfillment Systems: Assessing the Benefits of Automated Logistics. In Digital Transformation and Innovation in Emerging Markets (pp. 251-278). IGI Global.

Bentalha, B., & Boukare, M. (2024). AI-Driven Territorial Intelligence: An Integrated Approach to Enhancing Digital Sovereignty. In Generative AI and Implications for Ethics, Security, and Data Management (pp. 231-261). IGI Global.

Bentalha, B., & Alla, L. (2024). Revealing the subtleties: The art of qualitative studies in science and management. In *Applying qualitative research methods to management science* (pp. 1–21). IGI Global. DOI: 10.4018/979-8-3693-5543-5.ch001

Bentalha, B., Hmioui, A., & Alla, L. (2019). The digitalization of the supply chain management of service companies: a prospective approach. In *Proceedings of the 4th International Conference on Smart City Applications* (pp. 1-8). DOI: 10.1145/3368756.3369005

Benzaid, C., Taleb, T., & Song, J. (2022). AI-Based Autonomic and Scalable Security Management Architecture for Secure Network Slicing in B5G. *IEEE Network, 36*(6), 165–174. DOI: 10.1109/MNET.104.2100495

Berry, K., & Singh, A. (2024). AI-Driven Service Marketing: Transforming Customer Experience and Operational Efficiency. In *Innovation in AI in Service and Tourism Marketing* (pp. 35-56). IGI Global. DOI: DOI: 10.4018/979-8-3693-7909-7.ch003

Berry, L. L. (1983). Relationship Marketing. In Berry, L. L., Shostack, G. L., & Upala, G. D. (Eds.), *Emerging Perspectives on Services Marketing* (pp. 25–80). American Marketing Association.

Bharadwaj, A., El Sawy, O. A., Pavlou, P. A., & Venkatraman, N. (2013). Digital business strategy: Toward a next generation of insights. *Management Information Systems Quarterly, 37*(2), 471–482. DOI: 10.25300/MISQ/2013/37:2.3

Bhaskar, P., & Sharma, K. D. (2022). A critical insight into the role of artificial intelligence (AI) in tourism and hospitality industries. *Pacific Business Review International, 15*(3).

Bhattacharya, C., & Sinha, M. (2022). The role of artificial intelligence in banking for leveraging customer experience. *Australasian Accounting. Business and Finance Journal, 16*(5), 89–105.

Bilal, M., Zhang, Y., Cai, S., Akram, U., & Halibas, A. (2024). Artificial intelligence is the magic wand making customer-centric a reality! An investigation into the relationship between consumer purchase intention and consumer engagement through affective attachment. *Journal of Retailing and Consumer Services, 77*, 103674. DOI: 10.1016/j.jretconser.2023.103674

Bin Mofidul, R., Alam, M. M., Rahman, M. H., & Jang, Y. M. (2022). Real-Time Energy Data Acquisition, Anomaly Detection, and Monitoring System: Implementation of a Secured, Robust, and Integrated Global IIoT Infrastructure with Edge and Cloud AI. *Sensors (Basel), 22*(22), 8980. DOI: 10.3390/s22228980 PMID: 36433575

Birhane, M., Amentie, C., Borji, B., & Kant, S. Are Ethiopian Coffee Farmers Proficient to Predict Capital Structure with Mediation of AI Based Knowledge Systems and Asset Liquidity? In *AI in Agriculture for Sustainable and Economic Management* (pp. 199-215). CRC Press. http://dx.doi.org/DOI: 10.1201/9781003451648-15

Bojić, L., Cinelli, M., Ćulibrk, D., & Delibašić, B. (2024). CERN for AI: A theoretical framework for autonomous simulation-based artificial intelligence testing and alignment. *European Journal of Futures Research, 12*(1), 15. Advance online publication. DOI: 10.1186/s40309-024-00238-0

Boos, A., Herzog, O., Reinhardt, J., Bengler, K., & Zimmermann, M. (2022). A Compliance–Reactance Framework for Evaluating Human-Robot Interaction. *Frontiers in Robotics and AI, 9*, 733504. DOI: 10.3389/frobt.2022.733504 PMID: 35685618

Boppana, V. R. (2023). AI Integration in CRM Systems for Personalized Customer Experiences. *Available atSSRN* 4987149. DOI: 10.2139/ssrn.4987149

Bouaddi, M., & Khaldi, S. (2023). The Importance of Studying Consumer Behavior in Marketing Strategies: The Case of Moroccan Companies. The Interdisciplinary Journal of Human and Social Studies, 2(2).

Boudri, R., Bentalha, B., Andaloussi, O. B., & Abbass, Z. (2025). Leveraging the "Made in Morocco" Label for Smart Marketing and Sustainable Territorial Attractiveness. In Sustainable and Intelligent Territorial Marketing and Entrepreneurship (pp. 69-94). IGI Global.

Bouhtati, N., Alla, L., & Bentalha, B. (2023). Marketing Big Data Analytics and Customer Relationship Management: A Fuzzy Approach. In Integrating Intelligence and Sustainability in Supply Chains (pp. 75-86). IGI Global. DOI: 10.4018/979-8-3693-0225-5.ch004

Bouizgar, M., Aarabe, M., Khizzou, N. B., Alla, L., & Benjelloun, A. (2025). AI and Digital Technologies for Transforming Territorial Branding Management: A Systematic Review. *Corporate Management in the Digital Age*, 35-68.

Bouizgar, M., Aarabe, M., Khizzou, N. B., Alla, L., & Benjelloun, A. (2025). Smart Territorial Marketing and Promotion of Customer Engagement Towards the Territorial Brand: A Systematic Review of Literature. Sustainable and Intelligent Territorial Marketing and Entrepreneurship, 129-158.

Bouizgar, M., Aarabe, M., Khizzou, N. B., Alla, L., & Benjelloun, A. (2025a). AI and Digital Technologies for Transforming Territorial Branding Management : A Systematic Review. *Corporate Management in the Digital Age*, 35-68.

Bouizgar, M., Aarabe, M., Khizzou, N. B., Alla, L., & Benjelloun, A. (2025b). Smart Territorial Marketing and Promotion of Customer Engagement Towards the Territorial Brand : A Systematic Review of Literature. *Sustainable and Intelligent Territorial Marketing and Entrepreneurship*, 129-158.

Bowen, J. T., & Morosan, C. (2018). Beware hospitality industry: The robots are coming. *Cornell Hospitality Quarterly*, *59*(3), 236–245.

Brady, M. (1984). Robotics and artificial intelligence. In M. Brady, L. A. Gerhardt, & H. F. Davidson (Eds.), *Artificial intelligence* (Vol. 26, Issue 1). Springer. https://link.springer.com/book/10.1007/978-3-642-82153-0

Brakus, J. J., Schmitt, B. H., & Zarantonello, L. (2009). Brand experience: What is it? How is it measured? Does it affect loyalty? *Journal of Marketing*, *73*(3), 52–68. DOI: 10.1509/jmkg.73.3.052

Brand, J., Israeli, A., & Ngwe, D. (2023). Using GPT for market research. *Harvard business school marketing unit working paper, 23-062*.

Brynjolfsson, E., & McAfee, A. (2022). The business of artificial intelligence: How AI creates new value. [URL: https://hbr.org/2022/07/the-business-of-artificial-intelligence]. *Harvard Business Review*, *100*(4), 58–67.

Budde, H., Williams, G. A., Winkelmann, J., Pfirter, L., & Maier, C. B. (2021). The role of patient navigators in ambulatory care : Overview of systematic reviews. *BMC Health Services Research*, *21*(1), 1166. DOI: 10.1186/s12913-021-07140-6 PMID: 34706733

Burlacu, C. (2023). *The Impact Of Ai-powered Content Generation on Customer Experience* (Bachelor's thesis, University of Twente).

Cain, L. N., Thomas, J. H., & Alonso, M.Jr. (2019). From sci-fi to sci-fact : The state of robotics and AI in the hospitality industry. *Journal of Hospitality and Tourism Technology*, *10*(4), 624–650. DOI: 10.1108/JHTT-07-2018-0066

Chaczko, Z., Slehat, S. S., & Salmon, A. (2015). Application of predictive analytics in telecommunications project management. *Journal of Networks*, *10*(10), 551.

Chae, H., Ahn, M. S., Noh, D., Nam, H., & Hong, D. (2021). BALLU2: A Safe and Affordable Buoyancy Assisted Biped. *Frontiers in Robotics and AI*, *8*, 730323. DOI: 10.3389/frobt.2021.730323 PMID: 34957224

Chan, L., Hogaboam, L., & Cao, R. (2022). Artificial intelligence in tourism and hospitality. In *Applied artificial intelligence in business : Concepts and cases* (pp. 213–229). Springer. DOI: 10.1007/978-3-031-05740-3_14

Charitsis, V., & Lehtiniemi, T. (2023). Data Ableism: Ability Expectations and Marginalization in Automated Societies. *Television & New Media*, *24*(1), 3–18. DOI: 10.1177/15274764221077660

Chaudhuri, R., Chatterjee, S., & Vrontis, D. (2022). Digital transformation of the organisations using AI integrated partner relationship management. In *Business advancement through technology Volume I: Markets and marketing in transition* (pp. 21-45). Cham: Springer International Publishing. DOI: 10.1007/978-3-031-07769-2_2

Cheah, T. S. (1998). Clinical pathways–the new paradigm in healthcare? *The Medical Journal of Malaysia*, *53*(1), 87–96. https://europepmc.org/article/med/10968144 PMID: 10968144

Cheng, X., Cohen, J., & Mou, J. (2023). AI-enabled technology innovation in e-commerce. *Journal of Electronic Commerce Investigation*, *24*(1), 1–6.

Chen, J. S., Tran-Thien-Y, L., & Florence, D. (2021). Usability and responsiveness of artificial intelligence chatbot on online customer experience in e-retailing. *International Journal of Retail & Distribution Management*, *49*(11), 1512–1531. DOI: 10.1108/IJRDM-08-2020-0312

Chen, Y., & Liu, H. (2024). Combining Neural Networks with Transformer-Based Embeddings for Enhanced Sentiment Analysis. *Journal of Computational Linguistics and Applications*, *36*(2), 125–138.

Chen, Y., & Prentice, C. (2024). Integrating Artificial Intelligence and Customer Experience. *Australasian Marketing Journal*, •••, 14413582241252904. DOI: 10.1177/14413582241252904

Chen, Y., Zhang, Z., Wu, C., Davaasuren, D., Goldstein, J. A., Gernand, A. D., & Wang, J. Z. (2020). AI-PLAX: AI-based placental assessment and examination using photos. *Computerized Medical Imaging and Graphics*, *84*, 101744. Advance online publication. DOI: 10.1016/j.compmedimag.2020.101744 PMID: 32634729

Chohan, S. R., & Akhter, Z. H. (2021). Electronic government services value creation from artificial intelligence: AI-based e-government services for Pakistan. *Electronic Government*, *17*(3), 374–390. DOI: 10.1504/EG.2021.116003

Chung, K., Quach, S., & Thaichon, P. (2022). A framework of artificial intelligence (AI) applications in marketing. In *Artificial Intelligence for Marketing Management* (pp. 41–51). Routledge. DOI: 10.4324/9781003280392-4

Clark, A., Fox, C., & Lappin, S. (2010). *The handbook of computational linguistics and natural language processing*. Wiley-Blackwell., DOI: 10.1002/9781444324044

Clarke, T., Mackinnon, E., England, K., Burr, G., Fowler, S., & Fairservice, L. (2000). A review of intensive care nurse staffing practices overseas : What lessons for Australia? In *Intensive and Critical Care Nursing* (Vol. 16, Numéro 4, p. 228-242). DOI: 10.1054/iccn.2000.1524

Colodette, R. M., Moreira, T. R., Gomes, A. P., & Siqueira-Batista, R. (2018). The oral health team in the family health strategy : Trajectories and challenges. In *Open Public Health Journal* (Vol. 11, Numéro 1, p. 438-450). Bentham Science Publishers B.V. DOI: 10.2174/1874944501811010438

Corea, F. (2019). How AI Is Transforming Financial Services. DOI: .DOI: 10.1007/978-3-319-77252-3_3

Cruces, G. A., Amarante, V., & Lotitto, E. (2024). *Generative artificial intelligence and its implications for labor markets in developing countries: A review essay.* Universidad Nacional de La Plata.

Cuevas, A. G., O'Brien, K., & Saha, S. (2016). African American experiences in healthcare : « I always feel like I'm getting skipped over ». *Health Psychology: Official Journal of the Division of Health Psychology, American Psychological Association, 35*(9), 987–995. DOI: 10.1037/hea0000368 PMID: 27175576

Danneels, E. (2004). Disruptive technology reconsidered: A critique and research agenda. *Journal of Product Innovation Management, 21*(4), 246–258. DOI: 10.1111/j.0737-6782.2004.00076.x

Daqar, M. A. A., & Smoudy, A. K. (2019). The role of artificial intelligence on enhancing customer experience. *International Review of Management and Marketing, 9*(4), 22–31. DOI: 10.32479/irmm.8166

Das, I. R., Talukder, M. B., & Kumar, S. (2024). Implication of Artificial Intelligence in Hospitality Marketing. In *Utilizing Smart Technology and AI in Hybrid Tourism and Hospitality* (pp. 291–310). IGI Global. DOI: 10.4018/979-8-3693-1978-9.ch014

Davenport, T. H., Guha, A., Grewal, D., & Bressgott, T. (2020). How artificial intelligence will change the future of marketing. *Journal of the Academy of Marketing Science, 48*(1), 24–42. DOI: 10.1007/s11747-019-00696-0

Davenport, T., Guha, A., Grewal, D., & Bressgott, T. (2023). Generative AI for customer engagement: Opportunities and challenges. [DOI: 10.1016/j.jbusres.2023.113760]. *Journal of Business Research, 160*, 113760.

Davenport, T., & Kalakota, R. (2019). The potential for artificial intelligence in healthcare. *Future Healthcare Journal, 6*(2), 94–98. DOI: 10.7861/futurehosp.6-2-94 PMID: 31363513

Davis, F. D. (1989). Perceived Usefulness, Perceived Ease of Use, and User Acceptance of Information Technology. *Management Information Systems Quarterly, 13*(3), 319. DOI: 10.2307/249008

De Bleser, L., Depreitere, R., De Waele, K., Vanhaecht, K., Vlayen, J., & Sermeus, W. (2006). Defining pathways. *Journal of Nursing Management, 14*(7), 553–563. DOI: 10.1111/j.1365-2934.2006.00702.x PMID: 17004966

de Bruijn, H., Warnier, M., & Janssen, M. (2022). The perils and pitfalls of explainable AI: Strategies for explaining algorithmic decision-making. *Government Information Quarterly, 39*(2), 101666. Advance online publication. DOI: 10.1016/j.giq.2021.101666

De Man, J., Roy, W. M., Sarkar, N., Waweru, E., Leys, M., Van Olmen, J., & Criel, B. (2016). Patient-centered care and people-centered health systems in sub-Saharan Africa : Why so little of something so badly needed? *International Journal of Person Centered Medicine, 6*(3), 162–173. https://www.academia.edu/download/61640113/JeroenDeManRoyWilliamMayegaNandiniSarkarEvelynWaweruMartLeysJosefienVanOlmen-2016-Patient-CenteredCareandPeopl20191230-20568-yv2rg.pdf. DOI: 10.5750/ijpcm.v6i3.591

Deep, S., & Zanke, P. (2024). Digital Transformation Strategy with CRM and AI for SMB's Sustainable Growth. *ESP Journal of Engineering & Technology Advancements (ESP-JETA), 4*(3), 9-22. DOI: 10.13140/RG.2.2.35510.51529

Deepthi, B., & Bansal, V. (2023). Applications of Artificial Intelligence (AI) in the Tourism Industry : A Futuristic Perspective. In *Impact of Industry 4.0 on Sustainable Tourism : Perspectives, Challenges and Future* (p. 31-43). Emerald Publishing Limited.

Deloitte. (2024). *Generative AI: Unlocking the power of Technology*. Media and Telecommunications in APAC.

Demirel, D. (2022). The effect of service quality on customer satisfaction in digital age: Customer satisfaction based examination of digital CRM. *Journal of Business Economics and Management, 23*(3), 507–531. DOI: 10.3846/jbem.2022.15328

Dereso, C. W., Kant, S., Muthuraman, M., & Tufa, G. (2023). Effect of Point of Service on Health Department Student's Creativity in Comprehensive Universities of Ethiopia: Moderating Function of Public-Private Partnership and Mediating Function of Work Place Learning. In: Jain, S., Groppe, S., Mihindukulasooriya, N. (eds) Proceedings of the International Health Informatics Conference. Lecture Notes in Electrical Engineering, vol 990. Springer, Singapore. https://doi.org/DOI: 10.1007/978-981-19-9090-8_13

Desmal, A. J., Hamid, S., Othman, M. K., & Zolait, A. (2022). A user satisfaction model for mobile government services: A literature review. *PeerJ. Computer Science*, *8*, e1074. Advance online publication. DOI: 10.7717/peerj-cs.1074 PMID: 36091981

Devlin, J., Chang, M. W., Lee, K., & Toutanova, K. (2019). BERT: Pre-training of deep bidirectional transformers for language understanding. Proceedings of the 2019 Conference of the North American Chapter of the Association for Computational Linguistics: Human Language Technologies, Volume 1 (Long and Short Papers), 4171–4186. DOI: 10.18653/v1/N19-1423

Di Stefano, G., Gambardella, A., & Verona, G. (2012). Technology push and demand-pull perspectives in innovation studies: Current findings and future research directions. *Research Policy*, *41*(8), 1283–1295. DOI: 10.1016/j.respol.2012.03.021

Diallo, E. M., Traore, F. B., Camara, B. S., Langlet, A., Delamou, A., Diallo, O. O., Gerbaud, L., & Camara, A. (2024). Analysis of care-seeking pathways and factors influencing early and appropriate care-seeking for malaria patients in the Republic of Guinea : A cross-sectional study. *Malaria Journal*, *23*(1), 273. DOI: 10.1186/s12936-024-05102-x PMID: 39256721

Doborjeh, Z., Hemmington, N., Doborjeh, M., & Kasabov, N. (2022). Artificial intelligence : A systematic review of methods and applications in hospitality and tourism. *International Journal of Contemporary Hospitality Management*, *34*(3), 1154–1176. DOI: 10.1108/IJCHM-06-2021-0767

Doğan, S., & Niyet, İ. Z. (2024). Artificial Intelligence (AI) in Tourism. In *Future Tourism Trends Volume 2 : Technology Advancement, Trends and Innovations for the Future in Tourism* (p. 3-21). Emerald Publishing Limited.

Durga, P., Godavarthi, D., Kant, S., & Basa, S. S. (2024). Aspect-based drug review classification through a hybrid model with ant colony optimization using deep learning. *Discov Computing*, *27*(1), 19. DOI: 10.1007/s10791-024-09441-w

Du, S., & Xie, C. (2021). Paradoxes of artificial intelligence in consumer markets: Ethical challenges and opportunities. *Journal of Business Research*, *129*, 961–974. DOI: 10.1016/j.jbusres.2020.08.024

Dwivedi, Y. K., Pandey, N., Currie, W., & Micu, A. (2024). Leveraging ChatGPT and other generative artificial intelligence (AI)-based applications in the hospitality and tourism industry : Practices, challenges and research agenda. *International Journal of Contemporary Hospitality Management*, *36*(1), 1–12. DOI: 10.1108/IJCHM-05-2023-0686

Ed-Daakouri, I., Bouhtati, N., & Alla, L. (2025). *Smart Data Analytics for Efficient Mapping of Customers' Online Shopping Behavior: A Systematic Review of the Literature*. IGI Global., DOI: 10.4018/979-8-3693-7545-7.ch010

Egbuhuzor, N. S., Ajayi, A. J., Akhigbe, E. E., Agbede, O. O., Ewim, C. P. M., & Ajiga, D. I. (2025). AI and data-driven insights: Transforming customer association management (CRM) in financial services. *Gulf Journal of Advance Business Investigation*, *3*(2), 483–511.

Eibl, G., Lampoltshammer, T., & Temple, L. (2022). Towards Identifying Factors Influencing Mobile Government Adoption: An Exploratory Literature Review. *EJournal of EDemocracy and Open Government*, *14*(1), 1–18. DOI: 10.29379/jedem.v14i1.693

Elhissoufi, M., & Alla, L. (2024). Artificial Intelligence in Customer Acquisition: A Bibliometric Study. In AI and data engineering solutions for effective marketing (pp. 1-22). IGI Global Scientific Publishing.

El-Razek, A. (2019). Effect of Implementing Clinical Pathway to Improve Child-Birth and Neonatal Outcomes. *American Journal of Nursing Research*, *6*(6), 6. Advance online publication. DOI: 10.12691/ajnr-6-6-13

Ersek, J. L., Nadler, E., Freeman-Daily, J., Mazharuddin, S., & Kim, E. S. (2017a). Clinical pathways and the patient perspective in the pursuit of value-based oncology care. *American Society of Clinical Oncology Educational Book*, *37*(37), 597–606. https://www.academia.edu/download/53658904/2017_ASCO_Educational_Book.pdf#page=615. DOI: 10.1200/EDBK_174794 PMID: 28561657

Esmaili, H., Hosseinzadeh, A., & Soltani, R. (2022). A Mathematical Model to Evaluate Time, Cost and Customer Satisfaction in Omni-Channel Distribution. *International Journal of Supply and Operations Management*, *9*(2), 195–211.

Esteva, A., Kuprel, B., Novoa, R. A., Ko, J., Swetter, S. M., Blau, H. M., & Thrun, S. (2019). Dermatologist-level classification of skin cancer with deep neural networks. *Nature*, *542*(7639), 115–118. DOI: 10.1038/nature21056 PMID: 28117445

Fakhruzzaman, M. N., & Gunawan, S. W. (2022). CekUmpanKlik: An artificial intelligence-based application to detect Indonesian clickbait. *IAES International Journal of Artificial Intelligence*, *11*(4), 1232–1238. DOI: 10.11591/ijai.v11.i4.pp1232-1238

Faulkner, N., Jorgensen, B., & Koufariotis, G. (2019). Can behavioural interventions increase citizens' use of e-government? Evidence from a quasi-experimental trial. *Government Information Quarterly*, *36*(1), 61–68. DOI: 10.1016/j.giq.2018.10.009

Fernandes, Ó. B., Netshiombo, M., Gulácsi, L., Klazinga, N. S., Péntek, M., & Baji, P. (2020). *Patient experiences in a public primary health care clinic : A South African case study*. DOI: 10.1556/204.2020.00014

Fisher, K. (2022). The role of gender in providing expert advice on cyber conflict and artificial intelligence for military personnel. *Frontiers in Big Data*, *5*, 992620. DOI: 10.3389/fdata.2022.992620 PMID: 36247972

Fornell, C., & Larcker, D. F. (1981). Evaluating structural equation models with unobservable variables and measurement error. *JMR, Journal of Marketing Research*, *18*(1), 39–50. DOI: 10.1177/002224378101800104

Fukuyama, H., & Tan, Y. (2024). Investigating into the dual role of loan loss reserves in banking production process. *Annals of Operations Research*, *334*(1–3), 423–444. DOI: 10.1007/s10479-021-04365-w PMID: 34866730

Gabelaia, I., & Hendieh, J. The Transformative Power of Ai and its Influence on Business Strategy, Financial Operations, and Marketing Decision-Making: A Case Investigation Method. *Financial Operations, and Marketing Decision-Making: A Case Investigation Method.*

Gajić, T., Petrović, M. D., Pešić, A. M., Conić, M., & Gligorijević, N. (2024). Innovative Approaches in Hotel Management: Integrating Artificial Intelligence (AI) and the Internet of Things (IoT) to Enhance Operational Efficiency and Sustainability. *Sustainability (Basel)*, *16*(17), 7279. DOI: 10.3390/su16177279

Gama, F., & Magistretti, S. (2023). Artificial intelligence in innovation management: A review of innovation capabilities and a taxonomy of AI applications. *Journal of Product Innovation Management*.

Gao, Y., & Janssen, M. (2020). Generating Value from Government Data Using AI: An Exploratory Study. In V. P. G., J. M., L. H., L. I., R. B. M.P., S. H.J., & Z. A. (Eds.), 19th IFIP WG 8.5 International Conference on Electronic Government, EGOV 2020, held in conjunction with the IFIP WG 8.5 International Conference on Electronic Participation, ePart 2020, and the International Conference for E-Democracy and Open Government: Vol. 12219 LNCS (pp. 319–331). Springer Science and Business Media Deutschland GmbH. DOI: 10.1007/978-3-030-57599-1_24

Gartner. (2023). Future of AI in Service Industry. *Gartner Research*.

Gavalas, D., Konstantopoulos, C., Mastakas, K., & Pantziou, G. (2014). Mobile recommender systems in tourism. *Journal of Network and Computer Applications*, *39*, 319–333. DOI: 10.1016/j.jnca.2013.04.006

Gavrila, S., González-Tejero, C. B., Gómez Gandía, J. A., & Ancillo, A. D. L. (2023). The impact of automation and optimization on customer experience: A consumer perspective. *Humanities & Social Sciences Communications*, *10*(1), 877. Advance online publication. DOI: 10.1057/s41599-023-02389-0

Gearhart, A., Gaffar, S., & Chang, A. C. (2020). A primer on artificial intelligence for the paediatric cardiologist. In *Cardiology in the Young* (Vol. 30, Numéro 7, p. 934-945). Cambridge University Press. DOI: 10.1017/S1047951120001493

Gentile, C., Spiller, N., & Noci, G. (2007). How to sustain the customer experience: An overview of experience components that co-create value with the customer. *European Management Journal*, *25*(5), 395–410. DOI: 10.1016/j.emj.2007.08.005

Ghaffari, S., Yousefimehr, B., & Ghatee, M. (2024, February). Generative-AI in e-Commerce: Use-cases and Implementations. In 2024 20th CSI International Symposium on Artificial Intelligence and Signal Processing (AISP) (pp. 1-5). IEEE.

Ghesh, N., Alexander, M., & Davis, A. (2024). The artificial intelligence-enabled customer experience in tourism : A systematic literature review. *Tourism Review*, *79*(5), 1017–1037. DOI: 10.1108/TR-04-2023-0255

Go, H., Kang, M., & Suh, S. C. (2020). Machine learning of robots in tourism and hospitality : Interactive technology acceptance model (iTAM)–cutting edge. *Tourism Review*, *75*(4), 625–636. DOI: 10.1108/TR-02-2019-0062

Gök, Ö. A. (2020). How does omni-channel transform consumer behavior? In *Managing Customer Experiences in an Omni-channel World: Melody of Online and Offline Environments in the Journey of purchaser* (pp. 27–42). Emerald Publishing Limited.

Gretzel, U. (2011). Intelligent systems in tourism : A social science perspective. *Annals of Tourism Research*, *38*(3), 757–779. DOI: 10.1016/j.annals.2011.04.014

Gretzel, U. (2021). Conceptualizing the smart tourism mindset : Fostering utopian thinking in smart tourism development. *Journal of Smart Tourism*, *1*(1), 3–8. DOI: 10.52255/smarttourism.2021.1.1.2

Gretzel, U., Sigala, M., Xiang, Z., & Koo, C. (2015). Smart tourism : Foundations and developments. *Electronic Markets*, *25*(3), 179–188. DOI: 10.1007/s12525-015-0196-8

Groening, C., Sarkis, J., & Zhu, Q. (2018). Green marketing consumer-level theory review: A compendium of applied theories and further research directions. *Journal of Cleaner Production*, *172*, 1848–1866. DOI: 10.1016/j.jclepro.2017.12.002

GSMA. (2022). The Mobile Economy 2022. Retrieved from www.gsma.com

Gündüz, C. (2023). Customised Holiday Experiences through Artificial Intelligence : Case Studies from the Aviation and Hospitality Sectors. *Journal of Aviation*, *7*(3), 337–345. DOI: 10.30518/jav.1351472

Gupta, R., Nair, K., Mishra, M., & Ibrahim, B. (2024). Adoption and impacts of generative artificial intelligence: Theoretical underpinnings and research agenda. International Journal of Information Management, Elsevier.

Gupta, R., Nair, K., Mishra, M., Ibrahim, B., & Bhardwaj, S. (2024, April). Adoption and impacts of generative artificial intelligence: Theoretical underpinnings and research agenda. *International Journal of Information Management Data Insights*, *4*(1), 100232. DOI: 10.1016/j.jjimei.2024.100232

Gupta, S., Modgil, S., Lee, C.-K., Cho, M., & Park, Y. (2022). Artificial intelligence enabled robots for stay experience in the hospitality industry in a smart city. *Industrial Management & Data Systems*, *122*(10), 2331–2350. DOI: 10.1108/IMDS-10-2021-0621

Gursoy, D., & Cai, R. (2024). Artificial intelligence : An overview of research trends and future directions. *International Journal of Contemporary Hospitality Management*.

Gursoy, D., Chi, O. H., Lu, L., & Nunkoo, R. (2019). Consumers acceptance of artificially intelligent (AI) device use in service encounters: The role of perceived control, innovation, and machine learning orientation. *International Journal of Information Management*, *49*, 157–169. DOI: 10.1016/j.ijinfomgt.2019.03.008

Guyo, K., & Kero, C. A. "Mediation of Marketing Intermediaries and AI Adoption Among Livestock Products Marketing and Economic Status of Pastoralist in Ethiopia," *2023 International Conference on Communication, Security and Artificial Intelligence (ICCSAI)*, Greater Noida, India, 2023, pp. 311-316, https://doi.org/DOI: 10.1109/ICCSAI59793.2023.10421261

Haefner, N., Parida, V., Gassmann, O., & Wincent, J. (2023). Implementing and scaling artificial intelligence: A review, framework, and research agenda. *Technological Forecasting and Social Change*, *197*, 122878. DOI: 10.1016/j.techfore.2023.122878

Hair, J. F.Jr, Anderson, R. E., Tatham, R. L., & Black, W. C. (2014). *Multivariate Data Analysis* (5th ed.). Prentice Hall.

Hariguna, T., Ruangkanjanases, A., & Sarmini, . (2021). Public behavior as an output of e-government service: The role of new technology integrated in e-government and antecedent of relationship quality. *Sustainability (Basel), 13*(13), 7464. Advance online publication. DOI: 10.3390/su13137464

Hasan, M. (2024). *Regulating artificial intelligence: A study in the comparison between South Asia and other countries*. Legal Issues in the Digital Age. CyberLeninka.

Hasan, R., Thaichon, P., & Weaven, S. (2021). Are we already living with Skynet? Anthropomorphic artificial intelligence to enhance customer experience. In *Developing digital marketing* (pp. 103–134). Emerald Publishing Limited. DOI: 10.1108/978-1-80071-348-220211007

Hasbullah, N. N., Kiflee, A. K. R., Anwar, S., & Ramachandran, K. K. (2024). Mapping the trend of digital transformation in omni-channel retailing: a bibliometric analysis. *Marketing i menedžment innovacij, 15*(1), 29-40.

He, P., Liu, X., & Gao, J. (2021). DeBERTa: Decoding-enhanced BERT with disentangled attention. Proceedings of the 9th International Conference on Learning Representations (ICLR 2021). https://openreview.net/forum?id=XPZIaotutsD (Note: The paper cites ICML 2022, but the canonical DeBERTa paper is ICLR 2021. Using the provided citation's conference details leads to ambiguity, ICLR 2021 is standard.)

Hechinger, M., Hentschel, D., Aumer, C., & Rester, C. (2022). A Conceptual Model of Experiences With Digital Technologies in Aging in Place : Qualitative Systematic Review and Meta-synthesis. In *JMIR Aging* (Vol. 5, Numéro 3). JMIR Publications Inc. DOI: 10.2196/34872

Heimberger, H., Horvat, D., & Schultmann, F. (2024). Exploring the factors driving AI adoption in production: A systematic literature review and future research agenda. *Information Technology and Management.* Advance online publication. DOI: 10.1007/s10799-024-00436-z

He, K., Zhang, X., Ren, S., & Sun, J. (2016). Deep residual learning for image recognition. *2016 IEEE Conference on Computer Vision and Pattern Recognition (CVPR).* DOI: 10.1109/CVPR.2016.90

Hemachandran K et al. (2025). Predictive Analytics and Generative AI for Data-Driven Marketing Strategies. DOI: 10.1201/9781003472544

Hipp, R., Abel, E., & Weber, R. J. (2016). A Primer on Clinical Pathways. *Hospital Pharmacy, 51*(5), 416–421. DOI: 10.1310/hpj5105-416 PMID: 27303097

Hmioui, A., Alla, L., & Bentalha, B. (2017). Pilotage de la touristicité territoriale au Maroc Proposition d'un indice de touriscticité pour la destination Fès. Entrepreneuriat, Innovation, Gouvernance et Développement territorial, 120-143.

Hmioui, A., Alla, L., & Bentalha, B. (2022). Perception du tourisme durable par les clients étrangers: Cas du séjour dans un établissement hôtelier. Reconfigurations du tourisme en contexte de la crise du Covid-19: Quelles démarches pour quelles résiliences au Maroc et ailleurs?, 1(1), 5-38.

Hofstede, G. (1980). *Culture's Consequences: International Differences in Work-Related Values*. Sage Publications.

Holger Harreis et al. (2023). *Generative AI: Unlocking the future of fashion*. McKinsey & Company.

Holz, H. F., Becker, M., Blut, M., & Paluch, S. (2023). Eliminating customer experience pain points in complex customer journeys through smart service solutions. *Psychology and Marketing*, *41*(3), 592–609. DOI: 10.1002/mar.21938

Homburg, C., Ehm, L., & Artz, M. (2015). Measuring and managing consumer sentiment in an online community environment. *JMR, Journal of Marketing Research*, *52*(5), 629–641. DOI: 10.1509/jmr.11.0448

Homburg, C., Koschate, N., & Hoyer, W. D. (2006). The role of cognition and affect in the formation of customer satisfaction: A dynamic perspective. *Journal of Marketing*, *70*(3), 21–31. DOI: 10.1509/jmkg.70.3.021

Hossain, F., Ahmed, G. M. S., Shuvo, S. P. P., Kona, A. N., Raina, M. U. H., & Shikder, F. (2024). Unlocking artificial intelligence for strategic market development and business growth: Innovations, opportunities, and future directions. *Edelweiss Applied Science and Technology*, *8*(6), 5825–5846. DOI: 10.55214/25768484.v8i6.3263

Houy, C., Fettke, P., Loos, P., Van Der Aalst, W. M. P., & Krogstie, J. (2010). BPM-in-the-large-towards a higher level of abstraction in business process management. In J. M., L. W., P.-H. J., & R. M. (Eds.), Joint IFIP TC 8 International Conference on E-Government and E-Services, EGES 2010 and IFIP TC 6 International Conference on Global Information Systems Processes, GISP 2010 Held as Part of 21st IFIP World Computer Congress, WCC 2010 (Vol. 334, pp. 233–244). Springer Science and Business Media, LLC. DOI: 10.1007/978-3-642-15346-4_19

Hoyer, W. D., Kroschke, M., Schmitt, B., Kraume, K., & Shankar, V. (2020). Transforming the customer experience through new technologies. *Journal of Interactive Marketing*, *51*(1), 57–71. DOI: 10.1016/j.intmar.2020.04.001

Huang, A., Chao, Y., de la Mora Velasco, E., Bilgihan, A., & Wei, W. (2022). When artificial intelligence meets the hospitality and tourism industry : An assessment framework to inform theory and management. *Journal of Hospitality and Tourism Insights*, *5*(5), 1080–1100. DOI: 10.1108/JHTI-01-2021-0021

Huang, M. H., & Rust, R. T. (2018). Artificial intelligence in service. *Journal of Service Research*, *21*(2), 155–172. DOI: 10.1177/1094670517752459

Hunter, W. C. (2021). Cultural representations and experience in tourism : Two forms of mimesis. *Journal of Smart Tourism*, *1*(1), 65–67. DOI: 10.52255/smart-tourism.2021.1.1.8

Hussein, H., Albadry, O. M., Mathew, V., Al-Romeedy, B. S., Alsetoohy, O., Abou Kamar, M., & Khairy, H. A. (2024). Digital leadership and sustainable competitive advantage: Leveraging green absorptive capability and eco-innovation in tourism and hospitality businesses. *Sustainability (Basel)*, *16*(13), 5371. DOI: 10.3390/su16135371

Ivanov, S. H., Webster, C., & Berezina, K. (2017). Adoption of robots and service automation by tourism and hospitality companies. *Revista Turismo & Desenvolvimento (Aveiro)*, *27*(28), 1501–1517.

Jabeen, F., Al Zaidi, S., & Al Dhaheri, M. H. (2022). Automation and artificial intelligence in hospitality and tourism. *Tourism Review*, *77*(4), 1043–1061. DOI: 10.1108/TR-09-2019-0360

Jabo, B., & Kant, S. "Impact of Technical CRM on Ethiopia Bank Human-Computer Interface and Competitive Advantage as Mediators of Performance," *2024 IEEE International Conference on Computing, Power and Communication Technologies (IC2PCT)*, Greater Noida, India, 2024, pp. 679-682, https://doi.org/DOI: 10.1109/IC2PCT60090.2024.10486237

Jabo, D., Borji, B., & Kant, S. (2024, February). Influence of Technical CRM on Ethiopia Bank Human-Computer Interface and Competitive Advantage as Mediators of Sustainability. In *2024 IEEE International Conference on Computing, Power and Communication Technologies (IC2PCT)* (Vol. 5, pp. 679-682). IEEE.

Jabo, D., Kant, S., & Borji, B. (2025). Customer Orientation and Ethiopian Bank Sustainability With Mediation of Competitive Advantage. In *Leveraging AI for Operative Digital Association Marketing* (pp. 459–482). IGI Global.

Jain, A., Singh, K., & Jain, P. (2024). Understanding the Impact of Artificial Intelligence and Robotics in the Tourism and Hospitality Industry Through Customer Experience : A Systematic Literature Review. *Impact of AI and Tech-Driven Solutions in Hospitality and Tourism*, 329-350.

Jalal, A. N., Bahari, M., & Tarofder, A. K. (2021). Transforming traditional CRM into social CRM: An empirical investigation in Iraqi healthcare industry. *Heliyon*, *7*(5), e06913. DOI: 10.1016/j.heliyon.2021.e06913 PMID: 34027153

Janssen, M., Hartog, M., Matheus, R., Yi Ding, A., & Kuk, G. (2022). Will Algorithms Blind People? The Effect of Explainable AI and Decision-Makers' Experience on AI-supported Decision-Making in Government. *Social Science Computer Review*, *40*(2), 478–493. DOI: 10.1177/0894439320980118

Jiang, X., Wang, H., & Guo, X. (2020). Analyzing Service Quality Evaluation Indexes of Rural Last Mile Delivery Using FCE and ISM Approach. *Information (Basel)*, *11*(6), 327. DOI: 10.3390/info11060327

Jing, X., Tan, F., & Zhang, M. (2021). Digital application of intangible cultural heritage from the perspective of cultural ecology. *Journal of Smart Tourism*, *1*(1), 41–52. DOI: 10.52255/smarttourism.2021.1.1.6

Kamoonpuri, S. Z., & Sengar, A. (2023). Hi, May AI help you? An analysis of the barriers impeding the implementation and use of artificial intelligence-enabled virtual assistants in retail. *Journal of Retailing and Consumer Services*, *72*, 103258. DOI: 10.1016/j.jretconser.2023.103258

Kant, S., & Adula, M. (2025). Does Technology-Enabled Knowledge Management-Based Competitive Advantage Transfer?: Its Combined Influence on Ethiopian Banking Sustainability. In *Building Inclusive Global Knowledge Societies for Sustainable Development* (pp. 75-106). IGI Global Scientific Publishing.

Kant, S., Adula, M., & Duloma, H. (2025). The Rise of Product-as-a-Service Models in the Digital Era Redesigning Business Models for Circular Innovation in the Horn of Africa. In *Innovating Sustainability Through Digital Circular Economy* (pp. 133–160). IGI Global Scientific Publishing.

Katsamba, Ngonidzashe & Kandiero, Agripah & Chizwina, Sabelo. (2024). The Impact of Artificial Intelligence on Customer Satisfaction Levels in the Mobile Telephony Industry of Zimbabwe. DOI: .DOI: 10.1108/978-1-80455-342-820241003

Katterbauer, K., Syed, H., Cleenewerck, L., Özbay, R. D., & Yılmaz, S. (2024). Impact of Generative AI on FINTECH in Africa. *Yıldız Social Science Review*, *10*(1), 1–53. DOI: 10.51803/yssr.1440501

Kaur, G., & Chauhan, P. (2024). Artificial Intelligence and Invigoration of the Hospitality Industry : An Analysis. In *Artificial Intelligence for Smart Technology in the Hospitality and Tourism Industry* (p. 49-62). Apple Academic Press.

Kercsmar, C., & Myers, T. (2002). Clinical pathways in treatment of asthma. *Current Opinion in Allergy and Clinical Immunology*, *2*(3), 183–187. DOI: 10.1097/00130832-200206000-00005 PMID: 12045412

Kerikmäe, T., & Pärn-Lee, E. (2021). Legal dilemmas of Estonian artificial intelligence strategy: In between of e-society and global race. *AI & Society*, *36*(2), 561–572. DOI: 10.1007/s00146-020-01009-8

Khan, H., Kushwah, K. K., Singh, S., Urkude, H., Maurya, M. R., & Sadasivuni, K. K. (2021). Smart technologies driven approaches to tackle COVID-19 pandemic: a review. 3 Biotech, 11(2), 50. DOI: 10.1007/s13205-020-02581-y

Khan, S., & Iqbal, M. (2020, June). AI-Powered Customer Service: Does it optimize customer experience? In *2020 8th International Conference on Reliability, Infocom Technologies and Optimization (Trends and Future Directions)(ICRITO)* (pp. 590-594). IEEE.

Khizzou, N. B., Aarabe, M., & Alla, L. (2024). Current trends in scientific research on managerial innovations in healthcare supply chain: A bibliometric analysis. In *2024 IEEE 15th International Colloquium on Logistics and Supply Chain Management (LOGISTIQUA)* (pp. 1-9). IEEE. DOI: 10.1109/LOGISTIQUA61063.2024.10571373

Khizzou, N. B., Aarabe, M., & Alla, L. (2024). Practices of Qualitative Studies in Medical Sciences: The Focus Groups Method Applied to Patients. In Data Collection and Analysis in Scientific Qualitative Research (pp. 229-252). IGI Global.

Khizzou, N. B., Aarabe, M., & Alla, L. (2024). The impact of digitalisation on the customer experience in medical tourism: A systematic review. *Impact of AI and tech-driven solutions in hospitality and tourism*, 408-428.

Khizzou, N. B., Aarabe, M., & Alla, L. (2024a). *Current trends in scientific research on managerial innovations in healthcare supply chain : A bibliometric analysis*. 1-9.

Khizzou, N. B., Aarabe, M., & Alla, L. (2024a). Current trends in scientific research on managerial innovations in healthcare supply chain : A bibliometric analysis. *2024 IEEE 15th International Colloquium on Logistics and Supply Chain Management (LOGISTIQUA)*, 1-9.

Khizzou, N. B., Aarabe, M., Bouizgar, M., Alla, L., & Benjelloun, A. (2025). The Digital Transformation of Medical Tourism : A Systematic and Bibliometric Review of the Literature. *Revolutionizing Healthcare Experience With Digital Medical Tourism*, 355-382.

Khizzou, N. B., Aarabe, M., Bouizgar, M., Alla, L., & Benjelloun, A. (2025). The Digital Transformation of Medical Tourism: A Systematic and Bibliometric Review of the Literature. *Revolutionizing Healthcare Experience With Digital Medical Tourism*, 355-382.

Khizzou, N. B., Aarabe, M., & Alla, L. (2024b). Practices of Qualitative Studies in Medical Sciences : The Focus Groups Method Applied to Patients. In *Data Collection and Analysis in Scientific Qualitative Research* (pp. 229–252). IGI Global. DOI: 10.4018/979-8-3693-8689-7.ch009

Kim, H., & Shon, T. (2022). Industrial network-based behavioral anomaly detection in AI-enabled smart manufacturing. *The Journal of Supercomputing*, *78*(11), 13554–13563. DOI: 10.1007/s11227-022-04408-4 PMID: 35340686

Kinsman, L., Rotter, T., James, E., Snow, P., & Willis, J. (2010). What is a clinical pathway? Development of a definition to inform the debate. *BMC Medicine*, *8*(1), 31. DOI: 10.1186/1741-7015-8-31 PMID: 20507550

Klein, K., & Martinez, L. F. (2023). The impact of anthropomorphism on customer satisfaction in chatbot commerce: An experimental study in the food sector. *Electronic Commerce Research*, *23*(4), 2789–2825. DOI: 10.1007/s10660-022-09562-8

Klumpp, M., & Ruiner, C. (2019). Human Role in Digital Logistics: Relevance of Intuition in Interacting with AI. In Lecture Notes in Logistics (pp. 32–44). Springer Science and Business Media B.V. DOI: 10.1007/978-3-030-29821-0_3

Knani, M., Echchakoui, S., & Ladhari, R. (2022). Artificial intelligence in tourism and hospitality : Bibliometric analysis and research agenda. *International Journal of Hospitality Management*, *107*, 103317. DOI: 10.1016/j.ijhm.2022.103317

Kokku, R. (2021). Omni and multi-channel: Association with utilitarian/hedonic benefits, shopping value and channel patronage. *International Review of Management and Marketing*, *11*(11), 11–22. DOI: 10.32479/irmm.11215

Kothapalli, K. R. V. (2022). Exploring the Influence of Digital Transformation on Business Operations and Customer Experience. *Global Disclosure of Economics and Business*, *11*(2), 103–114. DOI: 10.18034/gdeb.v11i2.760

Kotler, P., & Keller, K. L. (2016). *Marketing management*. Pearson.

Krishna, A. (2012). An integrative review of sensory marketing: Engaging the senses to affect perception, judgment and behavior. *Journal of Consumer Psychology*, *22*(3), 332–351. DOI: 10.1016/j.jcps.2011.08.003

Kühl, N., Schemmer, M., Goutier, M., & Satzger, G. (2022). Artificial intelligence and machine learning. *Electronic Markets*, *32*(4), 2235–2244. DOI: 10.1007/s12525-022-00598-0

Kumar, A., et al. (2022). Enhancing Roi Through Ai Powered Customer Interaction Models. International Journal of Applied Mathematics & Statistical Sciences (IJAMSS). ISSN (P): 2319–3972; ISSN (E): 2319–3980. Vol. 11, Issue 1, Jan–Jun 2022; 79–106

Kumar, P., Sharma, S. K., & Dutot, V. (2023). Artificial intelligence (AI)-enabled CRM capability in healthcare: The influence on service innovation. *International Journal of Information Management*, *69*, 102598. DOI: 10.1016/j.ijinfomgt.2022.102598

Kumar, V., Kotler, P., Gupta, S., & Rajan, B. (2024). Generative AI in Marketing: Promises, Perils, and Public Policy Implications. *Journal of Public Policy & Marketing*, •••, 1–23. DOI: 10.1177/07439156241286499

Kumar, V., & Reinartz, W. (2016). Creating enduring customer value. *Journal of Marketing*, *80*(6), 36–68. DOI: 10.1509/jm.15.0414

Kumlin, M., Berg, G. V., Kvigne, K., & Hellesø, R. (2022). Dilemmas and deliberations in managing the care trajectory of elderly patients with complex health needs : A single-case study. *BMC Health Services Research*, *22*(1), 1030. DOI: 10.1186/s12913-022-08422-3 PMID: 35962337

Kuo, F. I., Fang, W. T., & LePage, B. A. (2022). Proactive environmental strategies in the hotel industry: Eco-innovation, green competitive advantage, and green core competence. *Journal of Sustainable Tourism*, *30*(6), 1240–1261. DOI: 10.1080/09669582.2021.1931254

Kwilinski, A., Trushkina, N., Birca, I., & Shkrygun, Y. (2023). Organizational and Economic Mechanism of Customer Relationship Management under the Era of Digital Transformations. In *E3S Web of Conferences* (Vol. 456, p. 05002). EDP Sciences. DOI: 10.1051/e3sconf/202345605002

Laoute, C., Aarabe, M., Khizzou, N. B., Alla, L., Alj, B., & Benjelloun, A. (2025). Digital Marketing and Territorial Attractiveness of Innovative Entrepreneurship : Exploratory Qualitative Study. In *Sustainable and Intelligent Territorial Marketing and Entrepreneurship* (p. 33-68). IGI Global.

Laoute, C., Aarabe, M., Khizzou, N. B., Alla, L., Alj, B., & Benjelloun, A. (2025). Digital Marketing and Territorial Attractiveness of Innovative Entrepreneurship: Exploratory Qualitative Study. In Sustainable and Intelligent Territorial Marketing and Entrepreneurship (pp. 33-68). IGI Global.

Laveault-Allard, P. (2022). *Les effets de la défavorisation matérielle et sociale sur les coûts et les trajectoires de soins et services en périnatalité.*

Law, R., Lin, K. J., Ye, H., & Fong, D. K. C. (2024). Artificial intelligence research in hospitality : A state-of-the-art review and future directions. *International Journal of Contemporary Hospitality Management, 36*(6), 2049–2068. DOI: 10.1108/IJCHM-02-2023-0189

LeCun, Y., Bengio, Y., & Haffner, P. (1998). Gradient-based learning applied to document recognition. *Proceedings of the IEEE, 86*(11), 2278–2324. DOI: 10.1109/5.726791

Lemon, K. N., & Verhoef, P. C. (2016). Understanding customer experience throughout the customer journey. *Journal of Marketing, 80*(6), 69–96. DOI: 10.1509/jm.15.0420

Li, L., Lee, K. Y., Emokpae, E., & Yang, S.-B. (2021). What makes you continuously use chatbot services? Evidence from chinese online travel agencies. *Electronic Markets, 31*(3), 1–25. DOI: 10.1007/s12525-020-00454-z PMID: 35603227

Liu, Y., Ott, M., Goyal, N., Du, J., Joshi, M., Chen, D., & Le, Q. V. (2019). RoBERTa: A robustly optimized BERT pretraining approach. arXiv. https://arxiv.org/abs/1907.11692 (Note: The paper cites EMNLP 2019 proceedings, but the primary reference is often the arXiv version.)

Liu, B. (2020). *Sentiment analysis: Mining opinions, sentiments, and emotions* (2nd ed.). Cambridge University Press. DOI: 10.1017/9781108639286

Liu, X., & Han, L. (2022). Artificial Intelligence Enterprise Management Using Deep Learning. *Computational Intelligence and Neuroscience, 2422434*, 1–10. Advance online publication. DOI: 10.1155/2022/2422434 PMID: 35755746

Lopes, J. M., Gomes, S., Nogueira, E., & Trancoso, T. (2024). AI's invisible touch: How effortless browsing shapes customer perception, experience and engagement in online retail. *Cogent Business & Management, 12*(1), 2440628. DOI: 10.1080/23311975.2024.2440628

Luo, L., Zhang, Y., Pearson, B., Ling, Z., Yu, H., & Fu, X. (2018). On the Security and Data Integrity of Low-Cost Sensor Networks for Air Quality Monitoring. *Sensors (Basel), 18*(12), 4451. DOI: 10.3390/s18124451 PMID: 30558353

Luo, X., Tong, S., Fang, Z., & Qu, Z. (2019). Frontiers: Machines vs. Humans: The Impact of Artificial Intelligence Chatbot Disclosure on Customer Purchases. *Marketing Science*, mksc.2019.1192. Advance online publication. DOI: 10.1287/mksc.2019.1192

MacCormack, A., & Verganti, R. (2003). Managing the sources of uncertainty: Matching process and context in software development. *Journal of Product Innovation Management*, *20*(3), 217–232. DOI: 10.1111/1540-5885.2003004

Madanchian, M. (2024). Generative AI for Consumer Behavior Prediction: Techniques and Applications. *Sustainability (Basel)*, *16*(22), 9963. DOI: 10.3390/su16229963

Majeed, M., Chaudhary, A., & Chadha, R. (Eds.). (2025). *Digital Transformation in the Customer Experience*. CRC Press.

Mangano, G., Zenezini, G., & Cagliano, A. C. (2021). Value Proposition for Sustainable Last-Mile Delivery. A Retailer Perspective. *Sustainability (Basel)*, *13*(7), 3774. DOI: 10.3390/su13073774

Manktelow, M., Iftikhar, A., Bucholc, M., McCann, M., & O'Kane, M. (2022). Clinical and operational insights from data-driven care pathway mapping : A systematic review. *BMC Medical Informatics and Decision Making*, *22*(1), 43. DOI: 10.1186/s12911-022-01756-2 PMID: 35177058

Manthiou, A., Klaus, P., Kuppelwieser, V. G., & Reeves, W. (2021). Man vs machine : Examining the three themes of service robotics in tourism and hospitality. *Electronic Markets*, *31*(3), 511–527. DOI: 10.1007/s12525-020-00434-3

Mariani, M. M., & Borghi, M. (2024). Artificial intelligence in service industries: Customers' assessment of service production and resilient service operations. *International Journal of Production Research*, *62*(15), 5400–5416. DOI: 10.1080/00207543.2022.2160027

Maryam, H., & Shanthi, V. (2023). Unlocking Customer Engagement Through Strategic Content Marketing. Tuijin Jishu/Journal of Propulsion Technology. ISSN: 1001-4055. Vol. 44 No. 3 (2023)

Maryam, S., (2024). Generative AI-enabled Knowledge Base Fine-tuning: Enhancing Feature Engineering for Customer Churn. DOI: DOI: 10.21203/rs.3.rs-3823738/v1

Masrom, M., Ai Ling, E. L., & Din, S. (2015). E-participation behavioral in e-government in Malaysia. *Public Affairs and Administration: Concepts, Methodologies, Tools, and Applications*, *3*, 1490–1505. DOI: 10.4018/978-1-4666-8358-7.ch074

Master of Code Global. (2024). *The Finance Leader's Handbook to Generative AI: Solutions*. Insights, and Impact. Master of Code Global.

Mauri, L., & Damiani, E. (2022). Modeling Threats to AI-ML Systems Using STRIDE †. *Sensors (Basel)*, *22*(17), 6662. DOI: 10.3390/s22176662 PMID: 36081121

Mazumder, R. (2023). *Application of Generative AI in Big Data Visualization for Enhancing International Business Decision-Making. Final Projects. Spring 2023. International Business*. Oulu University of Applied Sciences.

McCarthy, J., and al. (2006). What is artificial intelligence? Stanford University. Retrieved from https://www-formal.stanford.edu/jmc/whatisai.pdf

McCarthy, J., Minsky, M. L., Rochester, N., & Shannon, C. E. (1956). A proposal for the Dartmouth summer research project on artificial intelligence. *Dartmouth Conference.* DOI: 10.1609/aimag.v27i4.1904

McKinsey & Company. (2022). *The state of AI in customer experience*. McKinsey Insights.

Medhat, W., Hassan, A., & Korashy, H. (2014). Sentiment analysis algorithms and applications: A survey. *Ain Shams Engineering Journal*, *5*(4), 1093–1113. DOI: 10.1016/j.asej.2014.04.011

Mehraliyev, F., Chan, I. C. C., & Kirilenko, A. P. (2022). Sentiment analysis in hospitality and tourism: A thematic and methodological review. *International Journal of Contemporary Hospitality Management*, *34*(1), 46–77. DOI: 10.1108/IJCHM-02-2021-0132

Mende, M., Scott, M. L., Van Doorn, J., Grewal, D., & Shanks, I. (2019). Service robots rising: How humanoid robots influence service experiences and elicit compensatory consumer responses. *JMR, Journal of Marketing Research*, *56*(4), 535–556. DOI: 10.1177/0022243718822827

Meyer, C., & Schwager, A. (2007). Understanding customer experience. *Harvard Business Review*, *85*(2), 116. PMID: 17345685

Meziane, B., Alla, L., & Bentalha, B. (2025). Transformational Trends of Territorial Economic Intelligence Strategies in the Digital Era: A Systematic Theoretical Exploration. In Utilizing Technology to Manage Territories (pp. 455-490). IGI Global.

Miller, D. D., & Brown, E. W. (2018). Artificial Intelligence in Medical Practice : The Question to the Answer? In *American Journal of Medicine* (Vol. 131, Numéro 2, p. 129-133). Elsevier Inc. DOI: 10.1016/j.amjmed.2017.10.035

Mir, U., Kar, A. K., & Gupta, M. P. (2022). AI-enabled digital identity – inputs for stakeholders and policymakers. *Journal of Science and Technology Policy Management, 13*(3), 514–541. DOI: 10.1108/JSTPM-09-2020-0134

Misischia, C. V., Poecze, F., & Strauss, C. (2022). Chatbots in customer service: Their relevance and impact on service quality. *Procedia Computer Science, 201*, 421–428. DOI: 10.1016/j.procs.2022.03.055

Mohamed, O. A. M. (2023). How generative AI transforming supply chain operations and efficiency?.

Mohammad, S., Kumar, P., & Jain, A. (2023). Evaluating Machine Learning Models for Sentiment Analysis: A Comparative Study of Logistic Regression and Naïve Bayes. *International Journal of Data Science and Analytics, 18*(4), 245–259. DOI: 10.1007/s41060-023-00408-z

Mousavi, P., Rahimnia, F., Mehraeen, M., & Shamizanjani, M. (2021). Customer experience management; trends and areas in investigation. *Journal of Business and Management, 13*(2), 502–523.

Munir, M. S., Dipro, S. H., Hasan, K., Islam, T., & Shetty, S. (2023). Artificial Intelligence-Enabled Exploratory Cyber-Physical Safety Analyzer Framework for Civilian Urban Air Mobility. *Applied Sciences (Basel, Switzerland), 13*(2), 755. Advance online publication. DOI: 10.3390/app13020755

Murphy, J., Hofacker, C., & Gretzel, U. (2017). Dawning of the age of robots in hospitality and tourism : Challenges for teaching and research. *European Journal of Tourism Research, 15*, 104–111. DOI: 10.54055/ejtr.v15i.265

Murungu, E. (2024). Generative AI and trade in Africa: Opportunities and challenges. International Journal of Sustainable Development. *SSRN.*

Mutanga et al. (2024). Adoption and impact of generative ai: perspectives from south african tech entrepreneurs. journal Business & IT, ISSN 2570-7434, Creative Commons license published by CTU in Prague, 2024, https://bit.fsv.cvut.cz/

Nadeem, M. (2024). Generative artificial intelligence [GAI]: Enhancing future marketing strategies with emotional intelligence [EI], and social skills. *British Journal of Marketing Studies, 12*(1), 1–15.

Nadeem, M. S. (2024). Omni-channel Retail Strategy: How to Meet the Needs of Today's Shoppers. *Open Journal of Business and Management, 12*(6), 4008–4019. DOI: 10.4236/ojbm.2024.126200

Nam, K., Dutt, C. S., Chathoth, P., Daghfous, A., & Khan, M. S. (2021). The adoption of artificial intelligence and robotics in the hotel industry : Prospects and challenges. *Electronic Markets*, *31*(3), 553–574. DOI: 10.1007/s12525-020-00442-3

Nasir, J. A., & Dang, C. (2017). An integrated model for home health care and patients cluster based care. *2017 International Conference on Robotics and Automation Sciences (ICRAS)*, 204-208. DOI: 10.1109/ICRAS.2017.8071945

Naslednikov, M. (2024). The Impact of Artificial Intelligence on Customer Relationship Management (CRM) Strategies. Haaga-Helia University of Applied Sciences, Degree in Business Information Technology, Bachelor Thesis.

Nawawi, I., Ilmawan, K. F., Maarif, M. R., & Syafrudin, M. (2024). Exploring tourist experience through online reviews using aspect-based sentiment analysis with zero-shot learning for hospitality service enhancement. *Information (Basel)*, *15*(8), 499. Advance online publication. DOI: 10.3390/info15080499

Nazir, S., Khadim, S., Asadullah, M. A., & Syed, N. (2023). Exploring the influence of artificial intelligence technology on consumer repurchase intention: The mediation and moderation approach. *Technology in Society*, *72*, 102190. DOI: 10.1016/j.techsoc.2022.102190

Nejjari, R., & Slaoui, S. (2024). Customer value creation and Moroccan hotels' performance : A multi-party and multi-phase vision. *Journal of Hospitality and Tourism Insights*, *7*(5), 2504–2524. DOI: 10.1108/JHTI-04-2023-0224

Nejjari, R., & Slaoui, S. (2025). Towards a comparison of three customer value perspectives in the hotel industry : Insights from Moroccan context. *Journal of Hospitality and Tourism Insights*, *8*(4), 1602–1620. DOI: 10.1108/JHTI-03-2024-0236

Neuhofer, B., Magnus, B., & Celuch, K. (2021). The impact of artificial intelligence on event experiences: A scenario technique approach. *Electronic Markets*, *31*(3), 601–617. DOI: 10.1007/s12525-020-00433-4 PMID: 38624486

Nguyen, H. N., & Tran, M. D. (2022). STIMULI TO ADOPT E-GOVERNMENT SERVICES DURING COVID-19: EVIDENCE FROM VIETNAM. *Innovative Marketing*, *18*(1), 12–22. DOI: 10.21511/im.18(1).2022.02

Nguyen, T. H., & Le, X. C. (2024). Artificial intelligence-based chatbots–a motivation underlying sustainable development in banking: Standpoint of customer experience and behavioral outcomes. *Cogent Business & Management*, *12*(1), 2443570. DOI: 10.1080/23311975.2024.2443570

Nguyen, T., Quach, S., & Thaichon, P. (2022). The effect of AI quality on customer experience and brand relationship. *Journal of Consumer Behaviour, 21*(3), 481–493. DOI: 10.1002/cb.1974

Niet, I., van Est, R., & Veraart, F. (2021). Governing AI in Electricity Systems: Reflections on the EU Artificial Intelligence Bill. *Frontiers in Artificial Intelligence, 4*, 690237. DOI: 10.3389/frai.2021.690237 PMID: 34396090

Niknezhad, M., Shokouhyar, S., & Minouei, M. (2020). Localization of Blockchain and E-Currency Model for E-Government Services. *Journal of Information Systems and Telecommunication, 8*(31), 157–166. DOI: 10.29252/jist.8.31.157

Nouhaila, B. K., Aarabe, M., & Alla, L. (2024). The impact of digitalisation on the customer experience in medical tourism : A systematic review. *Impact of AI and tech-driven solutions in hospitality and tourism*, 408-428.

Nouhaila, B. K., Aarabe, M., & Alla, L. (2024). The impact of digitalisation on the customer experience in medical tourism : A systematic review. *Impact of AI and tech-driven solutions in hospitality and tourism*, 408-428. https://www.igi-global.com/chapter/the-impact-of-digitalisation-on-the-customer-experience-in-medical-tourism/354144

Nouhaila, B. K., Aarabe, M., & Alla, L. (2024). The impact of digitalisation on the customer experience in medical tourism: A systematic review. *Impact of AI and tech-driven solutions in hospitality and tourism*, 408-428.

Nunnally, J. C., & Bernstein, I. H. (1994). *Psychometric theory* (3rd ed.). McGraw-Hill., DOI: 10.1177/073428299901700307

Nyoach, T. D., Lemi, K., Debela, T., & Kant, S. (2024). Does Organizational Commitment Mediate the Relationship among Employee Relationship Management and Bank Performance? The Case of Banks in Ethiopia. *International Journal of Organizational Leadership, 13*(2), 355–376. DOI: 10.33844/ijol.2024.60419

Nyuga, G., & Tanova, C. (2024). Assessing the mediating role of knowledge management in the relationship between technological innovation and sustainable competitive advantage. *Heliyon, 10*(23), e39994. DOI: 10.1016/j.heliyon.2024.e39994 PMID: 39654755

O'Lemmon, M. (2022). The worst mistake 2.0? The digital revolution and the consequences of innovation. *AI & Society*. Advance online publication. DOI: 10.1007/s00146-022-01599-5 PMID: 36465190

Obermeyer, Z., Powers, B., Vogeli, C., & Mullainathan, S. (2016). Dissecting racial bias in an algorithm used to manage the health of populations. *Science*, *366*(6464), 447–453. DOI: 10.1126/science.aax2342 PMID: 31649194

Ochuba, N. A., & Usman, F. (2024). Predictive analytics in the maintenance and reliability of satellite telecommunications infrastructure: A conceptual review of strategies and technological advancements. *Engineering Science & Technology Journal*, *5*(3), 704–715. DOI: 10.51594/estj.v5i3.866

Ogunseye, S., Aljanaideh, A., & Murungi, D. (2024). *Comparative advantage in the AI era: Leveraging generative AI for global competitiveness*. ResearchGate.

Ohenhen, P. E., Aderibigbe, A. O., & Nwaobia, N. K. (2023). Artificial intelligence in developing countries: Bridging the gap between potential and implementation. Academia.edu.

Ojha, A. (2024). Revolutionizing Enterprise Network Management: The Role of AI-Driven Solutions in Modern Computer Networking. Journal of Electronics. *Computer Networking and Applied Mathematics.*, *4*(44), 1–9. DOI: 10.55529/jecnam.44.1.9

Oladipo, O., Omidiora, E. O., & Osamor, V. C. (2022). Comparative analysis of features extraction techniques for black face age estimation. *AI & Society*. Advance online publication. DOI: 10.1007/s00146-022-01407-0

Oliver, R. L. (1999). Whence customer satisfaction? *Journal of Marketing*, *1*(1), 1–22. DOI: 10.1177/00222429990634s105

Oliver, R. L. (2014). *Satisfaction: A behavioral perspective on the consumer: A behavioral perspective on the consumer*. Routledge. DOI: 10.4324/9781315700892

Oliver, R. L., Rust, R. T., & Varki, S. (1997). Customer delight: Foundations, findings, and managerial insight. *Journal of Retailing*, *73*(3), 311–336. DOI: 10.1016/S0022-4359(97)90021-X

Olsson, J., Hellström, D., & Vakulenko, Y. (2022). Customer experience dimensions in last-mile delivery: An empirical study on unattended home delivery. *International Journal of Physical Distribution & Logistics Management*, *53*(2), 184–205. DOI: 10.1108/IJPDLM-12-2021-0517

Orozco, J., & Olga, W. (2024). What drives European organizations to invest in Generative AI, and what challenges do they face in 2023-2024? www.bth.se/mba. DEPARTMENT OF INDUSTRIAL ECONOMICS

Oyedeji, O. M. (2024). Optimizing customer relationship management with ai: Harnessing predictive analytics for strategic growth.

Page, M. J., McKenzie, J. E., Bossuyt, P. M., Boutron, I., Hoffmann, T. C., Mulrow, C. D., ... & Moher, D. (2021). The PRISMA 2020 statement: an updated guideline for reporting systematic reviews. *bmj, 372*.

Pang, B., & Lee, L. (2008). Opinion mining and sentiment analysis. *Foundations and Trends in Information Retrieval*, *2*(1–2), 1–135. DOI: 10.1561/1500000011

Panigrahi, A., Pati, A., Sahu, B., Das, M. N., Nayak, D. S. K., Sahoo, G., & Kant, S. (2023). En-MinWhale: An ensemble approach based on MRMR and Whale optimization for Cancer diagnosis. *IEEE Access : Practical Innovations, Open Solutions*, *11*, 113526–113542. DOI: 10.1109/ACCESS.2023.3318261

Pappas, A., Fumagalli, E., Rouziou, M., & Bolander, W. (2023). More than Machines: The Role of the Future Retail Salesperson in Enhancing the Customer Experience. *Journal of Retailing*, *99*(4), 518–531. DOI: 10.1016/j.jretai.2023.10.004

Parasuraman, A., Zeithaml, V. A., & Berry, L. L. (1985). A conceptual model of service quality and its implications for future research. *Journal of Marketing*, *49*(4), 41–50. DOI: 10.1177/002224298504900403

Parasuraman, A., Zeithaml, V. A., & Berry, L. L. (1988). Servqual: A multiple-item scale for measuring consumer perc. *Journal of Retailing*, *64*(1), 12.

Parasuraman, A., Zeithaml, V. A., & Berry, L. L. (1988). SERVQUAL: A multiple-item scale for measuring consumer perceptions of service quality. *Journal of Retailing*, *64*(1), 12–40.

Parasuraman, R., Sheridan, T. B., & Wickens, C. D. (2000). A model for types and levels of human interaction with automation. *IEEE Transactions on Systems, Man, and Cybernetics. Part A, Systems and Humans*, *30*(3), 286–297. DOI: 10.1109/3468.844354 PMID: 11760769

Patil, D., Rane, N. L., & Rane, J. (2024). The future of customer loyalty: How ChatGPT and generative artificial intelligence are transforming customer engagement, personalization, and satisfaction. In *The Future Impact of ChatGPT on Several Business Sectors* (pp. 48–106). Deep Science Publishing., DOI: 10.70593/978-81-981367-8-7_2

Patwala, A., Barker, D., Da Costa, A., Bayard, G., Brunner-La Rocca, H.-P., Fontes-Carvalho, R., De la Fuente, L., Goralski, M., Mahon, N. G., Roque, D., Santos, M., Yousef, Z., Ben Hamouda, H., Teal, M., Christory, F., Ahmed, F. Z., & Mebazaa, A. (2024). Optimizing heart failure pathways to enhance patient care : The Program to Optimize Heart Failure Patient Pathways (PRO-HF). *ESC Heart Failure*, *11*(5), 2578–2590. DOI: 10.1002/ehf2.14911 PMID: 38924644

Pearson, A. (2020). Personalisation the artificial intelligence way. *Journal of Digital & Social Media Marketing.*, *7*(3), 245. Advance online publication. DOI: 10.69554/JJGR7331

Peltzer, K. (2009). Patient experiences and health system responsiveness in South Africa. *BMC Health Services Research*, *9*(1), 117. DOI: 10.1186/1472-6963-9-117 PMID: 19602290

Peng, Z., Augusto, V., Perrier, L., & Xie, X. (2024). Optimal Process Mining of Traces With Events and Transition Attributes With Application to Care Pathways of Cancer Patients. *IEEE Transactions on Automation Science and Engineering*, *21*(3), 4364–4381. DOI: 10.1109/TASE.2023.3295947

Peruchini, M., da Silva, G. M., & Teixeira, J. M. (2024). Between artificial intelligence and customer experience: A literature review on the intersection. *Discover Artificial Intelligence*, *4*(1), 4. DOI: 10.1007/s44163-024-00105-8

Petty, R. E., & Cacioppo, J. T. (1986). The elaboration likelihood model of persuasion. *Advances in Experimental Social Psychology*, *19*, 123–205. DOI: 10.1016/S0065-2601(08)60214-2

Pinaire, J., Azé, J., Bringay, S., & Landais, P. (2017). Patient healthcare trajectory. An essential monitoring tool : A systematic review. *Health Information Science and Systems*, *5*(1), 1. DOI: 10.1007/s13755-017-0020-2 PMID: 28413630

Pizzi, G., Scarpi, D., & Pantano, E. (2021). Artificial intelligence and the new forms of interaction: Who has the control when interacting with a chatbot? *Journal of Business Research*, *129*, 878–890. DOI: 10.1016/j.jbusres.2020.11.006

Pontiki, M., Galanis, D., Papageorgiou, H., Androutsopoulos, I., Manandhar, S., Al-Smadi, M., & Eryiğit, G. (2016, January). Semeval-2016 task 5: Aspect based sentiment analysis. In International workshop on semantic evaluation (pp. 19-30).

Potla, R. T. (2024). Leveraging Generative AI for Enhanced Customer Relationship Management: Transforming Customer Interactions and Personalization in CRM Systems.

Potla, R. T. (2023). Enhancing Customer Relationship Management (CRM) through AI-Powered Tools and Machine Learning. *Distributed Learning and Broad Applications in Scientific Investigation*, *9*, 364–383.

Prentice, C., Dominique Lopes, S., & Wang, X. (2020). The impact of artificial intelligence and employee service quality on customer satisfaction and loyalty. *Journal of Hospitality Marketing & Management*, *29*(7), 739–756. DOI: 10.1080/19368623.2020.1722304

Pugna, I. B., Popescu, I. C., & Henson, M. (2023, June). AI and New Forms of Market Interaction to Enhance Customer Experience—A Management Perspective. In *International Conference on Economics and Social Sciences* (pp. 35-47). Cham: Springer Nature Switzerland.

Puntoni, S., Reczek, R. W., Giesler, M., & Botti, S. (2021). Consumers and artificial intelligence: An experiential perspective. *Journal of Marketing*, *85*(1), 131–151. DOI: 10.1177/0022242920953847

Qiu, H., Li, M., Shu, B., & Bai, B. (2019). Enhancing hospitality experience with service robots: The mediating role of rapport building. *Journal of Hospitality Marketing & Management*, *29*(3), 247–268. DOI: 10.1080/19368623.2019.1645073

Quigley, D. D., Reynolds, K., Dellva, S., & Price, R. A. (2021). Examining the Business Case for Patient Experience : A Systematic Review. *Journal of healthcare management / American College of Healthcare Executives, 66*(3), 200-224. DOI: 10.1097/JHM-D-20-00207

Rachmad, Y. E. (2022). The Influence And Impact of The Money Burning Strategy on The Future of Startups. Adpebi Science Series. (Note: Insufficient information for a standard APA citation. Treating as a report/series article.)

Rai, A., Constantinides, P., & Sarker, S. (2019). Next generation digital platforms: Toward human-AI hybrids. *Management Information Systems Quarterly*, *43*(1), iii–ix.

Rais, A., & Viana, A. (2011). Operations Research in Healthcare : A survey. *International Transactions in Operational Research*, *18*(1), 1–31. DOI: 10.1111/j.1475-3995.2010.00767.x

Ramesh, M. V. (2019). Integration of participatory approaches, systems, and solutions using IoT and AI for designing smart community: Case studies from India. TESCA 2019 - Proceedings of the 2019 1st ACM International Workshop on Technology Enablers and Innovative Applications for Smart Cities and Communities, Co-Located with the 6th ACM International Conference on Systems for Energy-Efficient Buildings, Cities, 4–5. DOI: 10.1145/3364544.3371501

Rane, N. (2023). Enhancing Customer Loyalty through Artificial Intelligence (AI), Internet of Things (IoT), and Big Data Technologies: Improving Customer Satisfaction, Engagement, Relationship, and Experience. DOI: 10.2139/ssrn.4616051

Rane, N., Choudhary, S., & Rane, J. (2023) Hyper-personalization for enhancing customer loyalty and satisfaction in Customer Relationship Management (CRM) systems. DOI: 10.2139/ssrn.4641044

Rane, N., Choudhary, S., & Rane, J. (2023) Metaverse for Enhancing Customer Loyalty: Effective Strategies to Improve Customer Relationship, Service, Engagement, Satisfaction, and Experience. DOI: 10.2139/ssrn.4624197

Ratti, M., Milicia, O., Rescinito, R., Coeckelberghs, E., Seys, D., Vanhaecht, K., & Panella, M. (2023). The determinants of expert opinion in the development of care pathways : Insights from an exploratory cluster analysis. *BMC Health Services Research*, *23*(1), 211. DOI: 10.1186/s12913-023-09139-7 PMID: 36869326

Rayyan : Plateforme de gestion des revues systématiques alimentée par l'IA. (s. d.). Consulté 18 février 2025, à l'adresse https://www.rayyan.ai/

Reichheld, F. (2003). The One Number You Need to Grow. *Harvard Business Review*, *81*, 46–54, 124. https://www.scirp.org/reference/referencespapers?referenceid=3074424 PMID: 14712543

Richter, P., & Schlieter, H. (2019). *Understanding patient pathways in the context of integrated health care services-implications from a scoping review*. https://aisel.aisnet.org/wi2019/track08/papers/6/

Richter, P., Hickmann, E., & Schlieter, H. (2021). Validating the Concept of Patient Pathways : A European Survey on Their Characteristics, Definition and State of Practice. *PACIS*, 32. https://www.researchgate.net/profile/Hannes_Schlieter/publication/354209554_Validating_the_Concept_of_Patient_Pathways_A_European_Survey_on_Their_Characteristics_Definition_and_State_of_Practice/links/6197875e3068c54fa5007579/Validating-the-Concept-of-Patient-Pathways-A-European-Survey-on-Their-Characteristics-Definition-and-State-of-Practice.pdf

Rizk, M., El-Samadicy, A., & Negm, E. (2024). The Influence of Omni-Channel Integration on Generation Z Purchase Intentions Towards FMCG Retailers: An Empirical Investigation on Egyptian FMCG Consumers. *The Journal of Business*, *12*(1), 1–12.

Rosa, W. E., Izumi, S., Sullivan, D. R., Lakin, J., Rosenberg, A. R., Creutzfeldt, C. J., Lafond, D., Tjia, J., Cotter, V., Wallace, C., Sloan, D. E., Cruz-Oliver, D. M., DeSanto-Madeya, S., Bernacki, R., Leblanc, T. W., & Epstein, A. S. (2023). Advance Care Planning in Serious Illness : A Narrative Review. In *Journal of Pain and Symptom Management* (Vol. 65, Numéro 1, p. e63-e78). Elsevier Inc. DOI: 10.1016/j.jpainsymman.2022.08.012

Rossmann, A. & Zimmermann, A. & Hertweck, D. (2020). The Impact of Chatbots on Customer Service Performance. DOI: .DOI: 10.1007/978-3-030-51057-2_33

Rotolo, D., Hicks, D., & Martin, B. R. (2015). What is an emerging technology? *Research Policy*, *44*(10), 1827–1843. DOI: 10.1016/j.respol.2015.06.006

Rotter, T., Kugler, J., Koch, R., Gothe, H., Twork, S., Van Oostrum, J. M., & Steyerberg, E. W. (2008). A systematic review and meta-analysis of the effects of clinical pathways on length of stay, hospital costs and patient outcomes. *BMC Health Services Research*, *8*(1), 265. DOI: 10.1186/1472-6963-8-265 PMID: 19094244

Roy, S. K., Singh, G., Sadeque, S., & Gruner, R. L. (2024). Customer experience quality with social robots: Does trust matter? *Technological Forecasting and Social Change*, *198*, 123032. DOI: 10.1016/j.techfore.2023.123032

Russell, S. J., & Norvig, P. (2020). *Artificial intelligence: A modern approach* (3rd ed.). Pearson.

Rust, R. T., & Huang, M. H. (2021). The AI revolution: The role of artificial intelligence in marketing. [DOI: 10.1007/s11747-020-00748-9]. *Journal of the Academy of Marketing Science*, *49*(1), 24–42.

Sadhu, A. K. R., Parfenov, M., Saripov, D., Muravev, M., & Sadhu, A. K. R. (2024). Enhancing customer service automation and user satisfaction: An exploration of ai-powered chatbot implementation within customer relationship management systems. *Journal of Computational Intelligence and Robotics*, *4*(1), 103–123.

Salama, W. M., Suliman, M. A., Hassanin, M., Khairy, H. A., Al Asrag, A. S. A., & Fahmy, N. S. (2024). Catalyzing green competitiveness in hotel and tourism businesses: Leveraging digital dynamic capability and green creativity. *Environment and Social Psychology*, *9*(9), 2978. DOI: 10.59429/esp.v9i9.2978

Saleem, F., Al-Ghamdi, A. S. A.-M., Alassafi, M. O., & AlGhamdi, S. A. (2022). Machine Learning, Deep Learning, and Mathematical Models to Analyze Forecasting and Epidemiology of COVID-19 : A Systematic Literature Review. *International Journal of Environmental Research and Public Health*, *19*(9), 5099. DOI: 10.3390/ijerph19095099 PMID: 35564493

Salehzadeh, R., Javani, M., & Esmailian, H. (2024). Leveraging green artificial intelligence for green competitive advantage: Testing a mediated moderation model. *The TQM Journal*. Advance online publication. DOI: 10.1108/TQM-04-2024-0152

Samala, N., Katkam, B. S., Bellamkonda, R. S., & Rodriguez, R. V. (2020). Impact of AI and robotics in the tourism sector : A critical insight. *Journal of tourism futures*, *8*(1), 73-87.

Samala, N., Katkam, B. S., Bellamkonda, R. S., & Rodriguez, R. V. (2020). Impact of AI and robotics in the tourism sector: a critical insight. *Journal of tourism futures, 8*(1), 73-87.

Sanh, V., Debut, L., Chaumond, J., & Wolf, T. (2019). DistilBERT, a distilled version of BERT: Smaller, faster, cheaper, and lighter. arXiv. https://arxiv.org/abs/1910.01108

Sankar, J. G., & David, A. (2023). Measuring the Service Quality of Artificial Intelligence in the Tourism and Hospitality Industry. In *Handbook of Research on Innovation, Differentiation, and New Technologies in Tourism, Hotels, and Food Service* (p. 133-155). IGI Global. DOI: 10.4018/978-1-6684-6985-9.ch007

Santoveña-Casal, S., & Pérez, M. D. F. (2022). Relevance of E-Participation in the state health campaign in Spain: #EstoNoEsUnJuego / #ThisIsNotAGame. *Technology in Society, 68*, 101877. Advance online publication. DOI: 10.1016/j.techsoc.2022.101877 PMID: 36540135

Saputra, F. E., Buhalis, D., Augustyn, M. M., & Marangos, S. (2024). Anthropomorphism-based artificial intelligence (AI) robots typology in hospitality and tourism. *Journal of Hospitality and Tourism Technology, 15*(5), 790–807. DOI: 10.1108/JHTT-03-2024-0171

Sarioguz, O.. (2024). AI-powered business model innovation: Analyzing the implications of generative AI on value creation, operational efficiency and market dynamics. *World Journal of Advanced Engineering Technology and Sciences, 13*(02), 216–229.

Sarker, I. H. (2022). AI-Based Modeling: Techniques, Applications and Research Issues Towards Automation, Intelligent and Smart Systems. *SN Computer Science, 3*(2), 158. DOI: 10.1007/s42979-022-01043-x PMID: 35194580

Savina, M.-D., & Boidin, B. (1996). Privatisation des services sociaux et redéfinition du rôle de l'État : Les prestations éducatives et sanitaires au Bénin. *Revue Tiers Monde*, •••, 853–874. https://www.jstor.org/stable/23592377

Saw, A. T. W., Ooi, A. Y., Yap, W. K., Patrick, Z., & Salam, S. N. (2022). Bank Ownership and Non-Performing Loans of Islamic and Conventional Banks in An Emerging Economy. *International Journal of Economics and Management, 16*(3), 339–349. DOI: 10.47836/ijeam.16.3.05

Saxena, D., Muzellec, L., & McDonagh, J. (2022). From Bureaucracy to Citizen-Centricity: How the Citizen-Journey Should Inform the Digital Transformation of Public Services. *International Journal of Electronic Government Research, 18*(1), 1–17. Advance online publication. DOI: 10.4018/IJEGR.305230

Schenk, B., Dolata, M., Schwabe, C., & Schwabe, G. (2021). What citizens experience and how omni-channel could help–insights from a building permit case. *Information Technology & People*. Advance online publication. DOI: 10.1108/ITP-06-2020-0374

Scholz, M., Haase, R., Schriefer, D., Voigt, I., & Ziemssen, T. (2021). Electronic health interventions in the case of multiple sclerosis : From theory to practice. *Brain Sciences, 11*(2), 180. https://www.mdpi.com/2076-3425/11/2/180. DOI: 10.3390/brainsci11020180 PMID: 33540640

Sealey, M., Breen, L. J., O'Connor, M., & Aoun, S. M. (2015). A scoping review of bereavement risk assessment measures : Implications for palliative care. In *Palliative Medicine* (Vol. 29, Numéro 7, p. 577-589). SAGE Publications Ltd. DOI: 10.1177/0269216315576262

Shamim, R., & Bentalha, B. (2023). Blockchain-enabled machine learning framework for demand forecasting in supply chain management. In *Integrating Intelligence and Sustainability in Supply Chains* (pp. 28–48). IGI Global. DOI: 10.4018/979-8-3693-0225-5.ch002

Shen, X., Zhang, Y., Tang, Y., Qin, Y., Liu, N., & Yi, Z. (2022). A study on the impact of digital tobacco logistics on tobacco supply chain performance: Taking the tobacco industry in Guangxi as an example. *Industrial Management & Data Systems, 122*(6), 1416–1452. DOI: 10.1108/IMDS-05-2021-0270

Shin, H., Bunosso, I., & Levine, L. R. (2023). The influence of chatbot humour on consumer evaluations of services. *International Journal of Consumer Studies, 47*(2), 545–562. DOI: 10.1111/ijcs.12849

Sigala, M., Ooi, K. B., Tan, G. W. H., Aw, E. C. X., Cham, T. H., Dwivedi, Y. K., Kunz, W. H., Letheren, K., Mishra, A., Russell-Bennett, R., & Wirtz, J. (2024). ChatGPT and service: Opportunities, challenges, and research directions. *Journal of Service Theory and Practice, 34*(5), 726–737. DOI: 10.1108/JSTP-11-2023-0292

Sikandar, M. A., Munari, P. K., & Arli, M. (2020). A Systematic Literature Review of the Impact of Artificial Intelligence on Customer Experience. *Machine Learning for Business Analytics*, 117-127.

Singh, L., & Dhankhar, D. (2024). Artificial Intelligence for Innovative Customer Services in the Hospitality Industry of India. In *Leveraging AI and Emotional Intelligence in Contemporary Business Organizations* (pp. 219–239). IGI Global.

Singh, P., & Kumar, A. (2024). Beyond Automation: Exploring the Function of AI in Enhancing Digital Marketing Influence and Management Innovation. *Journal of Informatics Education and Investigation, 4*(2).

Smith, A., & Hutson, J. (2024). From concept to creation: The role of generative artificial intelligence in the new age of digital marketing. *Design, 1*(1), 4776. DOI: 10.36922/dp.4776

Son, S. C., Bae, J., & Kim, K. H. (2021). The influence of perceived agility on intention to reuse Omni-channel: Focused on mediating influence of integration quality of Omni-channel. *Journal of Global Fashion Marketing, 12*(4), 375–389. DOI: 10.1080/20932685.2021.1947151

Soriano, B. & Dougherty, S. & Soublet, B. & Triepke, K. (2014). Autonomous Vehicles: A Perspective from the California Department of Motor Vehicles. DOI: DOI: 10.1007/978-3-319-05990-7_2

Sovrano, F., Vitali, F., & Palmirani, M. (2020). Modelling GDPR-Compliant Explanations for Trustworthy AI. In K. A., F. E., K. G., K. I., & T. A.M. (Eds.), 9th International Conference on Electronic Government and the Information Systems Perspective, EGOVIS 2020: Vol. 12394 LNCS (pp. 219–233). Springer Science and Business Media Deutschland GmbH. DOI: 10.1007/978-3-030-58957-8_16

Storm Reply. (2024). Unlock Real Value With Generative Ai. Increase revenue. Decrease costs. Attract and retain customers.

Stoumpos, A. I., Kitsios, F., & Talias, M. A. (2023a). Digital transformation in healthcare : Technology acceptance and its applications. *International Journal of Environmental Research and Public Health, 20*(4), 3407. https://www.mdpi.com/1660-4601/20/4/3407. DOI: 10.3390/ijerph20043407 PMID: 36834105

Sucupira Furtado, L., da Silva, T. L. C., Ferreira, M. G. F., de Macedo, J. A. F., & de Melo Lima Cavalcanti Moreira, J. K. (2023). A framework for Digital Transformation towards Smart Governance: using big data tools to target SDGs in Ceará, Brazil. Journal of Urban Management. DOI: 10.1016/j.jum.2023.01.003

Sułkowski, Ł., Kolasińska-Morawska, K., Brzozowska, M., Morawski, P., & Schroeder, T. (2022). Last Mile Logistics Innovations in the Courier-Express-Parcel Sector Due to the COVID-19 Pandemic. *Sustainability (Basel), 14*(13), 8207. Advance online publication. DOI: 10.3390/su14138207

Swartz, M. K. (2021). PRISMA 2020 : An update. *Journal of Pediatric Health Care, 35*(4), 351. DOI: 10.1016/j.pedhc.2021.04.011 PMID: 34243844

Taboada, M., Brooke, J., Tofiloski, M., Voll, K., & Stede, M. (2011). Lexicon-based methods for sentiment analysis. *Computational Linguistics, 37*(2), 267–307. DOI: 10.1162/COLI_a_00049

Taherdoost, H., & Madanchian, M. (2023). Artificial intelligence and sentiment analysis: A review in competitive research. *Computers, 12*(2), 37. Advance online publication. DOI: 10.3390/computers12020037

Tang, D., Qin, B., & Liu, T. (2015). Document modeling with gated recurrent neural network for sentiment classification. *Proceedings of the 2015 Conference on Empirical Methods in Natural Language Processing*, 1422–1432. DOI: 10.18653/v1/D15-1167

Toll, D., Lindgren, I., Melin, U., & Madsen, C. Ø. (2020). Values, benefits, considerations and risks of ai in government: A study of ai policy documents in sweden. *EJournal of EDemocracy and Open Government, 12*(1), 40–60. DOI: 10.29379/jedem.v12i1.593

Touretzky, D., Gardner-McCune, C., Breazeal, C., Martin, F., & Seehorn, D. (2019). A year in K-12 AI education. *AI Magazine, 40*(4), 88–90. DOI: 10.1609/aimag.v40i4.5289

Tran, M. T. (2024). Unlocking the AI-Powered Customer Experience: Personalized Service, Enhanced Engagement, and Data-Driven Strategies for E-Commerce Applications. In *Enhancing and Predicting Digital Consumer Behavior with AI* (pp. 375-382). IGI Global.

Tranfield, D., Denyer, D., & Smart, P. (2003). Towards a methodology for developing evidence-informed management knowledge by means of systematic review. *British Journal of Management, 14*(3), 207–222. DOI: 10.1111/1467-8551.00375

Tula, S. T., Kess-Momoh, A. J., Omotoye, G. B., Bello, B. G., & Daraojimba, A. I. (2024). Ai-enabled customer experience enhancement in business. *Computer Science & IT Research Journal, 5*(2), 365–389. DOI: 10.51594/csitrj.v5i2.789

Tung, V. W. S., & Au, N. (2018). Exploring customer experiences with robotics in hospitality. *International Journal of Contemporary Hospitality Management, 30*(7), 2680–2697. DOI: 10.1108/IJCHM-06-2017-0322

Turing, A. (1950). Computing machinery and intelligence. *Mind, 59*(236), 433–460. DOI: 10.1093/mind/LIX.236.433

Ullman, S. (2019). Using neuroscience to develop artificial intelligence. *Science, 363*(6428), 692–693. DOI: 10.1126/science.aau6595 PMID: 30765552

Utomo, S., John, A., Rouniyar, A., Hsu, H. C., & Hsiung, P. A. (2022). Federated Trustworthy AI Architecture for Smart Cities. ISC2 2022 - 8th IEEE International Smart Cities Conference. DOI: 10.1109/ISC255366.2022.9922069

Vakulenko, Y., Shams, P., Hellström, D., & Hjort, K. (2019). Online retail experience and customer satisfaction: The mediating role of last mile delivery. *International Review of Retail, Distribution and Consumer Research, 29*(3), 306–320. DOI: 10.1080/09593969.2019.1598466

Vanasse, A. (s. d.). *Cohorte sur les trajectoires de soins des personnes ayant une condition propice aux soins ambulatoires.*

Verganti, R. (2011). Radical design and technology epiphanies: A new focus for research on design management. *Journal of Product Innovation Management, 28*(3), 384–388. DOI: 10.1111/j.1540-5885.2011.00807.x

Verhoef, P. C., Lemon, K. N., Parasuraman, A., Roggeveen, A., Tsiros, M., & Schlesinger, L. A. (2009). Customer experience creation: Determinants, dynamics and management strategies. *Journal of Retailing, 85*(1), 31–41. DOI: 10.1016/j.jretai.2008.11.001

Vetrova, M. & Tatiana, S. & Arenkov, I. & Ivanova, D. (2023). The Impact of Digitalization on the Telecommunications Sector ESG Transformation. . DOI:DOI: 10.1007/978-3-031-30351-7_15

Vijverberg, J. R., Daniels, K., Steinmann, G., Garvelink, M. M., van der Voort, M. B. R., Biesma, D., Bos, W. J. W., van Merode, F., & van der Nat, P. (2022). Mapping the extent, range and nature of research activity on value-based healthcare in the 15 years following its introduction (2006–2021) : A scoping review. [abstract]. *BMJ Open, 12*(8), e064983. https://bmjopen.bmj.com/content/12/8/e064983. DOI: 10.1136/bmjopen-2022-064983 PMID: 35973705

Wallin, M. T., Culpepper, W. J., Nichols, E., Bhutta, Z. A., Gebrehiwot, T. T., Hay, S. I., Khalil, I. A., Krohn, K. J., Liang, X., Naghavi, M., Mokdad, A. H., Nixon, M. R., Reiner, R. C., Sartorius, B., Smith, M., Topor-Madry, R., Werdecker, A., Vos, T., Feigin, V. L., & Murray, C. J. L. (2019). Global, regional, and national burden of multiple sclerosis 1990–2016 : A systematic analysis for the Global Burden of Disease Study 2016. *Lancet Neurology, 18*(3), 269–285. https://www.thelancet.com/journals/laneur/article/PIIS1474-4422(18)30443-5/fulltext. DOI: 10.1016/S1474-4422(18)30443-5 PMID: 30679040

Wang, L., Huang, N., Hong, Y., Liu, L., Guo, X., & Chen, G. (2020). Effects of voice-based ai in customer service: evidence from a natural experiment.

Wang, C.-N., Nguyen, N.-A.-T., & Dang, T.-T. (2022). Offshore wind power station (OWPS) site selection using a two-stage MCDM-based spherical fuzzy set approach. *Scientific Reports, 12*(1), 4260. DOI: 10.1038/s41598-022-08257-2 PMID: 35277582

Wang, C.-N., Nguyen, N.-A.-T., Dang, T.-T., & Hsu, H.-P. (2021). Evaluating Sustainable Last-Mile Delivery (LMD) in B2C E-Commerce Using Two-Stage Fuzzy MCDM Approach: A Case Study From Vietnam. *IEEE Access : Practical Innovations, Open Solutions*, *9*, 146050–146067. DOI: 10.1109/ACCESS.2021.3121607

Wang, X., Zhang, Y., & Li, J. (2023). Deep Learning Models for Sentiment Analysis: Performance and Optimization Challenges. *Artificial Intelligence Review*, *61*(3), 445–470. DOI: 10.1007/s10462-023-10501-w

Wang, Y., Font, X., & Liu, J. (2020). Antecedents, mediation effects and outcomes of hotel eco-innovation practice. *International Journal of Hospitality Management*, *85*, 102345. DOI: 10.1016/j.ijhm.2019.102345

Wang, Y., Xi, C., Zhang, S., Zhang, W., & Yu, D. (2015). Combined approach for government E-tendering using GA and TOPSIS with intuitionistic fuzzy information. *PLoS One*, *10*(7), e0130767. Advance online publication. DOI: 10.1371/journal.pone.0130767 PMID: 26147468

Wang, Y., Zhang, N., & Zhao, X. (2022). Understanding the Determinants in the Different Government AI Adoption Stages: Evidence of Local Government Chatbots in China. *Social Science Computer Review*, *40*(2), 534–554. DOI: 10.1177/0894439320980132

Wankhade, M., Rao, A. C. S., & Kulkarni, C. (2022). A survey on sentiment analysis methods, applications, and challenges. *Artificial Intelligence Review*, *55*(7), 5731–5780. DOI: 10.1007/s10462-022-10144-1

Weber, N. (2017). *Matching the business model with the unique journey of purchaser: a case investigation of a high-tech Dutch EMS provider* (Master's thesis, University of Twente).

Widjaja, Y. G., So, I. G., Setiowati, R. I. N. I., & Furinto, A. S. N. A. N. (2023). The influence of utilitarian value and hedonic value on omni-channel shopping intention through tam perceived usefulness and perceived ease of use. *Journal of Theoretical and Applied Information Technology*, *101*(8), 3187–3198.

Wien, A. H., & Peluso, A. M. (2021). Influence of human versus AI recommenders: The roles of product type and cognitive processes. *Journal of Business Research*, *137*, 13–27. DOI: 10.1016/j.jbusres.2021.08.016

Williams, S. J., & Radnor, Z. (2018). Using bandwidths to visualize and improve patient pathways. *Public Money & Management*, *38*(1), 21–28. DOI: 10.1080/09540962.2018.1389495

Wirtz, J., Patterson, P. G., Kunz, W. H., Gruber, T., Lu, V. N., Paluch, S., & Martins, A. (2018). Brave new world: Service robots in the frontline. *Journal of Service Management, 29*(5), 907–931. DOI: 10.1108/JOSM-04-2018-0119

Witten, I. H., Frank, E., & Hall, M. A. (2011). *Data mining: Practical machine learning tools and techniques* (3rd ed.). Morgan Kaufmann.

Wynne, R. (2004). Variable definitions : Implications for the prediction of pulmonary complications after adult cardiac surgery. In *European Journal of Cardiovascular Nursing* (Vol. 3, Numéro 1, p. 43-52). DOI: 10.1016/j.ejcnurse.2003.11.001

Xiang, Z. (2021). Journal of Smart Tourism. *Journal of Smart Tourism, 1*(1), 1–2. DOI: 10.52255/smarttourism.2021.1.1.1

Xiong, L., Wang, H., & Wang, C. (2022). Predicting mobile government service continuance: A two-stage structural equation modeling-artificial neural network approach. *Government Information Quarterly, 39*(1), 101654. Advance online publication. DOI: 10.1016/j.giq.2021.101654

Xu, J., & Cui, X. (2023). Investigation on the Game Association and Behavior Optimization among Banks and Customers in the Omni-Channel Environment. *Systems, 11*(4), 171. DOI: 10.3390/systems11040171

Ye, Y., Lau, K. H., & Teo, L. K. Y. (2018). Drivers and barriers of omni-channel retailing in China: A case investigation of the fashion and apparel industry. *International Journal of Retail & Distribution Management, 46*(7), 657–689. DOI: 10.1108/IJRDM-04-2017-0062

Yi, Z., & Ayangbah, S. (2024). *The Influence of AI Innovation Management on Organizational Productivity and Economic Growth: An Analytical Investigation*. DOI: 10.35409/IJBMER.2024.3580

Yim, D., Malefyt, T., & Khuntia, J. (2021). Is a picture worth a thousand views? Measuring the effects of travel photos on user engagement using deep learning algorithms. *Electronic Markets, 31*(3), 1–19. DOI: 10.1007/s12525-021-00472-5

Youssofi, A., Jeannot, F., Jongmans, E., & Dampérat, M. (2023). Designing the digitalized guest experience: A comprehensive framework and research agenda. *Psychology and Marketing, 41*(3), 512–531. DOI: 10.1002/mar.21929

Yunanda, R. A., Rusmanto, T., Tareq, M. A., & Putri, N. K. S. (2024). Can ai-driven features alone foster customers'trust in indonesian and malaysian banks? *Journal of Theoretical and Applied Information Technology, 102*(24).

Zaugg, V., Savoldelli, V., Sabatier, B., & Durieux, P. (2014). Améliorer les pratiques et l'organisation des soins: Méthodologie des revues systématiques. *Santé Publique (Vandoeuvre-Les-Nancy, France)*, *26*(5), 655–667. DOI: 10.3917/spub.145.0655 PMID: 25490225

Zeithaml, V. A. (1988). Consumer perceptions of price, quality, and value: A means-end model and synthesis of evidence. *Journal of Marketing*, *52*(3), 2–22. DOI: 10.1177/002224298805200302

Zhang, S., Makedon, F., Ford, J., Sudborough, C., Ai, L., Kapidakis, S., Karkaletsis, V., & Loukis, E. (2004). An international trade negotiation framework for e-government. In T. R. (Ed.), Lecture Notes in Computer Science (including subseries Lecture Notes in Artificial Intelligence and Lecture Notes in Bioinformatics) (Vol. 3183, pp. 211–217). Springer Verlag. DOI: 10.1007/978-3-540-30078-6_35

Zhang, H., Sun, A., & Li, Y. (2023). A comprehensive survey on pre-trained models and their applications. *Journal of Machine Learning Research*, *24*(288), 1–142. http://jmlr.org/papers/v24/22-1273.html

Zhilkina, A. N., Zhilkin, O. N., & Krylov, V. K. (2020). Financial and economic and information aspects of smart city – AI at citizens' service. In P. E.G. & S. B.S. (Eds.), Advances in Intelligent Systems and Computing: Vol. 1100 AISC (pp. 148–155). Springer. DOI: 10.1007/978-3-030-39319-9_16

Zhu, B., Guo, D., & Ren, L. (2022). Consumer preference analysis based on text comments and ratings: A multi-attribute decision-making perspective. *Information & Management*, *59*(3), 103626. Advance online publication. DOI: 10.1016/j.im.2022.103626

About The Contributors

Mourad Aarabe is a Ph.D. student in Management Sciences at the National School of Business and Management, Sidi Mohamed Ben Abdellah University, Fez. He specializes in customer experience and the impact of emerging technologies on the tourism, healthcare, and service sectors. Mourad is also a Management and Business Trainer, with a focus on digital marketing and organizational management. He has published numerous contributions in indexed books and conferences, and actively contributes to the scientific community as an editor of an upcoming book on AI innovations for optimizing customer experience in the service sector. Additionally, he serves as a reviewer for several esteemed scientific journals and publishers. His research interests center on optimizing customer experience, applying emerging technologies in marketing, and promoting eco-responsible tourism behavior.

Nouhaila Ben Khizzou is a doctoral researcher in management sciences at Sidi Mohamed Ben Abdellah University in Fez, specializing in healthcare management with a particular focus on enhancing patient care and the overall patient experience within healthcare facilities. She holds a Master's degree in Healthcare Management and Marketing from ENCG Agadir and a Bachelor's degree in Radiology Technology from ISPITS Laayoune. Nouhaila has gained significant professional experience as an educator at OFPPT, where she teaches biomedical materials management, irradiation management, and quality assurance. Additionally, she has served as a practitioner in diagnostic radiology and radiotherapy at the Ministry of Health and Social Protection. With a strong blend of academic knowledge and practical expertise, Nouhaila is dedicated to advancing research in healthcare management. She has contributed to indexed books and conferences and is an active member of the scientific community. She also serves as a co-editor of an upcoming book on AI innovations aimed at optimizing customer experiences in the service sector.

Lhoussaine Alla is a professor in management sciences at the National School of Applied Sciences, and a researcher at the LAREMEF laboratory, Sidi Mohamed

Ben Abdellah University, Fez, Morocco. He is a permanent professor of various marketing management modules at Sidi Mohamed Ben Abdellah University in Fez (Morocco) and in several public and private business graduate schools. He is an accredited professional expert in Training Engineering, Professional Coaching and Mentoring young entrepreneurs. After a PhD thesis on creating value for the customer and its impact on the overall performance of companies, Prof. Lhoussaine Alla invested more in scientific research in marketing, through various scientific contributions in the form of participation in international conferences and symposia and scientific publications, in various themes inherent to Marketing (customer value creation, customer behaviour, e-marketing, customer experience, sales performance, Marketing Data Analytics, territorial marketing, territorial attractiveness, territorial economic intelligence, ...), finance (stock market performance, financial analysts, financing package,...), entrepreneurship (entrepreneur profile, startups, entrepreneurial resilience,...), tourism (tourist attractiveness, visitor behaviour, tourism, performance of tourist destinations,...), logistics (SC, SCM, SSCM, Green SCM, logistics performance,...). Prof. Lhoussaine ALLA is also (co)editor of the e-book “Integrating Intelligence and Sustainability into supply chains. IGI Global. DOI: 10.4018/979-8-3693-0225-5” and Publication Director of the scientific journal “Managerial and Economic Alternatives - AME”, indexed on the IMIST portal. Prof. Lhoussaine ALLA is also (co)coordinator of many scientific events devoted to marketing research. As a scientific and educational accumulation, in his capacity as editor of numerous books, especially in collaboration with IGI Global, Prof ALLA has been able to mobilize a large community of imminent researchers and experts on a global scale, to share the fruits of their relevant and innovative research in the implementation, supervision, evaluation, control and reinvention of innovative solutions developed through data engineering and AI in marketing. He is co-editor of several collective works including: “Integrating Intelligence and Sustainability in Supply Chains”, “AI and Data Engineering Solutions for Effective Marketing”, “Data Collection and Analysis in Scientific Qualitative Research”, Applying Qualitative Research Methods to Management Science, Utilizing Technology to Manage Territories, Sustainable and Intelligent Territorial Marketing and Entrepreneurship. Prof ALLA is the coordinator of a team of young researchers very dynamic and talented, with complementary profiles, creating a friendly space for high-level scientific research.

Ahmed Benjelloun is an associate professor at the National School of Business and Management at Sidi Mohamed Ben Abdellah University in Fez, where he has been teaching since 2019. He earned his PhD in Economics and Management, specializing in marketing, digital marketing, and project management. He is actively involved in research within the LAREMEF laboratory and the ALESCO Chair and coordinates several academic and scientific events. In addition to his academic role, he serves as an expert consultant and mentor at hackathons and professional events. The author of the book "Fès, Destination de Tourisme Culturel" has also contributed to several events linked to marketing and cultural tourism. He has published numerous contributions in indexed books, academic journals, and conferences. His role as editor for a forthcoming book on artificial intelligence innovations to optimize customer experience in the service sector reflects his commitment to enriching the scientific community. His primary research areas include customer experience optimization, the application of emerging technologies in marketing, territorial branding, and the promotion of eco-responsible tourism behavior.

***

Zouhair Allal is a professor of management. His areas of expertise include entrepreneurship, organizational psychology, and finance. His doctorate focused on entrepreneurial failure and the psychological health of entrepreneurs. He has worked on frugal innovation, survival strategies, and stress coping. He is currently interested in artificial intelligence in the financial sector.

Badr Bentalha teaches Supply Chain and Operations Management at National School Of Business and Management – Fez, Sidi Mohamed Ben Abdellah University – Morocco. Dr. Bentalha investigates the structural dynamics and control of complex networks, applying his findings to supply chain management, Industry 4.0, risk analysis, and digital supply chains. His work emphasizes the intersection of supply chain management, operations research, industrial engineering, and digital technology. As a professor, he teaches undergraduate, graduate, and, doctoral courses in operations management, supply chain management, logistics, management information systems, and strategic management. Through guest lectures, webinars, and scholarly presentations, he engages students and fosters an active learning environment.Professor Bentalha specializes in supply chain and operations management, operations research, and service management. He is passionate about integrating knowledge across disciplines to solve real-world problems. He has delivered numerous invited plenary talks, keynotes, and panel discussions at conferences and global webinars.

Ikram Ed-Daakouri, PHD student at the LAREMEF Laboratory within the National School of Business and Management in Fez, at Sidi Mohamed Ben Abdellah University, Morocco. My research focuses on "Smart Marketing and Generative AI for Optimizing Customer Retention: Case of Morocco," where I aim to explore the integration of advanced AI technologies to enhance customer engagement strategies.

Throughout my academic journey, I've published several works on topics such as smart data analytics and generative AI, reflecting my deep interest in these emerging technologies. Currently, I serve as the Marketing and Communication Manager at a Swiss-Moroccan company, where I apply both my practical expertise and research insights to drive innovative strategies in the digital marketing domain. Driven by my passion for leveraging AI in marketing, I continue to explore new trends that shape the future of customer retention and marketing intelligence.

Lamyae Khattabi is an independent researcher based in Morocco. She holds a PhD in Economics and Management from Sidi Mohamed Ben Abdellah University in Fez, with a dissertation entitled: "Islamic Finance and Venture Capital: Future Prospects of Moudaraba and Moucharaka in Enhancing the Investor–Entrepreneur Relationship Framework in Morocco." Dr. Khattabi previously held the position of full-time lecturer at the Ecole Supérieure de Commerce et de Gestion (ESCG) in Tangier. She also earned a Master's degree in Accounting, Control, and Auditing from Mohammed V University in Rabat, and a Bachelor's degree in Audit and Management Control from Moulay Ismail University in Meknès. Her research interests include finance, entrepreneurship, and management. She has participated in several international conferences and published articles in peer-reviewed academic journals.

Hajar Kobi holds a PhD in Economics and Management from Mohammed V University in Rabat, where she completed a dissertation on the impact of entrepreneurship education on the entrepreneurial intentions of Moroccan university students. She also holds a Master's degree in Accounting, Control, and Auditing from the same institution. She is currently a full-time faculty member at the École Marocaine des Sciences de l'Ingénieur (EMSI-Rabat), after previously serving as a lecturer at the Polydisciplinary Faculty of Béni Mellal. Her research focuses primarily on entrepreneurship and management. She has published several peer-reviewed articles and regularly contributes to national and international academic conferences.

Elmahdi Lemrami is a PhD student in management science at the Kenitra University in the LSPP Laboratory. He holds a master's degree in strategy and management of tourism organizations and has joined the research laboratory, where he is continuing his work in the field of tourism marketing. He's the author of articles on tourism with Dr. CHAREF Fatima. He has also taken part in a number of national and international symposia and conferences on the influence of satisfaction and the tourism experience on behavioral intention and place attachment, as well as on entrepreneurial innovation in the service sector. His research focuses on consumer behavior, customer relationship management (CRM), loyalty, tourism experiences, travel behavior, and tourism marketing. He is also interested in the challenges posed by the digitalization of the tourism sector.

Achmad Nurmandi is a Professor at the Department of Government Affairs and Administration, Jusuf Kalla School of Government, Universitas Muhammadiyah Yogyakarta, Indonesia. His research interests are on e-government, urban governance and strategic management in the public sector and published in many international journal and Book Chapter, such as International Journal of Public Sector Management, Transforming Government: People, Policy and Process, Jamba Journal of Disaster Studies, Asian Review of Political Science, Journal of Human Behavior in the Social Environment, Public Policy and Administration, Global Encyclopedia of Public Administration, Public Policy, and Governance, Springer. He is currently the Secretary of the Asia Pacific Society for Public Affairs (APSPA). He is also the Editor-in-Chief of Jurnal Studi Pemerintahan (Journal of Government and Politics) and a Guest Editor of International Journal of Public Sector Performance Management and International Journal of Sustainable Society.

Nurlina Subair, M.Si., is a Professor of Sociology at Universitas Muhammadiyah Makassar (Unismuh) and a breast cancer survivor. She began her career as a lecturer in 1989 and earned her Doctorate in Sociology from Universitas Negeri Makassar in 2012. In addition to her academic achievements, including publishing books and scholarly articles on social and gender issues, Prof. Nurlina has been the Chairperson of the Makassar Cancer Care Community (MCCC) since 2013. Her experience as a cancer survivor has inspired her to support cancer patients and raise public awareness about cancer prevention. In 2023, she was inaugurated as a Professor and, in her inaugural speech, highlighted the issue of poverty among female heads of households. Her journey of perseverance and dedication serves as an inspiration in the academic and social fields.

Muhammad Younus, graduated in 2019 from the Karachi Institute of Economics and Technology University in Karachi, Pakistan, and got a Bachelor's degree in Computer Science. The four-year undergraduate program in Computer Science formed the basis of my perseverance towards achieving an in-depth knowledge in the field. After graduation, I worked for the past few years as a business IT analyst in the product and research development of a logistics startup in Pakistan called TPL Logistics. We aim to Digitize Logistics Operations in Pakistan from the First Mile to the Last Mile. After this, I graduated in 2024 from the Universitas Muhammadiyah Yogyakarta in Yogyakarta, Indonesia, and got a Master's Degree in Government Science. My research interest is transforming governance and the public sector through technology. This Experience has given me the confidence and also kindled a desire to do research. The interdisciplinary nature has convinced me in taking this decision as it is the ideal choice for an exciting research career. At the same time, I am confident of contributing originally to the ongoing work. By working under the guidance of distinguished Team, I shall certainly be able to exploit my pote

Laila Zamzami, Third-year doctoral studies at Cadi Ayyad University position her as part of the NPG (New Management Practices) program. The research topic of Organizational Psychology and Entrepreneurship at Cadi Ayyad University includes Mental Health in Entrepreneurial Psychology, Health and Entrepreneurship, and Recovery from Work. She investigates psychological mechanisms that influence entrepreneurs' mental state and recovery approaches as well as their performance outcomes in professional settings. Research findings add value to the field by demonstrating mental health's purpose for entrepreneurs as a factor that helps them maintain enduring business achievement.

Index

A

C

D

E

H

I

O

P

R

S

T

www.ingramcontent.com/pod-product-compliance
Lightning Source LLC
LaVergne TN
LVHW080559300926
849162LV00005B/1000
* 9 7 9 8 3 3 7 3 0 9 1 8 7 *